'C' PROGRAMMING & DATA STRUCTURE

CS-62

For

Bachelor of Computer Applications [B.C.A.]

Author

Dinesh Verma

MCA, BCA, 'A' & 'O' Level, SCJP(USA), JP

Dinesh Verma

MCA,B.SC.,DECM,DCPA,DECOM

Academic Consultant : Indira Gandhi National Open University

Academic Counsellor : ARSD College, Delhi University

Guest Lecturer : Delhi College, Delhi University

Useful For

IGNOU, Vinayaka Mission University, IP University, Delhi University, CCS University, JMI University, B. M. V. Open University (KOTA), M. P. Bhoj Open University(M.P.), Tamilnadu Open University, YCM Open University (Maharashtra), Mahatma Gandhi University (Kottyam), M. D. University, and all other Indian Universities.

AF529969

GULLYBABA PUBLISHING HOUSE (P) Ltd.

AN ISO 9001:2008 CERTIFIED CO.

GullyBaba Publishing House (P) Ltd.
2525 / 193, Ist Floor, Onkar Nagar-A,
Tri Nagar, Delhi-110035
Ph: 9350849407, 9312235086, 011-27387998

E-mail: info@gullybaba.com
info@degreewala.com
WebSite: www.gullybaba.com
www.ignouonline.com

Edition : 2011

ISBN: 978-81-89086-27-5
Price : 380/-

Preface

This book is mainly targeted for BCA exam of PC Software Application Skills. It has been introduced in market after seeing the huge demand of ready to grasp material for exams with high level of quality, and its un-availability in market. We the GullyBaba Publishing House took a step ahead to publish the quality material focusing on exams at the same time giving you indepth knowledge about the subject.

GPH Book is the pioneer effort that provides a unique methodology so as to perform better in exams. If your goal is to attain higher grade use this powerful study tool independently or along with your text.

*On the Web : **www.gullybaba.com** is the vital resource for your exams acting as catalyst to boost up your preparation. Now you can access us on the net through **www.doctorignou.com, www.doeacconline.com, www.gphindia.com, and www.gullybabapublishinghouse.com.***

Feedback about the book can be sent at **cs612writers@gullybaba.com.**

Acknowledgments :

We appreciate the staff and facility support provided by GullyBaba Publishing House. In particular, we appreciate the encouragement and professional advises received from Mr. Ajay Saini, Mr. Tarun Sharma, H. Faheem Ahmed and many more.

Also we would like to thank typesetting and designing team Mrs. Bhawna Verma, Mr. Shravan Vats, Mr. Mukesh.

We gratefully acknowledges the significant contributions of Mr. Mahesh Chand, Mrs. Bimla Devi, Mrs. Bhawna Verma and our experts in bringing out this publication.

New Delhi

TABLE OF CONTENTS

STUDY NOTES

SOLVED PAPERS

Chapter - 1

'C' Concepts & Programming Involving Pointers, Functions & Files

Introduction :

C is a programming language developed at AT & T's Bell Laboratories of USA in 1972. It was designed and written by a man named Dennis Ritchie. In the late seventies C began to replace the more familiar languages of that time like PL/I, ALGOL etc. Ritchie seems to have been rather surprised that so many programmers preferred C to older languages like FORTRAN or PL/I, or the newer ones like Pascal and APL.

KEYWORDS IN C

Auto	double	if	static
Break	else	int	struct
Case	enum	long	switch
Char	extern	near	typedef
Const	float	register	union
Continue	far	return	unsigned
Default	for	short	void
Do	goto	signed	while

Storage Classes :

1) auto - storage class

auto is the default storage class for local variables.

```
{
   int Count;
   auto int Month;
}
```

The example above defines two variables with the same storage class. Auto can only be used within functions, i.e. local variables.

2) register - Storage Class

register is used to define local variables that should be stored in a register instead of RAM. This means that the variable has a maximum size equal to the register size (usually one word) and cant have the unary '&' operator applied to it (as it does not have a memory location).

```
{
 register int  Miles;
}
```

Register should only be used for variables that require quick access - such as counters. It should also be noted that defining 'register' goes not mean that the variable will be stored in a register. It means that it MIGHT be stored in a register - depending on hardware and implementation restrictions.

3) static - Storage Class

static is the default storage class for global variables. The two variables below (count and road) both have a static storage class.

```
static int Count;
int Road;

main()
{
 printf("%d\n", Count);
 printf("%d\n", Road);
}
```

'Static' can also be defined within a function. If this is done, the variable is initialised at compilation time and retains its value between calls. Because it is initialized at compilation time, the initialisation value must be a constant. This is serious stuff - treated with care.

```
void Func(void)
{
 static Count=1;
}
```

Here is an example

There is one very important use for 'static'. Consider this bit of code.

```
char *Func(void);
main()
{
 char *Text1;
 Text1 = Func();
}
char *Func(void)
{
 char Text2[10]="martin";
 return(Text2);
}
```

'Func' returns a pointer to the memory location where 'Text2' starts BUT Text2 has a storage class of auto and will disappear when we exit the function and could be overwritten by something else. The answer is to specify:

```
static char Text[10]="martin";
```

The storage assigned to 'Text2' will remain reserved for the duration of the program.

4) Extern - storage Class

extern defines a global variable that is visible to ALL object modules. When you use 'extern' the variable cannot be initialized as all it does is point the variable name at a storage location that has been previously defined.

Source 1	**Source 2**
extern int count;	int count=5;
write()	main()
{	{
printf("count is %d\n", count);	write();
}	}

Count in 'source 1' will have a value of 5. If source 1 changes the value of count - source 2 will see the new value.

Type Casting :

In arithmetic expressions, we have seen that if operation is to be performed on operands of different data type with lower rank is converted to a value of higher rank, and then operation takes place. Similarly in an assignment statement, the value on the right hand side of the assignment operator is converted to type of the variable to which it is to be assigned, and then value is stored in that variable.

In addition to these situations, sometimes we need to force the compiler to convert a value to a particular data type. For example, suppose our program uses a variable named *temp* of type *float*, and at some point we want to calculate square root of its value. Turbo C contains a library function *sqrt()*, declared in *math.h* header file, that return the square root, but the argument sent to this function must be of type *double*, otherwise it will return a nonsense value. So there is need to convert variable *temp* to type double. To do this, we use the *cast* operator, which consists of putting parentheses around the name of the data type as shown below:

(type) exp

where *exp* is either a constant, a variable, an array element or a function. For the above example, we can write

result = sqrt ((double) temp);

The expression *(double)* causes the value of variable *temp* to be converted from type *float* to type *double* before it is used.

An operator must have operands of the same type before it can carry out the operation. Because of this, C will perform some automatic conversion of data types.

These are the general rules for binary operators (* + / % etc):

If either operand is long double the other is converted to long double.

Otherwise, if either operand is double the other is converted to double

Otherwise, if either operand is float the other is converted to float

Otherwise, convert char and short to int

Then, if an operand is long convert the other to long.

Output format specifier :

Format Specifier	Used For
%d	signed decimal integer
%ld	signed long decimal integer
%u	unsigned decimal integer
%f	single precision floating real number
%lf	double precision floating real number
%e	floating point (exponential notation)
%x	unsigned hexadecimal integer
%o	unsigned octal integer
%c	single character
%s	string

Escape Sequence	Represents	Effect
\n	Newline	has the effect of both a carriage return and linefeed i.e. the subsequent output starts from new line.
\r	tab	move over to the next eight-space-wide field.
\b	backspace	moves the cursor one space left.
\r	carriage return	carriage return.
\f	formfeed	advances to the top of the next page on printer.
\a	beep	produces one audio tone of the speaker.
\’	single quote	insert character’ in the output.
\”	double quote	insert character” in the output.
\\	backslash	insert character\ in the output.

Logical Operator Example :

A company insures its drivers in the following cases:

- If the driver is married.
- If the driver is unmarried, male & above 30 years of age.
- If the driver is unmarried, female & above 25 years of age.

In all other cases the driver is not insured. If the marital status, sex and age of the driver are the inputs, write a program to determine whether the driver is to be insured or not.

We can write a program for the above problem in two ways:

(a) Without using && and || operators
(b) Using && and || operators

Method (a)

```
/* Insurance of driver-without using logical operators */
main( )
{
char sex, ms:
int age:

printf ( " Enter age, sex, marital status" ) ;
scant ( " %d %c %c", &age, &sex, &ms) ;

if ( ms == M )
printf ( " Driver is insured" ) ;
else
{
if  ( sex  == 'M')
{
if (age > 30 )
printf ( " Driver is insured " ) ;

else
printf ( " Driver is not insured " ) ;

}
else
```

```
{
if ( age > 25 )
printf " Driver is insured" ) ;
else
printf ( " Driver is not insured " ) ;
}
}
}
```

Method (b)

As mentioned above, in this example we expect the answer to be either 'Driver is insured' or 'Driver is not insured'. If we list down all those cases in which the driver is insured, then they would be:

(a) Driver is married.
(b) Driver is an unmarried male above 30 years of age.
(c) Driver is an unmarried female above 25 years of age.

Since all these cases lead to the driver being insured, they can be combined together using && and ll as shown in the program below:

```
/* insurance of driver – using logical operators */
main ( )
{
char sex, ms :
int age:

printf ( " Enter age, sex, marital status " ) :
scanf ( " %d %c %c " &age, &sex, &ms ) :

if ( ( ms – 'M' ) ll (ms == 'U' && sex == 'M' && age > 30 ) ll
/ms == 'U' && sex == 'F' "&& age> 25 , ))
printf ( 'Driver is insured' ) ;
else
printf ( " Driver is not insured " ) ;
}
```

In this program it is important to note that :

➢ The driver will be insured only if one of the conditions enclosed in parentheses evaluates to true.

➢ For the second pair of parentheses to evaluate to true, each condition in the parentheses separated by && must evaluate to true.
➢ Even if one of the conditions in the second parentheses evaluates of false, then the whole of the parentheses evaluates to false.
➢ The last two of the above arguments apply to third pair of parentheses as well.

Thus, we can conclude that the && and || are useful in the following programming situations :

(a) When it is to be tested whether a value falls within a particular range or not.
(b) When after testing several conditions the outcome is only one of the two answers.

If & Switch

If statement
The syntax of the if statement is as follows:
if(expression)
statement);
The expression must be enclosed in parenthesis. The statement may be a compound statement.
for example
if (y>5)
x=0;

The statement will be executed only if the expression is true. The syntax of the if else statement is as follows:
if(expression)
statement-1;
else
statement-2;
if expression is true statement –1 is executed. If expression is false, statement –2 is executed. So depending on the truth value of expression, either statement-1 or statement 2 is executed,

Nested if statements :
The statement sequence of if or else may contain another statement i.e. the if else statement can be nested within one another as shown below:

Syntax of nested if statement :

```
if (expression-1)
{
     if(expression-2)
{
statement;
}
else
        if(expression-3)
        {
statement;
        }
        else
{
statement;
}
}
```

there may be one problem raised with nested if that is to decide "which if does the else match".

☞ Each else matches to its nearest unmatched preceding if.

For example

```
if(a<10)
{
if(b>5)
Sum=Sum + a + b;
else
Sum=Sum – a – b ;
```

Multiple if statement :

Syntax of multiple if statement :

```
if(expression-1)
statement –1;
else if (expression –2)
     statement –2;
else if(expression –3)
statement-3;
..
,.
else if(expression –n)
statement-n;
else
```

default statement;

the expression are evaluated in order and if any condition is true then the statement associated with it is executed and this terminated the whole chain. The last else part is execute as default statement.

The switch statement :

If you have a long series of conditions to check, a large block of if ; else statements can get tiresome and confusing to write (and read, later on). For this reason, C++ provides the switch statement. The general syntax is:

```
Switch (expression)
{
   case value1:
   statements
   [break;]
   case value 2:
   statements
   [break:]
   ....
         default:
    Statements
}
```

An expression is evaluated in the first line of a switch statement, and its value is used to determine the action or actions to take. The value of the expression is compared in turn with each value listed next to a case statement. If a match occurs, the statements following that case statement are executed. The break statement (shown in square brackets to indicate that it is optional; the square brackets are not actually part of the code), if present, causes the switch statement to be terminated after the statements in the current case block are executed., that is, control will pass to the statement immediately after the final brace ending the switch statement without any further case statements being tested, if the break statement is not present , the next case statement will be checked as well . In other words, a switch statement offers greater flexibility that an if.. Else statement in that it allows more than one block of statements to be executed.

Loop

The while Loop :

It is often the case in programming that you want to do something a fixed number of times. Perhaps you want to calculate gross salaries of then different persons, or you want to convert temperatures from centigrade to Fahrenheit for 15 different cities. The while loop is ideally suited for such cases. Let us look at a simple example which uses a while loop.

```
/* Calculation of simple interest for 3 sets of p, n and r*/
main( )
{
int p, n, count :
float r, sl ;

count = 1 :
while (count <= 3)
{
printf ("\Enter values of p, n, and r");
scanf ("%d %d %f, &p, &n, &r );
si = p * n * r / 100;
printf ( " Simple interest = Rs. %f, si );
count = count + 1 ;
}
}
```

And here are a few sample runs ....

```
Enter values of p, n and r 1000 5 13.5
Simple interest = Rs. 675,000000
Enter values of p, n and r 2000 5 13.5
Simple interest = Rs. 1350. 000000
Enter values of p, n and r 3500 5 3.5
Simple interest = Rs. 612.500000
```

The for Loop :

Perhaps one reason why few programmers use while is that they are too busy using the for, which is probably the most popular looping control. The for allows us to specify three things about a loop in a single line:

(a) Setting a loop counter to an initial value.

(b) Testing the loop counter to determine whether its value has reached the number of repetitions desired.

(c) Increasing the value of loop counter each time the program segment within the loop has been executed.

The general form of for statement is as under:

```
For ( initialize counter : test counter : increment counter)
{
do this ;
```

```
and this ;
and this ;
}
```

Let us write down the simple interest program using for. Compare this program with the one which we wrote using while.

```
/* Calculation of simple interest for 3 sets of p, n and r */
main ( )
{
int p, n, count ;
float r, si ;
for ( count = 1 ; count <= 3 ; count = count + 1)
{
printf ( "Enter values of p, n, and r ");
scanf ( " %d %d %f , &p, &n, &r ");
si = p * n * r /100 ;
printf ( * Simple interest = Rs. %f\n", si );
}
}
```

The do-while Loop :

The do-while loop looks like this :

```
Do
{
this ;
and this ;
and this ;
and this ;
} while ( this condition is true ) ;
```

There is a minor difference between the working of while and do-while loops. This difference is the place where the condition is tested. The while teste the condition before executing any of the statements within the while loop. As against this, the do-while tests the condition after having executed the statements within the loop.

This means that do-while would execute its statements at least once, even if the condition fails for the first time itself. The while, on the other hand will not execute its statements if the condition fails for the first time. This difference is brought about more clearly by the following program.

```
main ()
```

```
{
while (4<1)
printf ("Hello there \n") ;
}
```

Here, since the condition fails for the first time itself the printf () will not get executed at all. Let's now write the same program using a do-while loop.

```
main()
{
do
{
printf ("Hello there \n") ;
} while (4< 1) ;
}
```

In this program the printf ( ) would be executed once, since first the body of the loop is executed and then the condition is tested.

Functions

Why Use Functions :

Why write separate functions at all ? Why not squeeze the entire logic into one function, main ( ) ? Two reasons:

(a) Writing functions avoids rewriting the same code over and over. Suppose you have a section of code in your program that calculates area of a triangle. If, later in the program, you want to calculate the area of a different triangle, you won't like it if you are required to write the same instructions all over again. Instead, you would prefer to jump back to the place from where you left off. This section of code is nothing but a function.

(b) Using functions it becomes easier to write programs and keep track of what they are doing. If the operation of a program can be divided into separate activities, and each activity placed in a different function, then each be written and checked more or less independently. Separating the code into modular functions also makes the program easier to design and understand.

Passing Values between Functions :

Consider the following program. In this program, in main ( ) we receive the values of a, b and c through the keyboard and then output the sum of a, b and c. However, the calculation of sum is done in different function called calsum ( ). If sum is to be calculated in calsum ( ) and values of a,b and c are received in main( ), then we must pass on these values to calsum ( ), and once calsum ( ) calculates the sum we must return it from calsum( ) back to main( ).

```
/* Sending and receiving values between functions*/
main( )
{
int a, b, c, sum;
printf ("\nEnter any three numbers");
scanf ("%d %d %d, &a, &b, &c);
sum = calsum (a , b , c);
printf ("nSum = %d", sum );
}
calsum (x, y, z)
int x, y, z ;
{
int d ;
d = x + y + z ;
return (d) /; See what Happen if return (d) if not given.
}
```

And here is the output...

Enter any three numbers 10 20 30
Sum = 60

Array Pointer and Arrays ::

(1) An array is a collection of variables of the same type that are referenced by a common name. Arrays are a way to group a numbers of terms into a larger unit.

Arrays are of different type.

(1) One dimensional arrays.

(2) Multi dimensional arrays.

C++ a class arrays of mare than two dimensions, the exact limit, if any is determined by the computes you use.

Single Dimensional Arrays.

The Simplest form of an array is a single dimensional array. The array is given a name and its elements are referred it by their subscripts or indices.

The general form of an array declaration is as shown below.

```
Datatype array name [size]
int          age [4];
 ↓            ↓   ↘ size
Datatype Name of array
```

Syntax

Type array - name [size]:

The data type of array elements is known as the same as type of the array.

Accessing Array Elements

Scanf (“%d”, $age[0]);

me insert the a value into the array with line.

Printf (“%d”, age[0]);

it we read it out with the line.

(1) Initializing Array elements

```
# include <stdio.h>
void main ( )
int month, day, total day:
int days - per month [12] = {31, 28, 31, 30, 31, 30, 31, 31, 31, 30, 31, 30, 21};
```

Arrays can be created from any of the C data types int, float, char. I start with int and float as these are the easiest to understand. Then move onto int and float multi dimensional arrays and finally char arrays.

1) int or float arrays.
2) Two dimensional int or float arrays.
3) char arrays.
4) char multidimensional arrays.
5) int and float arrays

To define an integer or floating point variable you would say.

```
main()
{
 int   Count;           /* integer variable             */
 float Miles;           /* floating point variable      */
}
```

The syntax for an array is :

```
main()
{
 int   Count[5];        /* 5 element integer array          */
 float Miles[10];       /* 10 element floating point array */
}
```

Now, the important fact is that the elements start at 0 (ZERO), so, ‘Count’ above has elements 0, 1, 2, 3, 4.

To change the value of the 5th element we would code:

```
main()
 {
  int Count[5];
  Count[4] = 20;              /* code 4 to update the 5th element */
 }
```

If we want to initialise 'Count' at definition we can say:

```
main()
{
 int i;
 int Count[5]={10, 20, 30};
 for (i=0; i< 5; i++)
 {
  printf("%d ", Count[i]);
 }
 puts("");
}
```

The result will be:

10 20 30 0 0

We can see from the example above that the elements that have NOT been initialised have been set to zero.

One last thing to show you. If all the elements are being initialized when the variable is being defined, the compiler can work out the number of elements for you.

So this example will create an array with 3 elements.

```
main()
  { int i;
    int Count[]={10, 20, 30};
  }
```

Don't forget, all the stuff so far also applies to float.

Two dimensional int and float arrays

C does not actually support multidimensional arrays, but you can emulate them.

```
main()
{ int Count[5];
  int Matrix[10][4];
}
```

Count has been seen before, it defines an array of 5 elements.

Matrix is defined as 10 arrays, all with 4 elements.

To initialise Matrix at definition, you would code the following.

```
main()
{ int Matrix[4][2]={{1, 2},
                   {3, 4},
                   {5, 6},
                   {7, 8}};
}
```

Don’t forget the last element will be Matrix[3][1]

char arrays

char arrays work in the same way as int and float

```
main()
{
  char Letter;
  char Letters[10];
}
```

‘Letter’ can only hold one character but ‘the ‘Letters’ array could hold 10. It is important to think of ‘char’ as an array and NOT a string.

To initialise ‘char’ variables you can use the following syntax.

```
main()
{
  char Letter=’x’;
    char Letters[10]=’f’,’a’,’x’,’ ‘,’m’,’o’,’d’,’e’,’m’,’\0';
  char Text[10]=”fax modem”;
}
```

☞ Note that the double quotes mean ‘text string’ and so they will add the NULL automatically. This is the only time that text can be loaded into an array in this way. If you want to change the contents of the array you should use the function strcpy.

Two dimensional char arrays :

Two dimensional arrays are a different kettle of fish! We can follow the rules above to define the array like this.

```
main()
{
```

```
    char Colours[3][6]={"red","green","blue"};
    printf ("%c \n", Colours[0][0]);      /* O/P 'r' */
    printf ("%s \n", Colours[1]);         /* O/P 'green' */
}
```

Pointer

First Principles :

To understand pointers, it may be worth understanding how normal variables are stored. If you disagree, Click here to move on.

What does the following program really mean?

```
main()
{
   int Length;
}
```

In my mind, it means, reserve enough storage to hold an integer and assign the variable name 'Length' to it. The data held in this storage is undefined. Graphically it looks like:

Address	Data	
f1		← Width
f2		
f3		
f4		

To put a known value into 'Length' we code,

```
main()
{
int Length;
   Length = 20;
}
```

the decimal value 20 (Hex 14) is placed into the storage location.

Address	Data	
f1	00	← length
f2	00	
f3	00	
f4	14	

Finally, if the program is expanded to become

```
main()
{
   int Length;
   Length = 20;
   printf("Length is %d\n", Length);
   printf("Address of Length is %p\n", &Length);
}
```

The output would look something like this .....

```
Length is 20
Address of Length is 0xF1
```

☞ Please *note the '& Length' on the second printf statement. The &means address of Length. If you are happy with this, you should push onto the pointers below.*

Pointer definition :

A pointer is a variable which contains the address in memory of another variable. We can have a pointer to any variable type.

The ***unary*** or ***monadic*** operator **&** gives the "address of a variable".

The ***indirection*** or ***deference*** operator ***** gives the "contents of an object ***pointed to*** by a pointer"

☞ *When a pointer is declared it does not point anywhere. You must set it to point somewhere before you use it.*

A pointer to any variable type is an address in memory — which is an integer address. A pointer is definitely NOT an integer.

The reason we associate a pointer to a data type is so that it knows how many bytes the data is stored in. When we increment a pointer we increase the pointer by one "block" memory. So for a character pointer ++ch_ptr adds 1 byte to the address. For an integer or float ++ip or ++flp adds 4 bytes to the address.

An example of code defining a pointer could be...

```
main()
{
   int *Width;
}
```

A graphical representation could be...

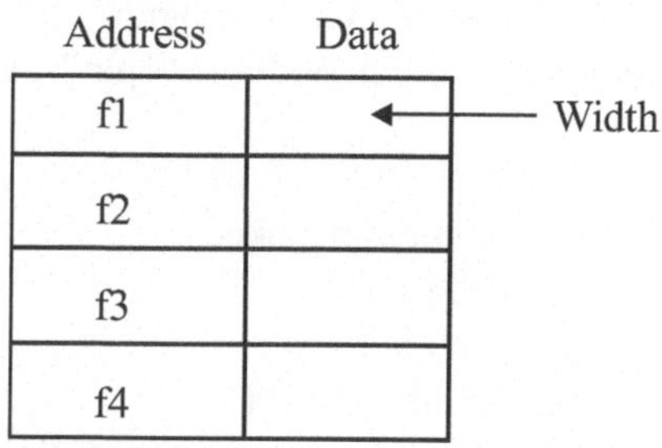

So far, this variable looks the same as above, the value stored at 'Width' is unknown. To place a value in 'Width' you could code.

```
main()
{
   int *Width;                                  /* 1 */
   Width = (int *)malloc(sizeof(int));  /* 2 */
   *Width = 34;                             /* 3 */
}
```

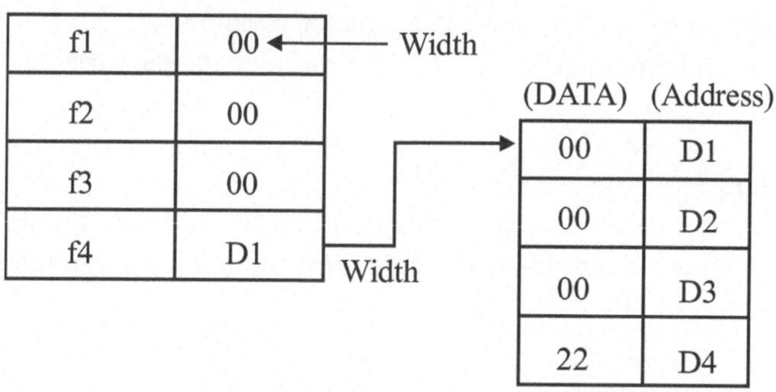

Statements 2 and 3 are important here:

2) The malloc function reserves some storage and puts the address of the storage into Width.

3) *Width puts a value into the storage pointed to by Width.

Unlike the Length = 20 example above, the storage pointed to by 'Width' does NOT contain 34 (22 in Hex), it contains the address where the value 34 can be found. The final program is...

```
main()
{
    int *Width;
    Width  = (int *)malloc(sizeof(int));
    *Width = 34;
    printf("  Data stored at *Width is %d\n", *Width);
    printf("       Address of Width is %p\n", &Width);
    printf("Address stored at Width is %p\n",  Width);
}
```

The program output is something like.

```
Data stored at *Width is 34
     Address of Width is 0xF1
Address stored at Width is 0xD1
```

A pointer can point to any data type, i.e. int, float, char. When defining a pointer you place an * (asterisk) character between the data type and the variable name, here are a few examples.

```
main()
{
    int   count;           /* an integer variable              */
    int   *pcount;         /* a pointer to an integer variable */
    float  miles;          /* a floating point variable.       */
    float *m;              /* a pointer                        */
    char   ans;            /* character variable               */
    char   *charpointer;   /* pointer to a character variable  */
}
```

Void Pointers :

There are times when you write a function but do not know the datatype of the returned value. When this is the case, you can use a void pointer.

```
    int func(void *Ptr);
main()
{
    char *Str = "abc";
    func(Str);
}
int func(void *Ptr)
{
    printf("%s\n", Ptr);
}
```

Please note, you cant do pointer arithmetic on void pointers.

Advantages of Using Pointers :

Some of the advantages offered by the use of pointers are:

✓ to return more than one value from a function

✓ to pass arrays and strings more efficiently as arguments to a function

✓ to create complex data structures, such as *linked lists, binary trees* and *graphs*, where one data structure element must contain references to the other data structures of same type

✓ to communicate with operating system about memory. For example, the function *malloc()* returns the location of free memory block by using a pointer and the function *free()* returns the memory block pointed to by a pointer to the operating system.

✓ the pointer notation compiles into faster and more efficient code.

Q1. Differentiate between the following with an example $\left[2\frac{1}{2}\times 2=5\right]$

[DEC04,Q4(a)(i)]

(i) Arrays vs Pointers

Refer to Page No. 207

Q2. List atleast 4 differences between Arrays and Pointers in 'C' language.

[JUNE03,Q2(c)][4]

Array

1) array uses continues memory allocation.
2) array size is declared in advance.
3) array size cannot be increased and decreased at run time.
4) array stores the value.
5) declaration of array is

    int arr_name[size];

6) for example

```
char arr[20]="dinesh "
char brr[20]="verma"
arr=brr; // not valid
```

you cannot assign the value of one complete array to other array.
But you can do this by using pointer,
declare

```
char *c="dinesh"
char *d="verma";
c=d this is valid
```

Pointer

1) pointer is called dynamic memory allocation.
2) pointer size is not declared in advance

3) because its size is not declared in advance so there size is increased and decreased at runtime.
4) there is no space is allocated for pointer.
5) declaration of pointer is :
int *point;
6) pointer stores the address of variable.

Q3. Write a program EXPR in C language which evaluates a Reverse Polish expression from the command line, where each operator or operand is a separate argument. For example, EXPR 2 3 4 + * evaluates 2 × (3 + 4). [JUN01,1(a)][10]

```
#include <stdio.h>
#include <ctype.h>
 int max=50;
main (int argc, char *argv [])
  {
  int stack[50],i;
  char *p;
  int j=0;
  if(argc<2)
  {printf("Insufficient number of arguments");
  getch();
  exit(0);
  }
  p=argv[1];
  for(i=0;i<strlen(argv[1]);i++)
  {
  if(*(p+i)>=48&&*(p+i)<=57)
  {
  stack[j]=*(p+i)-48;
  j++;
  }
  else
  if(*(p+i)=='+')
  {
  stack[j-2]=stack[j-1]+stack[j-2];
  j=j-1;
  }
  else
  if(*(p+i)=='-')
  {
```

```
 stack[j-2]=stack[j-1]-stack[j-2];
j=j-1;
}
else
 if(*(p+i)=='*')
{
 stack[j-2]=stack[j-1]*stack[j-2];
j=j-1;
}
else
 if(*(p+i)=='/')
{
 stack[j-2]=stack[j-1]+stack[j-2];
j=j-1;
}
}
j--;
printf("Final evaluation is %d",stack[j]);
 getch();
}
```

Structures & Union :

Just as the entity we call a 'book' is a collection of things such as title, author, isbn number, publisher, number of pages, date of publication etc. As you can see all this data is dissimilar, for example author is a string, whereas number of pages is an integer. For dealing with such collections, C provides a data type called 'structure'. A structure gathers together, different atoms of information that comprise a given entity.

Declaring A Structure

The following statement declares the structure type:

```
Struct book
{
char name;
float price;
int pages;
};
```

This statement defines a new data type called struct book. Each variable of this data type will consist of a character variable called name, a float variable called price and an integer variable called pages. The general form of a structure declaration statement is given below :

```
Struct <structure name>
{
structure element 1 ;
structure element 2 ;
structure element 3 ;
........
........
};
```

Once the new structure data type has been defined one or more variables can be declared to be of that type. For example the variables b1, b2, b3, can be declared to be of the type struct book, as,

```
Struct book b1, b2, b3;
```

How Structure Elements are Stored

```
Struct book
{
char name ;
float price;
int pages ;
};
struct book b1 = { 'B', 130.0, 500 };
```

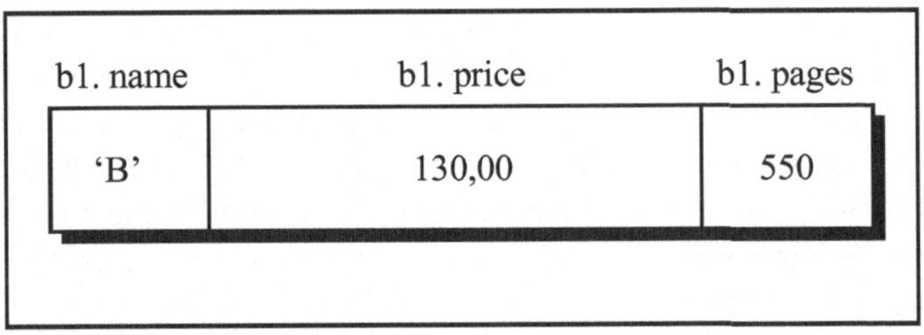

Unions ::

Both structures and unions are used to group a number of different variables together. But while a structure enables us to treat a number of different variables stored at different places in memory, a union enables us to treat the same space in memory as a number of different variables. That is, a union offers a way for a section of memory to be treated as a variable of one type on one occasion, and as a different variable of a different type on another occasion. You might wonder why it would be necessary to do such a thing, Let us take a look at a simple example :

```
/* Demo of union at work*/
main( )
{
```

```
union a
{
int I ;
char ch [2]
};
union a key ;
key, I = 512 ;
printf ("\nkey, I = %d" , key, I ) ;
printf ("\nkey, ch [0] = %d" , key. Ch [0] ) ;
printf ("\nkey, ch [1] = %d" , key. Ch [1] )
}
```

And here s the output ....

Key. I =512

Key,ch[0] = 0

Key,ch[1] = 2

```
struct a
int ;
char ch[2] ;
} ;
struct a key ;
```

This data type would occupy 4 bytes in memory, 2 for key. I and one each for key.ch[0] and key.ch[1], as shown below.

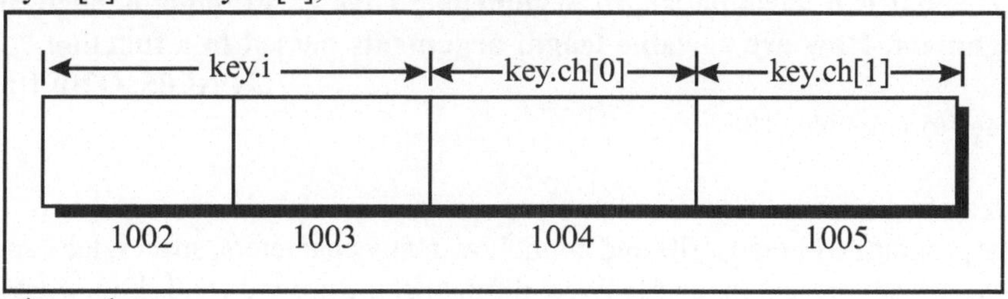


```
union a {
Int I ;
char ch [2] ;
} ;
union a key ;
```

Representation of this data type in memory is shown below .

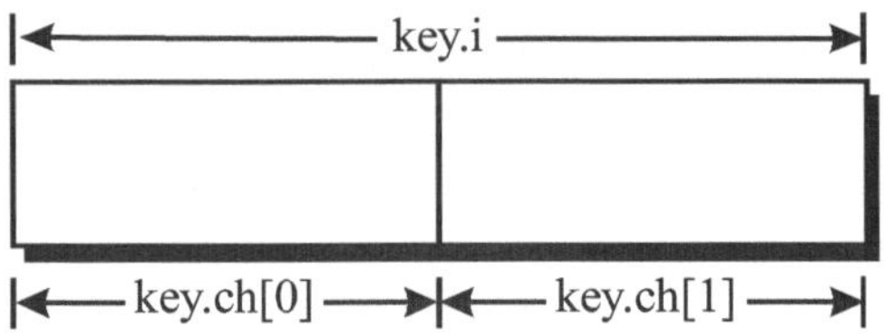

Q4. Write at least two differences between a Structure and a Union in 'C' language. Give an example each of a structure and Union.
[JUNE05, Q5(b)][5]

Please Refer to Page No. 196

Q5. Write the syntax of any five file handling commands supported by 'C'. **[JUNE05, Q1(a)][5]**

Refer to Page No. 178

Q6. Write a 'C' program to count the number of characters and lines in a text whose name is supplied command line. **[JUNE05, Q1(b)][5]**

Refer to Page No. 178

Q7. What is a variable length argument ? Give an example of such an argument. How are variable length arguments passed to a function ?
[JUNE05, Q2(b)][5]

Refer to Page No. 184

Files ::

Our program will read a file and count how many characters, spaces, tabs and newlines are present in the file. We will first list the program and show what it does, and then dissect it line by line. Here is the listing.

```
/* Count chars, spaces, tabs and newlines in a file */
#include "stdio.h"
main( )
{
FILE *fp;
char ch;
int not= 0, nos = 0, noc = 0;
fp = fopen ("PR1.C", "r");
While ( 1 )
{
```

```
ch = fgetc ( fp ) ;
if ( ch = = EOF )
break
noc ++ ;
if ( ch = = ' ' )
nob ++;
if ( ch = = '\n' )
nol ++ ;
if ( ch = = '\t' )
nol ++ ;
fclose ( fp ) ;
printf ( "\nNumber of  characters = %d" , noc ) ;
printf ( "\nNumber of  blanks  = %d" , nob ) ;
printf ( "\nNumber of  tabs  = %d" , not ) ;
printf ( "\nNumber of  lines  = %d" , nol ) ;
}
```

And here is a sample run ....

Number of character = 155
Number of blanks = 20
Number of tabs = 14
Number of tabs = 28

The above statistics are true for a file "PRI.C", which we had on our disk. You may give any other filename and obtain different results. More important than the actual statistics, is how the program calculates these. So let us now take a look at how it does it.

Opening A File

Before we can write information to a file on a disk or read it, we must open the file. Opening a file establishes a link between the program and the operating system, about, which file we are going to access and how. We provide the operating system with the name of the file and whether we plan to read or write to it. The link between our program and the operating system is a structure called FILE which has been defined in the header file "stdio.h" (standing for standard input/output header file). Therefore, it is necessary to always include this file when we are doing high level disk I/O. When we request the operating system to open a file, what we get back (if the request is indeed granted), is a pointer to the structure FILE. That is why, we make the following declaration before opening the file.

FILE *fp ;

Each file we open will have its own FILE structure. The FILE structure contains information about the file being used as its current size, its location in memory etc. More importantly it contains a character pointer which points to the character that is about to get read.

Now let us understand the following statements,

FILE *fp ;

fp = fopen ("PR1.C", "R") ;

fp is a pointer variable, which contains address of the structure FILE which has been defined in the header file stdio.h".

fopen () will open a file "PRI.C" in 'read mode, which tells the C compiler that we would be reading the contents of the file. Note that "r" is a string and not a character; hence the double quotes and not single quotes. In fact, fopen() Performs three important tasks when you open the file in "r" mode :

(a) Firstly it searches on the disk the file to be opened.

(b) If the file is present, it loads the file from the disk into memory. Of course if the file is very big, then it loads the file part by part.

If the file is absent, fopen( ) returns a NULL, NULL is a macro defined in "stdio.h" which indicates that you failed to open the file.

(c) It sets up a character pointer (which is part of the FILE structure) which points to the first character of the of if memory where the file has been loaded.

Reading from A File

Once the file has been opened for reading using fopen ( ), as we have seen be file's contents are brought into memory (partly or wholly) and a pointer points to the very first character. The read the file's contents from memory there exists a function called fgetc( ). This has been used in our sample program through,

ch = fgetc (fp) ;

fgetc ( ) reads the character from current pointer position, advances the pointer position so that it now points to the next character, and returns the character that is read, which collected in the variable ch. Note that once the file has been opened, we no longer refer to the file by its name, but through the file pointer fp.

We have used the function fgetc( ) within an indefinite while loop. There has to be a way to break out of this while. When shall we break out… the moment we reach the end of file. But what is end of file? End of file is signified by a special character, whose ASCII value is 26. This character is inserted beyond the last character in the file, when it is created. This character can also be generated from the keyboard by typing ctrl z.

While reading from the file, when fgetc( ) encounters this special character, instead of returning the character that it has read, it returns the macro EOF. The EOF macro has been defined in the file "stdio.h". In place of the function fgetc( ) we could have as well used the macro getc( ) with the same effect. In our sample program, we go on reading each character from the file till end of file is met. As each character is being read we keep running totals of number of characters, number of blanks, number of tabs and number of lines read. Note that the end of the line is marked by a \n. Once out of the loop, we print these running totals.

Using argc and argv

To execute program we are required to first type the program, compile it, and then execute it. This program can be improved in two ways:

(a) There should be no need to compile the program everytime to use the file-copy utility. It means the program must be executable at command prompt (A> or C> if you are using MS DOS, $ if you are using Unix).

(b) Instead of the program prompting us to enter the source and target filenames, we must be able to supply them at command prompt, in the form:

C>filecopy PR1.C PR2.C

Where, PR1.C is the source filename and PR2.C is the target filename.

The first improvement is simple. In MS-DOS, the executable file (the one which can be executed at DOS prompt and has an extension.EXE) can be created in Turbo C by using the key F9 to compile the program.

The second improvement is possible by passing the source filename and target filename to the function main( ). This is illustrated below:

```
#include "stdio.h"
main(int argc, char * argv[])
{
FILE *fs, *ft ;
char ch ;
If (argc ! = 3 )
{
puts("Insufficient arguments" ) ;
exit( ) ;
}
fs = fopen ( argv[1}, "1") ;
if (fs = = NULL)
{
puts ("Cannot open source file") ;
exit ( ) ;
}
ft = fopen(argv [2], "w") ;
if ( ft = = NULL )
puts ("Cannot open target file") ;
```

```
fclose(fs) ;
exit( ) ;
}
while ( 1 )
{
ch = fgetc ( fs ) ;
if (ch = = EOF )
break ;
else
fputc ( ch, ft ) ;
}
fclose ( fs ) ;
fclose ( ft ) ;
}
```

The arguments that we pass on to main ( ) at the command prompt are called command line arguments. The function main ( ) can have two arguments, traditionally named as argc and argv. Out of these, argv is an array of pointers to strings and argc is an int whose value is equal to the number of strings to which argv points. When the program is executed, the strings on the command line are passed to main ( ). More precisely, the strings at the command line are stored in memory and address of the first string is stored in argv [0], address of the second string is stored in argv [1] and so on. The argument argc is set to the number of strings given on the command line. For example, in our sample program, if at the command prompt we give,
argc would contain 3
argc [0] would contain base address of the string "filecopy"
argc [1] would contain base address of the string "PR1.C "
argc [2] would contain base address of the string "PR2.C "

Chapter - 2

DATA STRUCTURE

ARRAYS

Consider the following problem:

Read 25 numbers and print them in reverse order.

The problem requires all the numbers as they are read. Further we cannot print anything until all 25 numbers are read; therefore, we need to store all the twenty five numbers. Reading 25 numbers in 25 different variables will be quite cumbersome and so would be writing these numbers in reverse order. It is much simpler to call the numbers NUM_1 NUM_2, NUM_3 .... NUM_{25}.

Each number is a NUM, and numbers are distinguish by subscripts. Also they are read in succession. Thus we can abbreviate this sequence as NUM_i for i = 0,1, 2. .... 24. Such a subscripted variable is called an Array. More formally an array is a Finite ordered set of homogenous elements which are stored in adjacent cells in memory. Arrays are usually used when a program include a list of recovering elements.

In C subscripts are Placed in square brackets [ ]. Repetition over a sequence Of values of i may also be implemented using a loop construct. For example, the following statement reads all 25 values:

```
for ( i = 0; i<25;++1) { scanf ("%d",&NUM[i]);
```

Operations on Arrays

The array is a homogenous structure, i.e. the elements of an array are of the same type. Following set of operations are defined for this structure.

(i) creating an array
(ii) initialising an array
(iii) storing an element

(iv) retrieving an element
(v) inserting an element
(vi) deleting an element
(vii) searching for an element
(viii) sorting elements
(ix) printing an array

Storage

in a 2-dimensional array we think of data being arranged in rows and columns. However Machine's memory is arranged as a row of memory cells. Thus the rectangular structure of a 2-dimensional array must be simulated. We first calculate the amount of storage area needed and allocate a block of contiguous memory cells of that size. One way to store the data in the cells is row by row. That is, we store first the first row of the array, then the second row of the array and then the next and so on. For example the array defined by A which logically appears as given in Figure; appears physically as given in Figure. Such a storage scheme is called Row Major Order.

The order alternative is to store the array column by column. It is called Column Major Order. The array of Figure.

$$\begin{bmatrix} A[0][0] & A[0][1] & A[0][2] & A[0][3] \\ A[1][0] & A[1][1] & A[1][2] & A[1][3] \\ A[2][0] & A[2][1] & A[2][2] & A[2][3] \end{bmatrix}$$

Figure Logical Representation

$$\begin{bmatrix} A[0][0] \rightarrow A[0][1] \rightarrow A[0][2] \rightarrow A[0][3] \\ A[1][0] \rightarrow A[1][1] \rightarrow A[1][2] \rightarrow A[1][3] \\ A[2][0] \rightarrow A[2][1] \rightarrow A[2][2] \rightarrow A[2][3] \end{bmatrix}$$

Figure Row Major Representation

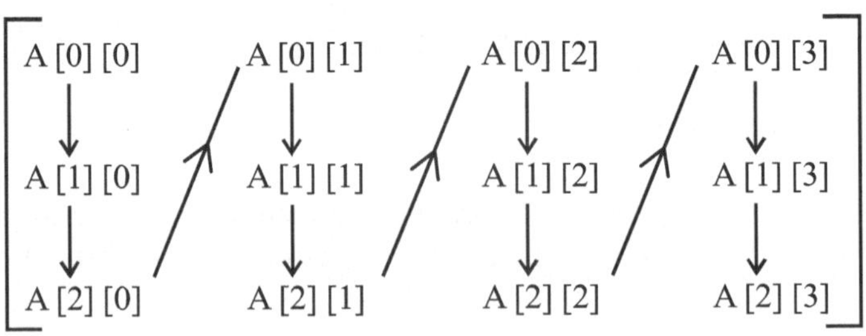

Column Major Representation

Let us now see how do we calculate the address of an element of a 2-dimensional array, which is mapped in Row Major Order. Consider a 4x6 array A[4] [6]. Take B as the array's base address and S as the size of element of the array.

To locate element A [I] [J] we must skip (I-1) rows; each having 6 elements, each element of S length and (J- 1) elements of Ith row, each of length S. Therefore, the address of element A[I] [J] would be
B+I*6*S + J*S
We may now generalize this expression for a 2-dimensional array
$A[U_0], [U_1]$
where (U_0-1) and (U_1-1) are the upper bounds of the two subscript ranges. The location of an element A[I],[J] for such an array would be
$B+I * (U_1*S + J*S$

Let us see how the above expressions work out for a column major order.

We once again consider a 4x6 array A[4] [6]. Also take B as base address and S as size of each element. Then the address of A[I,J] would be

B+J*4*S+ I*S

To reach A[I] [J] we shall skip J-1 columns, each of length 4* S and I-1 elements each of lengths. We further generalize it for an array $A[U_1] [U_2]$.

Following the same logic, the address of A[I] [J] would be given as

$B+(J*U_1*S)+(I*S)$

The column major order varies the subscripts in left to right order. For example the elements of a 2-dimensional array A[4] [3] would be stored in the sequence as given below:

A[0] [0]
A[1] [0]
A[2] [0]
A[3] [0]
.
.
.
A[0] [2]
A[1] [2]
A[2] [2]
A[3] [2]

Q1. What are Row major and Column major representations of arrays? For a character array defined as A[20] [20], if A[0] [0] is located at memory address 100, where is element A[10] [1] located in Column major representation and in Row major representation.

[JUNE04,Q1(b)][10]

Row major representation of arrays

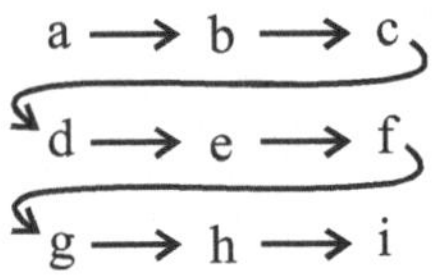

Column major representation of arrays

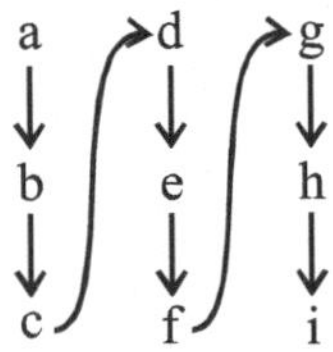

In column major representation, first column of array occupies the first set of memory locations reserved for the array, the second column occupies the next set and so on.

Given,

A[20][20]

And A[0][0] is located at memory address 100.

In row major

Formula = base address + $(i1*r^2+i2)$*size.

So address of A[10][1] = 100 + (1*20 + 10)*1

= 100 + 30

= 130.

Q2. Define the following terms : [DEC04,6(b)(iii)][5]

(i) Column major order

Refer to Page No. 214

Q3. Write an algorithm to add two polynomials. Use the array implementation. If the polynomials have M and N terms respectively, what is the time complexity of your algorithm? [DEC03, Q1(a)]

A node of linked list can represent a polynomial expression of one or two variables. Representation of polynomial expression of one variable

The structure of a node of linked list represent polynomial of one variable will be as follows:

Structure
{
int power;
int coef;
}* head = NULL ;

One polynomial term will be mapped to one node of linked list. The field "power" of a node is used represent the power of the term & the "coeff" of the node is used to represent coefficient of the term.

Example :-

Suppose we have a polynomial expression of variable.

$2x^2 + 3x^3 + 5x^5$

It will be represented as follows :

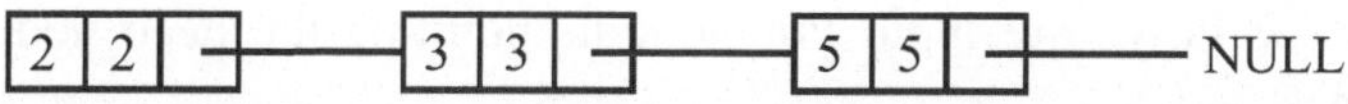

Now the polynomial expression of two variables can also be represented through linked list. The linked list representing two variable-polynomial addition will be a two way list in which a node containing the power of X will also contain all the coefficient & power of Y for which power of X is same. In this way we will maintain two linked list in which the node of first linked list will have the following fields. (i) Power of X (ii) Pointer to next node (iii) pointer to the node of second linked list.

The second list will have the fields. (i) co-efficient (ii) Power of y (iii) Pointer to next node.

Example :-

Suppose we have a two variable polynomial expression $3x^2 y^2$ then it will be represented as follows:

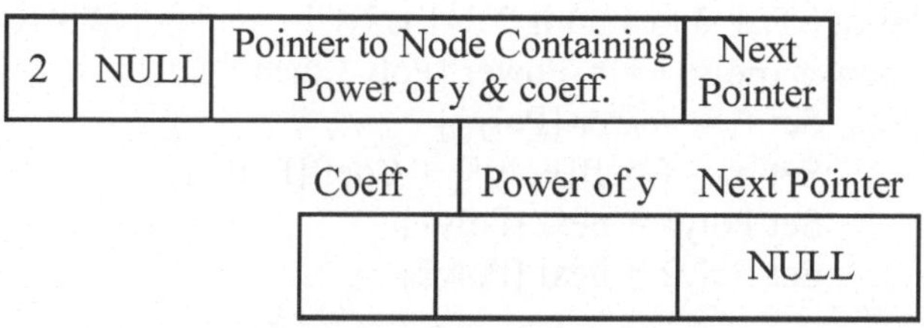

The structure of a node of linked list to represent polynomial of two variable is as follow:

structure list_y // Structure of second list
{
    int Pow_y ;

```
        int coeff;
        struct list_y *next_y;
}
struct list_x //Structure of first list
{
        int pow_x;
        structure list_y *next_xy;
        structure list_x *next_x;
}
struct list_x node_x;
```

Algorithm to add two Polynomials.

Assumption of Algorithm

(i) Here we are performing one-variable polynomial addition

(ii) Poly1 & Poly2 are input Polynomials pointing the head node of two polynomials

(iii) Poly3 is the output Polynomial which is the outcome of addition of two polynomials.

Logic of the algorithm is as follows :-

The logic of one-variable polynomial addition is that if power of corresponding terms of both Polynomials is equal, their coefficient are added and a new output term is created with the power of input term and added coefficient, otherwise, the input term having smallest power becomes new output terms. Now we move to next term of input polynomial. This process continues until any of the two input polynomials end. The rest terms of the polynomial, which did not end are added to output polynomials.

Algorithm :-

```
STEP-1 : Start
STEP-2 : Repeat STEP 3 to 4 until Poly1 is NULL and poly2 is NULL
STEP-3 : If power [poly1] = = Power [Poly2]then
                Set P = Power [Poly1]
                Set m = Coeff[Poly1] + Coeff[Poly2]
                Set Poly1 = next [Poly1]
                Set Poly2 = next [Poly2]
else
        if Power [Poly1]<Power [Poly2]then
        Set P = Power [Poly1]
        Set m = Coeff[poly1]
        Set poly1 = next [Poly1]
else
```

Set P = Power [Poly2]
Set m = Power [Poly2]
Set Poly2 = next [Poly2]

SETP-4 : Create a new node in Poly3
Set power [poly3] = p
Set coeff[Poly3] = m

STEP-5 : If Poly1 is not NULL then repeat following statements until

Poly1 is NULL
Create new node in Poly3
Set Power [Poly3] = Power [Poly1]
Set coeff [Poly3] = Coeff [Poly1]
Set poly1 = next[Poly1]

else
If Poily2 is not NULL then repeat following statements until Poly2 is NULL
Set Power [Poly3] = Power [Poly2]
Set coeff[Poly3] = Power[Poly2]
Set Poly2 = next [Poly2]

STEP-6 : Print Poly3
STEP-7 : END

Time Complexity

When the two Polynomials have m & n terms respectively, then the computing time is O(m+n), because maximum number of executions of any of the statements is bounded by m+n.

This means that if the algorithm is implemented & run on a computer, the time taken will be $C_1m+C_2n+C_3$ Where C_1, C_2, C_3, are constants. Since any algorithm that adds two Polynomials must look at each non zero term at least once, every algorithm must have a time requirement of

$C_1m+C_2n+C_3$

Q4. Write an algorithm to convert an Infix Expression which includes the operators (,), +, -, * and / to Postfix Expression. [DEC03,(b)][10]

Convert Infix expression to postfix.

Algorithm

1) pick an element from the expression E
2) if element =operand then
   [print element goto step 1]

```
3) if element = operator then
   [while (priority(element) <=priority(stack[top])) and stack[top]<>'(' )
   [pop an element from stack and print it]
   [push element on the stack ];
   goto step 1]

4) if element ='(' then
   [push element on the stack ; goto step1]

5) if element =')' then
   [while stack[top]<>'(' ]
   [pop an element from stack; if element <> '(' then print it ]
   go to step 1;]

6) if element =';' then
   [while (stack is not empty)]
   [pop an element from stack and print it]
   goto step 7]

7) end
```

Q5. Given two Sorted Lists, L_1 and L_2, write an algorithm to compute $L_1 \cup L_2$. L_1 and L_2 are to be implemented as Arrays.

[JUNE03,Q1(b)][10]

```
#include<stdio.h>
#include<conio.h>
void main()
{
    int p,q,m,n,c;
    int array1[100],array2[100],array3[200];
    puts("Enter number of element of the first sorted array");
    scanf("%d",&p);
    puts("Enter element of the first sorted array");

    for(m=0;m<=p;m++)
    scanf("%d",&array1[m]);
    puts("Enter number of element of the second sorted array");
    scanf("%d",&q);
    puts("Enter element of the second array");
    for(n=0;n<=q;n++)
    scanf("%d",&array2[n]);
      c=0;
```

```
    m=0;
    n=0;

   while((m<q)&&(n<q))
   {
    if(array1[m]<=array2[n])
    array3[c]=array1[m++];
    else
    array3[c]=array2[n++];
    c++;
   }

   while(m<p)
   {
    array3[c]=array1[m];
    c++;
    m++;
   }
   while(n<q)
   {
    array3[c]=array2[n];
    c++;
    n++;
   }
   puts("Merged array in ascending order");
   for(m=0;m<=c;m++)
   printf("%d",array3[m]);
}
```

Q6. Write an algorithm for the addition of two matrices. The second matrix will be a sparse matrix. The first matrix is not a sparse matrix. [JUNE03,Q3(b)][5]

This question tells us to write an algorithm to add two metrices in which second input matrix is a sparse, matrix but the first input matrix is not a sparse matrix.

In a sparse matrix, three are large number of zero entries.

Here we do addition of sparse and another non-sparse matrix according to the rules of sparse additions rules:

(a) If jth column of ith row of one sparse matrix has a non-zero entry & the jth column of the ith row of second sparse matrix has also non-zero entry and the data value of both are added and inserted in the resultant sparse matrix according to the rules of sparse addition. The resultant matrix will also be treated as sparse matrix.

Assumptions :-

(a) Sparse1[5][5] is a sparse matrix also one of the input matrix
(b) Array1 [5][5] is non-sparse matrix
(c) The resultant matrix is Result[5][5]
(d) Addsparse( )

This function adds two matrices sparse [5][5] and Array[5][5] according to the rules of addition of sparse matrix, since one input array is sparse & other is non-sparse.

Step-1 : Set i = 0
Set j = 0

Step-2 : Repeat step 3 to 6 until i>= 5

Step-3 : Repeat step 4 to 5 until j>= 5

Step-4 : CHECK [Sparse [i][j] ! = 0]
Set Result [i][j] = Sparse [i][j] + Array 1 [i][j];
Else
CHECK [Sparse [i][j] = = 0]
Set Result [i][j] = Sparse [i][j] + Array 1 [i][j];
Else
CHECK [Sparse [i][j] = = 0]
Set Result[i][j] = Array1 [i][j]]

Step-5 : Set j = j + 1

Step-6 : Set i = i + 1

Step-7 : END

Q7. Write an algorithm for multiplication of two matrices.

[DEC02, Q3(b)][5]

Step 1 : [Check condition of multiplicity]

If $Col_1 = Row_2$ [When we are taking column of firs matrix and multiplying it with rows of second matrix]

Repeat for I = 0, 1, 2, …… $Row_1 - 1$
Repeat for J = 0, 1, 2, ……$Col_1 - 1$
Mat_res[I][J] = 0

Repeat for k = 0, 1, 2, …… $Col_1 - 1$
Mat_res[I][J] = Mat_res[I][J] = Mat_1 [I][J]*Mat_2[K][J]
Else if $Row_1 = Col_2$ [When we are taking rows of first matrix and multiplying it with the columns of the second matrix]
Repeat for I = 0, 1, 2, ……. $Col_1 - 1$
Repeat for J = 0, 1, 2,…….. $Row_2 - 1$
Mat_res[I][J] = 0
Repeat for K = 0, 1, 2, …… $Col_2 - 1$
Mat_res[I][J] = Mat_res[I][J] + Mat_1[I][J]*Mat_2[K][J]
Else
Output "Multiplication is not possible" and Exit
Step 2: Exit

Q8. If A = (a_1, a_2, ……, a_n) and B = (b_1, b_2, …., b_m) are ordered lists and are represented by Arrays, then write an algorithm for the concatenation of the above ordered lists. [JUNE02, Q1(a)][10]

```
#include<stdio.h>
#include<conio.h>
void main()
{
int p,q,m,n,c;
int array1[100],array2[100],array3[200];
puts("Enter number of element of the first sorted array");
scanf("%d",&p);
puts("Enter element of the first sorted array");
for(m=0;m<p;m++)
scanf("%d",&array1[m]);
puts("Enter number of element of the second sorted array");
scanf("%d",&q);
puts("Enter element of the second array");
for(n=0;n<q;n++)
scanf("%d",&array2[n]);
c=0;
m=0;
n=0;
while((m<q)&&(n<q))
{
if(array1[m]<=array2[n])
array3[c]=array1[m++];
else
array3[c]=array2[n++];
c++;
```

```
}
while(m<p)
{
array3[c]=array1[m];
c++;
m++;
}
while(n<q)
{
array3[c]=array2[n];
c++;
n++;
}
puts("Merged array in ascending order");
for(m=0;m<=c;m++)
printf("%d",array3[m]);
}
```

Q9. Write an algorithm for the addition of two sparse matrices (use proper representation for sparse matrices). [JUNE02,Q3(b)][5]

Sparse Matrices can be represented either through linked list or double dimensional array. The linked representation of sparse Matrices represent it in dynamic data structure & the array representation of sparse matrices represent it in sequential data structure.

Here for this question, we are representing sparse matrices through linked list. The structure of a node of linked list to represent one value of sparse matrices will be

Row - No	Col - No.	Data	Pointer to Next Node

The linked list for sparse matrix is represented through array of pointers.

The logic for the addition of two sparse matrices are as follows:

(i) If row number & column number of corresponding node of both input sparse matrices are equal then add their data value & Create a node in resultant sparse matrix with row number, column number & added Data value.

(ii) If row number of corresponding nodes of both input sparse Matrices are same but the col. Numbers are not same then the node with row no. & smallest column value will be attached to resultant sparse matrix.

(iii) If row number of corresponding nodes are not equal then the node with smallest row number will be copied to resultant sparse matrix.

Assumptions of algorithm

(i) The input sparse matrices are being represented as:

```
struct sparse
{
int data ;
int rowno ;
int colon ;
struct sparse *next ;
} *s1[ ROW ], *s2[ ROW ], *s3[ ROW ] ;
```

Where s1 [ROW], s2 [ROW] are input sparse matrices & s3 [ROW] is resultant sparse matrix.

(ii) We assume that the input sparse matrices are already created & given to us, we have to only design the algorithm for adding them.

Algorithm

```
Step-1 : Start

Step-2 : set i = 0

Step-3 : while (i < ROW)
{
    Set p = s1[ i ] ; [ p is pointer to sparse s1 [ROW]]
    Set q = s2[ i ] ; [ q is the pointer to sparse s2 [ROW ]]

Step-4 : While (p ! = NULL && q ! = NULL)
{
            if(colon[p] = = colon[q])
            {
                Create a node n in sparse matrix s3 [ i ] & put
                set colon[ n ] = colon[ p ] ;
                set rowno [ n ] = i ;
                set data[ n ] = i ;
                set data[ n ] = data[ p ] + data[ q ] ;
                set p = next[ p ] ;
                set q = next[q] ;
            }
else
{
        if (colon[p] < colon[q] )
        {
                create a node n in sparse matrix s3[ i ] & put
                set rowno[ n ] = i ;
                set colon[ n ] = colon[ p ] ;
```

```
                set data[n] = data[ p ] ;
                set p = next[ p ];
        }
else
{
                Create a node n in sparse matrix s3 [ i ] & put
                Set colon[ n ] = colon[ q ] ;
                Set data[ n ] = data[ q ] ;
                Set rowno[ n ] = i ;
                Set q = next[ q ] ;
        }
        } / * end of second while * /

Step-5 : if (p ! = NULL && q = = NULL)
        {
                While (p ! = NULL)
                {
                Create a node n in sparse matrix s3 [ i ] & put
                Set colon[ n ] = colon[ p ] ;
                Set data[ n ] = data[p] ;
                        Set rowno [ n ] = i
                        Set p = next [ p ] ;
        }
}
else
{
if (p = = NULL && q ! = NULL)
{
        While (q ! = NULL)
        {
                Create a node n in sparse matrix s3 [ i ] & put
                Set colon[ n ] = colon[ q ] ;
                Set data[ n ] = data[ q ] ;
                Set rowno[n] = i ;
                Set q = next[ q ] ;
        }
}
}
Set i = i + 1 ;
} [ end of while ]
Step-6 : End
```

Now we write the algorithm to print the value of s3[ROW] matrices.

```
Step-1 : Set i = 0

Step-2 : While (i < ROW)
         {
Step-3 : Step p = s1 [ i ] ;

Step-4 : While (p ! = NULL)
             {
                 Print data[ p ] ;
                 Set p = next [ p ] ;
             {
             i = i + 1 ;
           }
Step-5 : Set i = 0
         While (i < ROW)
             {
             Set p s2[ i ] ;
                 While (p ! = NULL)
              {
                 Print data[ p ] ;
                 Set p next[ p ] ;
              }
             i = i + 1
              }

Step-7 : Set i = 0
         While (i < ROW)
         {
              Set p = s3 [ i ] ;
             While (p ! = NULL)
              {
                 Print data[ p ] ;
                 Set p = next[ p ] ;
              }
         }
Step-10 : End
```

Lists

➢ **Link or pointer :** A pointer also called a link or a reference, is defined to be a variable that gives the location of some other variable, typically of a structure containing data. If we use pointers to locate all the structures themselves are actually stored, since by using a pointer, we can let the computer system itself locate the structure when requires.

The figure shows links to several structures:

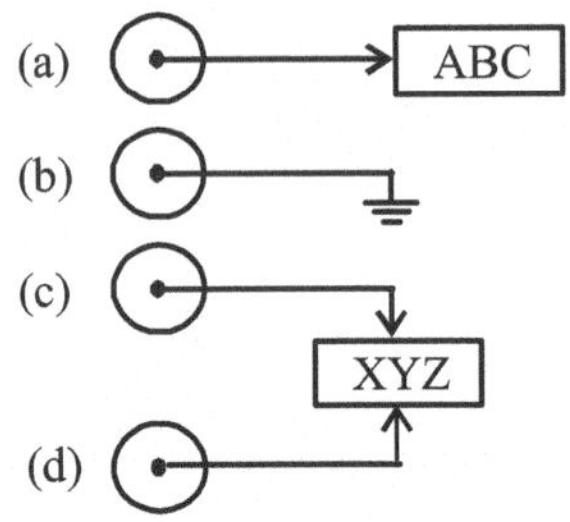

➢ **List :** First one is a dynamic data structure because its size. A list of numbers is type of structure whose size is variable, that is, a list for which numbers can be inserted or deleted, so that, if n = 3 then the list contain only 3 numbers and it n = 20 then it contain 20 numbers.

Generally the list is based on the concept of information hiding, that is if someone else had already written the functions for handling lists, then we could use them without need to know the details of how lists are kept in memory or how the list operations are actually done.

➢ **Linked list :** The idea of a linked list is for every structure in the list, to put a pointer into the structure giving the location of the next structure in the list. This idea is illustrated in Figure.

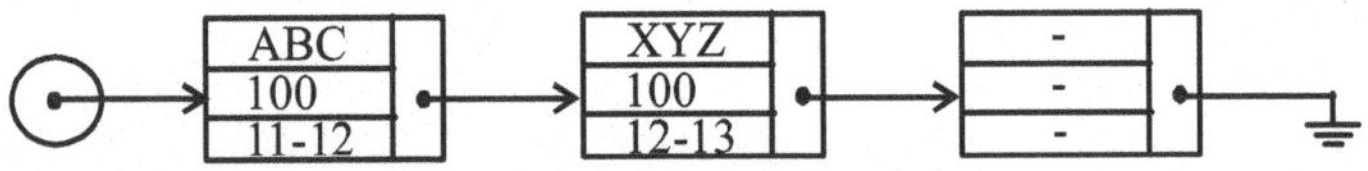

As you can see from the illustration, a linked list is simple in concept. A linked list may be considered analogous to following locations where each instruction is given out only upon completion of the previous task. There is then no inherent limit on the number of tasks to be done, since each task may specify a new instruction, and there is no way to specify a new instruction, and there is no way to tell in advance how many instructions are there.

➢ **Advantage & Disadvantage of linked list**

✓ ***Advantage***

1) Flexibility : The main advantage of linked list is dynamic storage which provides flexibility

2) Overflow : There is no overflow problem until the computer memory is actually exhausted. Especially when the individual records are quite large, it may be difficult to determine the amount of contiguous static storage. But with dynamic allocation, there is a no need to attempt to make such decisions in advance.

3) Changes : Changes, especially insertions and deletions, can be made in a middle of a linked list more quickly. If the structure are large, then it is much quicker to change the value of a few pointers then to copy the structures themselves from one location to another.

✓ ***Disadvantages:***

1) Space use : The first drawback of linked list is that the links themselves take space - space that might otherwise be needed for additional data.
In the most system the pointer requires the same amount of storage (one word) as does an integer. Thus, the lists of integers will require double the space in linked storage that it would require in contiguous storage.

2) Random access : The major drawback of linked lists is that they are not suited to random access. Because with a linked list, it may be necessary to traverse a long path to reach the desired node.

3) Access time : Access to a single node in linked storage may even take slightly more computing time, since it is necessary, first, to obtain the pointer and then go to the address.

4) Programming : The writing functions to manipulate linked list as a bit more programming effort, but, with practice, this discrepancy will decrease.

Contiguous storage is preferable :

✓ When the records are individually very small;
✓ When the size of limit is known when the program is written.
✓ When few insertion or deletion need to be made at the end of the list.

➢ **Types of link list**

1) Single or simple link list
2) Doubly linked list
3) Circular linked list
4) Double-Circular linked list.

✓ **Doubly linked list**

Some applications of link list require that we frequently move both forward and backward through the list. The idea is shown in figure is to keep two links in each node, pointing in opposite directions. Hence, by following the appropriate link, we can move either direction through the linked list with equal ease. We call such a list a doubly linked list.

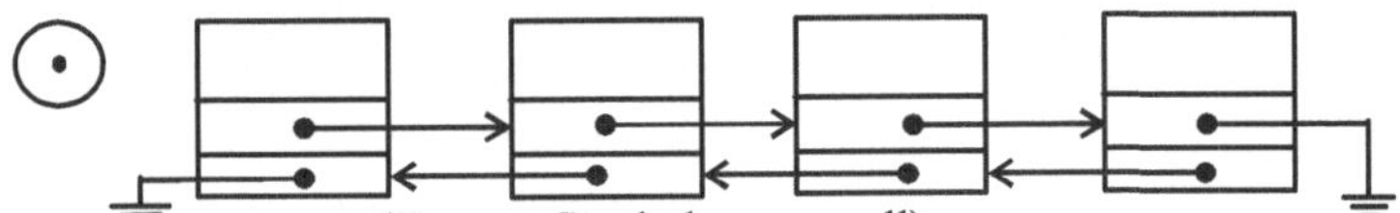

(Here ⏚ Symbol means null)

➢ **Circular link list**

A Circular link list, is a linked list in which the node at the tail of the list, instead of having a NULL Pointer, point, back to the node at the head of the list. We then need only one pointer tail to access both ends of the list, Since we know that tail next points back to the head of the list. The idea of list is shown in fig.

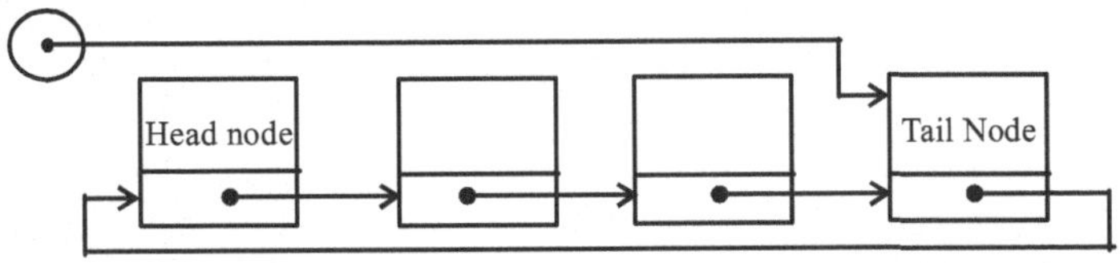

Fig. A circularly linked list with tail pointer

Q10. Write an algorithm for creation of a Singly Linked List. Also write algorithms for insertion and deletion of elements from the Singly Linked List. [JUNE04, Q4(a)][5]

➢ **Algorithm of Creation of a linked list**

An algorithm for creation of a linked list is given below :

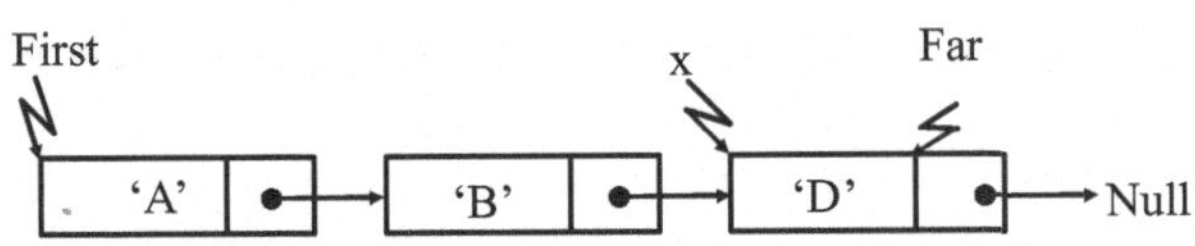

CREATE → In this algorithm a linked list of nodes is created. The list is pointed by a pointer first, the last node of the list points to NULL, indicating the end of the list. Each node is having two parts DATA and NEXT. Let us assume that a linked list of N number of nodes is to be created. The operator new will be used for the dynamic allocation of node. A variable I is being used as a counter to count the number of nodes in the created list.

Steps :

1. first=new node;{create the 1st node of the list pointed by first) ;
2. Read(Data (first));
3. NEXT(First) = NULL;
4. Far a First; [point Far to the first]
5. For I = 1 to N-1 repeat steps 6 to 10

6. X = new node;
7. Read (DATA (X)
8. NEXT (X) = NULL;
9. NEXT (Far) =X; {connect the nodes}
10. Far =X; [shift the pointer to the last node of the list]
 [end of For loop]
11. END

➢ Traversing a linked list

Many a times, it is required to traverse whole of a linked list. For example, counting of nodes in a list, printing data of all the nodes etc. an algorithm for traversing a linked list is given below:

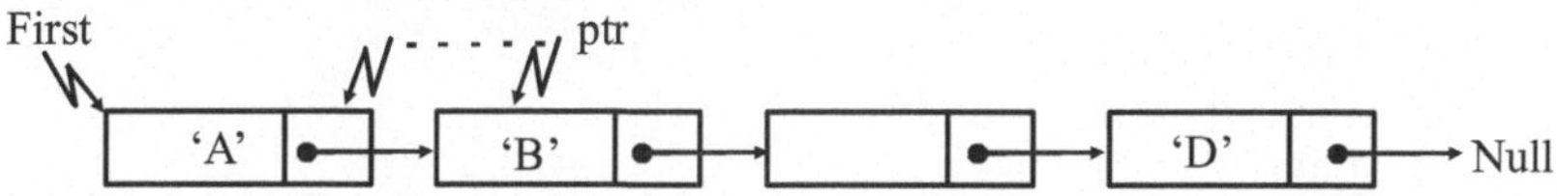

Travel : In this algorithm a linked list, pointed by first, is traversed. The number of nodes in the list is also counted during the traverse. A pointer ptr is being used to visit the various nodes in the list. A variable count is used to keep track of the number of nodes visited during the traverse. The traversal Stops when a NULL is encountered.

***Steps* :** 1. If First = NULL then {print " List empty" STOP;
 }
 2. count = 0; {initialize count}
 3. ptr = First; {point ptr to the 1 st node}
 4. While ptr<> NULL repeat steps 5 to 6
 5. count = count + 1;
 6. ptr = NEXT(ptr) [shift ptr to the next node]
 [end of while]
 7. print ('Number of nodes=', count)
 8. End

In the above algorithm, Step 6 is worth noting i.e. ptr = NEXT (ptr). This step means that the pointer Ptr should be shifted to the node which is being pointed by NEXT (ptr).

➢ *Searching a linked list*

Search is an operation in which an item is searched in a linked list. This operation is similar to traveling the list. An algorithm for search operation is given below:

Search : In this algorithm a linked list, pointed by First, is traversed. While traversing. The data part of each visited node is compared with an item 'x'. If the item is found then the search stops otherwise the process continues till the end of the list (i.e. NULL) is encountered. A pointer ptr is being used to visit the various nodes in the list.

Steps : 1. If first = NULL the {
Print "LIST empty"; STOP;}
2. ptr = First; [point ptr to the 1 st node]
3. while (ptr<> NULL) repeat steps 4 to 5
4. If (DATA (ptr) = 'X')
then {print " Item found;
STOP
}
5. ptr = NEXT (ptr); [shift ptr to the next node]
[end of while]
6. Print "item not found";
7. END

It may be noted in the above algorithm that if the item 'X' is found then the search stops.

Insert : In this algorithm a node X is inserted at the beginning of a linked list. The linked list is being pointed by a pointer First at the beginning.

Steps : 1. X = new node;
2. Read (DATA (X);
3. If (FIRST=NULL) then
{ First =X;
NEXT (X)= NULL;
}
else {NEXT (X) = First;
First = X;
}
4. END

The list structure before and after the insert operation is shown in following figure.

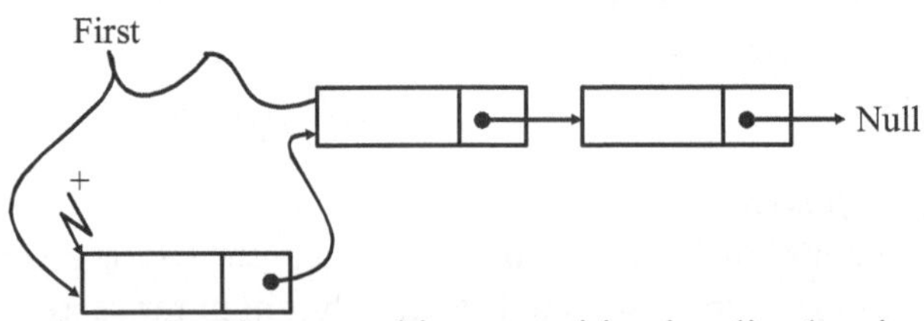

If we desire to insert data into an arbitrary position in a list then it can either be inserted after a node or before a node in the list. An algorithm for insertion of Data- after a selected node in a linked list is given below:

Insert [after a node] : Let List be a pointer to a linked list. In this algorithm a node X is inserted in the list after a node with data part equal to 'VAL'. A pointer ptr travels the list in such a way that each visited node is checked for data part equal to 'VAL'. If such a node is found then node X is inserted after the same.

Steps :
```
1.   ptr =  List;
2.   while  (ptr < > NULL)  repeat steps 3 to 4
3.   If  ( DATA (ptr)  = 'VAL') then
       {X= new node
        Read (DATA (X);
         NEXT (X) =  NEXT (ptr)
         NEXT (ptr) = X;
        Break;
4.   ptr =NEXT (ptr)
     [end of while]
5.   END
```

It may be noted in the above algorithm that in step 3 a function exit () has been used. The purpose of this function is to leave the while loop. The resulting list structure is shown in following Figure.

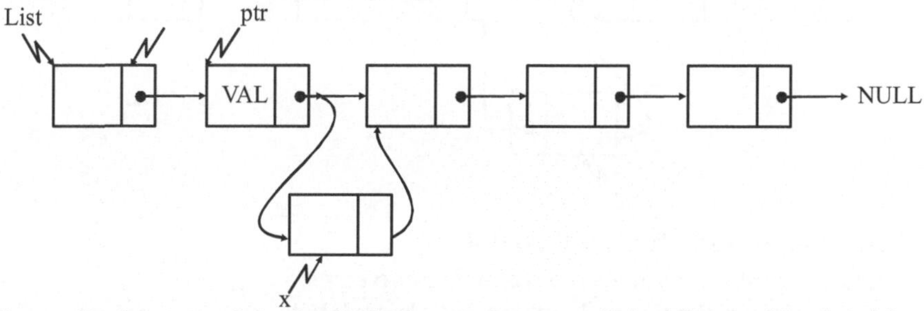

Insert[before a node] : Let LIST be a pointer to a linked list. In this algorithm a node X is inserted in the list before a node with data part equal to 'VAL' Two Pointers ptr & back travel the list in such a way that each visited node is checked for data part equal to 'VAL' . If such a node is found then ptr points to the selected node and back point to immediate previous node in the list. The node X is inserted before the selected node.

Steps :
```
1.  ptr =LIST
    [check if the first node is the desired one]
2.   If  (data (ptr) = 'VAL' ) then
      { X = new nod ;
      Read DATA (X);
    NEXT (X) =LIST;
    LIST = X;
```

```
STOP;
    }
3. While (ptr <> NULL ) repeat steps 4 to 6
4. back = ptr;
5. ptr =NEXT (ptr);
6. If (DATA (ptr) ='VAL' ) then
  { X = new node;
       read DATA (X);
       NEXT (X) = ptr;
NEXT (back) = X;
Exit;
}
[end of while loop]
7. END
```

The resulting structure of the list after the insert operation is shown in figure.

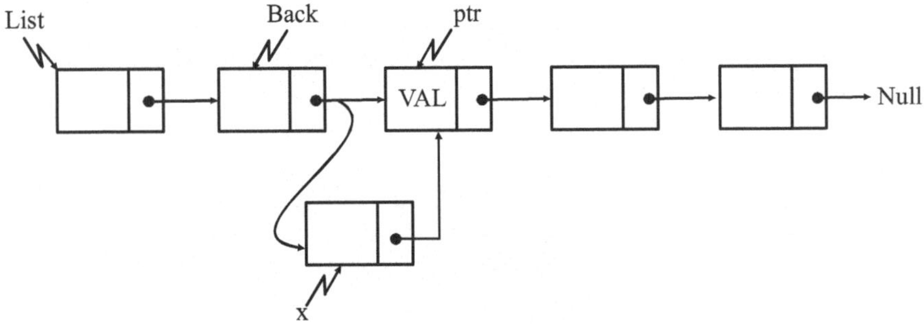

➢ Deleting a Node from a linked list

A delete operation involves the following two steps:

1. search the list for the node which is to be deleted.
2. delete the node.

An algorithm for the deletion of a node from a linked list is given below :

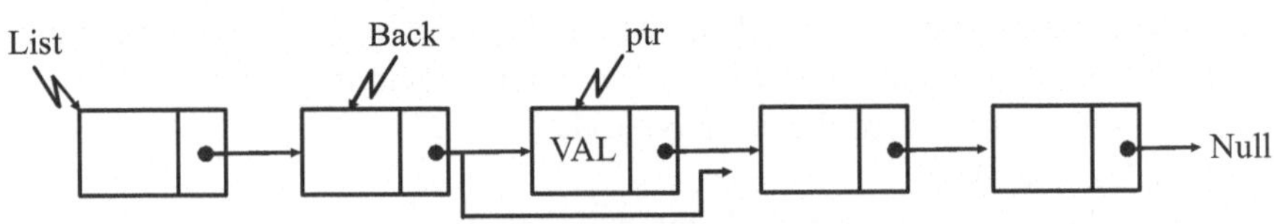

Delete: Let LIST be a pointer to a linked list. In this algorithm a node with data value equal to 'VAL'. Deleted from the list. Two pointers PTR& back travel the list in such a way that each visited node is checked for data part equal to 'VAL'. If such a node is found then ptr points to the selected node and back points to immediate previous node in the list. The selected node is deleted from the list.

Steps : [check if the first node is the desired one]

```
1.  If ( DATA (list) = 'VAL') then
                 {ptr = LIST;
          LIST = NEXT (list);
          Delete ptr;
           Stop ;
                 }
           back = list;
           ptr  =  list;
2.  while ( ptr < > NULL ) repeat steps 3 to 5
3.  If ( DATA ( ptr )  = 'VAL') then
                 {NEXT(back) =NEXT  (Ptr);
                 delete ptr;
          Exit;
4.  back  = ptr;
5.  ptr = next (ptr);
         [end of while loop]
6.  END
```

It may be noted here that the search operation had an upper hand over the insert and delete algorithms for linked lists. Therefore, efficiency and correctness of these algorithms are very much dependent upon the search operation.

➢ Algorithms and logics

Insertion in beginning of doubly linked list

(1)

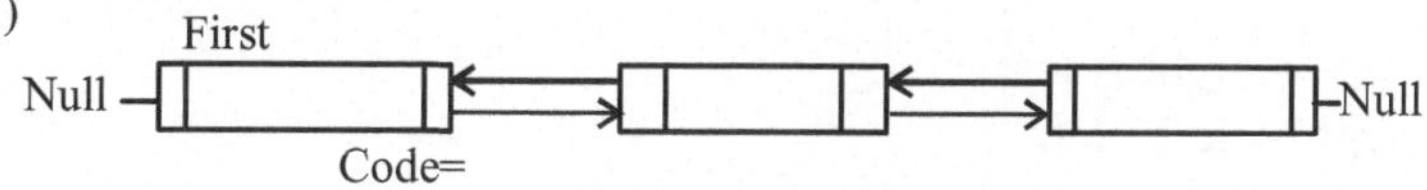

(1) Newpt $\rightarrow$ right=first;
(2) first $\rightarrow$ left = Newpt;
(3) first = Newpt;

(2)

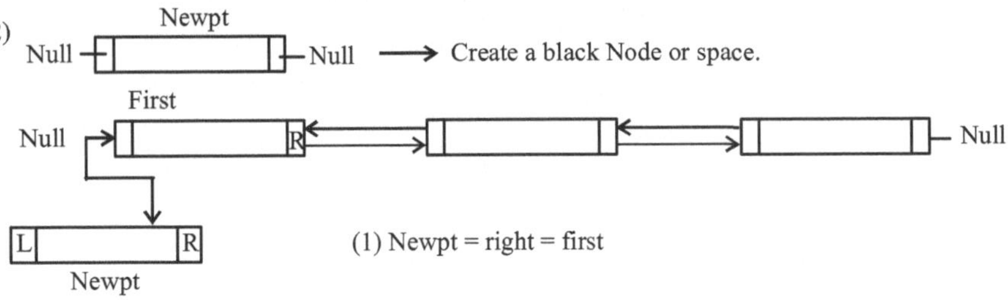

(3)

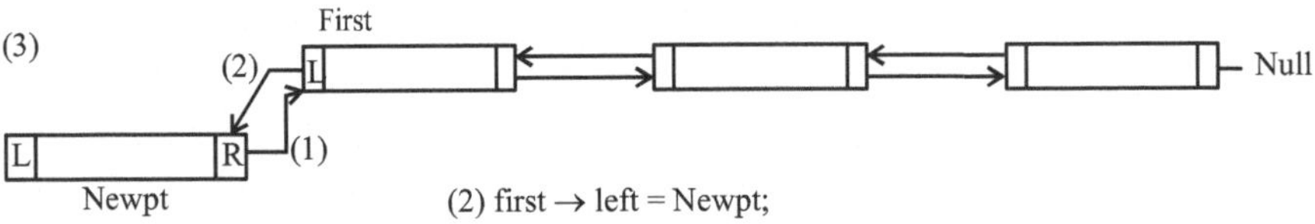

(4)

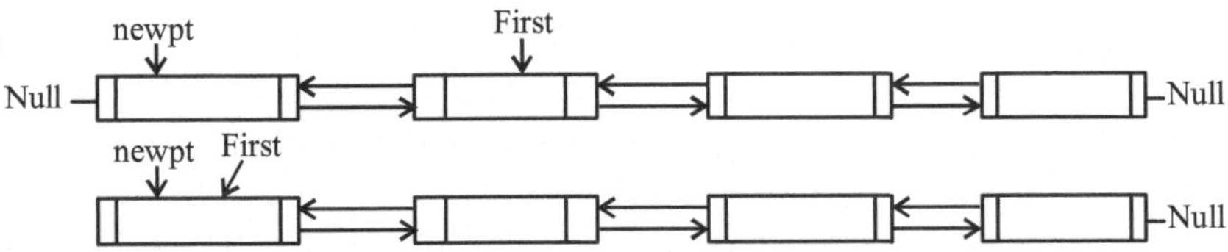

First = Newpt

(3) Shifting the pointer position.

Insertion in middle of the Node or before the Search node

Link code

(1) Newpt →right = last

(2) Newpt → left =left

(3) last → left → right = Newpt

(4) last → left = Newpt.

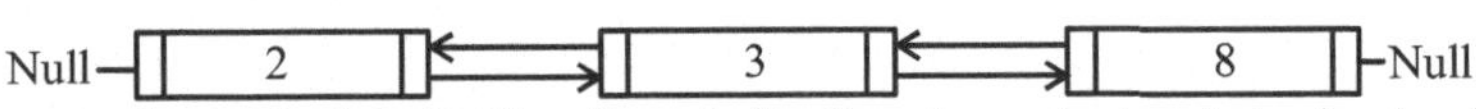

Suppose to insert before 8. You Search for 8 and you last pointer is also locate a Search node.

(1)

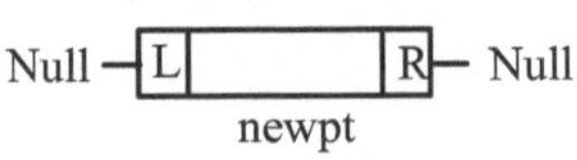

(1) Newpt → left = last → left

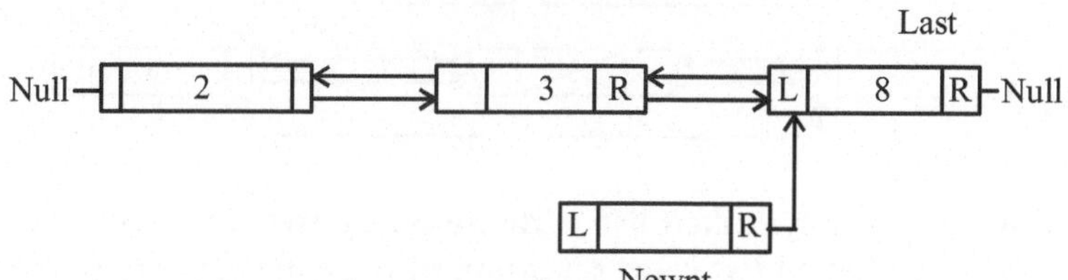

Here, Replace the value of b = a means all the addresses that are stored in last → left is not moved or replaced with the Newpt →left. So that Newpt automatic point the address of previous list.

(2) Last → Left → Right = Newptr

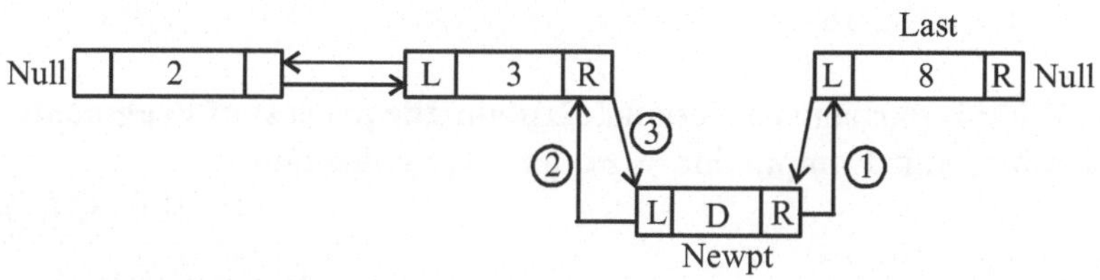

(3) Last → left = Newptr;

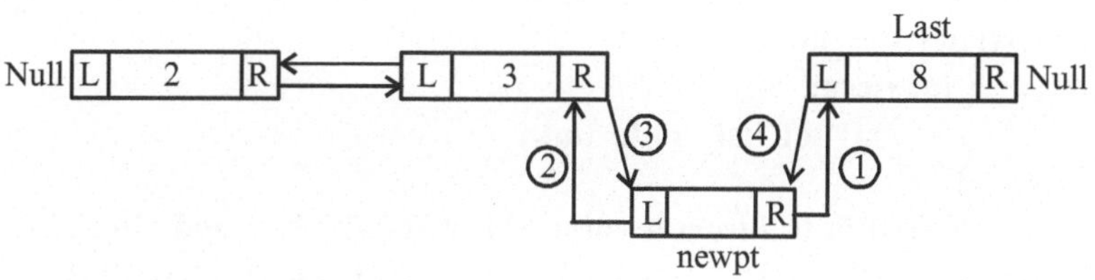

Deletion in double link list

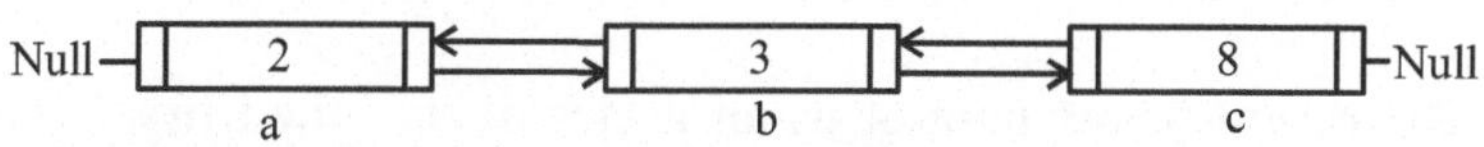

We want to delete b node then following Steps are followed :

(1) Search the node value that you want to delete

(2) Delete or free the memory location

(3) link the node or list.

(1) last → left → right = last;

last → right → left = last → left;

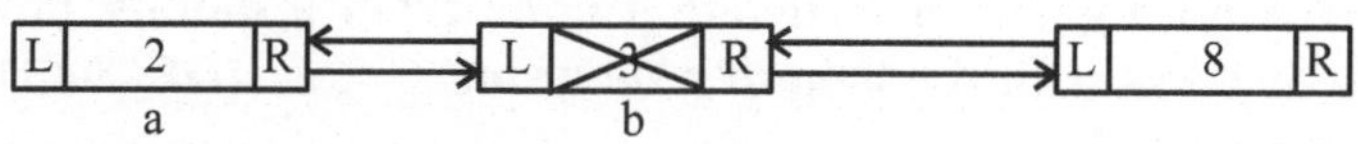

Want to delete 3

(2) last → left → right = last

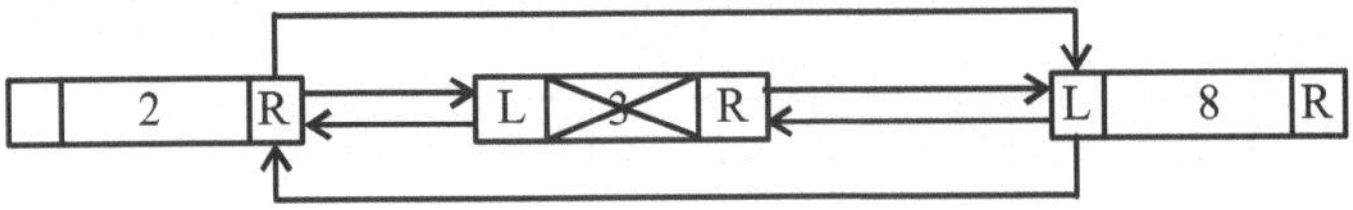

Q11. What is a singly linked list ? Mention any two advantage of singly linked list Give linked list representation of the following sparse matrix:

$$\begin{bmatrix} 0 & 1.2 & 0 & 3 \\ 0 & 0 & 0 & 0 \\ 0.5 & 0 & 1 & 0 \\ 0 & 1.5 & 0 & 0 \end{bmatrix}$$

[JUNE05,Q2(a)][5]

Refer to Page No. 183

Q12. What is garbage collection ? Explain the process of Fragmentation, Relocation, and Compaction w.r.t. garbage collection.
[JUNE05,Q4(a)][8]

Refer to Page No. 191

Q13. Consider the following declaration :

```
struct list_node
  { int data;
        struct list_node link;
   };
```

Write an algorithm to insert a value 'M' after the last node in the Singly Linked List. [JUNE05, Q4(b)][2]

Refer to Page No. 193

Q14. Represent a polynomial using a circularly inked list. Write an algorithm to subtract two polynomials using the representation above. What is the time complexity of your algorithm to subtract two polynomials using the representation above. What is the time complexity of your algorithm ? [DEC04, Q1(a)][10]

Refer to Page No. 198

Q15. Write an algorithm to delete a node from a doubly linked list. Show the process with the help of a diagram. [DEC04,Q2(b)][5]

Refer to Page No. 204

Q16. Write a function to multiply two polynomials, using a linked list implementation. You must make sure that the output polynomial is sorted by exponent and has atmost one term corresponding to any power. Assume appropriate representation for input polynomials.

[JUNE03, Q1(a)][15]

A node of linked list can represent one term of a polynomial. A node of linked list is able to represent polynomial expression of one or two variable.
Here in our question, we are taking the polynomials of one variables.
The structure of one variable polynomial term will be as follows:

```
struct link_type
{
int power;
int coeff;struct link_type *next;
} * polyhead;
```

One polynomial term will be mapped into one node of linked list. The field "power" of a node is used to represent the power of the term & the coefficient, will be used to represent the coefficient of the term.
E.g. Suppose we have a polynomial expression of one variable.
$2x^3 + 3x^3 + 5x^5$
It will be represented as :-

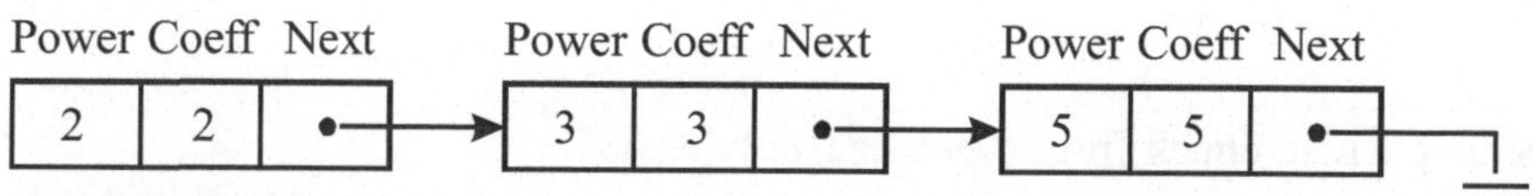

Assumption :-
(i) We have been given two input polynomials represented through linked list
(ii) The pointers polyhead1 & polyhead2 are used to point input polynomials respectively.
(iii) The resultant polynomial will also be represented through linked list & it will be pointed by the pointer polyhead3.
(iv) C-implementation of one node of polynomial will be declared as :

```
sruct polytype
{
int power;
int coeff;
struct poltype *next;
}
```

(v) We have two functions insert( ) & multiply( ). Multiply( ) will multiply the terms of two polynomials & insert( ) will insert the multiplied value into third resultant polynomial.

Step-1 : set p = polyhead2
Set q = polyhead1
Step-2 : Repeat step 3 to 6 unitl q is not = NULL.
Step-3 : set p = polyhead1
Step-4 : Repeat step 5 unitl p us not = NULL
Step-5 : set m = coeff[p] *coeff[q]
Set n = power[p] + power [q]
Call insert (m,n)
Set p = next[p]
Setp-6 : set q = nect [q]
Setp-7 : end
Insert (m,n)

The insert (m,n) insert a term resultant polynomial pointed by ployhead3. The power of term will be m & coefficient will be n

Step-1 : Check [polynomial3 is = NULL]
Set polynomial3 = call memory area equal to the size of a node of linked list representing polynomial
set power [polyhead3] = n;
set coeff. [polyhead3] = m;
set next [polyhead3] = NULL;

Step-2 : Else check [n is < power [[polyhead3]]
Set G = call a memory area equal to the size to the a node of lined list representing polynomial
Set power [G] = n;
Set coeff [G] = m;
Set next [G] = polyhead 3;
Set polyhead3 G

Step-3 : else
Set s = p[olyhead3
Repeat step 4 until power[s] is < n s is not = NULL

Step-4 : set T = s
Set s = next [s];

Step-5 : check [s is not = and power [s] is = n]
set coeff [s] = coeff [s] + m;

Step-6 : else
set G = call a memory area equal to the size of node of linked list representing polynomial
set power [G] = n;
set coeff [G] m;
set next [G] next[T]
set next[T] = G

Step-7 : END

Q17. Let 'P' be a pointer to a doubly linked list. Show how this list may be used as a queue by writing algorithms to add and delete elements. Specify the value for 'P' when the queue is empty. [DEC02, Q1(b)][10] [DEC01, Q1(b)]

Here we have to implement queue through circular linked list.
A circular linked list is a data structure in which last node's address field points to the first node.
To implement a queue through this circular list, we will have to keep two pointers say rear & front. Front will point the first node of the queue & rear will point to the last node of the queue. Here front will be the value of "p" given in question. We are assuming that the circular linked list is being implemented in dynamic data structure.
Thus the value of "P" will be NULL when the queue is empty.
A queue implemented as circular list is called circular queue.
It can be shown figuratively as follows:

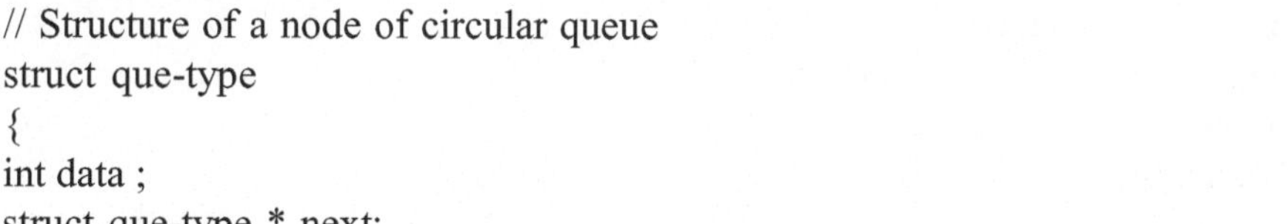

Global declarations

```
// Structure of a node of circular queue
struct que-type
{
int data ;
struct que-type * next;
};
struct que-type * rear = NULL, *front = NULL;
                                // rear will Point to the end of queue & front will
                                // point to the starting node of queue.
typedef struct que-type que;
```

```
void insertq (int);          // Function will insert a data
                             // in circular queue
                             // this function will delete an element
                             // from circular queue
void insertq (int value)     // Function definition
                             // value is the data item to
                             // be inserted in circular queue
{
que *p;
if(front = NULL && rear = NULL)
{
        rear = (que * )malloc (sizeof (que));
        rear -> data = value ;
        rear -> next = NULL ;
        front = rear ;
        rear-> next = front;        // Making the queue circular
}
else
        p = (que*) malloc (sizeof(que));
        p-> data = value;
        p-> next = rear -> next;
        rear = p;
}
}                            // end of function
int deletq (void)            // function definition
{
int p;
if (front = = NULL)          // underflow condition
        print ("n que empty");
else
{
p = front -> data ;
rear -> next = front -> next ;
front = front -> next ;
return (p);
}
}                            // end of function
```

Q18. A general polynomial A(x) can be written as
$a_n x^n + a_{n-1} x^{n-1} + ... + a_1 x + a_0$
where $a_n \neq 0$ and we say that the degree of A is 'n'. Each $a_i x^i$ is a term of

the polynomial. If $a_i = 0$, then it is a zero term, otherwise, it is a non-zero term. Now, write an algorithm which evaluates a polynomial at a value 'x_0'. [DEC01, Q1(a)] [10]

The algorithm is :

Step-0 : initialize the sum by 0
Step-1 : define the structure as –
coefficient – a, x
exponent – n
Step-2 : accept the exponent value
Step-3 : initialize the counter by 0
Step-4 : accept the value of 'x'
Step-5 : allocate memory for the structure
Step-6 : accept the value 'a' in the structure
Step-7 : evaluate the equation
- val = a × (x × x............n times)
sum = sum + val
Step-8 : decrease the value of n by 1
Step-9 : if n > = 0 then go to step-4
Step-10 : print the value of sum

Q19. Give the node structure for implementing a linked list containing two information fields viz. info 1, info 2. Let p be the pointer to the first node of the linked list. Traverse the linked list to go to the node containing the information info 1 = u and then print the info 1 and info 2 fields. [JUNE01, Q1(b)][10]

```
// Program to insert a node at the beginning of a linked list
// containing two info fields.
// The program also searches the list for a particular node
#include <stdio.h>
#include <conio.h>
#include <alloc.h>
typedef struct node
{
  int info1;
  int info2 ;
  struct node *link ;
}
node ;
void main ( )
{
```

```
    int data1, data2 ;
    node *head=NULL, *tail ;
    char ch ;
    node *add (node *, int, int) ;
    do
    {
      printf ( "Enter info1 : \n") ;
      scanf ( "%d" ,&data1) ;
      printf ( "Enter, infor2 : \n") ;
      scanf ( "%d", &data2) ;
      head=add (head, data1, data2) ;
      printf ( "Continue ?\n") ;
      ch=getche ( ) ;
    }
    while (ch != 'n'  &&  ch!= 'N') ;
    printf ("The list is \n") ;
    for (tail = head; tail!= NULL; tail=tail ->link)
    {
      printf( "%d ", tail->info1) ;
      printf( "%d\t ", tail->info2) ;
    }
    printf ( "\nEnter data to be searched as info1 \n") ;
    scanf ( "%d", &data1) ;
    for (tail=head; tail!=NULL && tail->info1 !=data1; tail=tail->link) ;
    if (tail ==NULL)
      printf ( "Node not found\n") ;
    else
      printf ("Info1=%d          Info2=%d\n" , tail->info1, tail->info2) ;
    getch ( ) ;
  }

  node *add (node *head, int data1, int data2)
  {
    node *save, *first ;
    first = (node *) malloc (sizeof (node)) ;
    first -> info1 = data1 ;
    first -> info2 = data2 ;
    if (head == NULL)
    {
      first->link=NULL ;
      return (first) ;
```

```
    }
    first->link=head ;
    return (first) ;
}
```

Q20. List the differences between a Singly Linked Circular List and Doubly Linked Circular List. List the advantages of each list.

[JUNE01, Q2(b)][5]

Singly linked circular List	**Doubly Linked**

1. The structure of a node of singly linked circular list is as follows :-
struct list_type
{
int data;
 	
struct list_type * next ;
}
	The structure of a node of doubly linked circular list is as follows :-
	{
	int data ;
	struct doubly list * previous
	struct doubly_list * next;
	}

2. Only one pointer is maintained in a node of singly list which contains the address of next node in sequence another will keep the address of.	Two pointers are maintained in a node of doubly list, one will keep the address of first previous node & first next node in sequence.
3. In singly, we can not move in backward direction because each in node has next node pointer which facilitates us to move in forward direction.	In doubly list, we can move backward as well as forward direction as each node keeps the address of previous & next node in sequence.
4. During deletion of a node in between the singly list, we will have to keep two nodes address one-the address of the node to be deleted & the node just previous of it	During deletion, we have to keep only one node address i.e. the node to be deleted. This node will give the address of previous node automatically.

This similarity between singly linked circular list & doubly linked circular list is that the next pointer of last node of both list will point to the first node. The advantage of singly linked circular list is that we can go to first node automatically when we are on last node we don't have to again set the pointer to first node.

The second advantage is that the next pointer of last node is utilized because it keeps the address of first node.

The advantage of doubly circular list is that we can move in backward as will as forward direction. Besides if we have reached at last node and have to go to first node then instead of using the previous pointers to reach to first node we will use the next pointer of last node because in doubly circular list the next pointer of last node contains the address of first node.

Q21. Write the advantages of arrays over linked list and advantages of linked list over arrays. [JUNE01, Q4(b)][5]

Array is an static data structure. Once the size of array is fixed then at execution time its size cannot be increased. An array can be of the type int, char, float etc.

(1) The advantage of using arrays over linked list is that manipulation of array within program is very easy while linked list includes pointer concept which makes is somewhat difficult & confusing.

Array are accessed through index. Thus, their access is easy.

(2) Another advantage of array is that there are certain application where the size of data is fixed use of array is more each than linked list.

(3) Another advantage of array is that whenever we deal with the array, it is very easy to access any arbitrary item while it is cumbersome & time consuming in linked list.

(4) Another advantage of array is that linked list will use more storage than an array with the same number of items because each item has a link field additionally.

LINKED LIST : A linked list is a dynamic data structure. The size of linked list can be increased at execution time. The size of a linked list be large enough to cover whole memory of system.

(1) One primary advantage of linked list over arrays is that linked list can grow or shrink in size during execution. A link list can be made as long as required.

(2) Another advantage is that linked list does not waste memory space like arrays. It uses the memory that is just needed for the list at any point of time.

(3) Another important advantage of link list on arrays is that linked lists provides flexibility in allowing the items to be rearranged efficiently. It is easier than array to insert & delete items by rearranging links.

Q22. Let List 1 = $(x_1, x_2, ..., x_n)$ and List 2 = $(y_1, y_2, ..., y_n)$ be two linked lists. Write an algorithm to merge the two lists to obtain the linked list, List 3 = $(x_1, y_1, x_2, y_2 .... x_m, y_m, ..., x_n)$ if $m \leq n$, and List 3 = $(x_1, y_1, x_2, y_2, ... x_n, y_n, x_{n+1}, ... x_m)$ if $m > n$. [JAN01, 1(b)][10]

It is an operation in which two ordered (ascending or descending) lists are merged into a single ordered list. The merging of two lists PAR1 and PAR2 can be done by examining the element at the head of the two lists and select the smaller of the two. The smaller element is then stored into a third list called FINAL. For example consider the lists PAR1 and PAR2 given in following Figure.

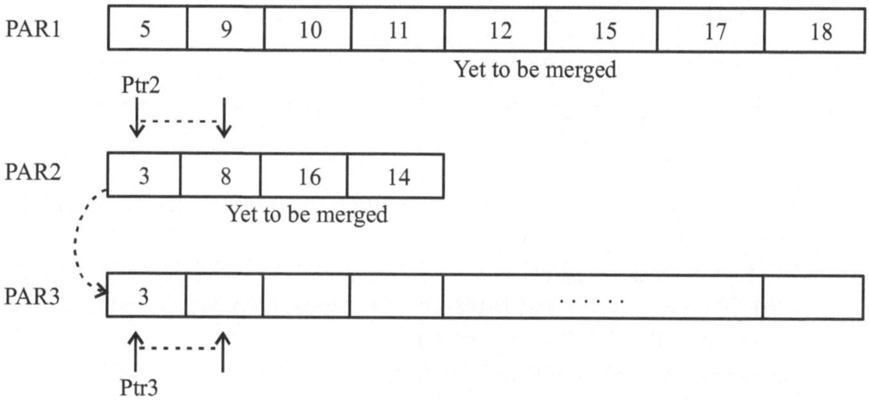

Let pointer Ptr2 and Ptr3 point to the first locations of arrays, PAR1, PAR2, and FINAL respectively. The comparison of PAR1 [ptr1] and PAR2 [ptr2] shows that the element of PAR2 (i.e. 3) is smaller. Thus ,this element will be placed into the array FINAL by the following operation.

FINAL [Ptr3] = PAR2 [Ptr2]

Since an element from PAR2 has been added into FINAL, its corresponding pointer ptr2 is shifted to the next location to point the *"Yet to be merged"* part to array of array PAR2 (see Fig. above). The pointer ptr3 is also shifted to the next location The process of comparing, storing and shifting is repeated till both the arrays are merged as shown in following Figure.

It may be noted here that during this merging process, a situation can arise when we run out of elements in one of the arrays. We must therefore stop the merging process and copy rest of the elements from the unfinished array into the final array.

An ***algorithm*** for merge sort is given below

In this algorithm, the two sorted arrays PAR1 [N] and PAR [N] are merged into an array FINAL [M + N]. Two variables Ptr1 and Ptr2 are being used to point to *"Yet to be merged parts"* of PAR1 and PAR2.

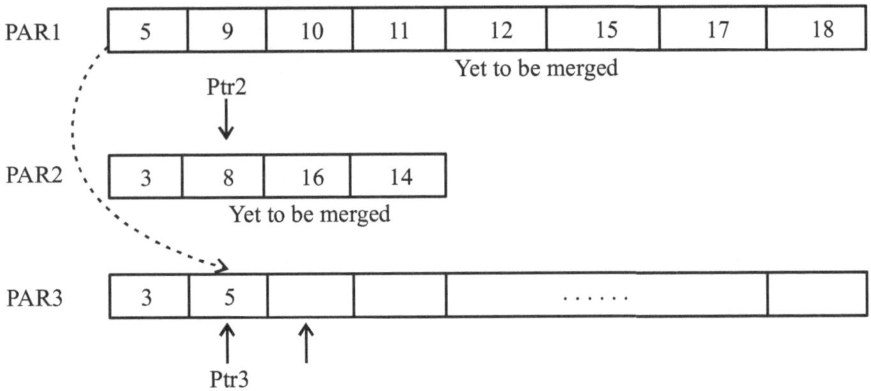

A third variable Ptr3 is used to point to the next location in FINAL where the merged element is to be added.

```
Steps: 1. Ptr1 = Ptr2 = 1; Ptr3 = 1;
    2. While ((Ptr1 <= N) and (Ptr2 <= M)) repeat step 3
    3. If (PAR1 [Ptr1] < PAR2 [Ptr2] )
       then [FINAL [ptrs] = PAR1 [Ptr1];
          Ptr1 = Ptr1 + 1
          Ptr3 = Ptr3 + 1; ]
       else
          [FINAL [Ptr3] = PAR2 [Ptr2]
          Ptr2 = Ptr2 + 1;
          Ptr3 = Ptr3 + 1; ]
       {end of while loop}
       {copy rest of the elements of array PAR2}
    4. While (Ptr2 <= M)
       FINAL [Ptr3] = PAR2 [Ptr2];
          Ptr3 = Ptr3 + 1;
          Ptr2 = Ptr2 + 1;
       {end of while loop}
       {copy rest of the elements of array PAR2}
    5. While (Ptr1 <= N)
       FINAL [Ptr3] = PAR1 [Ptr1];
          Ptr3 = Ptr3 + 1;
          Ptr1 = Ptr1 + 1;
       {end of while loop}
    6. END
```

Stacks & Queues

➢ **Stack**

A stack is data structure in which all insertions and deletions of entries are made at one end, called the top of stack. For example, it is to think of a stack of a plates on the counter in a busy cafeteria. Throughout the lunch hour, customers take plates off the top of the stack, and employees place returned plate back on top of the stack. The plate most recently put on the stack is the first one taken off. The bottom plate is the first one put on, and the last one to be used.

Note that the last item pushed onto a stack is always the first that will be popped from the stack. This property is called last in first out, or LIFO for short.

➢ **Advantages of stack**

(1) Help in information hiding :- If someone else had already written the functions for handling stacks, then we could use them without need to know the details of how stacks are kept in memory or how the stack operations are actually done.

(2) Change of implementation

(3) Clarity of programs :- One more advantage of stack is that the every appearance of the words push and pop will immediately alert a person reading the program to what is being done, whereas the instructions themselves night be more obscure.

(4) Top-down design :- A final advantage we shall find is that separating the use of data structures from their implementation will help us improve the top-down design of both our data structures and our programs.

➢ **Types of operations in stack**

✓ **Basic Operation**

(i) Push : When we add an item to a stack then we say that we push it onto the stack.

(ii) Pop : When we remove an item from the stack, then we say that we pop it from the stack.

✓ **Some other Operations**

(i) Stack TOP : When the stack exists and it is not empty, the item at the top of stack is returned without being removed, and the stack remains unchanged.

(ii) Stack Size : When the stack exists and has been initialized, the function returns the number of entries in the stack.

(iii) Clear Stack : When the stack exists and is been initialized, then all the entries in the stack have been deleted, and stack becomes empty.

✓ **Operations for checking status**

(i) Stack Empty :- When the stack exists and it has been initialized, then this return TRUE if the stack is empty, and FALSE otherwise.

(ii) Stack Full :- When the stack exists and it has been initialized, this return TRUE if the stack is full, and FALSE otherwise.

➢ ***Stack Related Terms :***

The method of writing all operators either before their operands, or after them, is called **polish notation.** When the operators are written before their operands, it is called the prefix form. When the operands, come after their operands, it is called the **postfix form** or sometimes, **reverse polish form** or **suffix form.**

The expression a×b becomes ×ab in prefix form and ab× in postfix form. And in the expression a+b×c, the multiplication is done first, so we convert it first, obtaining first a+(bc×) and then abc×+ in postfix form. The prefix form of this expression is +a×bc.

(a) Stack Implementation

The simplest way to represent a stack is by using a one-dimensional array, Say Stack [N] with room for N elements. The first element in the stack will be at STACK[0], the second element at STACK[1], and so on. An associated variable TOP points to the top element of stack. Type definition for a sequentially allocated stack is

```
# define  STACK_SIZE_MAX   100/* maximum stack size* /
Typedef   struct
{ int key;
} element;
element stack [STACK_SIZE_MAX];
int top = -1,/* denotes
an empty stack */
```

To check whether the stack is empty, we just need to check the value of TOP. If it is -1, the function may return 1 else 0.

```
int  stackempty( )
        { If  ( top == -1)
                return 1;
        else
                return 0; }
```

Given a sequentially allocated stack, and a value to be pushed, this procedure makes the newtop of stack be that value.

```
void add ( int *top, element item)
        {If (*top >= STACK_SIZE_MAX-1)
        { stackoverflow ( );
                return;
        }
        stack [ ++*top] = item;
        }
```

(b) Pointer Implementation

Although this method of allocating storage is adequate for many applications, there are many other applications where the sequential allocation method is inefficient and, therefore, unacceptable.

For such applications we store a stack element in a structure with a pointer to the next lower element on the stack.

```
        Type struct stack
                { int data;
                stack_pointer next;
                };
        typedef struct stack *stack_pointer;
                int *top;
```

Push, Pop and Top operations involve inserting, deleting and reading item at the top of this list structure.

Let us define push operation as given below :

```
void    push ( stack_pointer *top, int data)]
{ /* Push an element into Stack */
stack_pointer temp = (stack_pointer) malloc (size of (stack));
temp → data = data1;
temp → data = * top;
top = temp;}
```

Stack Applications

Two of the many applications of stacks are

(1) Convert Number Bases by Using Stacks

Changing a number from base 10 to an equivalent number in any other base 0 can be accomplished by repeated division of the number by the new base, until a zero result is obtained, saving the remainder after each division and then writing out the remainders in reverse order. This process is illustrated below.

Change (37) 10 to an equivalent number in base 2.

First Division	2)37	
Second Division	2)18	remainder 1
Third Division	2)9	remainder 0
Fourth Division	2)4	remainder 1
Fifth Division	2)2	remainder 0
Sixth Division	2)1	remainder 0
	0	
		remainder 1

The remainders are written out in reverse order giving following result:

(37) 10 = (100101)2 $(37)_{10} = (1001\ 01)_2$

The first remainder is the last to be written out while the last remainder is the first to be written out. We can model this LIFO situation very conveniently by means of a Stack.

(2) Infix to Postfix Conversion

You are already familiar with arithmetic expressions in infix notation. In this notation, a binary operator is placed between its operands. For example

A+B-C
A - (C-D)/(B * D)
A + B * D - E/F

The operations are normally carried out from left to right. We also have procedure rules for evaluating expressions. A typical evaluation sequence for A * B + C + D * E would be to multiply B and A; adding it to C; saving the result temporarily, say in RESULT., multiplying D and E and add it to the RESULT. Therefore we have followed the sequence as given below:

AB*C+DE*+

This notation is called the postfix notation or reverse polish notation.

An algorithm using stack is given below:

1. Initialise the stack to be empty.
2 For each character in the infix string

if operand append to output
else
if stack empty or the operator has higher precedence than the operator on top of the stack
then
push it onto the stack
else
pop the stack and append it to the output

3. If input end encountered
then
loop until stack not empty pop the stack and append to the output.

Queues

A Queue is a kind of data structure or type of list in which all additions to the list are made at one end, and all deletions from the list are made at the other end. For example, queue is defined as a waiting line, like a line of people waiting to purchase tickets, where the first person in line is the first person served. Queues are also called first in first out lists or FIFO for short.

Use of Queue

Applications of queues are, if anything, even more common that are application of stacks, since in performing tasks by computer, as in all parts of life, it is so often necessary to wait one's turn before having access to disk storage, or even, in a timesharing system, for use of the CPU. Within a single program, there may be multiple requests to be kept in a queue, or one task may create other tasks, which must be dine in turn by keeping them in a queue.

Queues Related terms

(i) Front : First entry that will be removed from the queue, we call the front of the queue or sometimes, the head of the queue.

(ii) Rear : The most recently added or the last entry in the queue, we call the rear of the queue sometimes, the tail of the queue.

OPERATIONS IN A QUEUE

(i) Create Queue : It will be used to create a queue which is initialized to be empty.

Operations for checking a status of queue

(i) Queue Empty :- When a queue is created on exits the function return true if queue is empty and false when the queue is not empty.

(ii) Queue Full :- When the queue is exists, then the function return true if the queue is full and return false when the queue is not full.

Fundamental operations on a queue.

(i) Append Queue :- When the queue exists and it is not full, then it will store some entry.

(ii) Serve Queue :- When the queue is exist and it is not empty, then it will remove the first entry of the queue and return as the value.

More Operations on a Queue

(i) Queue Size :- When the queue exists or created then the function returns the number of entries in the queue.

(ii) Clear Queue :- When queue exists previously, then the function will remove all entries that are present in queue and after this the queue becomes empty.

(iii) Queue Front :- When queue is created or exists and it is not empty, then a variable i.e. x is copy of the first entry in queue. And the present queue will remain unchanged.

Queues Implementation

(a) Vector or array Implementation

We here give a vector representation of a queue. We define a queue as a record structure containing the vector and two variables front and rear to denote the present position of its front and rear element.

We may define a Queue as given below:

```
const max = 100
struct  q_type
{ elementtype queue [max];
int front, rear;
};
```

As an example of this representation of a queue, consider a size 6. Assume that the queue is initially empty. It is required to insert element RED, BLACK and BLUE, followed by delete RED and BLACK and insert GREEN, WHITE AND YELLOW.

Following figure give a trace of the queue contents for this sequence of operations.

RED					

RED	BLACK				

RED	BLACK	BLUE			

	BLACK	BLUE			

		BLUE			

		BLUE	GREEN		

		BLUE	GREEN	WHITE	

		BLUE	GREEN	WHITE	YELLOW

(b) Pointer Implementation

The second approach for implementing queues is by using the dynamic storage allocation through the use of pointers. We can define a queue consisting of records where each record contains record that comes after it. Therefore we may declare a queue as

```
        struct  qrec
        { element type data;
        struct qrec * next;};
struct qrec *qptr;
```

we must also specify the items at the front and rear of the queue. This may be done by the following declaration.

```
        struct qtype
        { struct qrec * front;
                struct qrec * rear;
        };
        qtype q;
```

This kind of an implementation is a singly linked list implementation of the Queue.

Queues Applications

(a) They find their applications in CPU scheduling.
(b) Used in printer spooling
(c) Queueing in Computer Network.

Q23. A file stores a series of numbers. Write an algorithm using binary search tree that counts the occurrence of different numbers in the file. For example, file containing data 1, 50, 20, 1, 25 would produce output as [DEC04, Q1(b)][10]

Number	**Occurrence**
1	**2**
20	**1**
25	**1**
50	**1**

Refer to Page No. 201

Q24. How can a queue be represented using an array and a linked list ? Compare the two represented in terms of time and space complexities. [DEC04, Q3(a)][4]

Refer to Page No. 204

Q25. Write an algorithm to implement a Queue that allows insertion and deletion at both ends. [DEC04, Q4(b)][5]

Refer to Page No. 208

Q26. Write 'C' program which accepts a stack as input and reverses the elements of stack using one additional queue. [JUNE05, Q3(b)][5]

Refer to Page No. 189

Q27. What is a Circular Queue? Give an example of its application. Give an algorithm for the addition of a new element to the circular queue. Include necessary validation checks. [JUNE04, Q2(a)][5]

A Circular Queue : A circular queue is one in which the insertion of a new element is done at the very first locations of the queue if the last location of the queue is full. In other words if we have a queue Q of say n elements, then after inserting an element last (i.e., in the n-1 the) location of the array the next element will be inserted at the very first location (i.e., location with subscript 0) of the array. It is possible to insert new elements, if and only if those

locations (slots) are empty. We can say that a circular queue is one in which the first element comes just after the last element. It can be viewed as a mesh or loop of wire, in which the two ends of the wire connected together. Following figure shows a empty circular queue Q which can accommodate five elements.

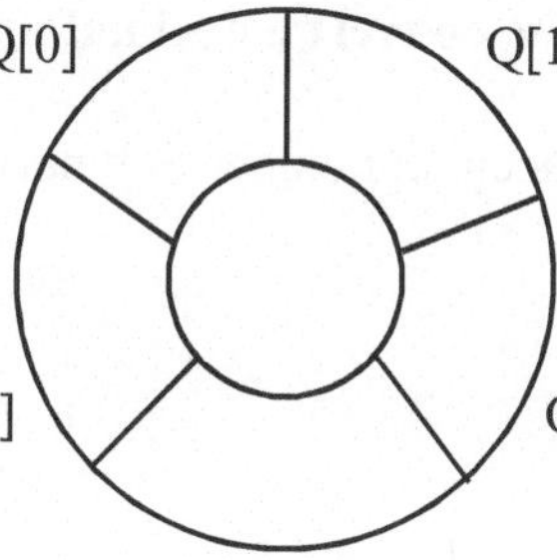

Circular Queue

A circular queue overcomes the problem of unutilized space in linear queues implemented as arrays. A circular queue also have a Front and Rear to keep the track of the elements to be deleted and inserted and therefore to maintain the unique characteristic of the queue.

The following assumptions are made:

1. Front will always be pointing to the first element (as in the linear queue).
2. If Front = Rear the queue will be empty.
3. Each time an new element is inserted into the queue the Rear is incremented by one.

Rear = Rear + 1

4. Each time an element is deleted from the queue the value of Front is incremented by one.

Front = Front + 1

Function for inserting value in the circular queue.

```
Insert (struct queue *q, int x)
{
        if (q → rear = = MAX – 1)
            q → rear = = 0;
        else
        (q → rear) + +;
        If (q → rear = = q front)
        {
                printf ("queue overflow");
                exit(1);
```

```
    }
    q → item [q → rear] = x;
    return;
}
```

Q28. Write an algorithm to convert a decimal number to binary number using stack(s). [JUNE04, 5(b)][5]

Algorithm for converting decimal number to binary number using stack.

```
D_to_B (struct start *s, int x)
{
    while (x! = 0)
    {
        If (x%2 = = 1)
        push (s, 1);
        else
        push (s, 0);
        x = x/2;
    }
    // pop stack while it be comes empty
    while (s.top! = - 1)
    pop(s);
}
```

Q29. Write the postfix form of the following expression: [DEC03, Q3(a)][5]

(i) a + b - c * d

= a b + c d * -

(ii) (a -b) * (c + d)

= a b - c d + *

Q30. Let 'P' be a pointer to a doubly linked list. Show how this list may be used as a queue by writing algorithms to add and delete elements. Specify the value for 'P' when the queue is empty. [DEC02, Q2(b)][10]

Here we have to implement queue through circular linked list.

A circular linked list is a data structure in which last node's address field points to the first node.

To implement a queue through this circular list, we will have to keep two pointers say rear & front. Front will point the first node of the queue & rear will point to the last node of the queue. Here front will be the value of "p" given in question. We are assuming that the circular linked list is being implemented in dynamic data structure.

Thus the value of "P" will be NULL when the queue is empty.
A queue implemented as circular list is called circular queue.
It can be shown figuratively as follows:

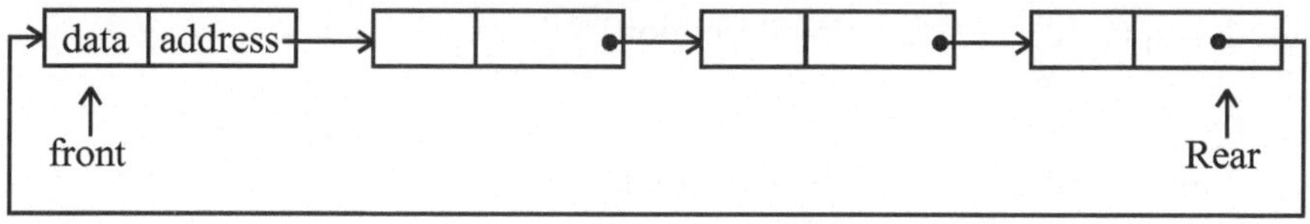


```
Global declarations
// Structure of a node of circular queue
struct que-type s
{
int data ;
struct que-type * next;
};
struct que-type * rear = NULL, *front = NULL;
                                    // rear will Point to the end of queue & front
will
                                    // point to the starting node of queue.
typedef struct que-type que;
void insertq (int);                 // Function will insert a data
                                    // in circular queue
                                    // this function will delete an element
                                    // from circular queue
void insertq (int value)            // Function definition
                                    // value is the data item to
                                    // be inserted in circular queue
{
que *p;
if(front = NULL && rear = NULL)
{
        rear = (que *)malloc (sizeof (que));
        rear -> data = value ;
        rear -> next = NULL ;
        front = rear ;
        rear-> next = front;        // Making the queue circular
}
else
        p = (que*) malloc (sizeof(que));
        p-> data = value;
        p-> next = rear -> next;
```

```
        rear = p;
}
}    // end of function

int deletq (void)     // function definition
{
int p;
if (front = = NULL)   // underflow condition
        print ("n que empty");
else
{
        p = front -> data ;
        rear -> next = front -> next ;
        front = front -> next ;
        return (p);
}
}   // end of function
```

Q31. Write an algorithm to transform an infix expression to a postfix expression. [JUNE02,1(b)][10]

 # Write an algorithm to convert an Infix Expression which includes the operators (,), +, -, * and / to Postfix Expression. [DEC03,1(b)][10]

Algorithm :

```
1)    pick an element from the expression E
2)    if element =operand then
        [print element goto step 1]
3)    if element = operator then
        [while (priority(element) <=priority(stack[top])) and stack[top]<>'('
)
        [pop an element from stack and print it]
        [push element on the stack ];
        goto step 1]
4)    if element ='(' then
        [push element on the stack ; goto step1]
5)    if element =')' then
        [while stack[top]<>'(' ]
        [pop an element from stack; if element <> '(' then print it ]
        go to step 1;]
6)    if element =';' then
        [while (stack is not empty)]
        [pop an element from stack and print it]
        goto step 7]
7)    end
```

Q32. Write the postfix form of the following expressions :

[JUNE02,3(a)][5]

(i) (c ÷ d) × (a + b)
(ii) a + b × c ÷ d

(i) (c ÷ d) * (a + b)
1) (cd ÷) * (ab+)
2) (cd ÷ ab +*
(ii) a + b * c ÷ d

Input character	Process	Stack contents	Output
a	Is written to output		a
+	is pushed out stack	+	
b	is written output		ab
*	pushed out stack	+*	abc
c	is writted out stack		
÷	since it has same procedure as * the stack is poped out and ÷ is pushed into stack	÷	abc*
d	is written out stack		abc*d
end	stack is poped		abc*d ÷ +

Q33. Write the postfix form of the following expressions :

[DEC01,Q3(a)][5]

(i) -A + B – C + D
(ii) AB**C**

(i) A – B + C – D +
(ii) AB ** C **

Q34. Write a program EXPR in C language which evaluates a Reverse Polish expression from the command line, where each operator or operand is a separate argument. For example,
EXPR 2 3 4 + *
evaluates 2 × (3 + 4). **[JUNE01,1(a)][10]**

For example:

```
  EXPR 2 3 4 +*
evaluates 2*(3+4)*/
//Program filename: EXPR.c
#include <stdio.h>
#include <ctype.h>
 int max=50;
main (int argc, char *argv [])
  {
  int stack[50],i;
  char *p;
  int j=0;
  if(argc<2)
  {printf("Insufficient no: of arguments");
   getch();
  exit(0);
  }
   p=argv[1];
   for(i=0;i<strlen(argv[1]);i++)
   {

   if(*(p+i)>=48&&*(p+i)<=57)
   {
   stack[j]=*(p+i)-48;
  j++;
   }
   else
    if(*(p+i)=='+')
    {
    stack[j-2]=stack[j-1]+stack[j-2];
   j=j-1;
    }
   else
    if(*(p+i)=='-')
    {
    stack[j-2]=stack[j-1]-stack[j-2];
   j=j-1;
    }
   else
    if(*(p+i)=='*')
    {
```

```
 stack[j-2]=stack[j-1]*stack[j-2];
j=j-1;
}
else
 if(*(p+i)=='/')
 {
 stack[j-2]=stack[j-1]+stack[j-2];
j=j-1;
}
}
j--;
printf("Final evaluation is %d",stack[j]);
 getch();

}
```

Q35. Draw the tree representation for the following prefix expression : +*/ABCDE** **[JUNE01,3(a)][5]**

We are assuming * * sign. as exponent sign.
Infix of above expression is :
A/B * *C*D+E
The tree is as follows:

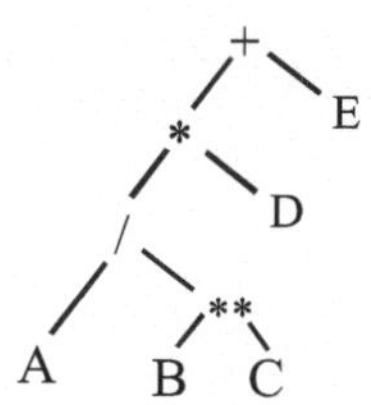

Q36. Show the stack evaluation of postfix notation : ab + c + d + e + **[JAN 01,1v(a)][2]**

Let us add a right parenthesis at the postfix expression :

Expression : ab + c + d + e +) and label each term as
Lable : 1 2 3 4 5 6 7 8 9 10 Now the evaluation :

LABLE NUMBER	SYMBOL FOUND	CONTAINS OF THE STACK		
1	a		a	
2	b	a		b
3	+	a	+	b
4	c	a+b		c
5	+	a+b	+	c
6	d	a+b+c		d
7	+	a+b+c+	+	d
8	e	a+b+c+d		e
9	+	a+b+c+d+	+	e
10	)			

Q37. Write a C-program using stack for implementing the following function : [JAN01,Q5][10]

(i) Function to determine if the parentheses in an expression are properly nested.

(ii) Function to determine if a word or phrase is a palindrome or not.

Sol. (i)
```
#include <stdio.h>
#include <conio.h>
#include <string.h>
#include <stdlib.h>
#define N 50
char stack[N] ;
int tos=-1 ;
void main ( )
{
char string[N],temp ;
int pointer,len ;
int pop( ) ;
void push(int);
clrscr( ) ;
printf("\n enter any arithmetic expression:") ;
scanf("%s", string) ;
len=strlen(string) ;
pointer=0 ;
while(string[pointer]!='\0')
{
if(string[pointer] == ')')
{
  temp=pop( ) ;
```

```
  while(temp!='(')
    temp=pop() ;
}
else
  push(string[pointer]) ;
pointer++ ;
}
while(tos!=-1)
{
temp=pop( ) ;
if(temp=='(' || temp==')')
{
 printf("\n improper string") ;
  getch();
 exit(0) ;
  }
 }
 printf("\n proper string") ;
 getch();
}

void push(int x)
{
 tos++ ;
 if(tos>=50)
   printf("\n stack overflow") ;
 else
   stack[tos]=x ;
}

int pop( )
{
 int out ;
if(tos==-1)
 {
  printf("\ improper string") ;
  exit(0) ;
}
else
{
  out=stack[tos] ;
```

```
  stack[tos]='\0' ;
  tos--;
  return(out);
  }
}
```

Input
enter any arithmetic expression ((a+b)+c)
Output
proper string

Input

enter any arithmetic expression a+b)+c)+d
Output.
improper string

Sol. (ii)

```
#include <stdio.h>
#include <conio.h>
#include <string.h>
#include <stdlib.h>
#define N 50

char stack[N];
int tos=-1;
void main( )
{
  char string[N],temp;
  char revstring[N];
  int pointer;
  int pop();
  void push(int);
  clrscr();
  printf("\n Enter any string:");
  scanf("%s",string);
  pointer=0;
  while(string[pointer]!='\0')
  {
     push(string[pointer]);
     pointer++;
  }
```

```
pointer=0;
while(tos!=-1)
{
  temp=pop();
  revstring[pointer]=temp;
  pointer++;
}
revstring[pointer]='\0';
if (strcmp(string,revstring)==0)
  printf("\n string is palindrome");

else
  printf("\n string is not palindrome");
 getch( );
}

void push(int x)
{
  tos++;
  if(tos>=50)
    printf("\n stack overflow");
else
    stack[tos]=x;
}

int pop( )
{
 int out;
 if(tos==-1)
 {
  printf("\n improper string");
  exit(0);
}
else
{
  out=stack[tos];
  stack[tos]='\0';
  tos--;
  return(out);
 }
}
```

```
/*
Input
  enter any string dinesh
Output
  string is not palindrome
Input
  enter any string mom
Output
    String is palindrome
*/
```

CHAPTER - 3

TREES & FILES ORGANISATION.

Trees

Different terms that are used in tree organisation :

- **Tree :** Tree is a an Acyclic graphs. Tree is a non empty collection of vertices and edges that satisfies certain requirements.
- **Vertex :** A vertex is simple object that can have a name and can carry other associated information.
- **Root/Parent :** Root does not have a parent. And called origin of the tree.
- **Child :** The node of a tree have a parent child relationship. A node may or may not have children.
- **Edge/branch :** An edge is connection between two vertices.
- **Acycle :** There is no loop.
- **Leaf :** The nodes that has no children is called a leaf node or terminal nodes.
- **Degree :** The degree of a node is number of non empty sub trees it has. A leaf node has a degree zero.
- **Sibling :** Child or node with the same parent are called siblings.
- **Length :** The length of the path is number of breaches on the path. Start with zero 0.
- **Depth :** Depth of any node n is length of the path from root to n. For example depth of the root is zero.
- **Height :** The height of the node n is the longest path from n to leaf. All the leaves are at height zero.
- **Level :** Depth of a node is sometimes also referred to as level of a node.
- **Ancestor/descendent :** If there is a path from n_i to n_j then n_j is ancestor of n_j and n_j is descendant of nj. All nodes in the tree are descendants of the root of the tree, while root is the ancestor of all nodes
- **Path :** A path in a tree is a list of distinct vertices in which successive vertices are connected by edge in the tree.

Types of tree

Binary tree

BST(Binary search tree)
B-tree
Avl tree(high balance tree)
Forest tree
Thread binary tree

1) Binary Tree

A **binary tree** is made up of finite elements called **nodes** (or **vertex**es). This set either is empty, or consists of a node called the root together with two binary trees, called the left and right **subtrees**, which are disjoin from each other and from the root. Either or both of a tree's two subtrees may be empty. The roots of these subtrees are **children** of the root. There is an edge from a node to each of its children, and a node is said to be the **parent** of its children.

Condition of binary tree

Properties of binary tree

1) A binary tree with N internal nodes has maximum of (n + 1) external nodes. Root is considered as an internal nodes.

Internal nodes = The nodes with degree 2 are called internal nodes.

External nodes = The node with degree 0 are called external or leaf nodes.

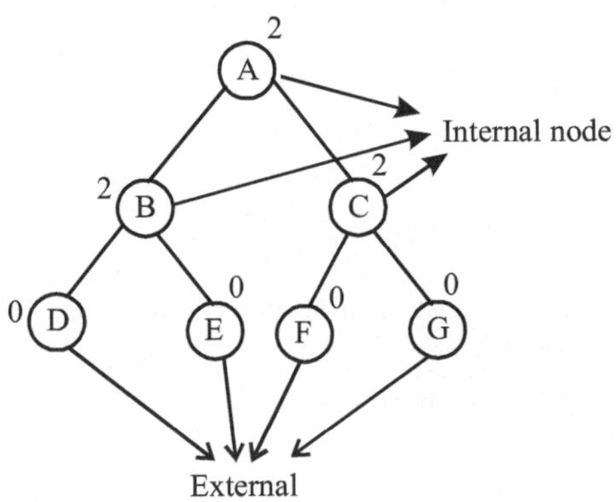

In the given binary tree

(a) A, B, C has 2 degree so total number of internal nodes are 3.

(b) External nodes one (n + 1) = (3 + 1) = 4.

2) Length of a full binary tree with N internal node is about $\log_2 N$.

(i) A full binary tree must fulfill the following condition.

Nodes = $2^{n+1} - 1$ h = height

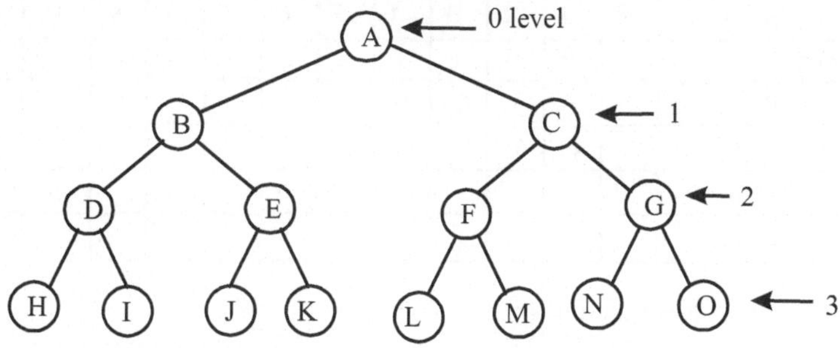

Total number of Node at level 0 is = $2^{0+1} - 1$ = 2-1 = 1
Total number of Node at level 1is = 2^{1+1} -1 = 4-1 = 3
Total number of Node at level 2is = $2^{2+1} - 1$ = 8-1 = 7
Total number of Node at level 3is = $2^{3+1} - 1$ = 16-1 = 15

And similar total no. of edges is = (n-1)
Total number of edge at level 0 is = (1-1) = 0
Total number of edge at level 1 is = (3-1) = 2
Total number of edge at level 2 is = (7-1) = 6
Total number of edge at level 3 is = (16-1) = 15

b) Representation of binary tree in internal memory
There are two type of binary representation use to store data in memory or disk
1) Sequential Representation
2) Linked list Representation

Tree in Array
A tree can be implemented in **array**. Here is an example with diagram :-

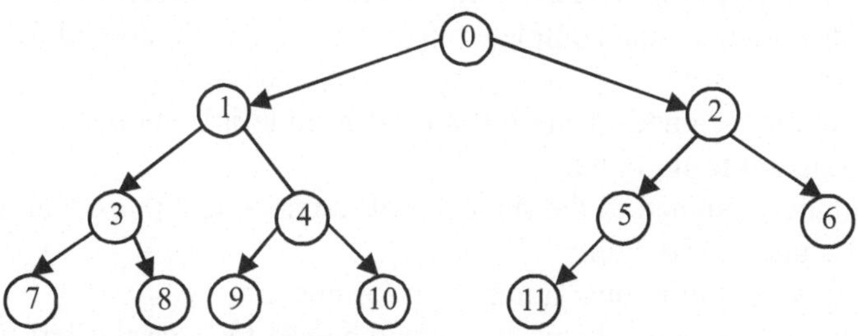

The array indices for the relatives of each node are shown below. A dash indicates that the relative does not exist.

Node/Index	**0**	**1**	**2**	**3**	**4**	**5**	**6**	**7**	**8**	**9**	**10**	**11**
Parent	-	0	0	1	1	2	2	3	3	4	4	5
Left child	1	3	5	7	11	-	-	-	-	-	-	-
Right child	2	4	6	8	10	-	-	-	-	-	-	-
Left sibling	-	-	1	-	3	-	5	-	7	-	9	-
Right Sibling	-	2	-	4	-	6	-	8	-	10	-	-

(1) Linked List Representation

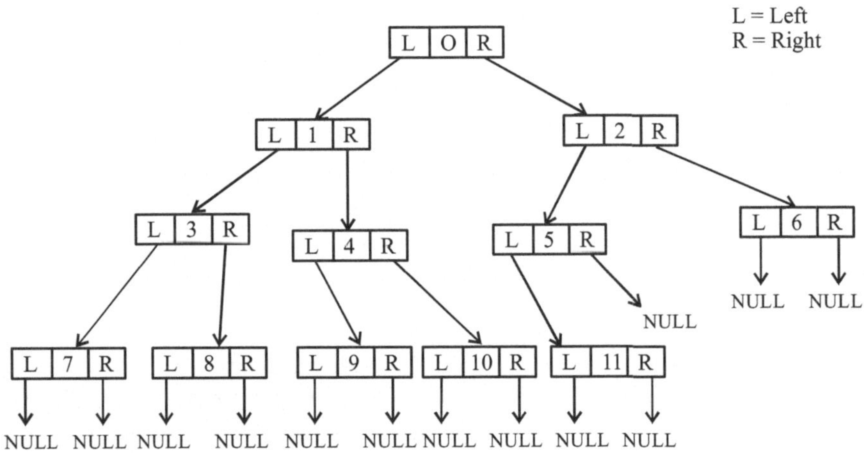

(2) Sequential Representation

0	1	2	3	4	5	6	7	8	9	10	11	
0	1	2	3	4	5	6	7	8	9	10	11	12

➢ **Sequential Representation (implicit Array Representation)**

1. The nodes of an almost complete binary tree can be numbered from 0 to n-1 such that:

(a) the number assigned to the left son of a node is 1 more than twice the number assigned to its father.

(b) the number assigned to the right son of the node is 2 more than twice the number assigned to its fathers.

2. this results in continuous numbering for nodes.

3. with this numbering scheme it is not required to have the left, right and father links.

4. Such a tree can be represented using an array of size n with the root at position 0 of the array.

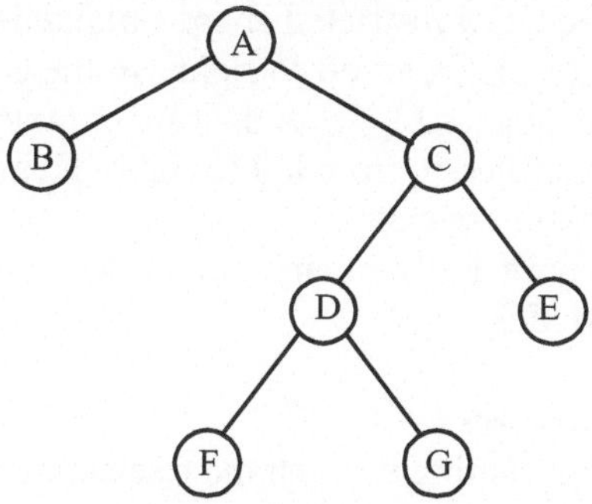

A Binary Tree

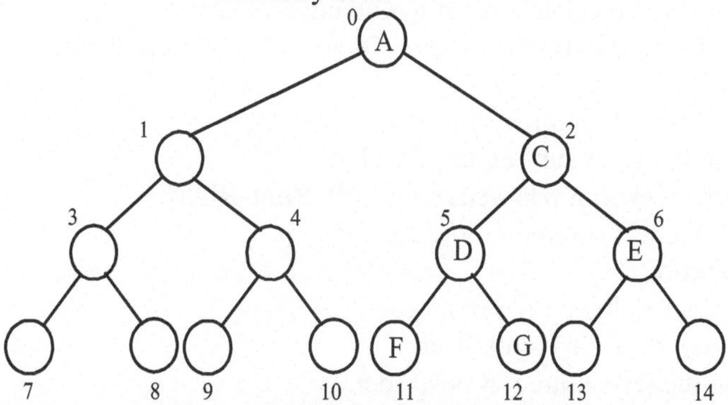

An almost binary tree Extension of the Binary Tree

A	B	C			D	E				F	G	
0	1	2	3	4	5	6	7	8	9	10	11	12

Sequential Representation

Sequential representation VS Linked representation

Sequential Representation	Linked Representation
Merits: 1. It is simpler 2. Saves storage space for tree that are almost complete binary trees. Demerits: 1. The maximum number of nodes must be known in advance.	Merits: 1. It allows a flexible use of the collection of nodes. 2. The tree shape and number of nodes could change dynamically. Demerits: 1. Require more space for the storage of left, right and father and brother nodes.

Fully binary tree

A **complete** binary tree has a restricted shape obtained by starting at the root and filling the tree by levels from left to right. In the complete binary tree of height d, all levels except possibly level d -1 are completely full. The bottom level has all of its nodes filled in from left to right. **Heap data structure** is an example of a complete binary tree.
One important property of Fully binary tree is that it must have 2i node at each level or 2^{n+1} -1 nodes.

➢ ***Operations on Binary trees***

✓ **Traverse :-** implies visiting through the tree enumerating each node once and only once.

There exist three mechanisms of traversing a binary three:

1. Preorder or depth-first order(DFS) or Root-Left-Right

a) Visit the root
b) Traverse the left subtree in preorder
c) Traverse the right subtree in preorder

2. Inorder or symmetric order or Left-Root-Right

a) traverse the left subtree in inorder
b) visit the root
c) traverse the right subtree in inorder

3. Postorder or Left-Right-Root

a) traverse the left subtree in postroder
b) traverse the right subtree in postorder
c) visit the root

TRAVERSAL IN BINARY TREE

(1) Preorder = Root, left, right
A B D E C F H I J K G

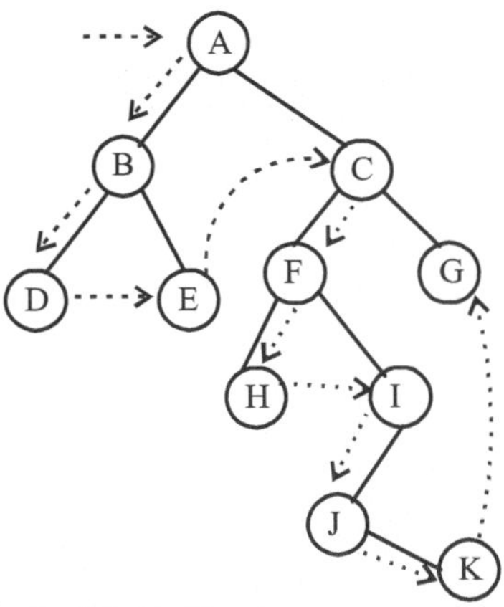

(2) Postorder = Left, Right, Root

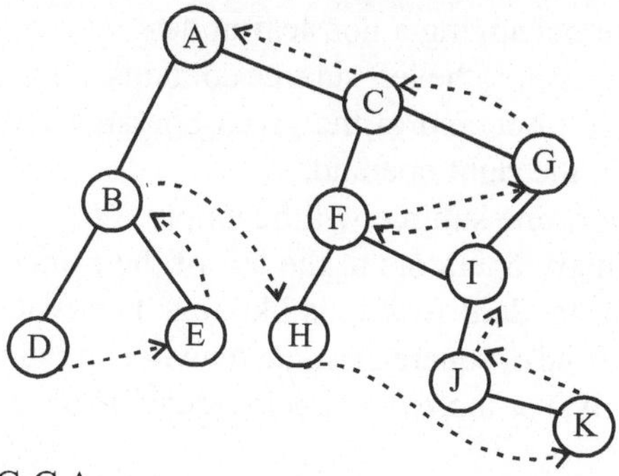

D E B H K J I F G C A

(3) Inorder = Left Root Right

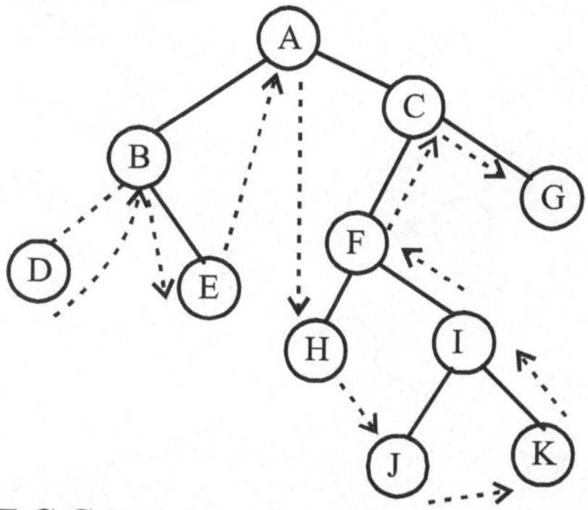

D B E A H J K I F C G

(4) Level by level

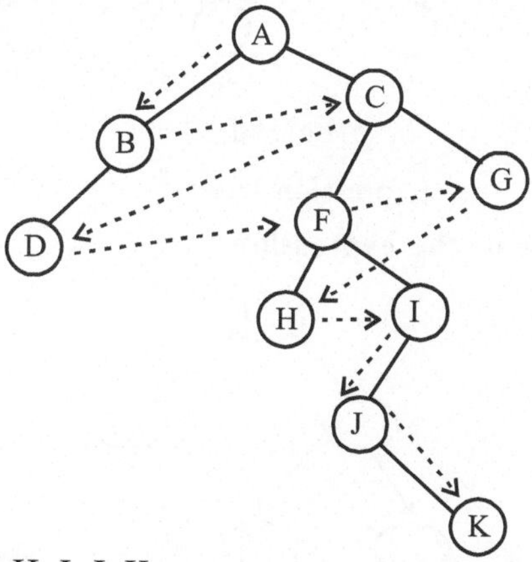

A B C D F G H I J K

➢ ***Expression Tree***

Binary Tree Representation of An Expression Tree

✓ The operands are occupying the leaf nodes.

✓ The operators are occupying a non leaf nodes.

✓ For each binary operator, the left subtree contains, all the simple operands and operators in the left operand of the given operator and the right subtree contains everything in the right operand.

✓ For unary operator, one subtree will be empty.

✓ We write some unary operators to the left of their operands (such as '_' unary notation or the standard functions like log( ) or cos0( ).

✓ Function like factorial or square of a number write on right of their operands.

✓ Derivatives (dy / dx) or increment operator can be occupied either side of their operands.

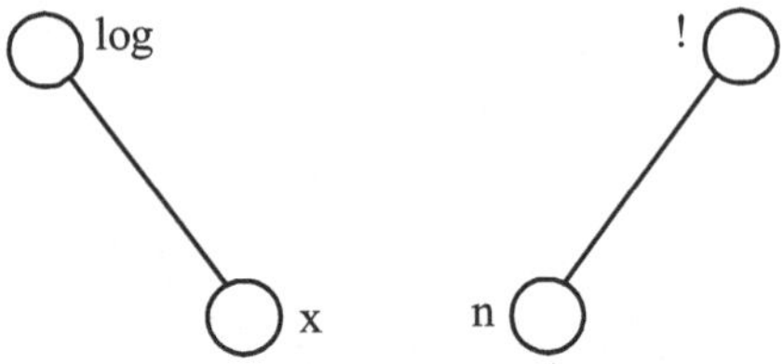

log x n!

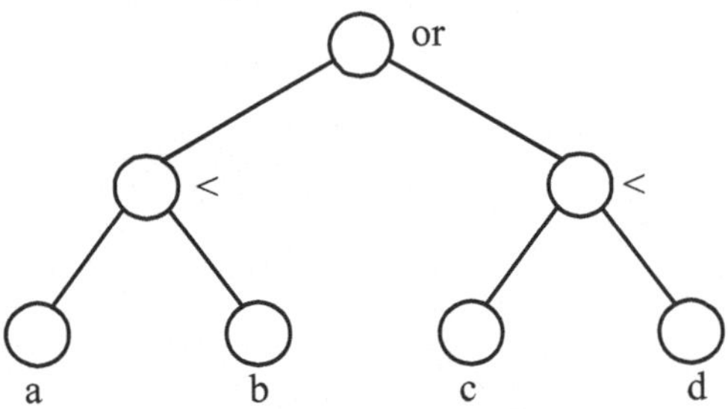

(a<b) or (c<d)

Expression Tree

Create expression tree of the expression :

9 / 5 * C + 32

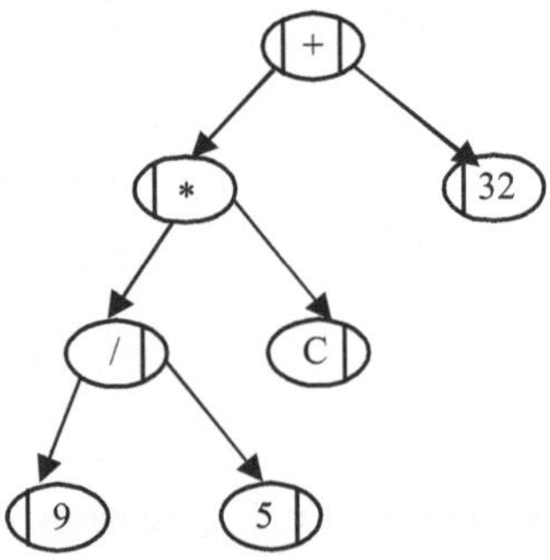

Preorder Traversal	+*/95C32
Inorder Traversal	9/5*C+32
Postorder Traversal	95/C*32+
Level-order Traversal	+*32/C95

Heap : complete binary tree

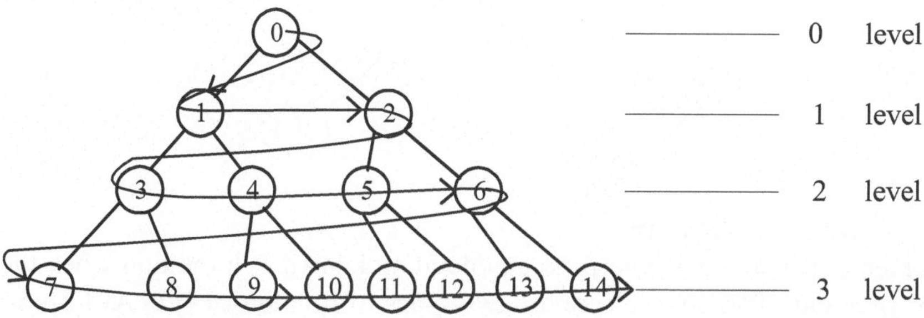

Figure : Full binary tree

A binary tree is said to be complete if it contains the maximum number of nodes possible for its length.
1) number of nodes at level 0 is $1 = 2^i = 2(0) = 1$
2) number of nodes at level 1 is $2 = 2^i = 2(1) = 2$

Note : Therefore, a complete binary tree with k levels contains $\sum_{i=0}^{k} 2^i$ nodes.

So, the total number of nodes at particular level is $\sum_{i=0}^{k} 2^i$ nodes.

where K is the level number

✓ ***Algorithm / Program***

1) Creation of binary tree
2) Insertion in binary tree
3) Counting number of nodes in binary tree
   Traversal in binary tree both recursive or non recursive
      In order
      Post order
      Pre order

➤ ***AVL tree***

An AVL tree is a binary tree in which the left and right subtrees of any node may differ in height by at most 1, and in which both the subtrees are themselves AVL trees (the definition is recursive). It is also called height balanced tree.

1. An AVL tree is constructed in the same manner as an ordinary binary tree, except that after the addition of each new node, a check must be made to ensure that the AVL balance conditions have not been violated. If all is well, no further action need to be taken. If the new node causes an imbalance in the tree, however, some rearrangement of the tree's nodes must be done.

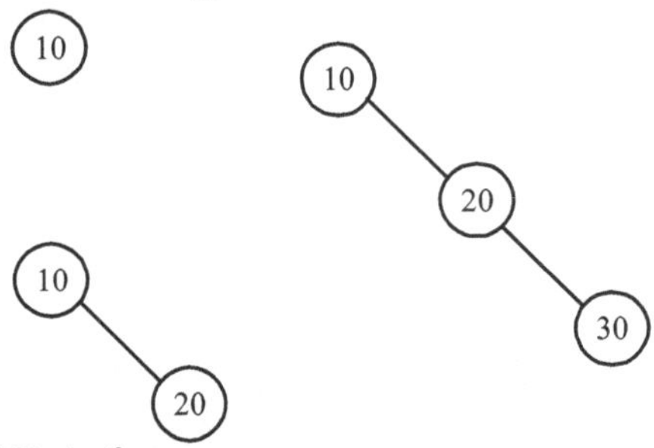

✓ Condition of Rotation

As mentioned above, we perform an operation known as a rotation when the tree goes out of balance. There are two types of rotation used in AVL trees: single and double rotations. The rules for deciding which type of rotation to use are quite simple:

1. When you have found the first node that is out of balance (according to the algorithm above), restrict your attention to that node and the two nodes in the two layers immediately below it (on the path you followed up from the new node).
2. If these three nodes lie in a straight line, a single rotation is needed to restore the balance.
3. If these three nodes lie in a dog-leg' pattern (that is, there is a bend in the path), you need a double rotation to restore the balance.

In our example here, the three nodes to consider are the only three nodes in the tree. The first node where an imbalance was detected was the root node (10). The two layers immediately below this node, and on the path up from the new node, are the nodes 20 and 30. These nodes lie in a straight line, so we need a single rotation to restore the balance.

A single rotation involves shifting the middle node up to replace the top node and the top node down to become the left child of the middle node. After performing the rotation on this tree, we obtain:

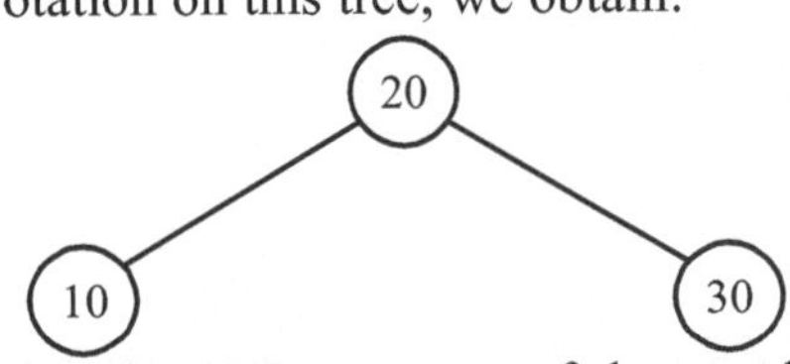

A check shows that the AVL structure of the tree has been restored by this operation.

We continue by adding two more nodes: 25 and 27. After adding 25, a check shows that the AVL nature of the tree has not been violated, so no adjustments are necessary. After adding 27, however, the tree looks like this:
Tracing a path back from the node 27, we find height differences of 0 at 27, + 1 at 25, and -2 to 30. Thus the first imbalance is detected at node 30. We restrict our attention to this node and the two nodes immediately below it (25 and 27). These three nodes form a dog-leg pattern, since there is a bend in the path at node 25. We therefore require a double rotation to correct the balance. A double rotation, as its name implies, consists of two single rotations. These two rotations are in opposite directions. The first rotation occurs on the two layers below the node where the imbalance was detected (in this case, it involves the nodes 25 and 27). We rotate the node 27 up to replace 25, and 25 down to become the left child of 27. The tree now looks like this:

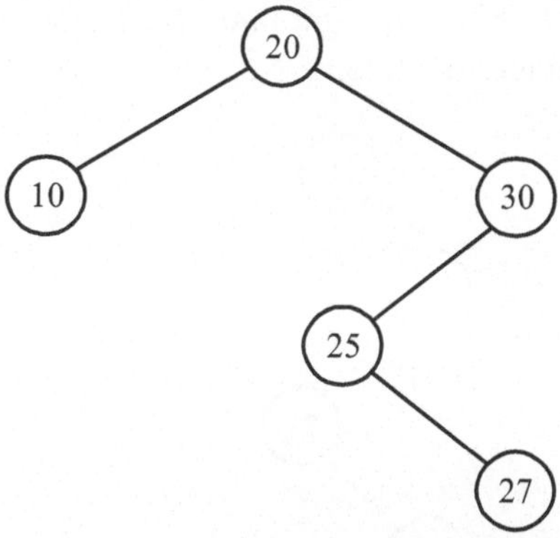

This operation obviously has not corrected the imbalance in the tree, so we must perform the second rotation, which involves the three nodes 25, 27, and 30. Node 27 rotates up to replace 30 and node 30 rotates down to become the right child of 27:

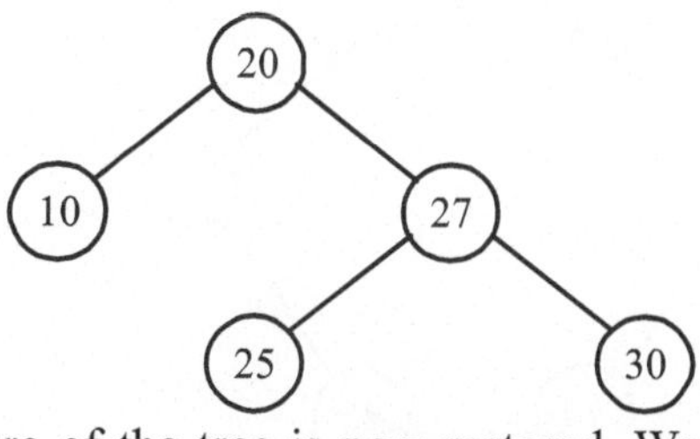

The AVL structure of the tree is now restored. We continue by adding the nodes 7 and 4 to the tree. Adding the 7 doesn't upset the balance, but adding the 4 does:

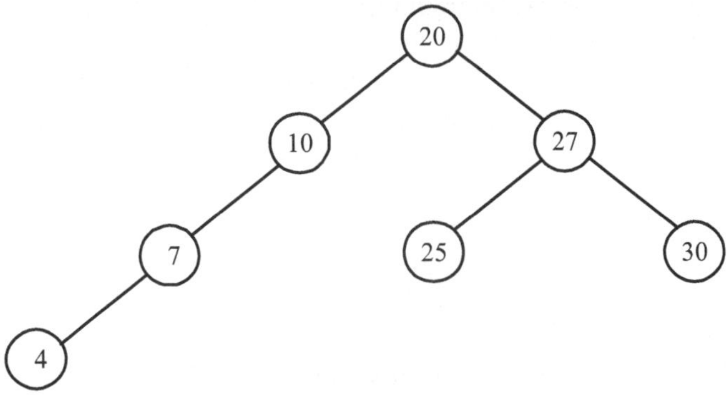

In this case, the first imbalance is detected at node 10, where a difference of -2 occurs. Considering this node and the two immediately below it, we see that the nodes 10, 7, and 4 lie in a straight line, so a single rotation is needed. Applying the rotation balances the tree:

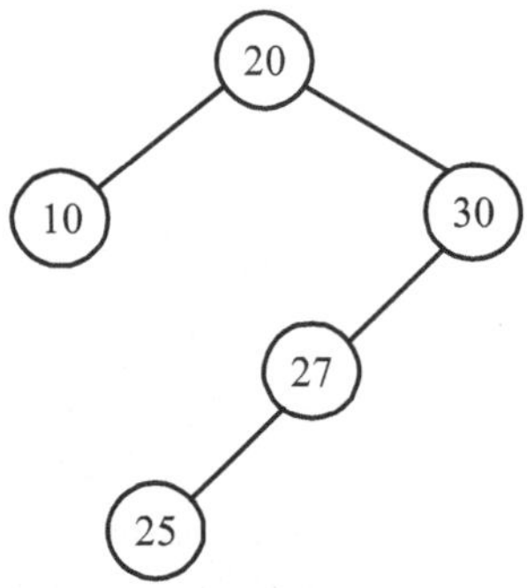

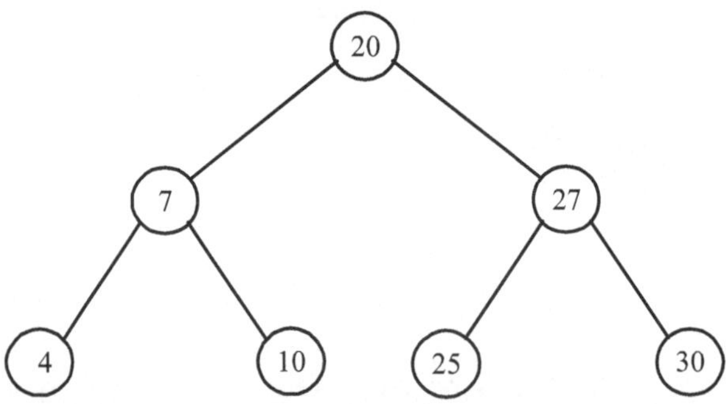

One final example, before we consider the general case. We add the nodes 23, 26, and 21 to the tree (the 23 and 26 do not disturb the balance, but the 21 does):

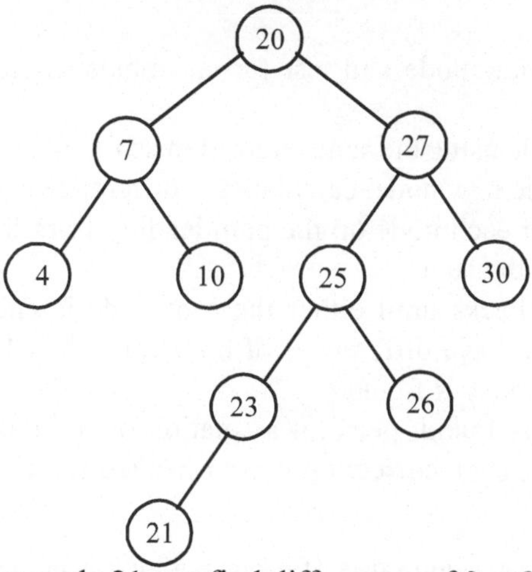

Working back from node 21, we find differences of 0 at 21, -1 at 23, -1 at 25, and -2 at 27. Node 27 is therefore the first node where an imbalance occurs. We examine this node and the two layers immediately below it on the path to the new node. This gives us the three nodes 27, 25, and 23, which lie in a straight line, so a single rotation is indicated. The middle node (25) rotates up to replace node 27 and node 27 rotates down to become the right child of 25. What happens to node 26, which is the old right child of 25? It must swap over to become the new left child of node 27. Making these modifications, we obtain:

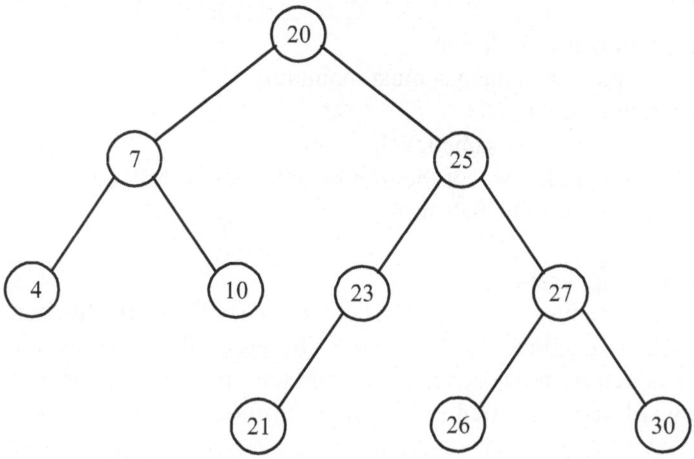

In summary, the steps involved in inserting a new node in an AVL tree are.

➢ ***Algorithm***

The insertion of a new node and test for an imbalance are done using the following algorithm:

1. Insert the new node using the same algorithm as for an ordinary binary tree.
2. Beginning with the new node, calculate the difference in heights of the left and right subtrees of each node on the path leading from the new node back up the tree towards the root.
3. Continue these checks until either the root node is encountered and all nodes along the path have differences of no greater than 1, or until the first difference greater than 1 is found.
4. If an imbalance is found, perform a rotation of the nodes to correct the imbalance. Only one such correction is ever needed for any one node.

➢ **B-Tree**

A **B-tree** is a multiway search tree of order ***n*** which is height balanced in that all leaves are on the same level and all non-leaves except possibly the root are at least half full of entries, that means has between *n /2* to *n* children. The root of a B tree is either a leaf or has at least two children.

➢ **Properties of B-tree**

✓ Alternate definition of B-tree of order *n* would say the tree has nodes with a maximum of *2n* keys and *2n + 1* children.

✓ The maximum number of keys is always even.

✓ The minimum number of keys in a non-root node is *n*.

➢ **In insertion and deletion**

B-tree undergoes the changes must maintain

✓ its height balance,

✓ all leaves are at the same level,

✓ all internal nodes except the root have to be half full, and

✓ all leaves have to be half full.

➢ **Inserting process**

Inserting a new entry into a full node of a B-tree will split the full node into two nodes. The two splited nodes become siblings on the same level in the tree. The two nodes are now each half full, and their median entry is promoted, i.e. sent upward, to be inserted into their parent node. B-tree grows towards its root.

Insertion Example 1:

Inserting with new entries 382, 518, and 508 into a B tree of order number, says 5, an **odd** number

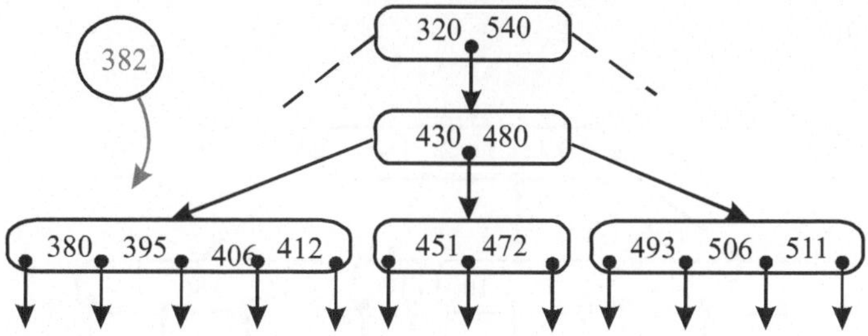

After inserting entry 382.

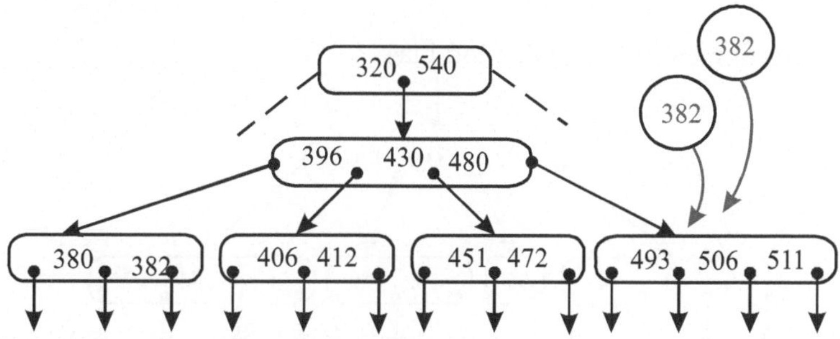

After inserting entries 518 and then 508.

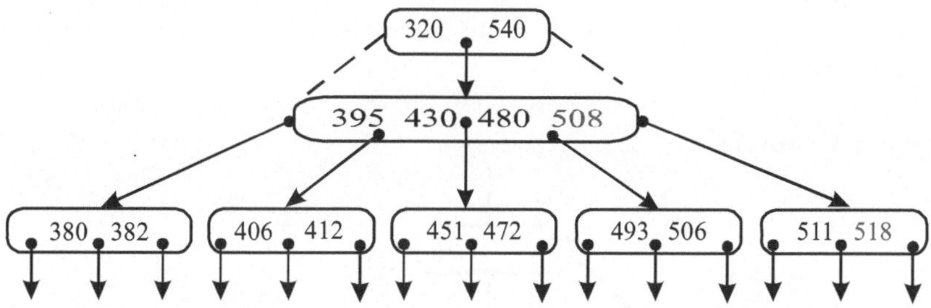

If the order of the B-tree is **even**, says n, then n - 1 keys must be divided into two unequal-sized groups: one of size $^{n}/_{2}$ and the other of size $^{(n-1)}/_{2}$. The larger sized group can be either the left leaf or the right leaf, i.e. left-biased or right-biased.

Insertion Example 2:

Inserting with new entries 102 into a B-tree of order number, says 4, an **even** number

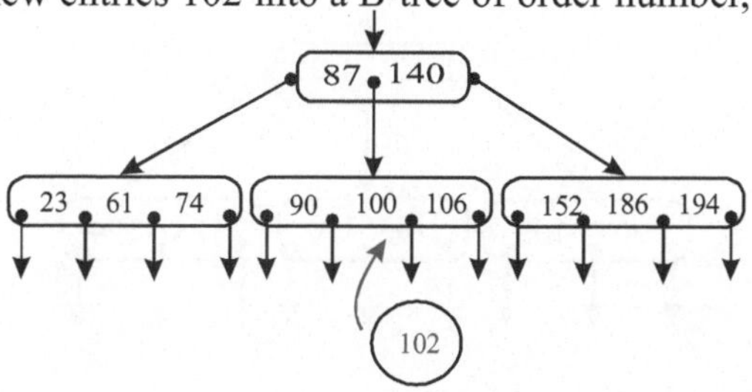

Original B-tree

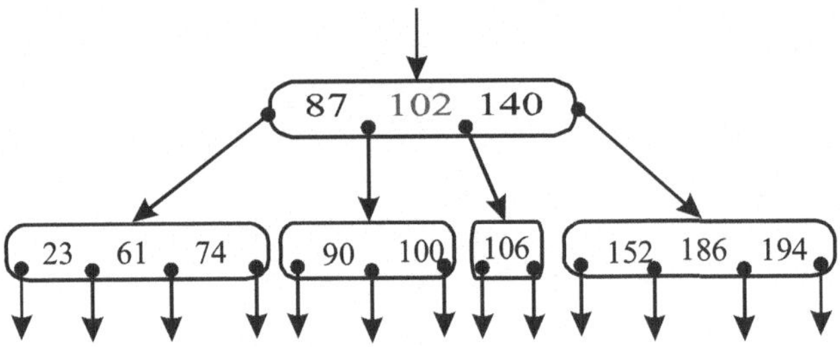

After inserting entry 102 with a left bias

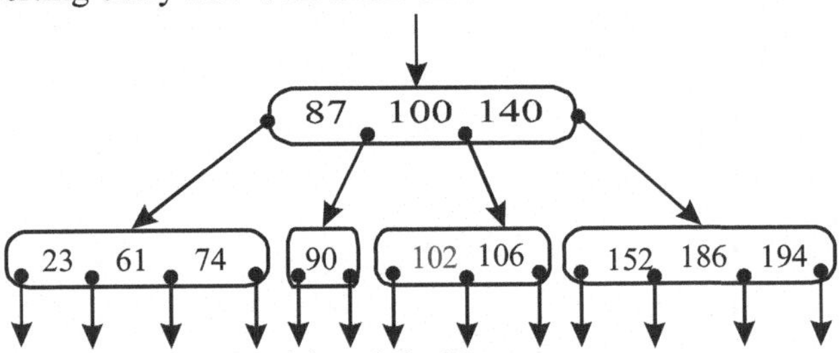

After inserting entry 102 with a right bias

Deleting an internal node will promote the immediate successor occupied by the deleted entry.

Deletion Example 1:

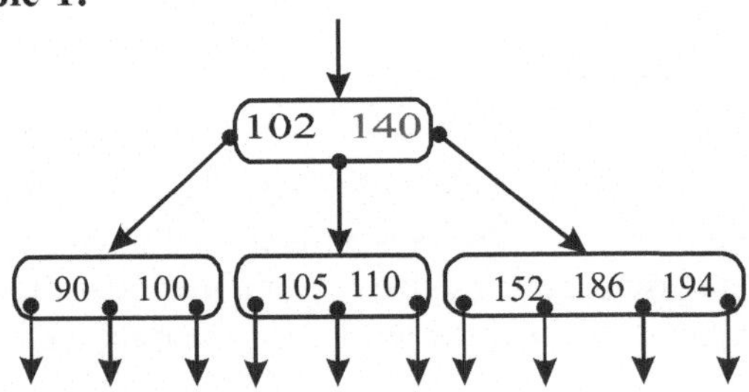

Original B-tree of order 4

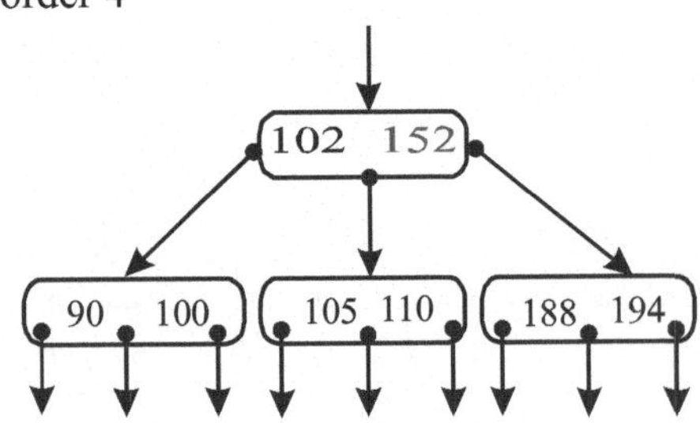

After deleting entry 140 from the B-tree

Deleting an entry from a leaf containing the minimum number of entries, and one of the two adjacent leaves has more than the minimum number of entries, then algorithm performs a rotation to **borrow** an entry from its sibling.

Deletion Example 2:

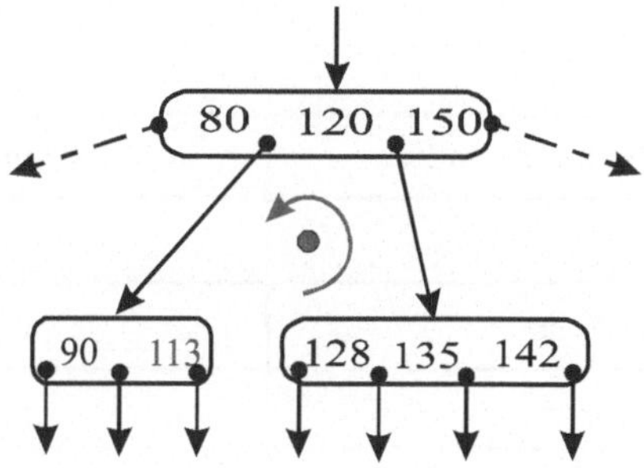

Deleting entry 113 will take a rotation from the above B-tree of order 5.

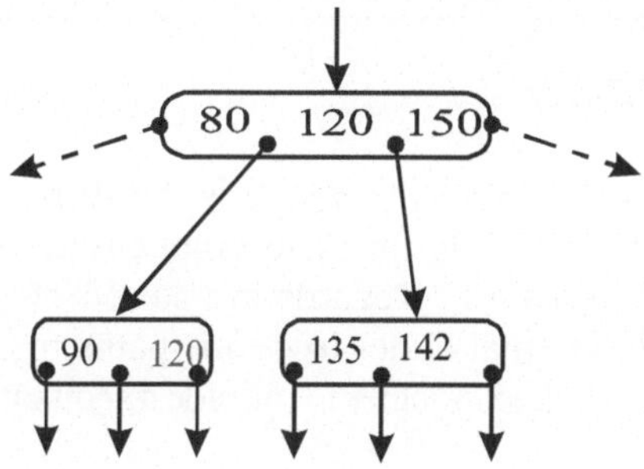

After deleting entry 113.

Deleting an entry from a leaf containing minimum number of entries, and its adjacent leaves have minimum number of entries also, then no sibling borrowing is possible. **Consolidation** of parent node and two leaves takes place. Such consolidation can propagates upward along the tree to decrease the tree height.

Deletion Example 3:

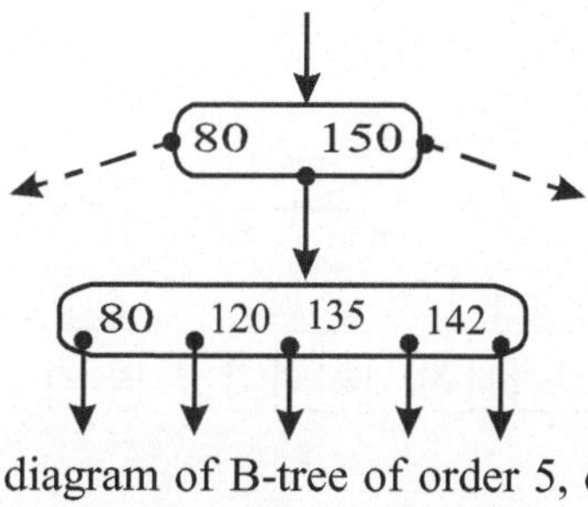

Based on the previous diagram of B-tree of order 5, delete entry 120 whose adjacent nodes have only minimum number of entries.

➢ B-tree analysis Big O Notion

Analysis on number of nodes and keys of a B-tree of order ***n*** , refer to the chart below. In the chart, d is the number of level of tree, as shown in the first column, and q equals $^{(n-1)}/_{2}$

Maximum number of node accesses to search one of keys in an order-*n*-B-tree is

$1 + \log_{q+1} ({}^{n}/_{2})$

Level	Maximum Nodes	Maximum Keys
0	1	n - 1
1	n	n (n-1)
2	n^2	n^2 (n-1)
i	n^i	n^i (n-1)
Total	$(n^{d+1} -1) / (n -1)$	$n^{d+1} - 1$

➢ *Disadvantages of B-tree*

B^+-Trees

One of the major drawbacks of the B-tree is the difficulty of traversing the keys sequentially. B^+-tree is designed to compensate this shortcoming. All keys are maintained in leaves. Records are stored only at the leaf nodes. Keys are replicated in internal nodes to define paths for searching individual records. The leaves are linked together to provide a sequential path for traversing the keys in the tree.

Insertion into B^+ -tree proceeds much as in a B-tree except when a node is split, the middle key is retained in the left half node as well as being promoted to the parent.

The B^+-tree retains the search and insertion efficiencies of the B-tree but increases the efficiency of searching the next record in the tree from **O**(ln n) to **O**(1).

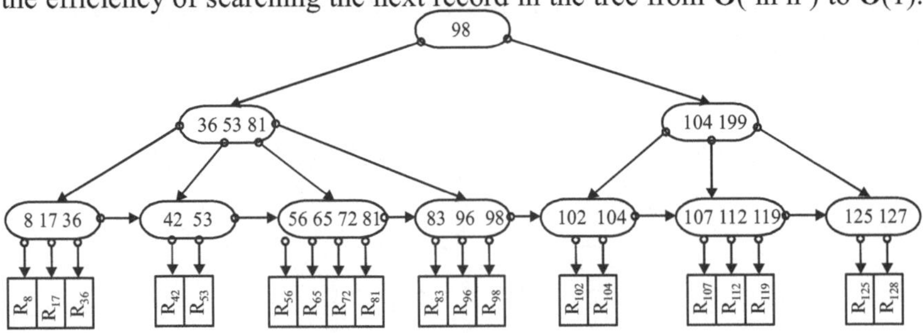

➢ Trees and Forests

✓ A tree is a finite-non-empty set of elements in which one element is called the root and the remaining elements are partitioned into m > = O disjoint subsets each of which is a tree itself.

✓ Each element in the time is called a node.

✓ The degree of a node in a tree is the number of its sons.

➢ ***Threaded Binary tree***

Threaded binary tree is like binary tree except that instead of containing a NULL pointer in its right field, a node with an empty right subtree contained in its right field a pointer to the node which is its inorder successor. Then there would no longer be a need for the stack like in binary trees. Such a pointer is called thread. Three are sight in threaded binary trees.

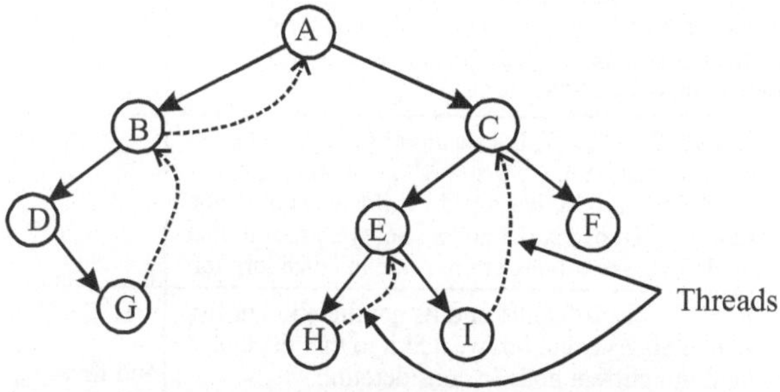

➢ Non-recursive traversal using a Threaded Binary Tree

As this is a non-recursive method for traversal, it has to be an iterative procedure; meaning, all the steps for the traversal of a node have to be under a loop so that the same can be applied to all the nodes in the tree.

I'll consider the INORDER traversal again. Here, for every node, we'll visit the left sub-tree (if it exists) first (if and only if we haven't visited it earlier); then we visit (i.e print its value, in our case) the node itself and then the right sub-tree (if it exists). If the right sub-tree is not there, we check for the threaded link and make the threaded node the current node in consideration. Please, follow the example given below.

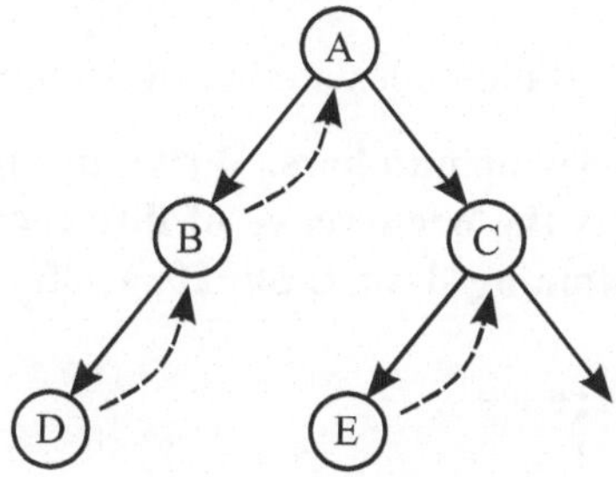

		List of visited nodes:	INORDER
Step 1	**'A'** has a left child i.e B, which has not been visited. So, we put B in our "list of visited nodes" and B becomes our current node in consideration.	B	
Step 2	**'B'** also has a left child, 'D', which is not there in our list of visited nodes. So, we put 'D' in that list and make it our current node in consideration.	B D	
Step 3	D' has no left child, so we *print 'D'*. Then we check for its right child. 'D' has no right child and thus we check for its thread-link. It has a thread going till node 'B'. So, we make 'B' as our current node in consideration.	B D	D
Step 4	'B' certainly has a left child but its already in our list of visited nodes. So, we *print 'B'*. Then we check for its right child but it doesn't exist. So, we make its threaded node (i.e 'A') as our current node in consideration.	B D	D B
Step 5	'A' has a left child, 'B', but its already there in the list of visited nodes. So, we *print 'A'*. Then we check for its right child. 'A' has a right child, 'C' and its not there in our list of visited nodes. So, we add it to that list and we make it our current node in consideration.	B D C	D B A
Step 6	'C' has 'E' as the left child and its not there in our list of visited nodes even. So, we add it to that list and make it our current node in consideration.	B D C E and finally ...	D B A D B E A C

✓ ***Algorithm:-***

Step-1: For the current node check whether it has a left child which is not there in the visited list. If it has then go to step-2 or else step-3.

Step-2: Put that left child in the list of visited nodes and make it your current node in consideration. Go to step-6

Step-3: For the current node check whether it has a right child. If it has then go to step-4 else go to step-5

Step-4: Make that right child as your current node in consideration. Go to step-6.

Step-5: Check for the threaded node and if its there make it your current node.

Step-6: Go to step-1 if all the nodes are not over otherwise quit.

Q1. A file stores a series of numbers. Write an algorithm using binary search tree that counts the occurrence of different numbers in the file. For example, file containing data 1, 50, 20, 1, 25 would produce output as.

Number	**Occurrence**
1	**2**
20	**1**

25	**1**
50	**1**

[DEC04,Q1(b)][10]

We must read numbers from the file and insert the numbers in Binary Search Tree i.e. Parent is > Left child and parent < right child.

Then we write the entries in inorder, thus numbers will be arranged in increasing order with repeating numbers written adjacent. We count number of occurrences of repeating numbers with a loop and thus result is arrived at.

Algorithm :

```
1. declare tree node with left, right, child. Declare array A[100]
2. open file "ABC.TXT"
3. while(! EOF)
do read h
if TREE IS EMPTY,
then parent = n.
else
if n< parent.
then parent —> left =n.
else
parent —> right=n.
end if.
; Traverse the tree
4. P=parent, i = 0;
5. while (p!=NULL)
do
p=p—> left
A[i]=p—>info
i=i+1
p=p—>right
; count occurrences
6. count = a[j], k=1, occurrence[20], l=0
7. for j=1 to i-1
do
if count = a[j]
k=k+1
else
occurrence[l]=k
l=l+1
k=1
print "No :" a[j] "has occurrences" occurrence [l-1]
end if
8. Stop
```

Q2. Write an algorithm construct a binary tree from the given in order as well as preorder traversal. [DEC04,Q3(b)][4]

Refer to Page No. 206

Q3. Define the following terms : [DEC04,Q6(b)(i)(ii)][5]
(i) Height balanced tree
(ii) Post-order traversal

Refer to Page No. 214

Q4. What do you understand by a height balanced tree. Construct a height balanced tree for the following list : [JUNE05,Q1(e)][5]

5, 10, 0, 7, 8, 2, 6, 3

Refer to Page No. 182

Q5. Write an algorithm that takes a pointer to the root of a binary tree T and another variable which indicates whether preorder, postorder or inorder traversal of the tree is required. Depending on this variable, the function should print the tree in either preorder, poster or inorder. [JUNE04,Q1(c][10]

```
struct tree
{
int info ;
struct tree * left ;
struct tree * right ;
} node ;
void post (node *) ;
void pre (node *) ;
void in (node * ) ;
void main ( ) ;
{ char choice;
clrscr ( ) ;
do
{
printf ("Traverse postorder ; 1") ;
printf ("Traverse preorder ; 2") ;
printf ("Inorder 3") ;
printf ("Exit 4) ;
scanf ("%c" & change) ;
switch (choice)
{
```

```
case 1 : post (root 1) ;
break ;
case 2 : pre (root, 2) ;
break ;
case 3 : in (root, 3) ;
break ;
}
while (choice ! = 4) ;
}
void pre (node * root) ;
{
if (root)
        {
        print f ("%d\t", root → info) ;
        pre (root → left) ;
        pre (root → right) ;
        }
}
void in (node * root)
        {
        if (root)
        { in (root → left) ;
        print f ("% d", root → info) ;
        in (root → night) ;
        } }
void post (node * root)
        { if (root)
            {
                post (root → left);
                post (root → right);
                printif ("%d", root → info);
        }
}
```

Q6. The following are the inorder and preorder traversal of a Binary Tree. [JUN04,Q3(a)][5]

Inorder : NTCGOISU

Preorder : IGNCTOUS

Construct the Binary Tree.

Inorder : NTCGOISU $= L\ R_0\ R$

Preorder : IGNCTOUS $= R_0\ L\ R$

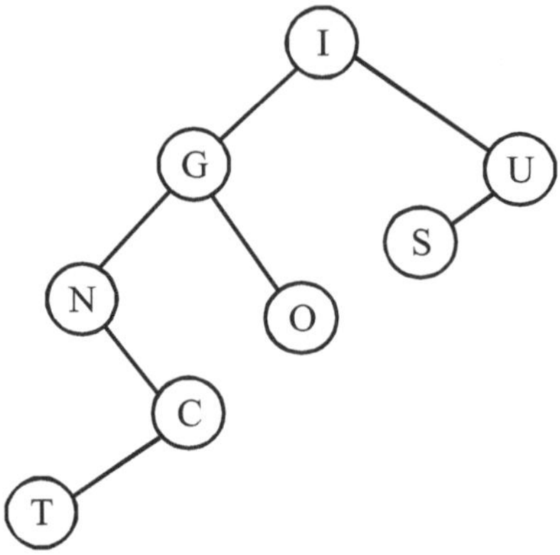

left right

Pre	I	G	N	C	T	O	U	S
In	N	T	C	G	O	I	S	U

left right

left right

Pre	G	N	C	T	O
In	N	T	C	G	O

right

left

right

Pre	N	C	T
In	N	T	C

right

Pre	C	T
In	T	C

left

Pre	U	S
In	S	O

left

Q7. Define the following: [JUNE04,Q3(b)(i)(iv)][5]
(i) Tree
(ii) Binary Tree

Tree → Tree is an a cycle graph. Tree is non empty collection of vertices and edges that satisfies certain requirements.

Binary tree → Binary tree is made up of a finite set of elements called nodes. This set either is empty or consists of node called the root together with two binary trees called the left and right subtrees.

Q8. Write an algorithm to list the nodes of a Binary Tree in the following way: List the root, then nodes at depth 1, followed by nodes at depth 2, and so on. Your algorithm should have linear time complexity. [JUNE04,Q4(b)][5]

```
Traverse (Node *s)
{
        dqueue = the empty queue;
While (s! = NULL)
                visit (s);
                insert (dqueue, s);
                while (empty (dqueue) = = FALSE)
                {
                        x = remove (dqueue);
                        If (x left! = NULL)
                        {
                                visit (x left);
                                insert (dqueue, x left);
                        }
                        if (x right!  NULL)
```

```
                        {
                              visit(x right)
                              insert (dqueue, x right);
                        }
                }
}
}
```

Q9. Write a function that takes a pointer to the root of a binary tree T and computes the number of full nodes in T. What is the running time of your function? [DEC03,Q1(c)][10]

Recursive method is used: Start with an initial call of fullNodes(root). If the root is null, there are no full nodes (by definition), otherwise, if the root has a left and a right child, then it is full, otherwise the number of full nodes is the number full nodes in the right subtree. We traverse on the subtrees until they are empty.

```
private int fullNodes( BinaryNode t )
{
    if( t == null )
    return 0;
    else if( ( t.left != null ) && ( t.right != null ) )          /* it's full */
    return( 1 + fullNodes( t.left ) + fullNodes( t.right ) );
else
    return( fullNodes( t.left ) + fullNodes( t.right ) );
}
```

All these methods visit each node once and do a constant amount of work at each node. Therefore, the running time is linear, O(n).

Q10. Draw the internal memory representation of the following Binary Tree using Sequential Representation. [DEC03,Q2(a)][5]

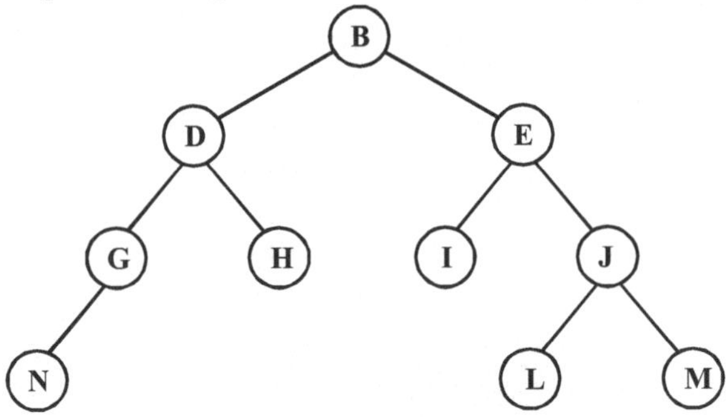

B	D	E	G	H	I	J	N	.	.	.	.	.	L	M
0	1	2	3	4	5	6	7	8	9	10	11	12	13	14

Q11. What is the minimum number of external nodes for a Binary Tree with height 'h'? Justify your answer. [DEC03,Q2(b)][5]

Minimum number of external nodes for binary tree with height 'h' will be 1. See in the figure

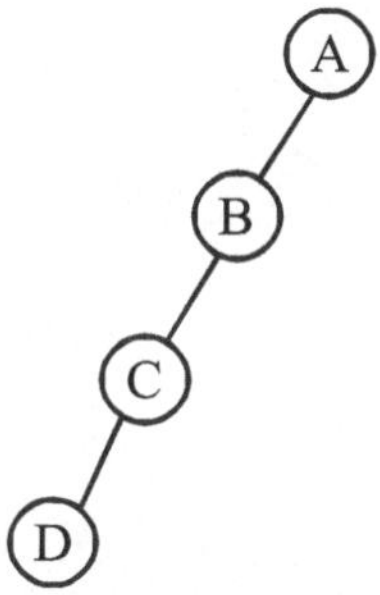

In this binary tree leaf node i.e. external node is only one i.e. D. So a binary tree with height 'h' will have minimum one external node.

Q12. Write a function that takes only a pointer to the root of a binary tree T and computes the number of nodes in T. [JUNE03,Q1(c)][5]

```
// count total number of nodes in binary tree
int countnode(node *root)
{
    if(root==NULL)
    {
      return 0;
    }
    else
    {
      return (countnode(root→left) + countnode(root→right) + 1);
    }
}
```

Q13. Draw the Internal memory representation of the following Binary Tree using Sequential Representation. Assume that nodes appear in the following physical sequence:

A, B, C, D, E, F, G, H [JUNE03,Q2(a)][3]

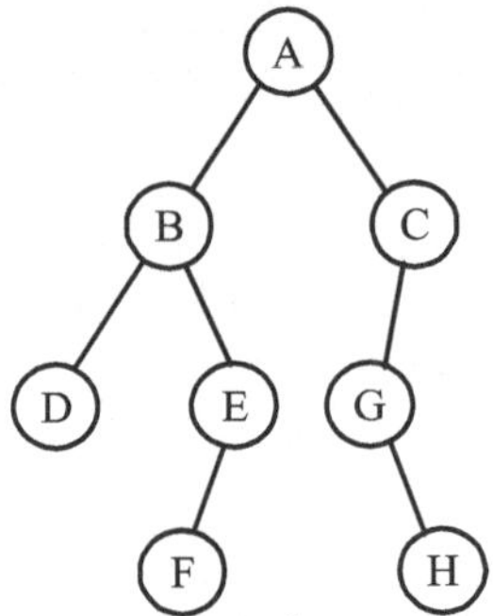

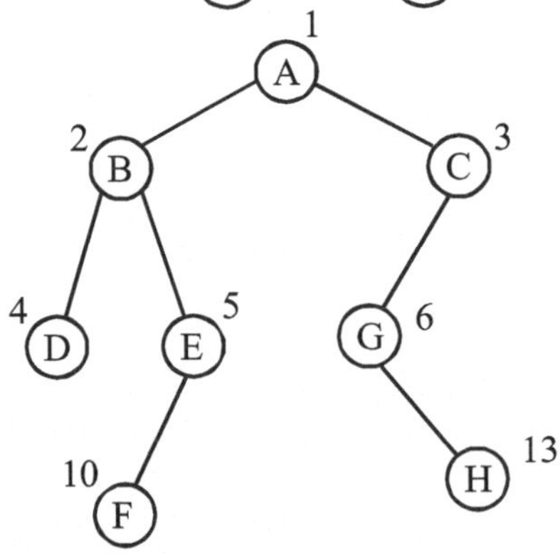

Internal memory representation.

A	B	C	D	E	G				F			H
1	2	3	4	5	6	7	8	9	10	11	12	13

Q14. Consider the tree in the following figure: [JUNE03,Q2(b)][3]

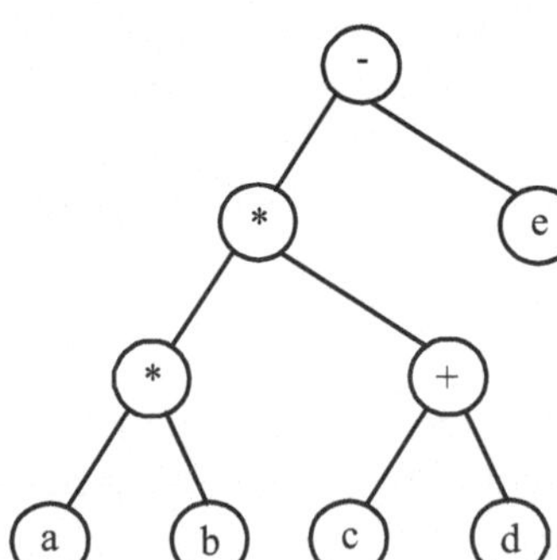

Give the Postfix, Prefix and Infix expressions corresponding to the above tree.

left right root	postfix	ab*cd+*e-
root left right	prefix	-**ab+cde
left root right	infix	d * b * c + d - c

Q15. What is an AVL Tree? How does it differ from a Binary Tree? [JUNE03,Q3(c)][3]

An AVL tree is a binary tree in which the left and right subtrees of any node may differ in height by at most 1, and in which both the subtrees are themselves AVL trees (the definition is recursive).

An AVL tree is constructed in the same manner as an ordinary binary tree, except that after the addition of each new node, a check must be made to ensure that the AVL balance conditions have not been violated. If all is well, no further action need to be taken. If the new node causes an imbalance in the tree, however, some rearrangement of the tree's nodes must be done.

Q16. Write a non-recursive procedure for traversing a Binary Tree in "Postorder". [DEC02,Q1(c)][10]

```
void travpost(node *root)
  {
  node *p=root,*q=NULL;
  stk.top=-1;
  do
    {
    while(p!=NULL)
      {
      push(p);
      p=p→left;
      }
    if(stk.top!=-1)
      {
      p=pop();
      if((p→right!=q)&&(p→right!=NULL))
              {
              push(p);
              p=p→right;
              }
      else
              {
              printf("%d \t",p→info);
              q=p;
              p=NULL;
              }
      }
```

```
        }
    while(stk.top!=-1);
    }
void push(node* p)
    {
    stk.arr[++stk.top]=p;
    }
node* pop()
    {
    return stk.arr[stk.top—];
```

Q17. Draw the internal memory representation of the following Binary Tree using sequential representation: [DEC02,Q2(a)][5]

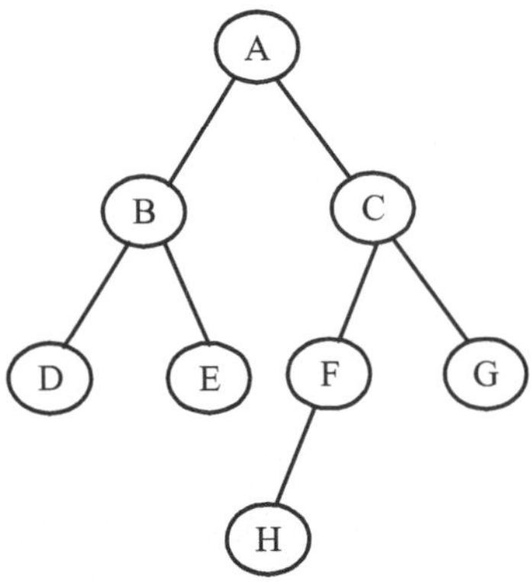

Sequential

Sol.

A	B	C	D	E	F	G					H
0	1	2	3	4	5	6	7	8	9	10	11

Q18. Draw the internal memory representation of the following Binary Tree using Sequential Representation. [JUNE02,Q2(a)][5]

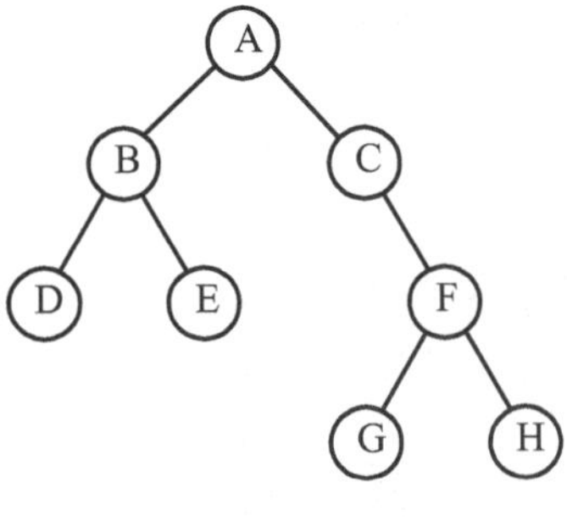

Sol.

A	B	C	D	E		E					G	H
0	1	2	3	4	5	6	7	8	9	10	11	12

Q19. Write a non-recursive procedure for traversing a Binary Tree in "Preorder". [DEC01,Q1(c)][10]

 # Write a non-recursive program in 'C' language to traverse a binary tree in preorder. [JUNE01,Q3(b)][5]

Assumptions :

We are assuming that a binary tree is already created & given.

```
//  Global Declarations
    #include<stdio.h>
    #define TRUE 1
    #define FALSE 0
    #include<alloc.h>

    struct node
    {
      struct node *l;
      int data;
      struct node *r;
    }*p=NULL;  //or *p here and p=NULL in main()

    typedef struct node node;

    /* structure of a node of stack used for preorder traversal of node*/
    struct stack_type
    {
    node *address;              // this will contain address of a node of node
    struct stack_type * next;
    };
    typedef struct stack_type stack;
    stack * top = NULL;         // It will point to top of stack
    void push (node*);
    node * pop (void);
    void preorder(void);
    int set=0;
    void insert(int);
    void main()
    {
```

```
int n,i,num;
clrscr();
printf("How many nodes to insert:");
scanf("%d",&n);
for(i=0;i<n;i++)
{
printf("\nEnter the data for the node:");
scanf("%d",&num);
insert(num);
if(set==1)
{
i--;
set=0;
printf("\nEnter other value");
}
}
printf("\nThe nodes in preorder traversal are:\n\n");
preorder();
getch();
}

void insert(int num)
{
int found;
node* t,*parent;
node *q;
found=FALSE;
parent=NULL;
if(p!=NULL)
{
q=p;
while(q!=NULL)
{
  if(q->data==num)
    found=TRUE;
  if(q->data>num)
  {
  parent=q;
  q=q->l;
  }
```

```
  else
  {
  parent=q;
  q=q->r;
  }
 }
 }

 if(found==TRUE)
 {
 printf("\nSuch node already exists");
 set=1;
 }
 else
 {
 t=(node*)malloc(sizeof(node));
 t->data=num;
 t->l=NULL;
 t->r=NULL;

 if(parent==NULL)
 p=t;
 else
 if(parent->data>num)
 parent->l=t;
 else
 parent->r=t;
 }
}
 void preorder (void)
 {
 node *t,*q;
 t=p;
 while(t!=NULL)
          /* Go to the left most node printing the value of each
                node & pushing their right child on to stack*/
 {
 printf("%d ",t->data);
 push(t->r);
 t=t->l;
 }
```

```
While(top!=NULL)
    /* Now Pop out each element from the stack, print its value & push its
right child (if any) on to stack  & then from this right child again go to left
most child until we encounter NULL. This process will continue till stack is
not empty          */

    {
    q=pop();
    if(q!=NULL)
    {
    t=q;
    while(t!=NULL)
    {
    printf("%d ",t->data);
    push(t->r);
    t=t->l;
    }
    }
    }
    }

    void push(node *g)
    {
    stack *p;
    if (top==NULL)
    {
    top = (stack *) malloc (sizeof (stack));
    top -> address = g;
    top -> next = NULL;
    }
    else
    {
    p = (stack *) malloc (sizeof (stack));
    p -> address = g;
    p -> next = top;
    top = p;
    }
    }

    node * pop (void)
    {
```

```
node * g;
g = top -> address;
top = top -> next;
return (g);
}
```

Q20. Draw the internal memory representation of the following Binary Tree using sequential representation : [DEC01,Q2(a)][5]

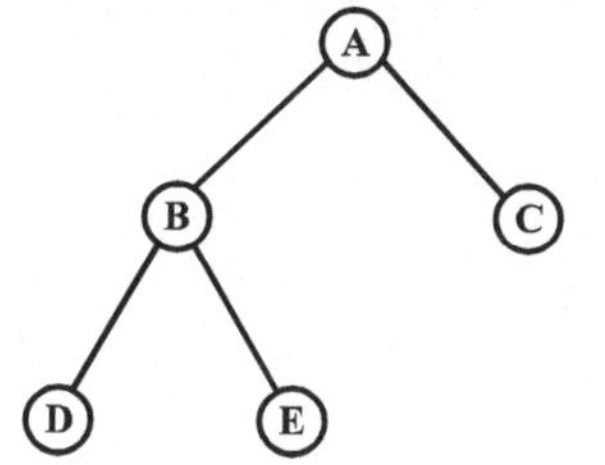

Sequential

A	B	C	D	E		
0	1	2	3	4	5	6

Q21. Write an algorithm to construct the binary tree with a given preorder and inorder sequence. [DEC01,Q2(b)][5]

1. Here we get the root as starting node of preorder.
2. All members to left of that root in inorder come to left and all members to right of that root come to the right.
3. The left subtree sequence in inorder appearing in preorder sets the left subtree root as the first node in the sequence present in preorder.
4. All nodes to left of this node in order form left subtree & on right form right subtree.
5. Repeat step 3 for right subtree sequence from step 2
6. Repeat step 2 to 5 for newly formed left a right subtrees in order till you get single nodes.

Preorder → Root Left Right

Inorder → Left Root Right

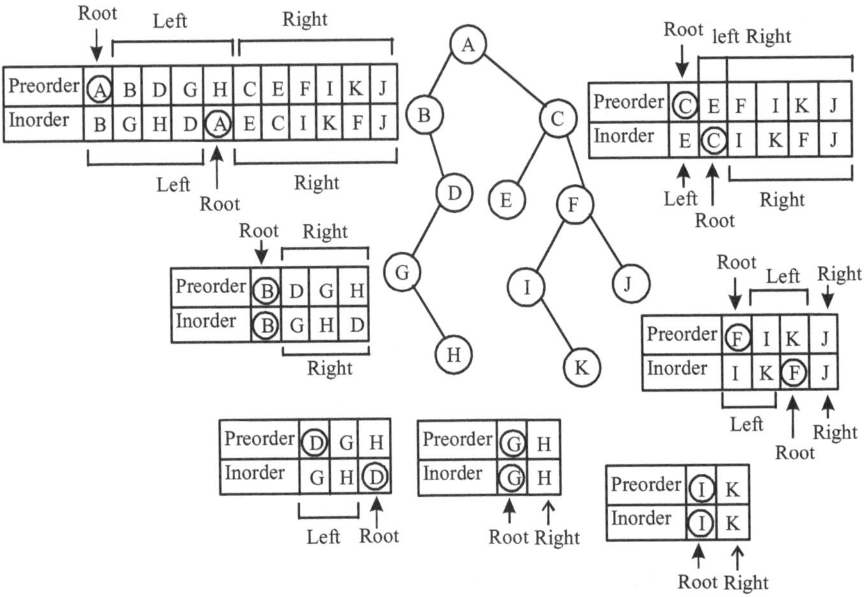

Q22. Define binary search tree. Write a function in 'C' to create a binary search tree. [JUNE01,Q1(c)] [10]

A binary search tree T is a binary tree that may be empty. A nonempty binary search tree satisfies the following properties:

1. Every element have a key(or value) and no two elements have the same key i.e. all keys are unique.

2. The key, if any, in the left subtree of the root are smaller than the key in the node.

3. The keys, if any, in the right subtree of the root are larger than the key in the node.

4. The left and right subtrees of the root are also binary search trees.

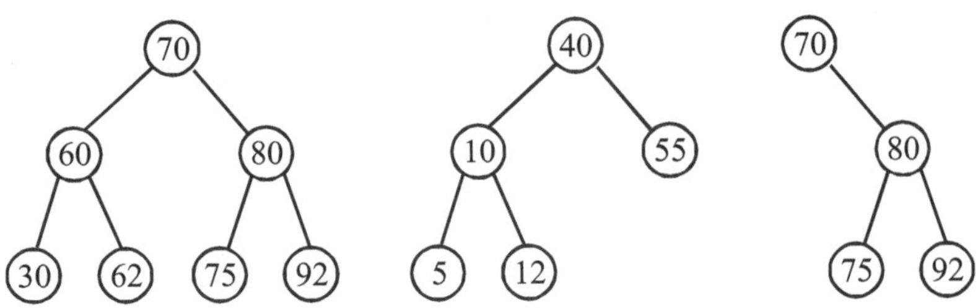

Function to Create BST :

```
Typedef struct node
{
        struct node * left;
        int info;
        struct node *right;
} bnode;
bnode *root;
void Createtree(node **tree)
{
        *tree = (bnode*) NULL;
}
```

Q23. The order of nodes of a Binary Tree in Preorder and Inorder Traversal are as follows :
Preorder : A B C D F H J M K E G I L N
Inorder : A D J M H K F C I N L G E B
Draw the corresponding Binary Tree. [JUNE01,Q2(a)][5]

Preorder	A	B	C	D	F	H	J	M	K	E	G	I	L	N	Root Left Right
Inorder	A	D	J	M	H	K	F	C	I	N	L	G	E	D	Left Root Right

Step (1)
Here, A Root

B	C	D	F	H	J	M	K	E	G	I	L	N
D	J	M	H	K	F	C	I	N	L	G	E	B

2) Now second Step find the left part of A and right part of A. After the root in preorder it is left part while in inorder the root is in middle and all the elements left to the root comes under left part of (A).

Step (2)
Here, there is no left part of Root (A) because when we examine inorder there is no element present before Root(A).

Step (3)
Here, all part is Right part of (A).

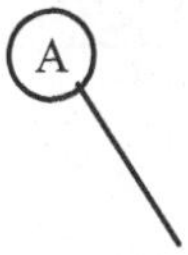

B	C	D	F	H	J	M	K	E	G	I	L	N
D	J	M	H	K	F	C	I	N	L	G	E	B

Step 4 Repeat all there step.

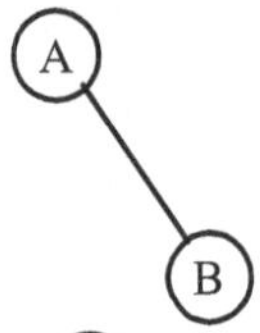

B	C	D	F	H	J	M	K	E	G	I	L	N
D	J	M	H	K	F	C	I	N	L	G	E	B

Left

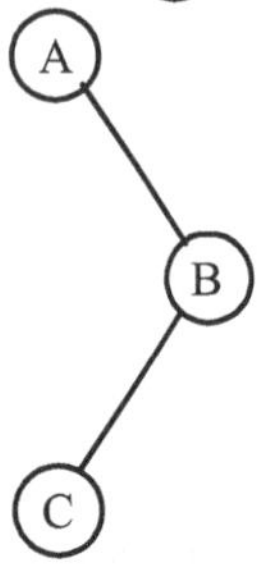

Preorder	C	D	F	H	J	M	K	E	G	I	L	N
Inorder	D	J	M	H	K	F	C	I	N	L	G	E

Left Root Right

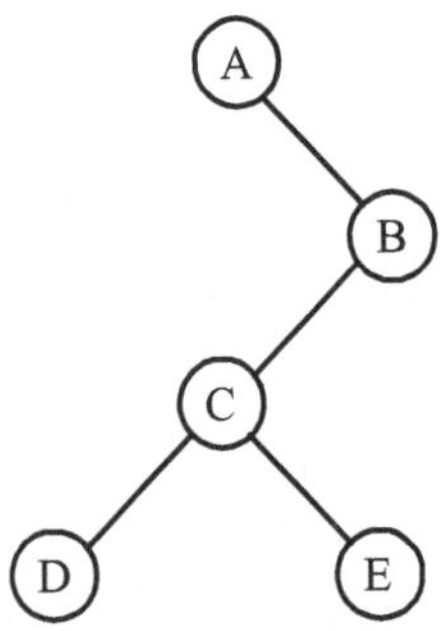

Root

Preorder	D	F	H	J	M	K
Inorder	D	J	M	H	K	F

Right

Root

Preorder	E	G	I	L	N
Inorder	I	N	L	G	E

Left

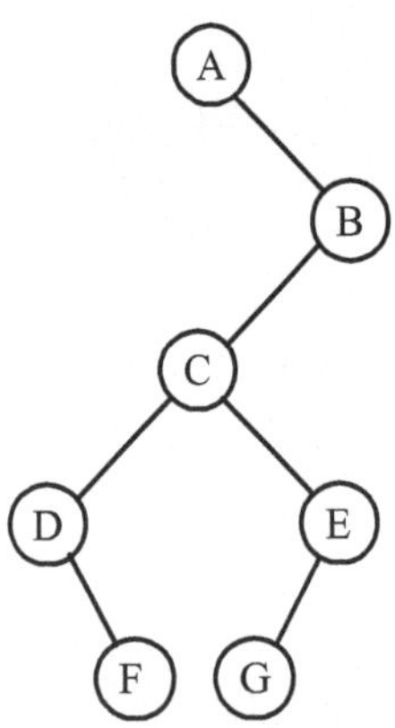

Root

Preorder	F	H	J	M	K
Inorder	J	M	H	K	F

Right

Root

Preorder	G	I	L	N
Inorder	I	N	L	G

Left

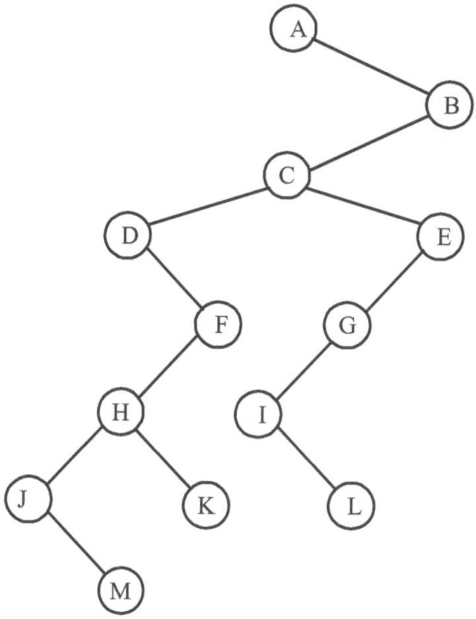

Root

Preorder	H	J	M	K
Inorder	J	M	H	K

Left Right

Preorder	J	M
Inorder	J	M

Root Right

Root

Preorder	I	L	N
Inorder	I	N	L

Left

Final tree is :

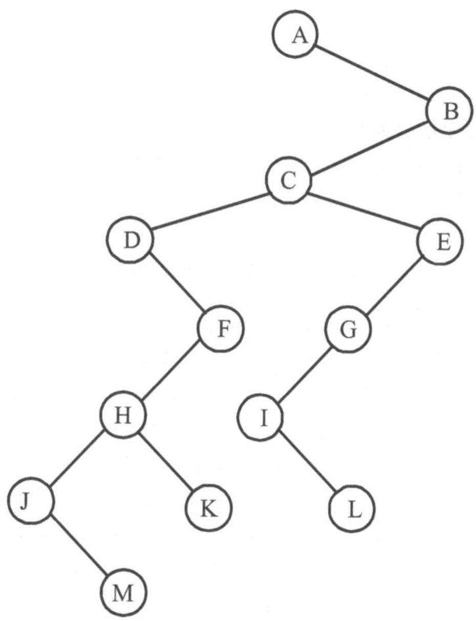

Q24. Draw the tree representation for the following prefix expression: +*/ABCDE** **[JUNE01,Q3(a)][5]**

We are assuming * * sign. as exponent sign.

Infix of above expression is :

A/B * *C*D+E

The tree is as follows:

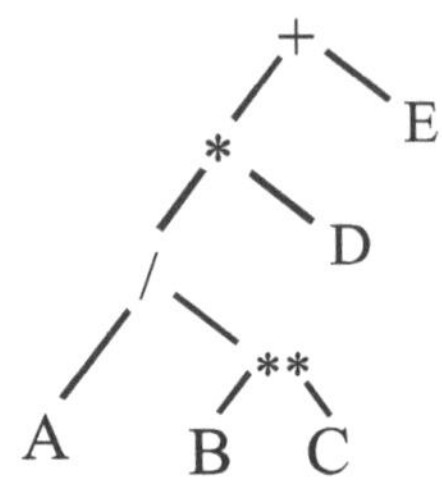

Files

Q25. Sequential file organization vs Direct file organization.
[DEC04,Q4(ii)]

Refer to Page No. 207

Q26. Discuss the differences between the following file organization techniques :

- **Sequential File Organization**
- **Index Sequential File Organization**
- **Direct File Organization**

To what type of applications are each of the above techniques suited?
[JUN01,Q5][10]

 # Differentiate between the following with an example $\left[2\frac{1}{2}\times 2=5\right]$

(i) Sequential file organization vs Direct file organization

Sequential File Organization : This organization refers to the storage method where the data records are stored in some specific sequence. This sequence may be the order of arrival of records, the ascending sequence of any key etc. Generally a key field is chosen which follows the sequence of insertion and the key field is such that it uniquely processes systems where a certain number of records can be collected and processed in batch which is called batch processing where a certain number of records can be collected together and then stored after some time. Also this kind of file organization requires sequential mode of storage like magnetic tapes and previously used punched cards etc. this file organization is best suited for maintaining a database and its backup. The major disadvantage of this organization is that none of the records can be accessed directly i.e. even if the last records has to be accessed then the process is to move sequentially from the first record only. The second disadvantage is that it can never be use used for on-line transaction, all the transactions are required to be batched together. The updates are also not easily handled.

Indexed Sequential File Organization : This is mixture of both the sequential and direct file organization. This file organization originated to allow random access to the sequential files. The data records are stored according to their specific sequence only but an index is maintained for each and every record. The most generally found application for this is a dictionary or a telephone directory. The basic idea is to store the main data file indexes separately. But whenever the data file is updated or changed then index file should also change simultaneously.

Direct File Organization : This organization refers to the storage method where the data records are stored with some relative position in the file. This helps in direct access of the records i.e. a record can be accessed directly. A field of the record is fixed as a key that helps in unique identification of the record. The new records to be inserted or deleted is performed through this key field. This organization is suited for interactive processing like the reservation system, booking counters so that the queries are solved as soon as they are raised. Any record can be accessed directly if the key is know. The faster access devices like floppy disk, hard disk etc. is used for implementing direct file organization.

Applications & Suitability : Sequential files are most frequently used in commercial, batch-oriented data processing where there is the concept of a master file to which details are updated periodically. Payroll, Customer Ledgers and Mark-sheet creation are such application areas.

Index-Sequential file organization represents some end of a balance between sequential and relative organization, the two extremes. It provides sequential storage and random access or random processing. In a library, catalogue of books or authors along with their details can be attracting such applications. Direct files are used extensively in application areas where interactive, on-line processing is used. Space programs, Query processing at reservation centers etc. are examples of such applications.

If the processing is going to be batch processing, then the sequential file can be used. But if on-line processing mode is going to be sued then the direct or indirect sequential file organization is more suitable. On line processing refers to update of file as and when any transaction takes place. For example, the airline ticketing system is a perfect example of online processing. As soon as a ticket is issued, the master file is updated. So that the file always stores the latest position. In such applications, the direct file organization is to be issued.

The activity rate is the percentage of records updated on every run. If the activity rate of a file is going to be high, then the sequential file organization can be adopted. If the activity rate is going to be low, then using a sequential file will lead to a lot of wastage of time. The whole file will have to be gone through to process a few records. In this case the direct file organization should be used.

Relative Files :- Each data record has a fixed place in a relative file. Each record must have associated with it in integer key value that will be sued for insertion and retrieval of the record. A record as well as sequential access is possible. Relative files can exist only on random, as well as sequential access is possible. Relative files can exists only on random access devices like disks.

Direct Files :- These are similar to relative files except that the key value need not to be an integer. The user can specify keys, which make sense to his application.

Index Sequential Files :- An index is added to the sequential file to provide random access. An overflow area needs to be maintained to permit insertion in sequence.

Indexed Files :- In this file organization, sequence is imposed on the storage of record in the data files. Therefore, no overflow area is needed. The index however, is maintained in strict sequence. Multiple indexes are allowed on a file to improve access.

Sequential Files :- In a sequential file organization, the records are stored in which they are written. Also the records can be read only in the order in which they are written.

Disadvantage of Sequential File Organization :- Random access of records is not possible. When the number of records in the file exceeds a certain limit, the maintenance of the file takes more time. When we have sequential master files, the update procedures, not only take more processing time, but also lead to the existence and maintenance of multiple files related to it. These occupy additional external storage space. Frequent sorting of files is necessitated for transaction processing. In an INDEX file organization the records can be accessed directly with the help of an index. They need to be accessed in the order in which they are written.

Advantage of Index File over Sequential Files : Maintenance of file becomes easier as the addition, deletion and modification of records is done without creating any intermediate files. Faster access of records is done without creating any intermediate files. Faster access or records, which leads efficient on-line operations. In case of addition of new records the file automatically sorts itself based on the record key. If a record is deleted, the entire file is re-organized automatically and processing time is minimized.

Chapter - 4

Graphs

Q1. Define a graph.

A Graph G consists of a set V of vertices (nodes) and a set E of edges (arcs). We write G=(V,E). V is a finite and non empty set of vertices. E is a set of pairs of vertices; these pairs are called edges. Therefore V(G), read as V of G, is set of vertices, and E(G), read as E of G, is set of edges.

An edge e = (v,w), is a pair of vertices v and w, and is said to be incident with v and w. A graph may be pictorially represented as given in Figure below.

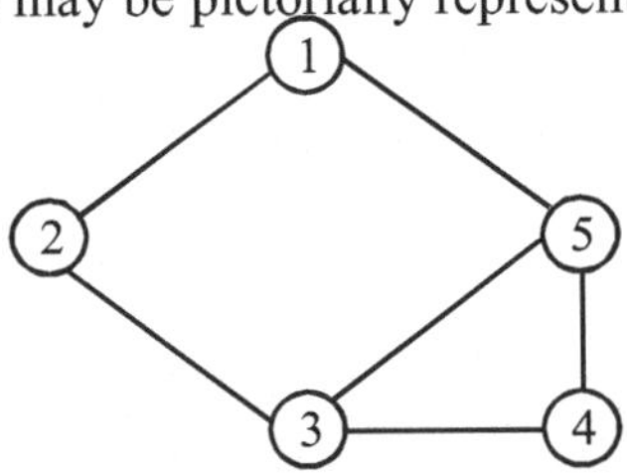

Terminology ::

Adjacent vertices : Vertex v1 is said to be adjacent to a vertex v2 if there is an edge (v1, v2) or (v2, v1)

2. Cyclic path - is a path in which first & last vertices are same:

3. Connected & unconnected graph :

A graph is called connected if there exists a path from any vertex to any other vertex. There are graphs which are unconnected. Consider the graph in figure.

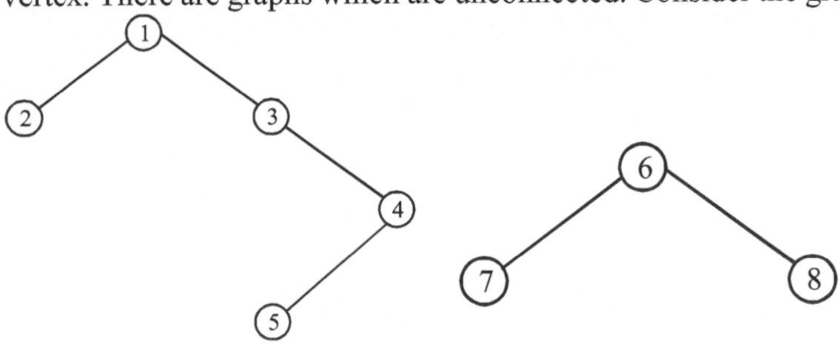

Figure : An Unconnected

4. Diagraph

In a Digraph the path is called a directed path and a cycle as directed cycle.

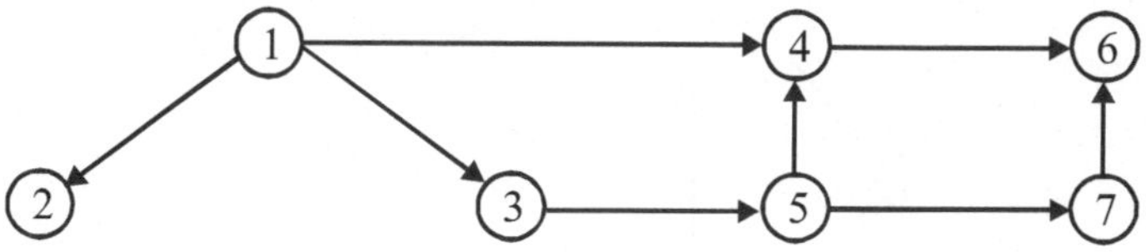

Figure : A Digraph

In the above Figure, 1,2 is a directed path; 1,3,5,7,6 is a directed path 1,4,5 is not a directed path.

A digraph is called strongly connected if there is a directed path from any vertex to any other vertex.

Representation

The adjacency matrix A for a graph G = (V,E) with n vertices, is an nxn matrix of bits, such that A

A_{ij} = 1, iff there is an edge from vi to vj and

A_{ij} = 0, if there is no such edge.

In this representation, we store a graph as a linked structure. We store all the vertices in a list and then for each vertex, we have a linked list of its adjacent vertices.

Traversal ways

Depth First Search (DFS)

In graphs, we do not have any start vertex or any special vertex singled out to start traversal from. Therefore the traversal may start from any arbitrary vertex. We start with say, vertex v. An adjacent vertex is selected and a Depth First Search is initiated from it, i.e. let V_1, V_2 .. V_k are adjacent vertices to vertex v. We may select any vertex from this list. Say, we select v_1 . Now all the adjacent vertices to v1 are identified and all of those are visited; next V2 is selected and all its adjacent vertices visited and so on. This process continues till all the vertices are visited. It is very much possible that we reach a traversed vertex second time. Therefore we have to set a flag somewhere to check if the vertex is already visited.

Let us see it through an example. Consider the following graph on the next page :

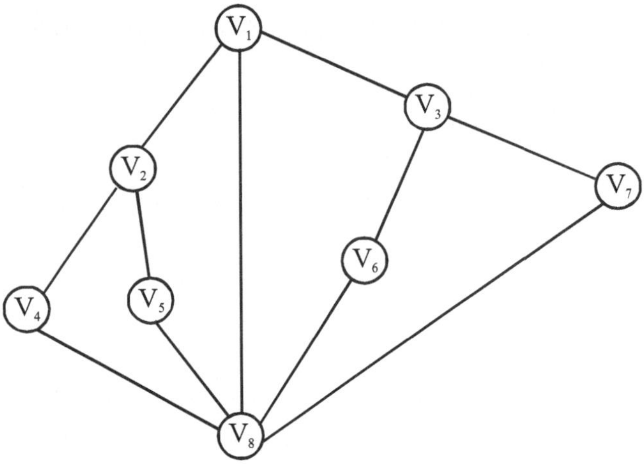

Let us start with V_1.
Its adjacent vertices are V_2, V_8 and V_3. Let us pick on V_2.
Its adjacent vertices are V_1, V_4, V_5. V_1 is already visited. Let us pick on V_4.
Its adjacent vertices are V_2, V_8. V_2 is already visited. Let us visit V_8. Its adjacent vertices are V_4, V_5, V_1, V_6, V_7.
V_4 and V_1, are already visited. Let us traverse V_5. Its adjacent vertices are v_2, V_8. Both are already visited Therefore, we back track. We had V_6 and V_7 unvisited in the list of V_8. We may visit any. We visit v_6. Its adjacent are v_8 and V_3. Obviously the choice is V_3. Its adjacent vertices are V_1, V_7 . We visit V_7. All the adjacent vertices of V_7 are already visited, we back track and find that we have visited all the vertices.

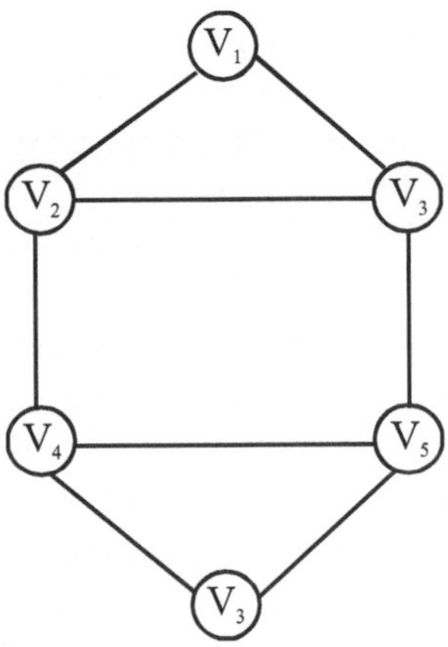

Therefore the sequence of traversal is
V_1,V_2 ,V_4 , V_8 , V_5 , V_6 , V_3 , V_7.

Breadth First Search (BFS)

In DFS we pick on one of the adjacent vertices; visit all of its adjacent vertices and back track to visit the unvisited adjacent vertices. In BFS, we first visit all the adjacent vertices of the start vertex and then visit all -the unvisited vertices adjacent to these and so on. Let us consider the same example, given in Figure. We start say, with V_1. Its adjacent vertices are V_2, V_8, V_3. We visit all one by one. We pick on one of these, say V_2. The unvisited adjacent vertices to V_2 are V_4, V_5. We visit both. We go back to the remaining visited vertices of V_1 and pick on one of those, say V_3. The unvisited adjacent vertices to v_3 are V_6, V_7. There are no more unvisited adjacent vertices of V_8, V_4, V_5, V_6 and V_7.

Thus, the sequence so generated is V_1, V_2, V_8, V_3, V_4, V_5, V_6, V_7.

Shortest Path

Consider the weighted graph in Figure with 8 nodes A,B,C,D,E,F,G and H.

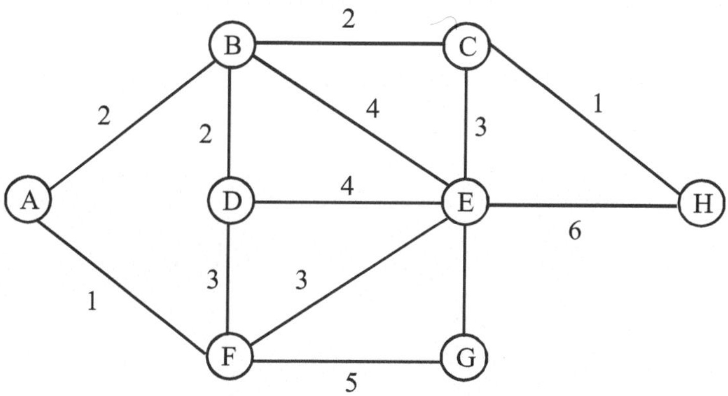

There are many paths from A to H. Length of path AFDEH = 1 + 3 + 4 + 6 = 14. Another path from A to H is ABCEH. Its length is 2+2+3+6 = 13.

We may further look for a path with length shorter than 13, if exists. For graphs with a small number of vertices and edges, one may exploit all the permutations combinations to find shortest path.

Minimal Spanning Tree

Tree is a connected acyclic graph. If we are given a graph G = (V,E), we may have more than one V tree structures. Let us see what do we mean by this statement. Consider the graph given in Figure some of the tree structures for this graph are given in Figure (a), (b) and (c).

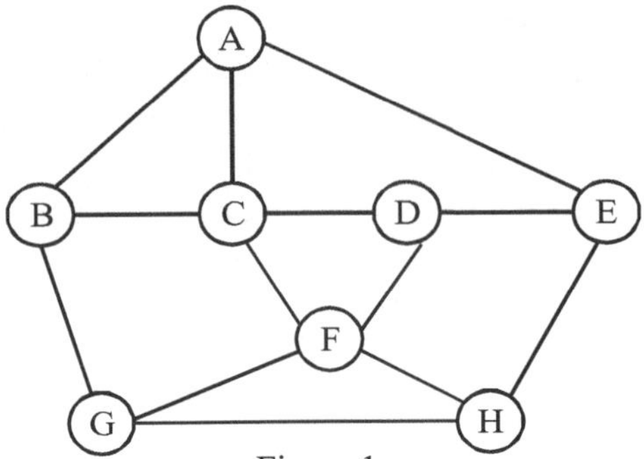

Figure 1

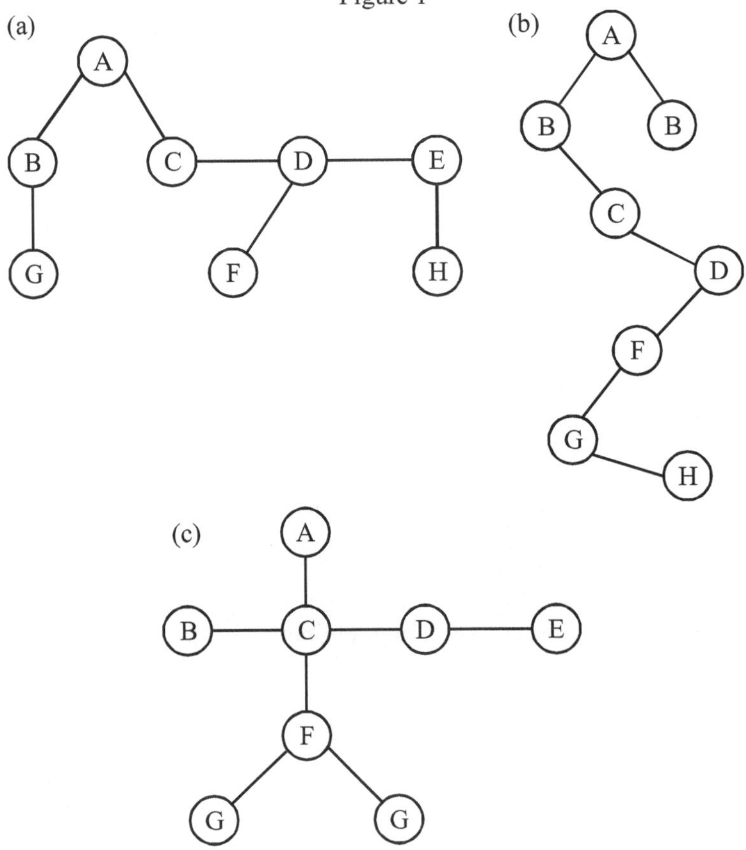

Figure (a), (b), (c)

You may notice that they differ from each other significantly, however, for each structure

(i) the vertex set is same as that of Graph G

(ii) the edge set is a subset of G(E); and
(iii) there is no cycle.
Such a structure is called spanning tree of graph. Let us formally define a spanning tree. A tree T is a spanning tree of a connected graph G(V,E) such that 1) every vertex of G belongs to an edge in T and
2) the edges in T form a tree.
Actually we need to construct a spanning tree with minimum cost or a **Minimal Spanning Tree**.

Q2. What is a graph ? How can it be represented in a C program? Describe two important applications of graphs. [DEC04,2(a)][5]
Refer to Page No. 203

Q3. Consider the graph :

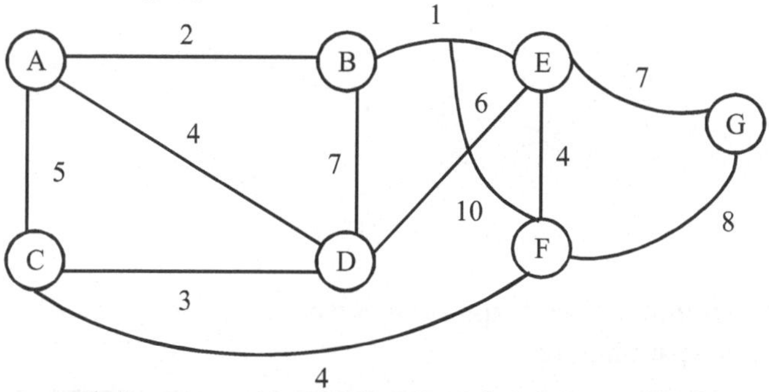

Construct a minimum cost spanning tree for the graph above. Also give the cost of this tree. [DEC04,5(a)][5]
Refer to Page No. 211

Q4. Define an adjacency matrix and an adjacency list. Create an adjacency list and an adjacency matrix for the following graph: [JUNE05,1(c)][6]

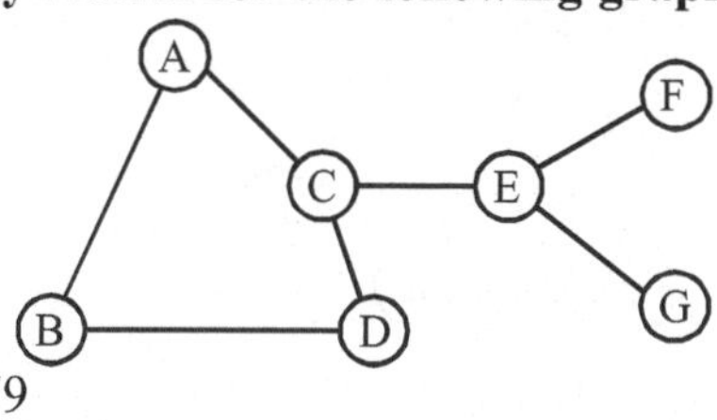

Refer to Page No. 179

Q5. Describe the steps involved in creating a minimum cost spanning tree from a graph with the help of an example of a graph consisting of at least 4 vertices. [JUNE05,5(a)][5]
Refer to Page No. 193

Q6. Define the following: [JUNE04,Q3(b)(ii)(iii)(v)][5]
(i) Strongly Connected Graph
(ii) Adjacency Matrix
(iii) Directed Graph

Directed Graph → A graph is directed graph if the edge have a direction, if they are armed with a head and a tail.

Connected Graph → An undirected graph is connected if there exists path between every pair of nodes.

Adjacency Matrix → Adjacency Matrix shows relations among different nodes in matrix format If there is relation between two nodes, we represent it with 1 otherwise 0. The relation between the nodes cannot be bidirectional in graphical representation.

Q7. Consider the following graph: [JUNE04,5(a)][5]

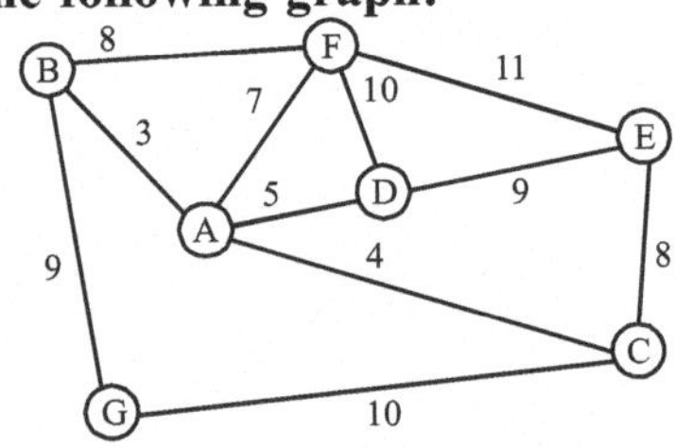

Construct a minimum cost spanning tree. Give the cost.

Minimum cost spanning tree

Edge	A B	A C	A D	A F	B F	E C	B G	D E	F D	G C	F E
Cost	3	4	5	7	8	8	9	9	10	10	11
Selection	✓	✓	✓	✓	✗	✓	✗	✗	✗	✗	✗

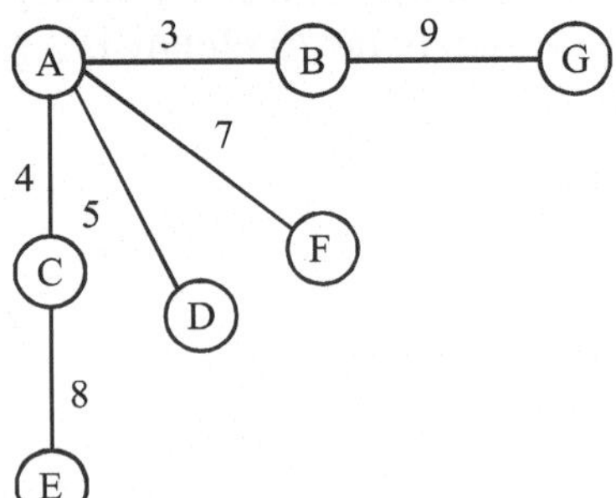

AB = 3
AC = 4
AD = 5

AF = 7
CE = 8
BG = 8
Total = 36

Q8. Write an algorithm to solve the Single-Source Shortest-Path problem. **[JUNE03,4(a)][5]**
#. Write Dijkstra's Algorithm. **[DEC03,4(b)] [5]**

Dijkstra's algorithm is usually used with directed graphs, though it works equally well with undirected graphs if each edge is considered as two directed edges, one in each direction.

The algorithm is as follows:

1. Choose the source vertex.
2. Define a set *S* of vertices and initialize it to contain only the source vertex. The set *S* will store those vertices to which a shortest path has been found as the algorithm progresses.
3. Label each vertex *not* in the set *S* (at this stage, this simply means 'any vertex other than the source') with the minimum distance from the source vertex, but only if this vertex can be connected *by a single edge* with the source. If there is no single edge connection between the source and the vertex not in *S*, label the vertex not in *S* with a distance of infinity.
4. Add to S that vertex with the smallest distance as determined in step 3 (or step 5 on subsequent iterations of the algorithm).
5. Check the distances to all vertices not in *S*. If the latest addition to *S* in step 4 provides a single edge connection between a vertex in *S* and the vertex. Otherwise, do not change the distance.
6. Repeat the algorithm from step 4 until either all vertices are in the set *S* or all vertices not in *S* have an infinite distance to them. In the latter case, these vertices are not reachable from the source vertex at any cost.

Q9. Is the Minimum Cost Spanning Tree found by using Prim's Algorithm unique? Justify your answer. **[DEC03, 5(b)][5]**

No the Minimum Cost Spanning Tree found by using Prims algorithm is not unique any algorithm used to create minimum cost spanning tree will produce the same spanning tree as in DEC03, Q. No.5(a) Tree will be same path weight, same connectivity of nodes and same cost also in that spanning tree. In Question 5(a), we use the Prism's algorithms to find out the minimum cost spanning tree of above same spanning tree, we show it as follows:
Spanning tree of the graph of Q. No.5(a) created using kruskal's algorithm.

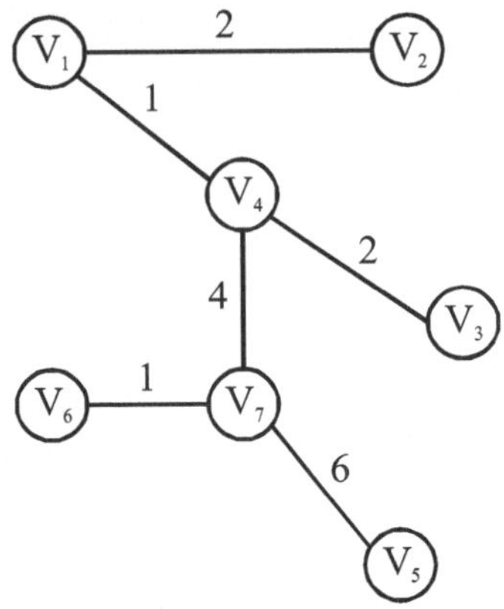

Here the total cost is 16 and the node connectivity is also same. So any algorithm can be used to create minimum cost spanning tree.

Q10. Draw the transitive closure of the directed graph shown in the following figure: **[DEC03,4(a)][5]**

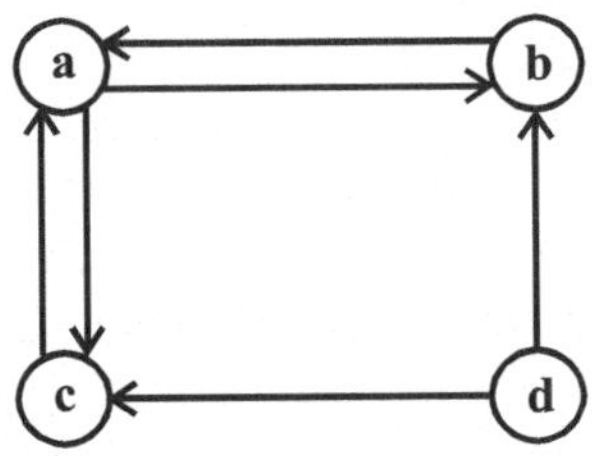

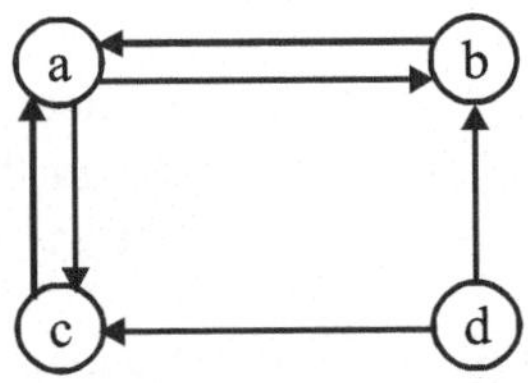

For finding transitive closure we firs find the adj matrix of given graph.

	A	B	C	D
A	0	1	1	0
B	1	0	0	0
C	1	0	0	0
D	0	1	1	0

This is the adj matrix
Find adj 1. i.e. adj*adj

	A	B	C	D
A	1	0	0	0

B	0	1	1	0
C	0	1	1	0
D	1	0	0	0

Now adj2 i.e. adj*adj1;

	A	B	C	D
A	0	1	1	0
B	1	0	0	0
C	1	0	0	0
D	0	1	1	0

Now Adj 3.

	A	B	C	D
A	1	0	0	0
B	0	1	1	0
C	0	1	1	0
D	1	0	0	0

Transitive closure

Path [I][j] = adj || adj1 || adj2 || adj3.

	A	B	C	D
A	1	1	1	0
B	1	1	1	0
C	1	1	1	0
D	1	1	1	0

Transitive closure graph:

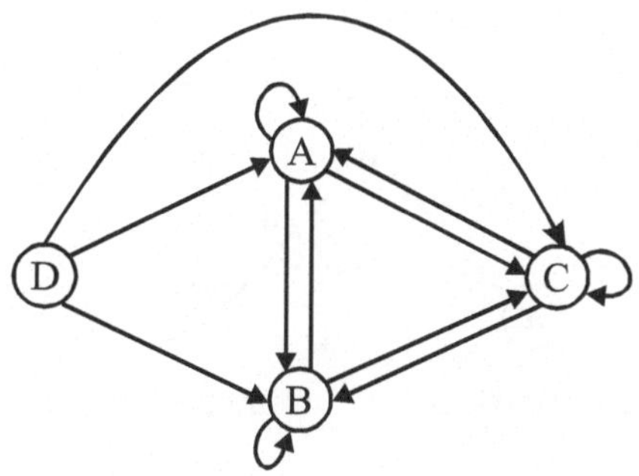

Q11. Consider the following graph : [JUNE02, 5(a)][5]

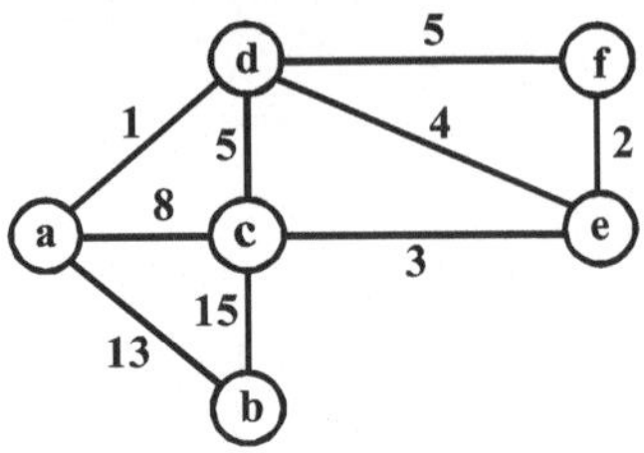

Find the minimum cost spanning tree for the above graph using Prim's algorithm.

Step 1 : We take 'a' as initial node.

Step 2 : Now due to most less weight, we take 'd'

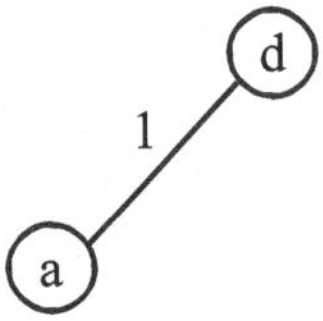

Step 3 : Now we add 'e'

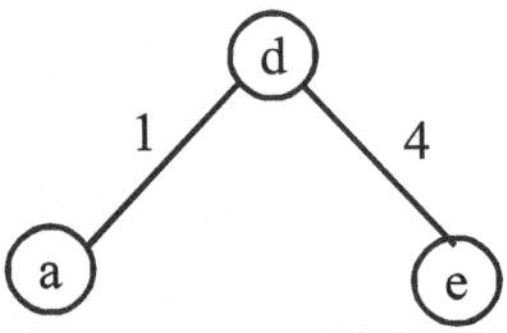

Step 4 : Now we add 'f'

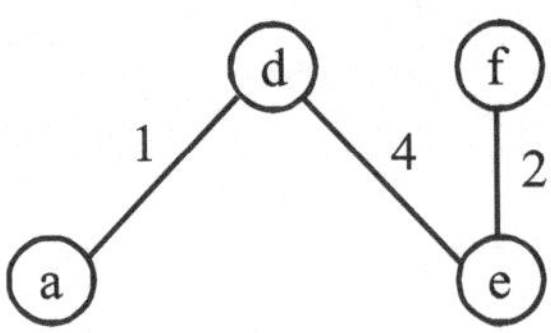

Step 5 : Since 'd' is already existing in minimum spanning tree so we take 'c'

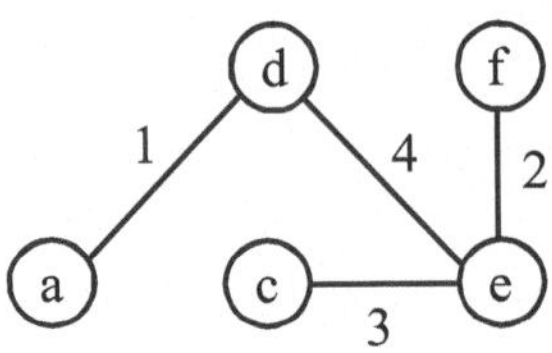

Step 6 : Finally 'b' is included as following.

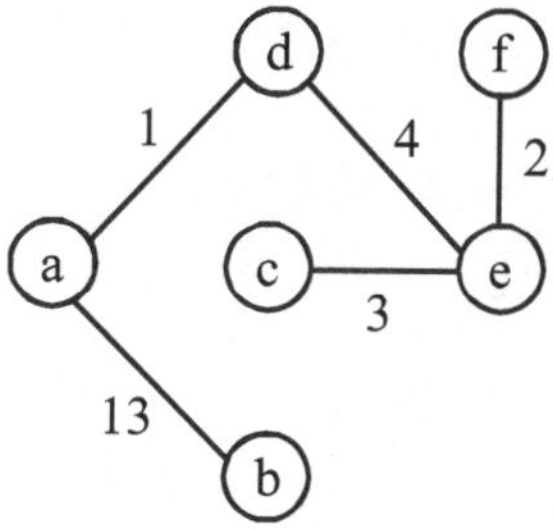

Minimum spanning cost = 1 + 4 + 2 + 3 + 13 = 23

Q12. Prove that if the edge weights on an undirected graph are distinct, there is only one minimum-cost spanning tree. [JUNE02, 5(b)][5]

Assumption.

1. Graph is undirected
2. Weights on the edges are all distinct

Let T1 be the minimum cost spanning tree. For a graph G with n vertices it will require n = 1 distinct edges.

To apply reduction we assume that there exists another minimum cost spanning tree T_2.

Clearly T_2 has at least one edge which is not in T_1. Let e_2, T_2 and e_1 T are the said edges. As all the edges are distinct, either $e_2 > e_2$. In case if $e_1 > e_2$ then dearly, $W(T_2) > W(T_1)$ and therefore T_1 is not a minimum cost spanning tree. Contradiction the proposition. On the other hand if $e_2 > e_1$ then $W(T_2)>W(T_1)$ implying that T_2 is not a minimum cost spanning tree but T_1 is a minimum cost spanning tree.

In either case it is established that for a graph having distinct edge weight there will be – minimum cost spanning tree.

Q13. Prove that the number of edges in an n-vertex complete graph is $\frac{n(n-1)}{2}$. [DEC01, 4(a)][5]

In a complete graph G every node u is adjacent to every node VEG by definition. Clearly, for an n vertex graph degree of each vertex V will b(n-1). Also, the degrees of n vertices combined together will be:

$$\sum_{i=1}^{h} d(v_i) = n(n-1) \qquad \text{(i)}$$

Further, we know that

$$\sum_{i=1}^{h} d(v_i) = 2e \qquad \text{(ii)}$$

Comparing (i) and (ii) we get

$2e = n(n-1)$ [Here e is an edge]

$\Rightarrow$ $e = n(n-1)/2$ Q.E.D.

Q14. Consider the following graph : [DEC01, 5(a)][5]

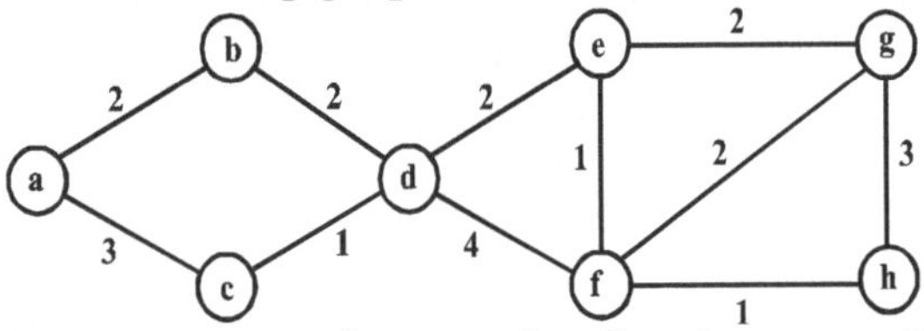

Find the minimum cost spanning tree for the above graph using Prim's Algorithm.

ab = 2
cd = 1
bd = 2
dc = 2
cf = 1
fg = 1
fh = 2
11

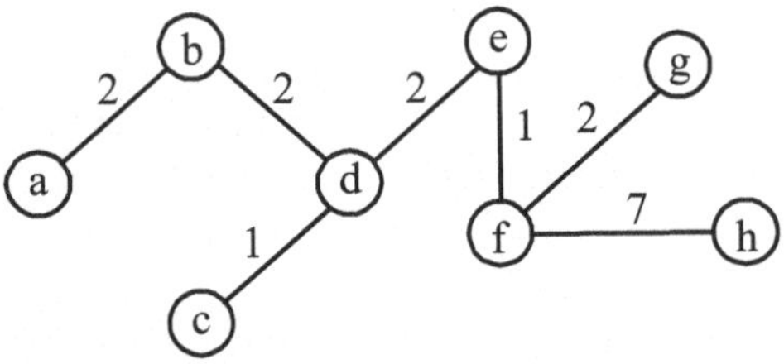

Q15. Write a program to determine whether a directed graph of 'n' vertices has a cycle. [DEC 01 5(b)][5]

```
/*first we calculate its transitive closure and if there is a non-zero element on
the diagonal then a cycle exists in the graph G.*/
    main( )
    { int i, j, k, m, a[10][10], t[10][10];
      /*a[] is adjacency matrix and t[] is transitive closure of G */
      printf("Input number of vertices");
      scanf("%d", &m);
      printf("\n Input value for adjacency matrix");
      for(i=0;i<m;++i)
         for (j=0;j<m;++j)
                 scanf("%d",&a[i][j]);
      for(i=0;i<m;++i)
```

```
  for(j=0;j<m;++j)
          t[i][j]=(a[i][j]>0)?1:0;
for(k=0;k<m;++k)
  for(i=0;i<m;++i)
          for(j=0;j<m;++j)
                  t[i][j]=(t[i][j]|(t[i][k]&t[k][j]));
for(i=0;i<m;++i)
  if (t[i][i]>0)
          printf ("vertex % d has a cycle\n", i+1);
getch();
}
```

Q16. Consider the following diagraph : [JUNE01, 4(a)][5]

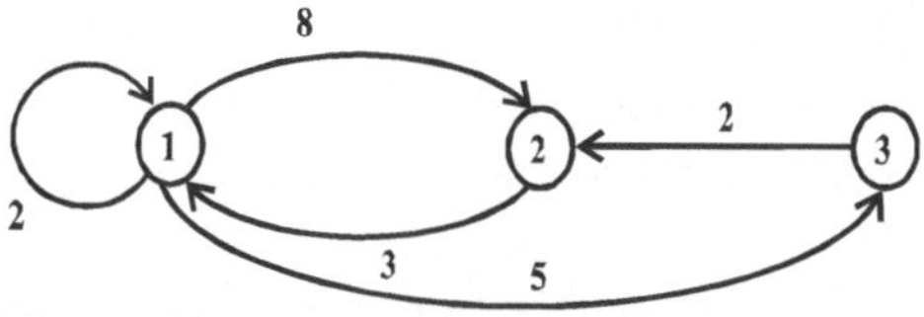

Write an algorithm which accepts an adjacency matrix as input and prints the corresponding graph as output.

Convert (Node_list, n)

Step 1 : [Initialize]

a[n] → where a is an array & n is number of element.

node k → where k is temporary node

Temp = list, where temp is temporary node

Step 2 : Repeat step through 8 while temp ! = NULL

Step 3 : Repeat step through 4 for i = 0 , 1, 2, ….., n – 1.

Step 4 : Repeat step through 5 for j = 0, 1, 2, ……, n – 1.

K = temp;

Step 5 : Repeat step through 6 while temp! = NULL.

Step 6 : if(temp next! = NULL) then

A(i,j) = 1

else

A[i,j)=0

temp = temp → next;

Step 7 : temp = k

Step 8 : temp = temp → next;

Step 9 : End

Q17. For the following graph [JAN01, 1(iii)][3]

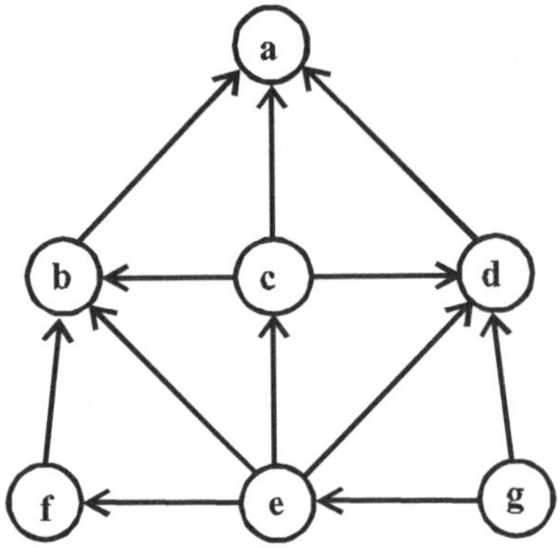

Obtain :

(a) In-degree and out-degree of each vertex

(b) Its adjacency matrix

(c) Its adjacency list representation

(a) In-degree and **Out-degree** of each vertex are :

Vertex	(a)	(b)	(c)	(d)	(e)	(f)	(g)
In-degree	3	3	1	3	1	1	-
Out-degree	-	1	3	1	4	1	2

(b) Adjacent Matrix : Let the set of vertices be V, then V = {a, b, c, d, e, f, g} And Set of edges be E = {(b, a), (c, a), (c, d), (d, a), (e, b), (e, c), (e, d), (e, f), (f, b), (g, d), (g, e)}

The adjacency matrix graph(G) is as follows :

	a	b	c	d	e	f	g
a	0	0	0	0	0	0	0
b	1	0	0	0	0	0	0
c	1	1	0	1	0	0	0
d	1	0	0	0	0	0	0
e	0	1	1	1	0	1	0
f	0	1	0	0	0	0	0
g	0	0	0	1	1	0	0

(c) Its adjacency list representation :

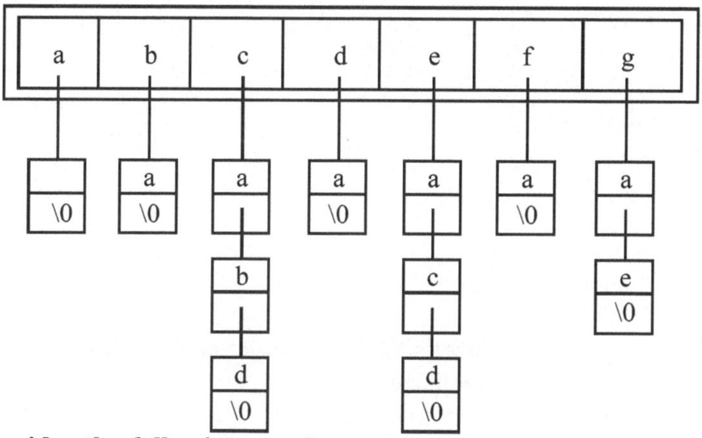

Q18. Consider the following graph : **[JAN01, 2(i)][3]**

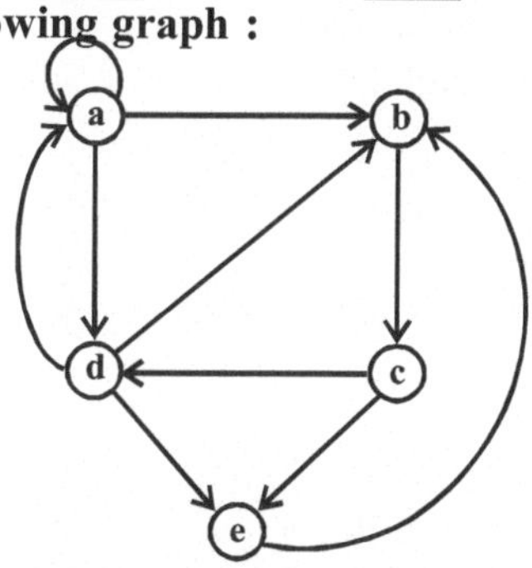

(a) How many arcs are there?
(b) How many acyclic paths are there from node a to d?
(c) How many simple cycles are there? List them.

(a) (9)
(b) 2
(c) 6

Cycles are
(a to d to a), (a to a), (a to b to c to d to a), (a to d to c to b to a), (a to c to e to b) & (c to d to e to b to c).

Q19. Write a C-program to implement Dijkstra's algorithm for finding shortest paths. Describe the algorithm in terms of data structure used, functioning and its running time. **[JAN01,2(ii)][7]**

```
#include<stdio.h>
#define size 20
#define P 1
#define T 0
```

```
#define infinity 9999
struct Label
{
int predecessor;
int length;
int flag;
};
int k, min, count;
struct Label state[size];
int visit_path[size];
int Short_Path(int a[size][size],int,int,int,int path[size],int*);
void Input(int,int a[size][size]);
void Output(int,int a[size][size]);
/* Shortest path computing function*/
int Short_Path(int a[size][size], int n, int s, int t, int path[size], int*dist)
  {
  int i;
  int k;
  int t1, t2;
  *dist=0;
  for (i=1;i<n;i++)
  {
    state[i].predecessor = 0;
    state[i].length = infinity;
    state[i].flag = T;
  }
 /*Make source vertex permanent*/
 state[s].predecessor = 0;
 state[s].length = 0;
 state[s].flag = P;
 /* Start from source vertex*/
 k=s;
 do
 {
 /* check all the paths from kth vertex and find their distance from kth
vertex*/
 for(i=1;i<n;i++)
 {
   if((a[k][i]>0)&&(state[i].flag==T))
   {
   if(state[k].length+a[k][i]<state[i].length)
```

```
    {
    state[i].predecessor=k;
    state[i].length=state[k].length+a[k][i];
    }
    }
  }
  min = infinity;
  k = 0;
  for(i=1;i<n;i++)
  {
    if((state[i].flag==T)&&(state[i].length<min))
    {
    min=state[i].length;
    k=i;
    }
  }
  if(k==0)
    return(0);
  state[k].flag=P;
  }while(k!=t);
  /*store optimal path*/
  k=t;
  count = 1;
  do
  {
    visit_path[count]=k;
    count++;
    k = state[k].predecessor;
  }while(k!=0);
  /*Reverse the vertices since algorithm stores path in reverse direction*/
  count--;
  for(i=1;i<=count;i++)
    path[i] = visit_path[count-i+1];
  for(i=1;i<count;i++)
    {
    t1=path[i];
    t2=path[i+1];
    *dist+=a[t1][t2];
    }
  return (count);
  }
```

```
/*input function*/
void Input(int n, int a[size][size])
  {
  int i, j;
  printf("\n Input adjacency matrix \n");
  for(i=0;i<n;i++)
  {
    for(j=0;j<n;j++)
    scanf("%d",&a[i][j]);
  }
     }
/*Output function*/
void Output(int n, int a[size][size])
  {
  int i,j;
  printf("\n Adjacency matrix \n");
  for(i=0; i<n;i++)
    {
    for(j=0;j<n;j++)
  {
  printf("   %d",a[i][j]);
  }
  printf("\n");
  }
}
/* function main */
void main()
{
  int a[size][size];
  int path[size];
  int org, dest, dist;
  int count, i, n;
  printf("\n Input the number of vertices in the graph:");
  scanf("%d",&n);
  Input(n,a);
  Output(n,a);
  printf("\n Input starting vertex:");
  scanf("%d", &org);
  printf("\n input destination:");
  scanf("%d", &dest);
  count=Short_Path(a,n,org,dest,path,&dist);
```

```
    if(dist)
    {
    printf("\n Shortest path : %d", path[1]);
    for(i=2;i<=count;i++);
    printf("=>%d",path[i]);
    printf("\n Minimum distance = %i", dist);
    }
    else
      printf("\n Path does not exist \n");
    getch();
}
```

Q20. Find out the sequence of nodes visited through depth first search and breadth first search of the following graph : [JAN01,4(i)][3]

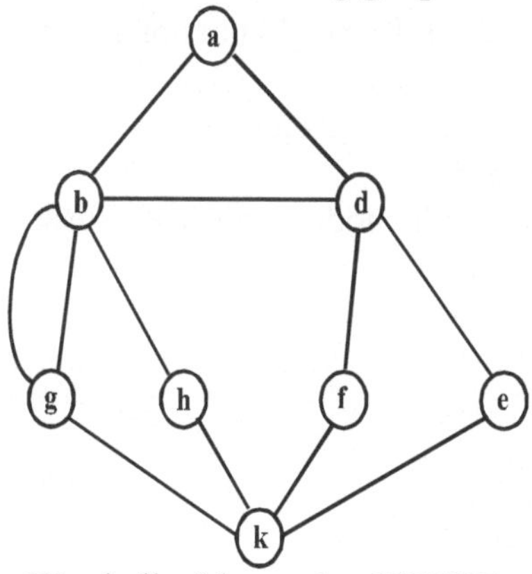

Bredth First Search : We shall add **a** to the QUEUE and set origin ORIG to NULL.

FRONT = 1, QUEUE : **a**
REAR = 1 ORIG : 0

Remove **a** from the front of the queue and **insert** neighbours of **a** from the rear of the queue.

FRONT = 2, QUEUE : **a, b, d**
REAR = 5 ORIG : **0, a, a**

Remove **b** from the front of the queue and **insert** neighbours of **b** from the near of the queue.

FRONT = 3, QUEUE : **a, b, d, g, h**
REAR = 5 ORIG : **, a, a, b, b**

Remove **d** from the front of the queue and **insert** neighbours of **d** from the near of the queue.

FRONT = 4, QUEUE : **a, b, d, g, h, f, e**
REAR = 7 ORIG : **, a, a, b, b, d, d**

Remove **g** from the front of the queue and **insert** neighbours of **g** from the near of the queue.

FRONT = 5, QUEUE : **a, b, d, g, h, f, e, k**
REAR = 8 ORIG : **, a, a, b, b, d, d, g**

We step now, as the final node k is already added to the queue.
We remove, the rest of the nodes from the front of the queue one after another.
The required sequence of nodes visited in **BFS** as :
a→b→d→g→h→f→e→k

Depth First Search : We shall push **a** on to the stack.

STACK : **a**

Pop and print **a** and push all the neighbours of **a** on to the stack.

STACK : **b, f, e**

Pop and print **e** and push all the neighbours of **e** on to the stack.

STACK : **b, f, k**

Pop and print **k** and push all the neighbours of **k** on to the stack.

STACK : **b, f, g, h**

At this point we stop as all the nodes have been pushed to the stack. Popping one by one we get the sequence of nodes visited in **DFS** as :
a→d→e→k→h→g→f→b

Chapter - 5

Searching & Sorting

Searching

➢ **Sequential search**

Both searching algorithms we will consider in this chapter work on one-dimensional lists of data. The data may be stored in an array or a linked list. The examples in this chapter all assume that the data are stored in an array.

A searching algorithm requires a *target* for which to search. The list is searched until either the target is located or the algorithm has determined that the target is not in the list. For simple data types, such as ints, a simple comparison is performed between the target and the data stored at each node in the list. For more complex data types such as user-defined classes, often one of the fields is chosen as a *key* field. The target is then compared only to the key field, with other fields being ignored for the purpose of the search. For example, a database may store customer information for a company. A customer is represented by a class in which the surname, first name, address, phone number, and so on are stored. For searching purposes, an ID number unique to each customer may be defined. This number is then used as the key field in the class, and the searching algorithm would expect the target to be an ID number.

The sequential search in simple: we start at the first array element and compare each key with the target until we have either found the target or reached the end of the list without finding it. The index of the corresponding array element is returned if the search is successful, and some flag value, such as -1, is returned if the search fails.

We can formalize the algorithm as follows:

1. Read in Target; initialize Marker to first array index (0).
2. While Target ! = Key at location Marker and not at the end of the list:
3. Marker ++.
4. If Target == Key at location Marker, then return Marker.
5. Else, return -1.

➢ **Binary search**

There are two forms of the binary search algorithm, both of which are designed to be applied to lists of *sorted* data. The condition that the data be sorted is a constraint not present for the sequential search, and could mean that extra computing is required to sort the list before the binary search is used. Since sorting algorithms are always less efficient than searching algorithms, this could mean that even though binary search on its own is much more efficient than sequential search, the combination of (sort + binary search) may actually be less efficient than sequential search on its own. The binary search algorithm is best used on lists that are constructed and sorted once, and then repeatedly searched.

We will only study one form of the binary search algorithm in depth here. The form we will look at here is sometimes called the *forgetful binary search* because it doesn't bother to check if the target node has been found until the very end of the algorithm. The forgetful algorithm looks less efficient than it needs to be, but as we will see, it is in most cases more efficient than the other form of the binary search.

The basic idea behind either binary search algorithm is to chop the list in half at each step, so that you only have half as many keys to search at each stage. The forgetful binary search continues to chop the list in half until there is only one element left, and then checks to see if this single remaining element is the target. The more traditional form of binary search checks at each stage to see if the target has been found.

The formal statement of the forgetful binary search algorithm is as follows: We use three markers (top, bottom, middle) to mark positions in the list.

1. Set top = numdata - 1; set bottom = 0.
2. While top > bottom do:
3. set middle = (top + bottom) / 2 [using integer division]
4. if key at index middle is less than target key, then set bottom = middle + 1
5. Else, set top = middle.
6. If top == -1, return -1 indicating that the list is empty.
7. If key at location top is the target key, return location top indicating that the target has been found.
8. Else, return -1 indicating target has not been found.

Sorting

Many sorting algorithms are available. Different environment require different sorting methods. Sorting algorithms can be characterized in the following two ways:

1. Simple algorithms which require the order of n^2 (written as $O(n^2)$) comparisons to sort n items.
2. Sophisticated algorithms that require the $O(n\log_2 n)$ comparisons to sort n items.

The difference lies in the fact that the first method moves data only over small distances in the process of sorting, whereas the second method moves data over large distances, so that items settle into the proper order sooner, thus resulting in fewer comparisons. Performance of a sorting algorithm can also depend on the degree of order already present in the data.

There are two basic categories of sorting methods: Internal Sorting and External Sorting. Internal sorting are applied when the entire collection of data to be sorted is small enough that the sorting can take place within main memory. The time required to read to write is not considered to be significant in evaluating the performance of internal sorting methods. External sorting methods are applied to larger collection of data which reside on secondary devices read and write access time are major concern in determining sort performances.

➢ Insertion sort

Insertion sort inserts the items into the sorted list at a time by beginning at the beginning of the list and stepping through the list at a time until the correct position is found. The arrow shows the location of marker1 as we progress through the algorithm. Beginning with array element 1 (the number 9), we compare the element with its immediate predecessor. In this case, $9 > 3$ so no data shifting needs to be done. We move marker2 along to element 2 (the number 1). In this case, $1 < 9$ so we need to shift some elements over to the right to make a space into which we can insert 1. We store the 1 in the temp location, and then shift the 9 and the 3 over to make a space for 1, into which it is inserted. The process is repeated for the remaining elements in the array (7 and 2) until we achieve a fully sorted list.

Insertion sort

✓ **Algorithm**

Our algorithm is as follows, for a list Element of L items stored in an array with elements numbered from 0 to L – 1.

1. Initialize marker1 to 1 (the second element in the list).
2. While marker1 < L
3. If Element [marker1] < Element [marker – 1], store Element [marker1] in a temporary location temp.

Initialize marker2 to marker1 – 1 (the location just before marker1).

4. While Element [marker2] > temp and marker2 >= 0, shift Element [marker2] to location marker2 + 1. (This slides the element over to make room to its left.} Decrease marker2 by 1.
5. Insert temp into the location last vacated by a shift.
6. Increase marker1 by 1.

✓ **Implementation in C**

```
void insertsort(int arr[])
    {
    int i,j,x;
    for(i=1;i<SIZE;i++)
      {
      x=arr[i];
      j=i-1;
      while((j>=0)&&(arr[j]>x))
        {
        arr[j+1]=arr[j];
        —j;
        }
      }
    }
```

➢ **Selection sort**

For large lists, this shifting can be the dominant operation, especially if each item contains a large amount of data that must be moved (as in a personal record with name, phone number, and other data, for example). We will quantitatively analyse the various sorting methods for efficiency later, but for now, it appears that an alternative algorithm in which the amount of shifting was reduced would be an advantage. Selection sort was designed with this in mind.

The data behind selection sort is that each shift of data moves an item directly into its final, correct place.

Selection sort will shift only (at most) two items at each step, and possibly none, if the item is already in the correct location. Its main overhead is in the determination of the maximum element in each sublist. This requires a scan of all remaining unsorted elements at each iteration, but this scanning does not actually move any data and so should be relatively fast.

For a list with L elements numbered from 0 to L – 1, the selection sort algorithm is:

1. Set marker to L – 1 (begin with the last element in the list).
2. While marker > 0:
3. Find the largest element in the range numbered from 0 to marker;
4. Swap that element with the element at location marker;
5. Increase marker by 1.

An example of selection sort is shown in following figure. The position of the arrow indicates the location of marker at each step. In the first step, marker points to the end of the list, and the maximum value in the entire list is found (9). In the next step, the 9 is swapped with the 2. Note that a swap requires an auxiliary storage location (shown in the diagram). To swap two values a and b, for example, we must define an extra location temp. Then a is copied into temp, b is copied into a, then temp is copied into b. Thus each swap requires three shifts of data.

In the next step, marker is moved back one step in the list, so that it now points to the second last element (7). The largest element from the beginning of the list up to marker is now found. This turns out to be the value at which marker is currently pointing. We have also not bothered to ask the algorithm to detect when the largest element coincides with marker, so 7 is swapped with itself. This decision is a trade-off between the extra comparison that would need to be done at each stage in the algorithm and the extra swap that may need to be done occasionally if the largest element in the unsorted part of the list happens to be at location marker.

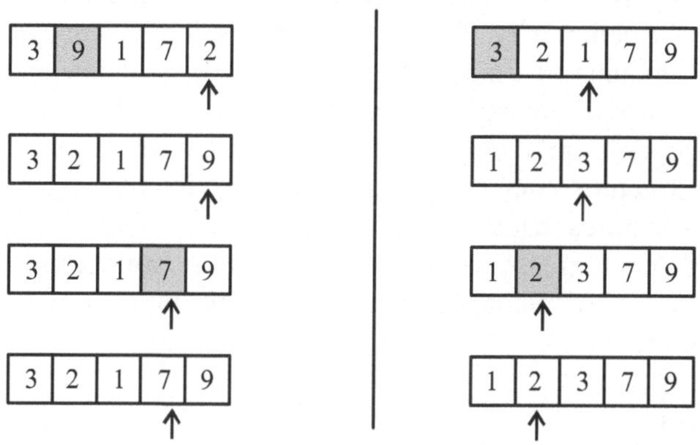

Selection sort

✓ **Implementation in C**

```
void selesort(int arr[])
    {
    int i,j,min,pos;
    for(i=0;i<SIZE-1;i++)
      {
      min=arr[i];
      pos=i;
      for(j=i+1;j<SIZE;j++)
        {
        if(arr[j]<min)
                {
                min=arr[j];
                pos=j;
                }
        }
      arr[pos]=arr[i];
      arr[i]=min;
      }
    }
```

➢ **Efficiency of insertion sort and selection sort**

✓ *Comparison and assignments*

There are two types of operations involved in sorting a list of data: comparisons and assignments. Since these two operations require different resources in terms of computing, we need to evaluate them separately.

A comparison requires that those parts of the data structure being used for sorting are compared to determine whether they are in the correct order. Depending on the complexity of the data structures being compared, this can take different amounts of time. If we are sorting lists of integers (or only using an integer field of a more complex data structure to determine the sorting order (a comparison is relatively fast. If we must compare several fields in a complex data structure, comparisons can take considerably longer.

An assignment requires that data be physically moved within the computer's memory. Assignments are therefore almost always more time consuming than comparisons. In general, algorithms that minimize the number of assignments are to be preferred.

1. Insertion sort

What order will this be? Let us look at the amount of work that is required to insert the last element into its proper place. If the list length is L, we expect about L/2 comparisons and L/2 assignments to be made. For the first element to be sorted (remember that the first element that actually needs sorting is the second element in the list), we expect that 1 comparison and either 0 to 1 assignments must be made. The average of these two extremes gives us about L/4 comparisons and L/4 assignments (very roughly) as an average number of comparisons and assignments per element. Since we have L – 1 elements to sort (remember that the first element in the list is not actually sorted on its own), we would expected about (L – 1)L/4 comparisons and assignments to be made in total. The leading term in this expressions is $L^2/4$, so we can predict that insertion sort is an $O(n^2)$ algorithm for both comparisons and assignments, with a proportionality constant of about 0.25 in both cases.

2. Selection sort

First, consider the number of comparisons. In the first iteration of the algorithm, we must find the largest element in the entire list. With a list of a length L, we must therefore do L – 1 comparisons. To see this, look at it this way. We first compare elements 1 and 2. Then we pick whichever is the larger of these two elements and compare it with element 3, and so on, until we compare the largest element in the first L – 1 elements the last element.
This makes one comparison for the first two elements, and then another comparison for all the remaining elements, for a total of L - 1.

3. Merge sort

Merge sort therefore has two stages: the initial division of the list into sub-lists of a single element each, and the merging of these sublists to produce the final sorted list. The first stage of merge sort is illustrated in Fig. a.
The second stage merges each of the sublists, starting at the bottom level and working upwards, sorting each pair of sublists to an ordered list at the next higher level at each stage (see Fig. b).

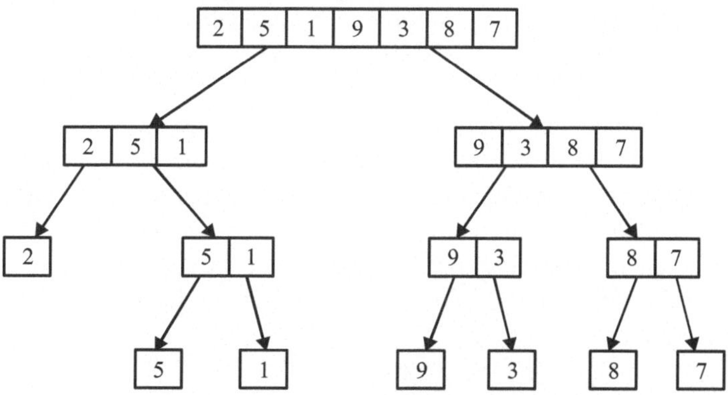

Fig. (a). Subdivision of the list in mergesort.

If we attempt to use merge sort for linked list, we don't need any extra space since we can perform the sorts by redirecting pointers. However, we need to be able to divide a linked list in half, which means we must be able to access the central node. Since the only way we can do this is to follow a chain of pointers from one end of the list, we use a lot of time in continually locating the centre of a linked list.

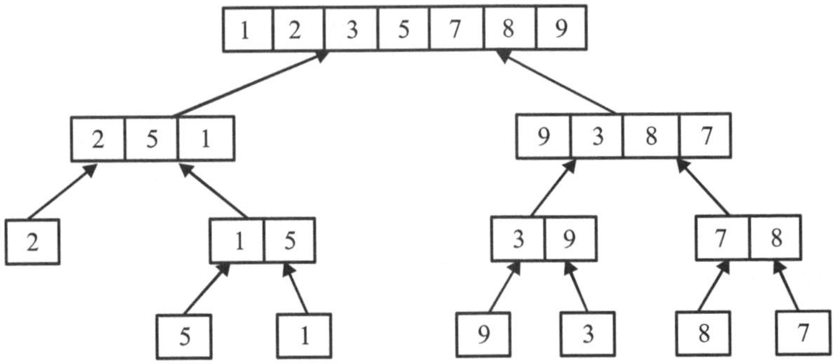

Fig. (b). Merging the sublists.

Q1. Discuss difference between Quick sort and Merge sort.

The main difference between merge sort and quick sort is that in quick sort, the list is divided into two parts in such away that all the element in the first sublist are less than all the elements in the second.

The two sublists are then sorted independently as in merge sort, but because of the condition used to separate the list as the first place the final merge is not required. The list is divided by choosing one of the list elements and using it as a pivot. If we are dealing with lists initially in random order, we can simply choose the first element in the list as the pivot. If the list is known to have some partial order, a different choice may be more appropriate. Ideally, the pivot should be chosen so that it divides the lists exactly in half, according to the relative sizes of the keys. For example, if we had a list of the integers from 1 through 10, 5 or 6 would be the ideal pivots, while 1 or 10 would be poor pivots.

Once the pivot has been chosen, it is used to sort the remainder of the list into two sublists: one where all keys are less than the pivot, and the other where all elements are greater than or equal to the pivot. These two partial is then produced by concatenating the first sublist, the pivot, and the second sublist, in that order, into a single list. The first stage in quick sort is the recursive partitioning of the list until all sublists consist of only a single element. This stage is illustrated in following figure.

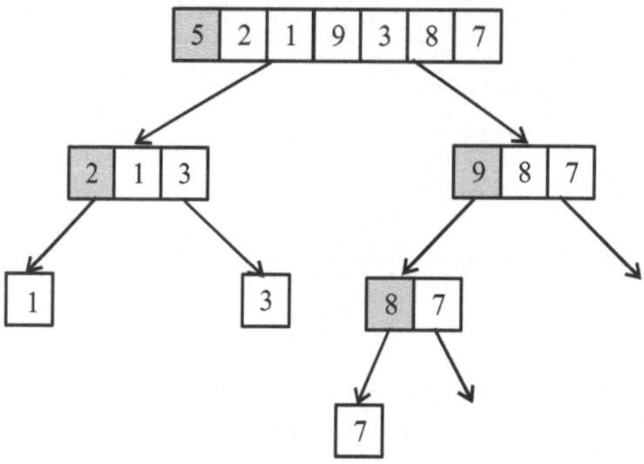

Partitioning the list in quicksort.

In this example, we use the first element in each list (or sublist) as the pivot for that list (the pivot element is shaded in each sublist). In the first step, the element 5 is used as the pivot, so the list is to be partitioned into two sublists, the first containing elements less than 5, and the second, elements greater than or equal to 5. These two sublists are shown on the second level in the diagram. Note that the pivot itself does not form part of either sublist.

In the second stage of the partitioning, each sublist is partitioned in the same way. The lower sublist uses the element 2 as the pivot and is partitioned into two sublists, each containing a single element, so the partitioning of the that portion of the list is now complete. In the upper list (9, 8, 7) 9 is used as the pivot. Since all the other elements of this sublist are less than 9, only one sublist is formed, consisting of the elements 8 and 7. The arrow pointing into empty space at this stage shows that no upper sublist is produced when 9 is used as the pivot.

In the first three steps in following diagram, the marker m is moved along the array until the first element larger than the pivot is found. This element is labelled with the marker s to indicate it is the starting point of the upper sublist. The marker m is then moved along from s. The next element (3) is less than the pivot, so it is swapped with the element at location s (first step in the second column in the diagram) and s is advanced by one. In the next two steps, m is advanced further, but the remaining two elements (8 and 7) are both larger than the pivot so no further swaps are required. In the final step, the pivot (5) is swapped with the element just prior to s. This swap places the pivot between the two sublists, so when these sublists are sorted recursively, it will be in the correct place relative to the sublists. It is this swap of the pivot into the correct location which ensures that the final concatenation step is not required. Note, however, that swapping the pivot into this location alters the order in the lower sublist. In our example above, the lower sublist had the order 2, 1, 3, while here it has the order 3, 2, 1.

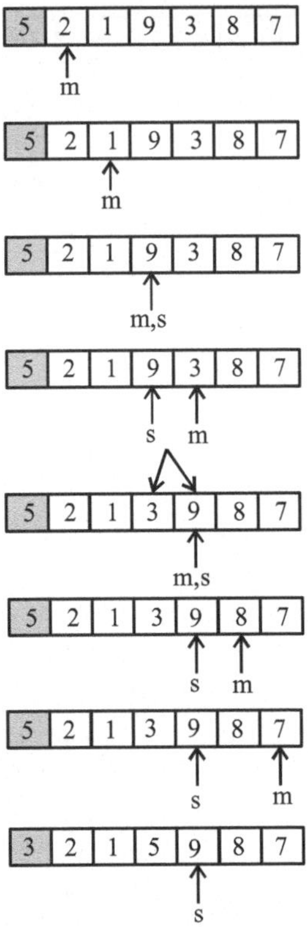

This will, of course, affect the pivot that is chosen for partitioning the sublist in the next stage of the algorithm. In our case, it will make the second partition less efficient than in our original example, but in other cases, of course, it may improve the efficiency so on average, this step will not adversely affect the efficiency of the algorithm overall.

Quick sort Algorithm Analysis :

The quick sort is an in-place, divide-and-conquer, massively recursive sort. As a normal person would say, it's essentially a faster in-place version of the merge sort. The quick sort algorithm is simple in theory, but very difficult to put into code (computer scientists tied themselves into knots for years trying to write a practical implementation of the algorithm, and it still has that effect on university students).

The recursive algorithm consists of four steps (which closely resemble the merge sort):

If there are one or less elements in the array to be sorted, return immediately. Pick an element in the array to serve as a "pivot" point. (Usually the left-most element in the array is used.)

Split the array into two parts - one with elements larger than the pivot and the other with elements smaller than the pivot. Recursively repeat the algorithm for both halves of the original array. The efficiency of the algorithm is major impacted by which element is chosen as the pivot point. The worst-case efficiency of the quick sort, $O(n^2)$, occurs when the list is sorted and the left-most element is chosen. Randomly choosing a pivot point rather than using the left-most element is recommended if the data to be sorted isn't random. As long as the pivot point is chosen randomly, the quick sort has an algorithmic complexity of O(n log n).

Pros: Extremely fast.

Cons: Very complex algorithm, massively recursive.

Empirical Analysis

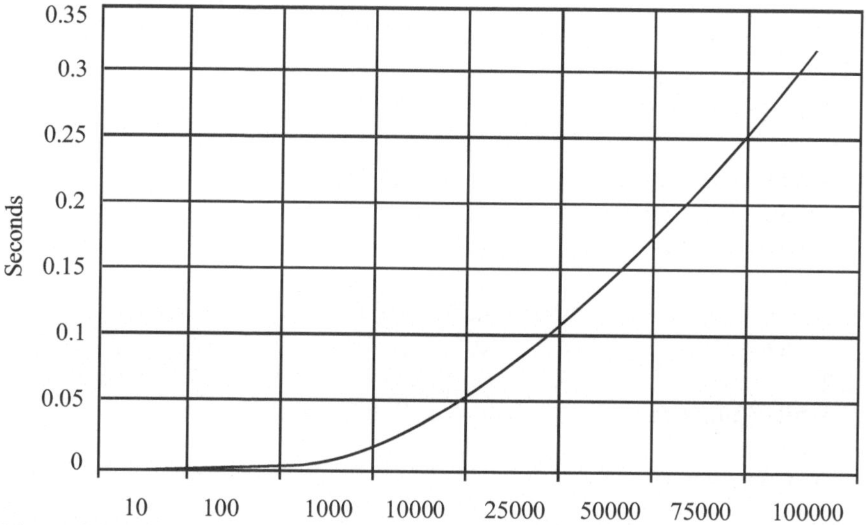

The quick sort is by far the fastest of the common sorting algorithms. It's possible to write a special-purpose sorting algorithm that can beat the quick sort for some data sets, but for general-case sorting there isn't anything faster. As soon as students figure this out, their immediate impulse is to use the quick sort for everything - after all, faster is better, right? It's important to resist this urge - the quick sort isn't always the best choice. As mentioned earlier, it's massively recursive (which means that for very large sorts, you can run the system out of stack space pretty easily). It's also a complex algorithm - a little too complex to make it practical for a one-time sort of 25 items, for example. With that said, in most cases the quick sort is the best choice if speed is important (and it almost always is). Use it for repetitive sorting, sorting of medium to large lists, and as a default choice when you're not really sure which sorting algorithm to use. Ironically, the quick sort has horrible efficiency when operating on lists that are mostly sorted in either forward or reverse order - avoid it in those situations.

SourceCode :

Below is the basic quick sort algorithm.

```
void quickSort(int numbers[], int array_size)
{
  q_sort(numbers, 0, array_size - 1);
}
void q_sort(int numbers[], int left, int right)
{
  int pivot, l_hold, r_hold;

  l_hold = left;
  r_hold = right;
  pivot = numbers[left];
  while (left < right)
  {
    while ((numbers[right] >= pivot) && (left < right))
      right—;
    if (left != right)
    {
      numbers[left] = numbers[right];
      left++;
    }
    while ((numbers[left] <= pivot) && (left < right))
      left++;
    if (left != right)
    {
      numbers[right] = numbers[left];
      right—;
    }
  }
  numbers[left] = pivot;
  pivot = left;
  left = l_hold;
  right = r_hold;
  if (left < pivot)
    q_sort(numbers, left, pivot-1);
  if (right > pivot)
    q_sort(numbers, pivot+1, right);
}
```

Q2. Write a recursive algorithm to implement Quick Sort.

[JUNE03,Q6(a)][5]

QuickSort Recursive (a, lb, ub)

Here is an array of size n(>1) in memory. This algorithm sorts this array in ascending order using quick sort technique. The variable loc is used to hold the index of splitting element.

```
begin
        if (lb < ub) then
        Call Split Array(a, lb, ub, loc)
        Call QuickSort Recursive (a, lb, loc – 1)
        Call QuickSort Recursive (a, loc + 1, ub)
endif
End.
```

SplittArray(a, beg, end, loc)

Here, is an array in memory, and beg and end represents the lower bound and upper bound of the sub array in question.

```
begin
        Set left = be, right = end, loc = beg
        Set done = false
        while (not done) do
        while(a[loc] ≤ a[right]) and [loc ≠ right)) do
                Set right = right – 1
endwhile
if (loc = right) then
         Set done = true
else if (a[loc]>a[right]) then
        Interchange a[loc] and a[right]
        Set loc = right
endif
if (not done) then
        while (a[loc] ≥ a[left]) and (loc ≠ left) do
                Set left = left + 1
        endwhile
        if(loc = left) then
                Set done = true
        else if (a[loc] < a[left]) then
                Interchange a[loc] and a[left]
                Set loc = left
        endif
    endif
endwhile
```

End.

Q3. The input sequence to a Quick Sort' algorithm which sorts in increasing order is [JUNE03,Q6(b)][5]

75, 73, 65, 82, 55, 90

Show the Sorting Process step-wise.

(1) (75), 73, 65, 82, 55, 90

pivot = 75. 55 < 75 exchange.
scan from right.

(2) 55, 73, 65, 82, (75), 90

pivot = 75 82 > (75), 90

Scan from left

(3) {(55), 73, 65, 75} 82 {90}

pivot = 55. but it is its place

(4) So, we have

55, {(73), 65, 75} 82 {90}

65 < 73 exchange

pivot = 73

(5) 55, {65, (73), 75} 82 {90}

P root = 73 but at its place

So, finally 55, 65, 73, 75, 82, 90

Q4. Write an algorithm to implement Heap Sort. [DEC02,Q6(a)[6]

Heap Sort:-

Heapsort(array, N)

Array represents the list of element & N represents the number of elements

Step 1 : Repeat through step 9
    for k = n, n-1, ….., 2

Step 2 : array[1] = array[k]

Step 3 : temp = array[1]
    i = 1
    j = 2

Step 4 : if(j+1) <k then
    If array[j + 1] > j then
    j = j + 1

Step5 : Repeat through step 9
    while j <= k - & array [j] > temp

```
Step6 : array[j] = array[i]
Step7 :          i = j
                 j = 2 × I
Step 8 : if j+1 <k then
          if array[j+1] > array[j] then
          j = j + 1
          else if
          j > n then
Step 9 : array[j] = temp
         [End of loops]
Step 10 : exit
```

Q5. The input sequence to a Heap Sort Algorithm which sorts in increasing order is :

5 3 9 2 14 8.

Show the sorting process stepwise. **[DEC02,Q6(b)][4]**

Arrange in Heap

Step 1 Insert 5

Step 2 Insert 3

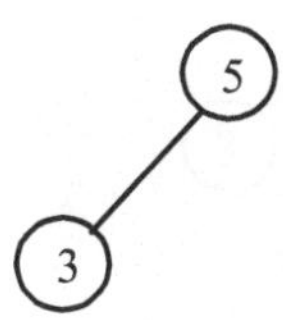

Step 3 Insert 9

Step 4 Insert 1

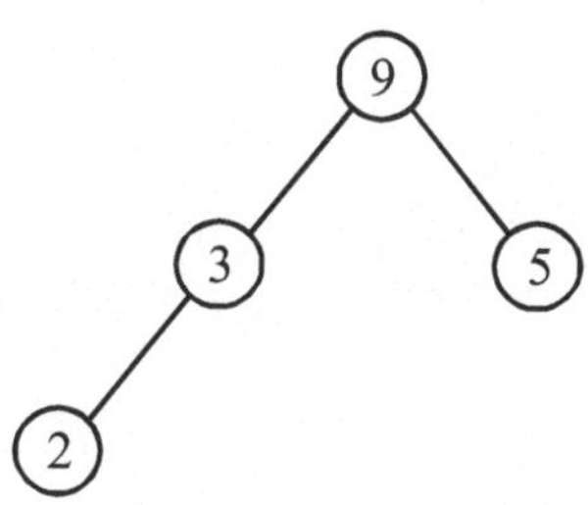

Step 5 Insert 14

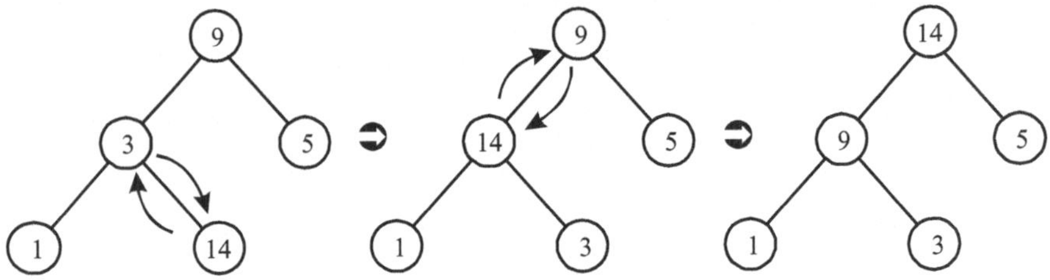

Step 6 Insert 8

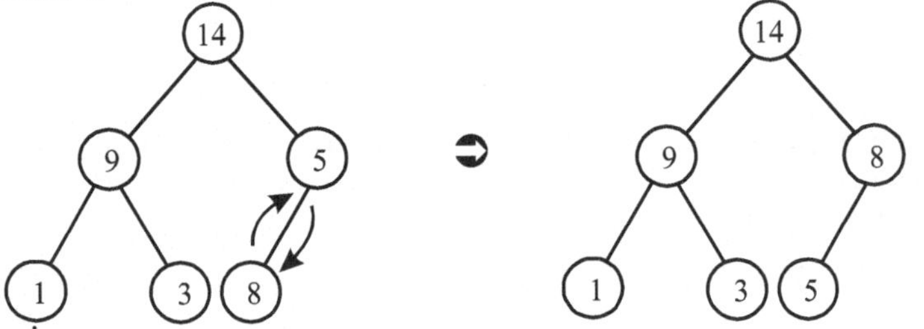

Final Heap is

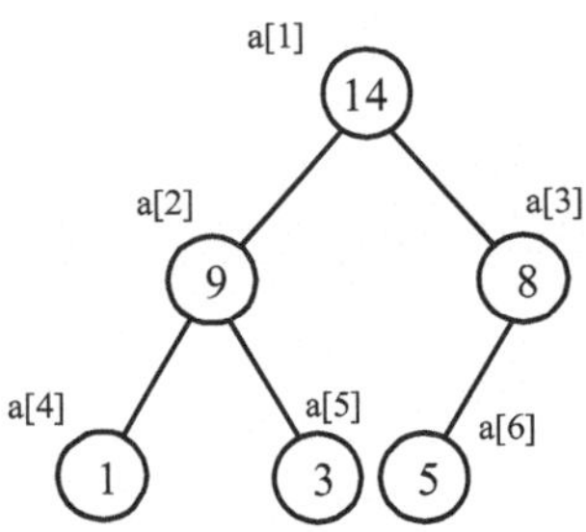

a	14	9	8	1	3	5
	1	2	3	4	5	6

a is array.

Remove from heap

Step I

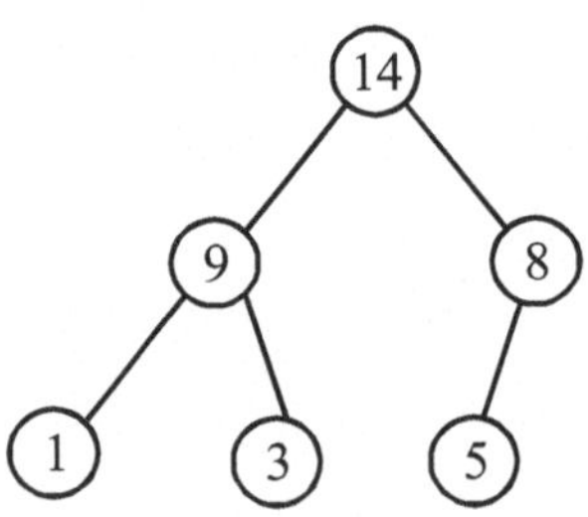

					14

Step II

Remove 14

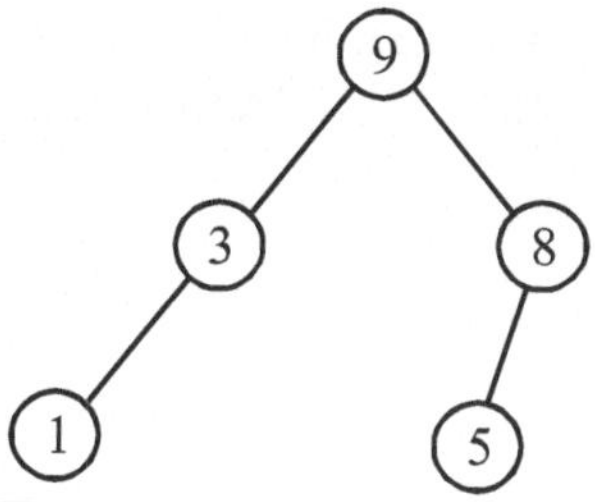

				9	14

Step III

Remove 9

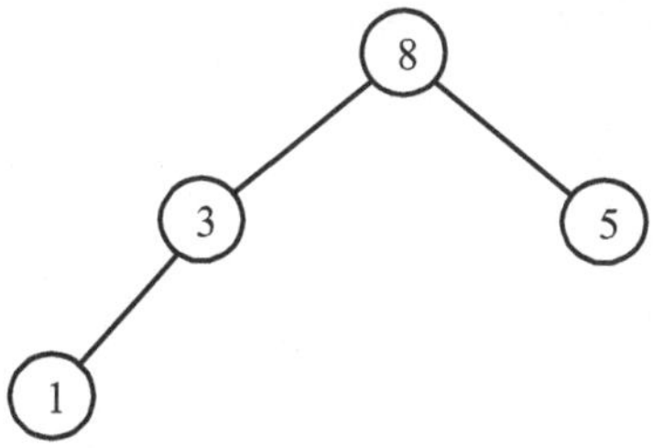

			8	9	14

Step IV

Remove 8

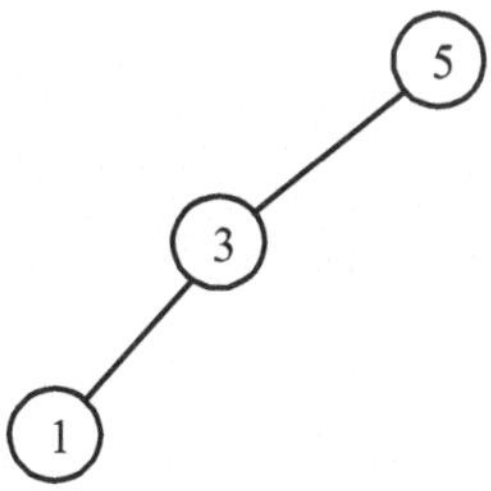

		5	8	9	14

Step V

Remove 5

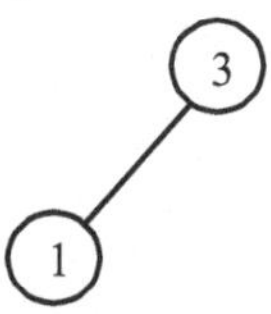

	3	5	8	9	14

Step VI

Remove 3

Hence Sort list is

1	3	5	8	9	14

Q6. Write a C-program to implement quicksort recursively. Show the status of the file at each recursive call of quicksort. The input file has 8 records with keys (15, 5, 25, 2, 40, 7, 50, 12). [JAN01, Q1(iv)][7]

```
#include<stdio.h>
#include<conio.h>
#define MAX 50
void main( )
{
int partition(int *,int,int);
void quick(int[], int, int); //Declaration of user defined function
int a[MAX],i,j,n,lb,ub,flag;; //Declaration of local variables
clrscr();
flag=0;
do
{
if(flag ==0)
{
flag = 1;

printf("\n Enter total number of elements in array");
        }
        else
        {
printf("\n You might have entered more than %d elements", MAX);
printf("\n\t\t\t\t OR \n");
printf("You have entered less than or equal to 0 elements");
printf("\n so please enter less than %d elements", MAX);
      }
scanf("%d",&n);
}while(n<=0 || n>MAX);
printf("\n Please enter %d elements\n",n);

for(i=0;i<n;i++)
scanf("%d",&a[i]);
quick(a,0,n-1); //User defined function call
printf("\n Sorted array is as under \n");
for(i=0;i<n;i++)
printf("%d\t",a[i]);
getch();
}
void quick(int a[],int p,int r)//User defined function definition
```

```
{
int q;
if(p<r)
{
 q=partition(a,p,r);
 quick(a,p,q-1);
 quick(a,q+1,r);
}
 }
int partition(int a[],int p,int r)
 {
 int x=a[r];
int i=p-1,j;
int temp;
 for(j=p;j<=r-1;j++)
 {
if(a[j]<=x)
 {
i+=1;
temp=a[i];
a[i]=a[j];
a[j]=temp;
}
}
temp=a[i+1];
a[i+1]=a[r];
a[r]=temp;
return i+1;
}
```

Q7. The input sequence to a Heap Sort algorithm which sorts in increasing order is : [JUNE02, Q6(b)][5]

6, 5, 39, 32, 11, 41

Show the sorting process stepwise.

Arrange in Heap

Step 1 Insert 5

Step 2 Insert 3

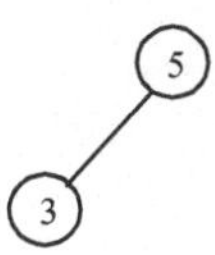

Step 3 Insert 9

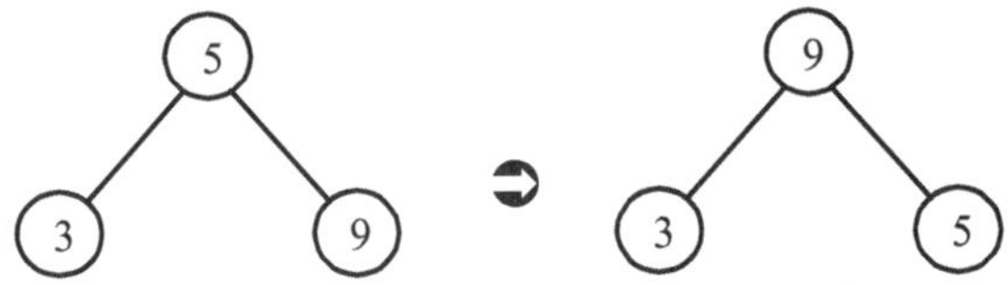

Step 4 Insert 1

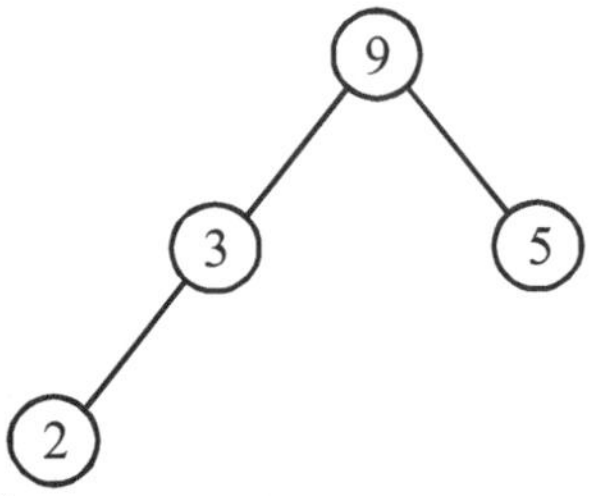

Step 5 Insert 14

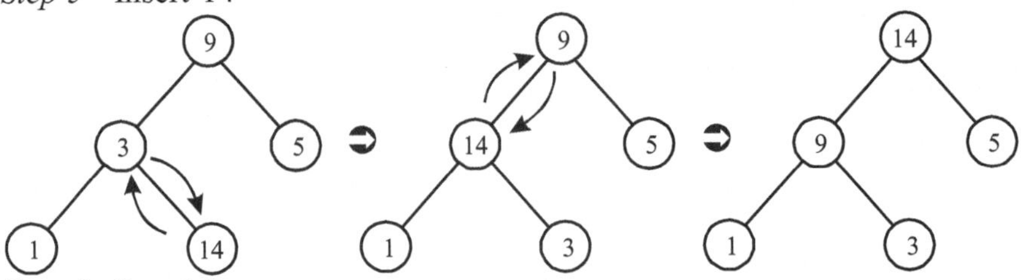

Step 6 Insert 8

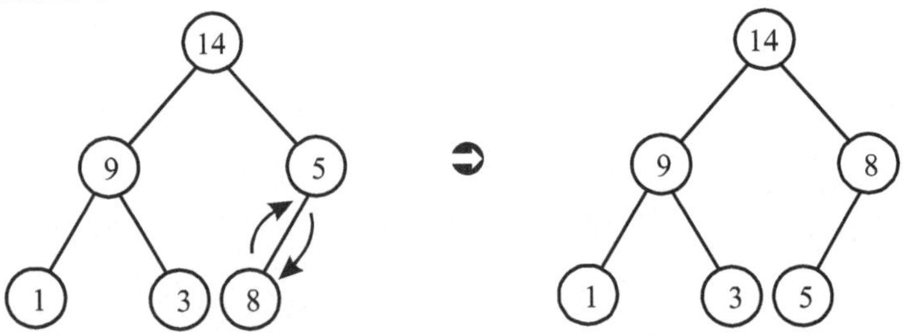

Final Heap is

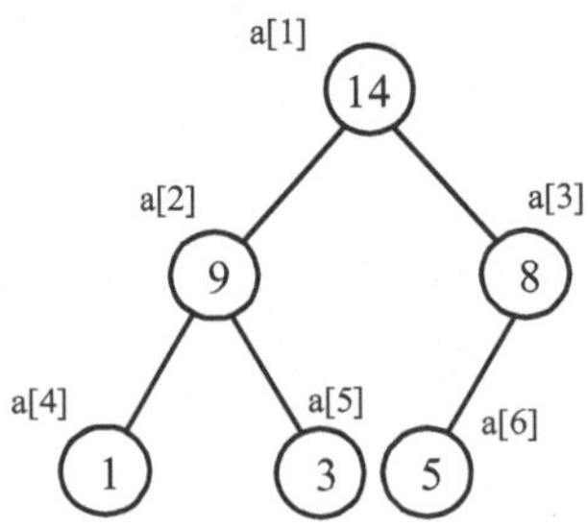

a	14	9	8	1	3	5
	1	2	3	4	5	6

a is array.

Remove from heap

Step I

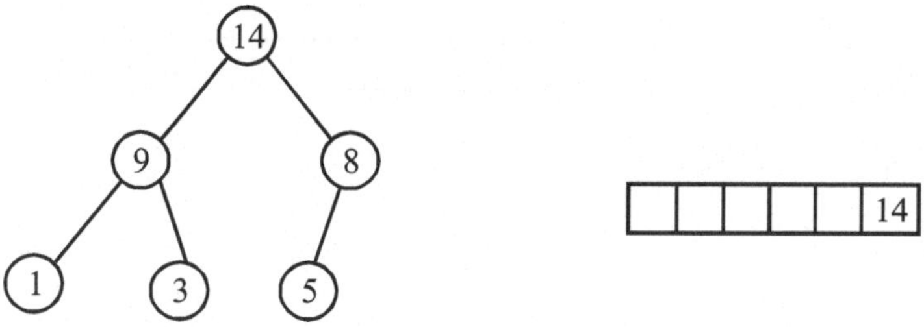

Step II

Remove 14

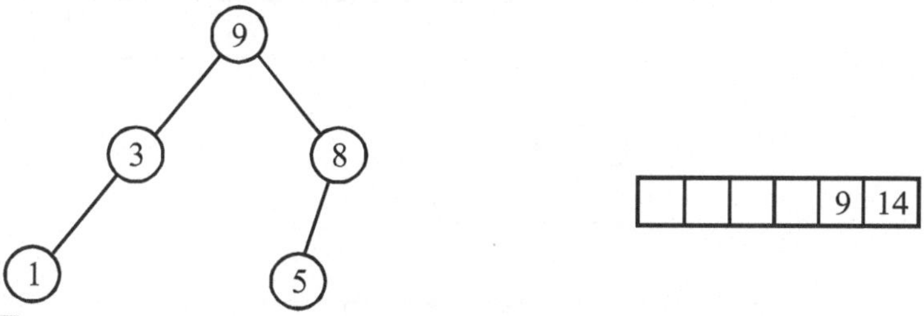

Step III

Remove 9

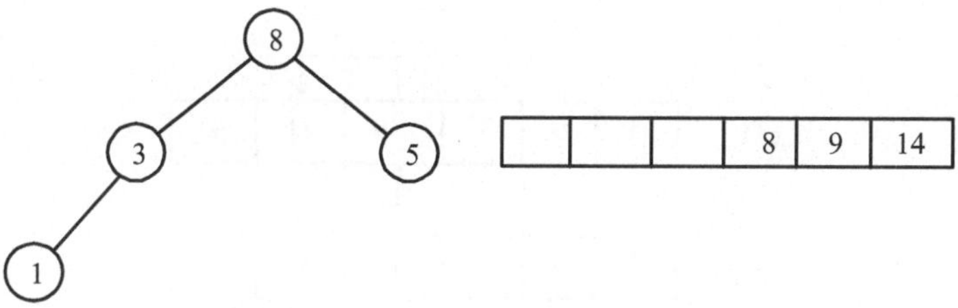

Step IV

Remove 8

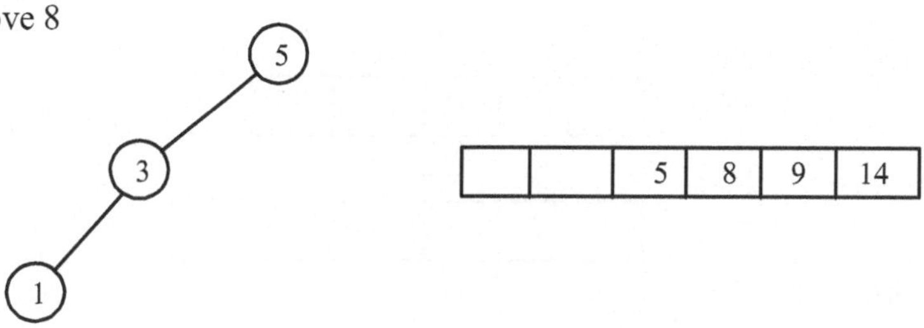

Step V

Remove 5

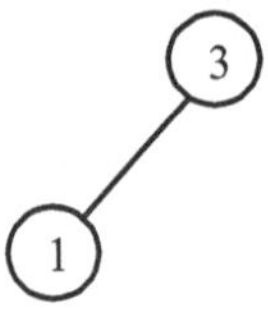

	3	5	8	9	14

Step VI

Remove 3

Hence Sort list is

1	3	5	8	9	14

Bubble Sort

6	5	39	32	11	41

Step I

(1)

6	5	39	32	11	41

(2)

5	6	39	32	11	41

(3)

5	6	32	39	11	41

(4)

5	6	32	11	39	41

Step II

(1)

5	6	32	11	39	41

(2)

5	6	11	32	39	41

Final sorted list.

Q8. Write an algorithm to implement insertion sort. [DEC01,Q6(a)[5]

Suppose an array A with n elements A [1], A [2] … A [N] is in memory. The insertion sort algorithm scans A from A[1] to A[N] inserting each element A[K] into proper position in the previously sorted subarray A[1], A[2] …….

A[K-1] That is :

Pass 1 : A[1] by itself is trivially sorted

Pass 2 : A [2] is inserted either before or after A[1]
so that : A[2] is sorted

Pass 3 : A [3] is inserted into its proper place in A[1]
A [2], that is before A[1], between A[1] & A[2]
or after A[2], so that : A[1], A[2], A[3] is sorted.

Pass 4 : A[4] inserted into its proper position in
A[1], A[2], A[3] so that
A[1], A[2], A[3], A[4] is sorted

Pass n : A[N] is inserted into its proper place in
A[1], A[2]…A[N-1] so that
A[1], A[2]…A[N] is sorted.

Algorithm :

This algorithm sorts away A with N elements

1. set A[0] = [Initialize sentinel value]
2. repeat step 3 to 5 for k = 2,3,….N
3. Set Temp = A [K] and ptr = K – 1
4. Repeat while Temp < A [PTR]

(a) set A [PTR + 1] = A [PTR] [Moves element forward]

(b) Set PTR = PTR – 1

[END OF LOOP]

5. Set A [Ptr + 1] = Temp [Insert element in proper place]

[END of step2 Loop]

6. Return

Time complexity of Insertion sort

worst case	Average case
$\frac{n(n-1)}{2} = o(n^2)$	$\frac{n(n-1)}{4} = o(n^2)$

Q9. The input sequence to a Quick Sort Algorithm which sorts in decreasing order is : [DEC01,Q6(b)][5]

4, 5, 25, 23, 11, 15, 16, 18

Show the sorting process stepwise.

Let the list be {(4), 5, 25, 23, 11, 15, 16, 18}

Let 4 be pivot and we initiate scan from 18.

Exchange the position of 18 which 4 to get

{18, 5, 25, 23, 11, 15, 16, (4)} None on the left of pivot is smaller than 4. Therefore 4 partitions the list and achieve final position.

Now, 18 is assumed as pivot in list sub list

{(18), 5, 25, 23, 11, 15, 16,} 4 [23>18]

{23, (18), 25, 5, 11, 15, 16,} 4 [5>18]

{23, (18), 25, 5, 11, 15, 16,} 4 [25>18]

{23, 25} 18 {5, 11, 15, 16,} 4

{23, 25} 18 {5, 11, 15, 16,} 4

We take the right sublist first let 5 be the pivot and scanning being right to left from 16.

As 16>5 Exchange takes place.

{23, 25} 18 {16, 11, 15} 5 4

No element on the left of 5 is smaller then 5 therefore, pivot achieves its final position and partitions the list as:

{23, 25} 18 {16, 11, 15} 5 4

{16, 11, 15} 5 4

{11, 15}

{15, 11}

{23, 25}

{25} 23

Now, no sublist is left therefore, we have a list sorted in decreasing order i.e.,

{25, 23, 18, 16, 15, 11, 5, 4}

Algorithm : Insertion sort (x, n)

Step 1 : Start.
Step 2 : For i = 2 to n
Step 3 : hold = x [i].
Step 4 : position = 1
Step 5 : while (hold>x [position])
Step 6 : Position = position + 1
[End while]
Step 7 : If position < i, then
Step 8 : for j = i down to position
Step 9 : x[j] = x[j-1]
End for.
Step 10 : x[position] = hold
End if.
End for.
Step 11 : Stop.

Q10. Write an Algorithm to implement Two Way Merge Sort. Discuss its efficiency. [JUNE01,Q6(a)][5]

Here we are giving recursive algorithm of merge sort.

```
Void merge_sort (int low, int high)
{
// a [low:high] is a global array to be sorted
// small [p] is true if there is only one element
// to sort. In this case the list is already sorted

int mid;
        if (low<high) // If there are more than one element
// divide p into subprograms
// Find where slit the set
                mind = (low + high)/2;
// solve the subprograms
                mergesort(low,mid);
                mergesort (mid + 1, high);
// combine the solution
                merge(low, mid, high)
}
}/* end of function

void merge (int low, mid,int high)
{
int h = low, i = low, j = mid + 1, k;
while (h < = mid && j <= high)
{
        If  (a[h] < = a [j])
        {
                b [i] = a [h];
                h ++;
        }

        else
        {
                b[i] = a [j];
                j ++;
        }
        i ++;
}
```

```
if (h > mid)
{
        for (k = j; k< = high; k ++)
        {
                b [i] = a [k];
i ++;
} }
else
{       for (k = h; k < = mid; k++)
        {
                b [i] = a [k];
                i ++;.
                }
        }
        for (k = low; k < = high ; k ++)
        a [k] = b [k];
}/* end of function */
```

The efficiency of mergesort can be shown by following table:

Algorithm merge sort	worst case behaviour n long = o (n long)	average case n long = O (n long n)	Extra memory o(n)

Where n is the number of input data to be sorted.

Q11. The input sequence to a Quick Sort Algorithm which sorts in increasing order is: [JUNE01,Q6(b)][[5]
11, 2, 23, 14, 15, 66, 22. Show the sorting process stepwise.

(1) (11) 2,23,14,15,66,22. pivot=11,2<11 Exchange. Scan from right.

(2) 2, (11), 23, 14, 15, 66, 22. pivot=11 is at it place

(3) {2}, 11 {23, 14, 15, 66, 22}. pivot=23 scan from right 22 < 23 exchange

(4) 2, 11 {22, 14, 15, 66, (23)}. pivot=23 scan from left 66 > 23

(5) 2, 11, {22, 14, 15, (23), 66}. pivot=23 is at it place

(6) 2, 11, {(22), 14, 15} 23 {66}

pivot = 22 scan from right 15 < 22 exchange

(7) 2, 11, {15, 14, (22)} 23 {66} 22 is at it place

(8) 2, 11, {(15), 14}, 22, 23, 66 pivot=14<15 exchange then all elements get placed finally,2,11,14,15,22,23, 66.

Solution Papers CS-62

CS-62 : 'C' PROGRAMMING AND DATA STRUCTURE
JAN 2001

Note : *There are* **6** *questions in this paper. Question* **1** *is* **compulsory**. *Answer any* **three** *questions from the rest. All algorithms should be written nearer to 'C' language.*

1(i) What are the advantages and disadvantages of C-pointer? What types of operations can be implemented on pointers? Explain through examples. **[5]**

Advantage & Disadvantage of C-pointer : A C-pointer is a variable which holds the memory address of another variable. Complex data types can be declared & accessed easily with the help of pointers. They have many advantages over simple data types. Pointer provides functions which can modify their calling arguments. It supports dynamic allocation routines, improves the efficiency of certain routines, makes a function return more than one value, makes passing of arrays & string convenient from one function to another. Also we may manipulate arrays more easily by moving pointers to them, instead of moving the arrays themselves. On the other side, the operation complexity in pointers are more.

Followings are the operations which can be implemented on pointers :

(a) Addition : Addition of pointers with an integer constants :

Example :

```
int a = 3, *b, *c ;
b = &a ;
b = b + 2 ;
b + b + 3 ;
```

(b) Substraction : Substraction of an Integer Constant from a pointers.

Example :

```
int a = 3, *b, *c ;
b = &a ;
b = b – 2 ;
```

(c) Comparison : Comparison of two pointer variable can be done.

Example :

```
Main ( )
    {
    int *a, *b, x [ ] = {1, 2, 3, 4, 5, 6} ;
    a = &x[1] ;
    b = (x + 1) ;
    if(a !=b)
```

```
            Printf("Pointing to different location") ;
    else
            Printf("Pointing to same location") ;

    }
```

(ii) Let List 1 = $(x_1, x_2, ..., x_n)$ and List 2 = $(y_1, y_2, ..., y_n)$ be two linked lists. Write an algorithm to merge the two lists to obtain the linked list, List 3 = $(x_1, y_1, x_2, y_2 .... x_m, y_m, ..., x_n)$ if $m \le n$, and List 3 = $(x_1, y_1, x_2, y_2, ... x_n, y_n, x_{n+1}, ... x_m)$ if $m > n$. **[10]**

Refer to Ch-2, Q22.

(iii) For the following graph **[3]**

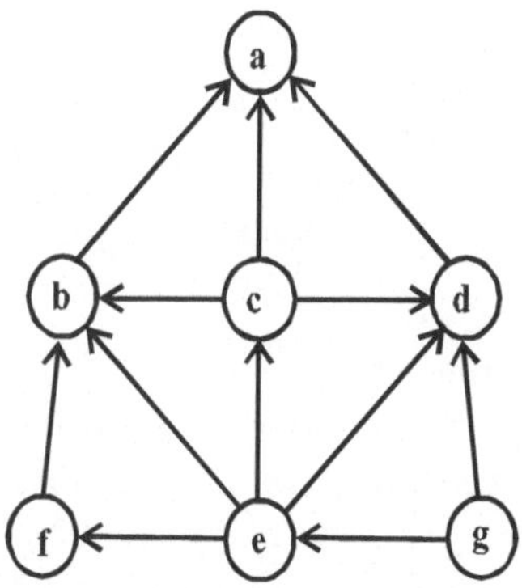

Obtain :

(a) In-degree and out-degree of each vertex

(b) Its adjacency matrix

(c) Its adjacency list representation

Refer to Ch-4, Q17.

(iv) Write a C-program to implement quicksort recursively. Show the status of the file at each recursive call of quicksort. The input file has 8 records with keys (15, 5, 25, 2, 40, 7, 50, 12). **[7]**

Refer to Ch-5, Q6.

(v)(a) Show the stack evaluation of postfix notation : **[2]**

ab + c + d + e +

Refer to Ch-2, Q36.

(b) List all data structures for representing tree. **[3]**

The equivalent infix expression is : a + b + c + d + e

Following are the data structure for representing tree.

(a) Binary tree
(b) Binary Search tree
(c) B-trees
(d) Threaded Binary tree
(e) AVL tree

2(i) Consider the following graph : [3]

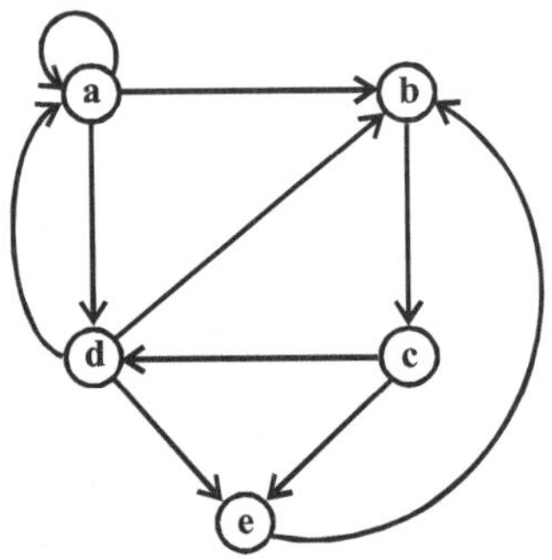

(a) How many arcs are there?
(b) How many acyclic paths are there from node a to d?
(c) How many simple cycles are there? List them.
Refer to Ch-4, Q18.

(ii) Write a C-program to implement Dijkstra's algorithm for finding shortest paths. Describe the algorithm in terms of data structure used, functioning and its running time. [7]
Refer to Ch-4, Q19.

3(i) List the main properties of Binary tree and make a proof of these properties by induction method. [5]

Properties of Binary Trees :

Property 1 : A binary tree with n elements, $n > 0$, has exactly n-1 edges.

Proof : Every element in a binary tree, except the root, has exactly one parent. There is exactly one edge between each child and its parent. So the number of edges is $n - 1$.

Property 2 : A binary tree of height h, h>0, has at least h and at most 2^h-1 elements in it.

Proof : Since there must be at least one element at each level, the number of elements is at least h. As each element can have at most two children. The number of elements at level k is at most $2^k - 1$ for k>0. For $h = 0$, the total number of elements is 0, which equals $2^0 - 1$. For h>0, the total number of elements can not exceed $\sum_{k=1}^{h} 2^k - 1 = 2^h - 1$

Property 3 : The height of the binary tree that contains n, $n \geq 0$, elements is at most n and at least [log2 (n + 1)].

Proof : Since there must be least one elements at each level, the height cannot exceed n. From property 2, we know that a binary tree of height h can have no more than $2^k - 1$ elements. So $n \leq^h - 1$. Hence $h \geq \log_2 (n + 1)$. Since h is an integer, we get $h \geq [\log_2(n + 1)]$.

Property 4 : Let $i, \leq i \leq n$, be the number assigned to an element of a complete binary tree. The following statements are true.

1. if $i = 1$, then this elements is the root of the binary tree. If i>1, then the parent of this element has been assigned the number [i/2].
2. If 2i>n, then this element has no left child. Otherwise, its left child has been assigned the number the number 2i.
3. If 2i + 1 >n, the this element has no right child. Otherwise, its right child has been assigned the number 2i + 1.

(ii) Write an algorithm of iterative version of preorder traversal. [5]

Preorder Traversal lterative (root) : Here root is pointer variable that holds address of the root node of the given tree. It uses a stack whose elements are pointers to type node. It uses a temporary pointer variable *ptr* to hold the address of current node.

```
Begin
        CreateEmptyStack(s)     // call procedure to create an empty stack
        Push(s, NULL)           // push NULL value as sentinel value
Set ptr = root
while (ptr ≠ NULL) do
        Print : ptr -> infor
        If (ptr->right ≠ NULL) then
        Push(s, ptr->right)
edif
if(ptr->left ≠ NULL) then
        Set ptr = ptr->left
else
        Set ptr = Pop(s)        // pop value from stack and assign to ptr
endif
endwile
End
```

4(i) Find out the sequence of nodes visited through depth first search and breadth first search of the following graph : [3]

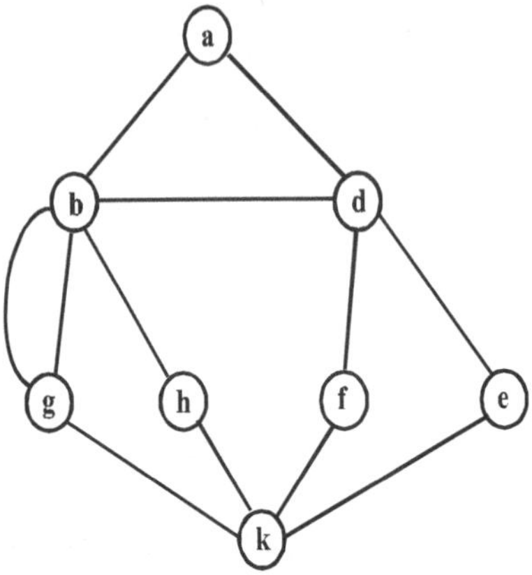

Breadth First Search : We shall add **a** to the QUEUE and set origin ORIG to NULL.

FRONT = 1, QUEUE : **a**
REAR = 1 ORIG : 0

Remove **a** from the front of the queue and **insert** neighbours of **a** from the rear of the queue.

FRONT = 2, QUEUE : **a, b, d**
REAR = 5 ORIG : **0, a, a**

Remove **b** from the front of the queue and **insert** neighbours of **b** from the near of the queue.

FRONT = 3, QUEUE : **a, b, d, g, h**
REAR = 5 ORIG : **, a, a, b, b**

Remove **d** from the front of the queue and **insert** neighbours of **d** from the near of the queue.

FRONT = 4, QUEUE : **a, b, d, g, h, f, e**
REAR = 7 ORIG : **, a, a, b, b, d, d**

Remove **g** from the front of the queue and **insert** neighbours of **g** from the near of the queue.

FRONT = 5, QUEUE : **a, b, d, g, h, f, e, k**
REAR = 8 ORIG : **, a, a, b, b, d, d, g**

We step now, as the final node k is already added to the queue.
We remove, the rest of the nodes from the front of the queue one after another.
The required sequence of nodes visited in **BFS** as :
a→b→d→g→h→f→e→k

Depth First Search : We shall push **a** on to the stack.

STACK : **a**

Pop and print **a** and push all the neighbours of **a** on to the stack.

STACK : **b, f, e**

Pop and print **e** and push all the neighbours of **e** on to the stack.

STACK : **b, f, k**

Pop and print **k** and push all the neighbours of **k** on to the stack.

STACK : **b, f, g, h**

At this point we stop as all the nodes have been pushed to the stack. Popping one by one we get the sequence of nodes visited in **DFS** as :

a→d→e→k→h→g→f→b

(ii) Write an algorithm/program to implement breadth first search and also describe the program/algorithm in terms of data structure and its functioning. **[7]**

Algorithm :

BreadthFirstSearch(adj, n, s)

Here adj is the adjacency-list of the graph with n vertices, and vertex s is the source vertex. This algorithm uses a FIFO queue q, and linear array color of size n, to keep track of the progress of BFS. It also uses a local variables u.

```
Begin
        For i = 1 to n by 1 do
        Set color[i] = WHITE
        endfor
        Set color[s] = GRAY
        Call CreateQueue(q) ;
        Call Enqueue(q, s)
        while (q is not empty) do
                Set u = Peek(q)
                Set ptr = adj[u]
                While(ptr ≠ NULL) do
                If (color[ptr->infor] = WHITE) then
                Set color[s] = GRAY
                Call Enqueue(q, ptr->infor)
                endif
        endwhile
        Print : u
        Set color[u] = BLACK
        endwhile
End
```

Description : Given an Input graph G = (V, E) & a source vertex S, from where to being. The BFS systematically explores the edges of G to discover every vertex that is reachable from S. it produces a breadth first tree with root S that contains all such vertices that are reachable from S. For every vertex V reachable from S, the path in the breadth first tree from S to V corresponds to shortest path. The algorithm works on both directed undirected graphs.

Q5. Write a C-program using stack for implementing the following function : [10]
(i) Function to determine if the parentheses in an expression are properly nested.
(ii) Function to determine if a word or pharse is a palindrome or not.
Refer to Ch-2, Q37.

Q6. Write insertion and deletion algorithms for B-trees. [10]

The algorithm for **insertion** into a B-Tree begins as do all the other search tree insertion algorithms: To insert item x, we begin at the root and conduct a search for it. Assuming the item is not already in the tree, the unsuccessful search will terminate at a leaf node. This is the point in the tree at which the x is inserted.

If the leaf node has fewer than M-1 keys in it, we simply insert the item in the leaf node and we are done. E.g., consider a leaf node with n<M subtrees and n-1 keys of the form

$$\mathbf{T = \{T_0; k_1; T_1; k_2; T_2;...; k_{n-1}; T_{n-1}\}.}$$

For every new key inserted in the node, a new subtree is required too. In this case because T is a leaf, all its subtrees are empty trees. Therefore, when we insert item x, we really insert the pair of items (x; θ). Suppose the key to be inserted falls between $\mathbf{K_1}$ and $\mathbf{K_{i+1}}$, i.e., $\mathbf{k_i < x < k_{i+1}}$. When we insert the pair (x; θ) into T we get the new leaf T' given by

$$\mathbf{T' = \{T_0; k_1; T_1; k_2; T_2;...;k_i; T_i; \theta\ k_{i+1}; T_{i+1};...; k_{n-1}; T_{n-1}\}.}$$

What happens when the leaf is full? I.e., suppose we wish to insert the pair, (x; θ) into a node T which already has M-1 keys. Inserting the pair in its correct position gives a result of the form

$$\mathbf{T' = \{T_0; k_1; T_1; k_2; T_2; ...; k_M; T_M\}.}$$

However, this is not a valid node in a B-tree of order M because it has M+1 subtrees and M keys. The solution is to split node T' in half as follows

$$\mathbf{T'_L = \{T0; k1; T1; ...; k_{[M/2]-1;}\ T_{[M/2]-1}\}}$$
$$\mathbf{T'_R = \{T_{[M/2]}; k_{[M/2]+1}; T_{[M/2]+1};...; k_m; T_M\}}$$

Note, $\mathbf{T'_L}$ is a valid B-tree node because it contains **[M/2]** subtrees and **[M/2] - 1** keys. Similarly, $\mathbf{T'_R}$ is a valid B-tree node because it contains **[(M + 1)/2]** subtrees and **[(M + 1/2)] - 1** keys. Note that there is still a key left over, namely **k[M/2'**. There are now two cases to consider—either T is the root or it is not. Suppose T is not the root. Where we once had the single node T, we now have the two nodes, T'_L and T'_{R}, and the left-over key, **k[M/ 2'.** This situation is resolved as follows: First, T'_L replaces T in the parent of T. Next, we take the pair **(k[M/2] : T'R)** and recursively insert it in the parent of T.

DELETE(T,X)

1. (P, i, j) < MSEARCH(T,X)
2. if j ! = 1 then return
3. let P be the form : A_0 (K_1 A_1), ……, (K_nA_n) and K_i = X
4. if A_0 ! = 0 then
5. [Q : = A_i
6. loop
7. let Q be of the form : n', A'_0 (K'_1,A'_1), ……,(K'_n A'_n)
8. if A_0 = 0 then exit
9. Q <-A'_0
10. forever
11. replace K_i in node P by K; an write the altered node P onto dism.
12. P : = Q, i : 1;
13. let n, A_0, (K_1, A_1……,(K_nA_n) be as defined by the new P]
14. from P : n, A_0,(K_1A_1),……,(K_nA_n) delete (k_iA_i) and replace it by n – 1
15. while n < [m/2]-1 and P! = T do
16. if P has nearest right sibling, Y then,
17. [let Y : n'', A_0(K'_1A_1),……, ($K''_nA''_n$) and
18. let Z : n',A'_0($K'_1A'_1$),……,($K'_1A'_n$) be the parent of P
19. and Y
20. let A'_1 = Y and A'_{j-1} = P
21. if n'' >= [m/2] then ($k'_{n=1}A'_{n=1}$) : = ($K'_jA''_0$) ;
22. n : = n + 1
23. K'_j : K''_1
24. output nodes P, Z and Y onto disk
25. return]
26. r : = [m/2] – 2
27. output r, A_0(K_1A_1),……..,(K_nA_n),($K'_1A''_0$),($K''_jA''_1$),……,($K''_nA''_n$) as new node P.
28. (n, A_0,….) <- (n' – 1,A'_0……,($K'_{j-1}A'_{j-1}$)($K'_{j=1}A'_{j=1}$……)
29. P : = Z]

CS-62 : 'C' PROGRAMMING AND DATA STRUCTURE
JUNE 2001

Note : *There are* **6** *questions in this paper. Question 1 is* **compulsory**. *Answer any* **three** *questions from the rest. All algorithms should be written nearer to 'C' language.*

1(a) Write a program EXPR in C language which evaluates a Reverse Polish expression from the command line, where each operator or operand is a separate argument. For example,
EXPR 2 3 4 + *
evaluates 2 × (3 + 4). [10]
For example:
Refer to Ch-1, Q3.

(b) Give the node structure for implementing a linked list containing two information fields viz. info 1, info 2. Let p be the pointer to the first node of the linked list. Traverse the linked list to go to the node containing the information info 1 = u and then print the info 1 and info 2 fields. [10]
Refer to Ch-2, Q19.

(c) Define binary search tree. Write a function in 'C' to create a binary search tree. [10]
Refer to Ch-3, Q22.

2(a) The order of nodes of a Binary Tree in Preorder and Inorder Traversal are as follows :
Preorder : A B C D F H J M K E G I L N
Inorder : A D J M H K F C I N L G E B
Draw the corresponding Binary Tree. [5]
Refer to Ch-3, Q23.

(b) List the differences between a Singly Linked Circular List and Doubly Linked Circular List. List the advantages of each list. [5]
Refer to Ch-2, Q20.

3(a) Draw the tree representation for the following prefix expression :
+*/ABCDE [5]**
Refer to Ch-2, Q35.

(b) Write a non-recursive program in 'C' language to traverse a binary tree in preorder. **[5]**

Refer to Ch-3, Q19.

4(a) Consider the following diagraph : **[5]**

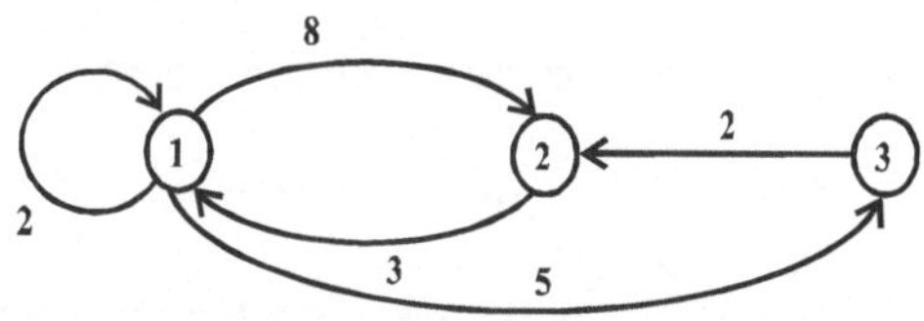

Write an algorithm which accepts an adjacency matrix as input and prints the corresponding graph as output.

Refer to Ch-4, Q16.

(b) Write the advantages of arrays over linked list and advantages of linked list over arrays. **[5]**

Refer to Ch-2, Q21.

Q5. Discuss the differences between the following file organization techniques :

- **Sequential File Organization**
- **Index Sequential File Organization**
- **Direct File Organization**

To what type of applications are each of the above techniques suited? **[10]**

Refer to Ch-3, Q26.

6(a) Write an Algorithm to implement Two Way Merge Sort. Discuss its efficiency. **[5]**

Refer to Ch-5, Q10.

(b) The input sequence to a Quick Sort Algorithm which sorts in increasing order is: **[5]**

11, 2, 23, 14, 15, 66, 22

Show the sorting process stepwise.

Refer to Ch-5, Q11.

CS-62 : 'C' PROGRAMMING AND DATA STRUCTURE
DEC 2001

Note : *There are* ***6*** *questions in this paper. Question* ***1*** *is* ***compulsory****. Answer any* ***three*** *questions from the rest. All algorithms should be written nearer to 'C' language.*

1(a) A general polynomial A(x) can be written as
$a_n x^n + a_{n-1} x^{n-1} + ... + a_1 x + a_0$
where $a_n \neq 0$ and we say that the degree of A is 'n'. Each $a_i x^i$ is a term of the polynomial. If $a_i = 0$, then it is a zero term, otherwise, it is a non-zero term. Now, write an algorithm which evaluates a polynomial at a value 'x_0'. [10]

Refer to Ch-2, Q18.

(b) Let 'P' be a pointer to a circularly linked list. Show how this list may be used as a queue by writing algorithms to add and delete elements. Specify the value for 'P' when the queue is empty. [10]

Refer to Ch-2, Q17.

(c) Write a non-recursive procedure for traversing a Binary Tree in "Preorder". [10]

Refer to Ch-3, Q19.

2(a) Draw the internal memory representation of the following Binary Tree using sequential representation : [5]

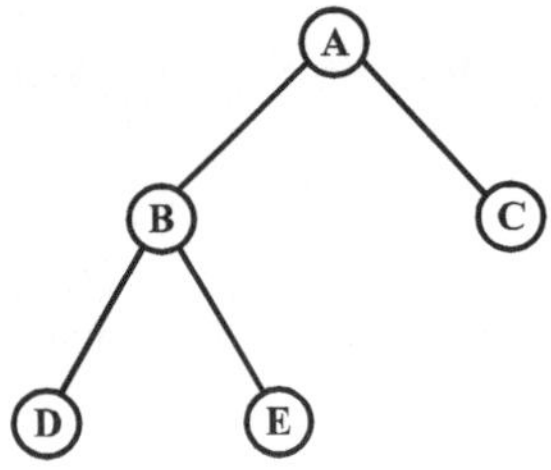

Refer to Ch-3, Q20.

(b) Write an algorithm to construct the binary tree with a given preorder and inorder sequence. [5]

Refer to Ch-3, Q21.

3(a) Write the postfix form of the following expressions : [5]
(i) -A + B – C + D
(ii) AB**C**

Refer to Ch-2, Q33.

(b) Write an algorithm for generating the transpose of a given sparse matrix. [5]

We are implementing sparse matrix through linked list
Function transpose( ) will transpose the sparse matrix
Global declarations

```
// structure of a node of sparse matrix
structure sparse-type
{
int data;
int col;
struct sparse-type *next;
}
typedef struct sparse sparse;
sparse * s[MAX] ;
void transpose (void) ; // function Prototype declaration.
// The logic for transposition is as follows:
if (i < j)
      {
(a) If node (i, j) & node (j, i) is present interchange their values
(b) If node (i, j) is present but node (j, i) is not present, remove node (j, i) &
connect it as node (j, i)
(c) If node (j, i) is present but node (j, i) is not present, remove node (j, i) &
attached it as node (i, j)
(d) It both are not present do nothing
}// end if
// We are assuming that sparse matrix s[MAX]
// is already created & we have to only transpose them
void transpose (void)
{
sparse * p, * q, * g, * m ;
int i = o, j = o, k ;
while (i< MAX)
{
         p = s[i] ;
While (p! = NULL)
{
```

```
        J = p → col ;
        if (i ! = j)
           {
                 if (s[j] → col = = i)
                 {
                         k = s[i] → data ; s[i]->data = s[i]->data;
                         s[j] → data = k ;
                 }
                 else
                 {
                         q = s[j] ;
                         while (q → col < i)
                              {
                                   g = q ; q = q → next ;
                         }
                         m = (sparse * ) malloc (sizeof (sparse)) ;
                         m → col = i ;
                         m → data = s[i] → data ;
                 m → next = g → next ;
                 g → next = m ; }                              }
p = p → next ;
}
i ++ ;
}
} // end of function
```

4(a) Prove that the number of edges in an n-vertex complete graph is $\frac{n(n-1)}{2}$. **[5]**

Refer to Ch-4, Q13.

(b) Write Kruskal's Algorithm. **[5]**

Refer to DEC02, Q5(b)

5(a) Consider the following graph : **[5]**

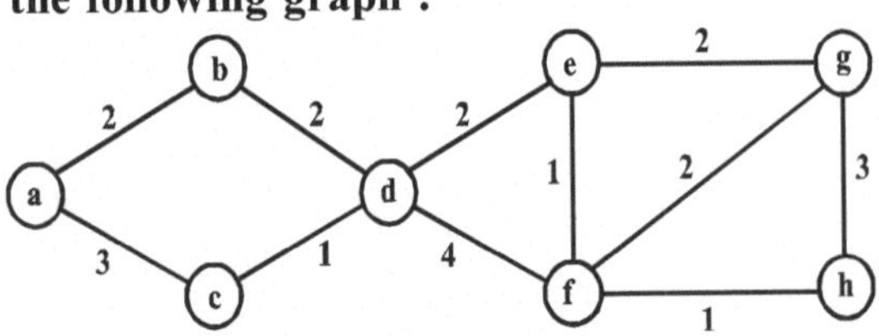

Find the minimum cost spanning tree for the above graph using Prim's Algorithm.

Refer to Ch-4, Q14.

(b) Write a program to determine whether a directed graph of 'n' vertices has a cycle. [5]

Refer to Ch-4, Q15

6(a) Write an algorithm to implement insertion sort. [5]

Refer to Ch-5, Q8.

(b) The input sequence to a Quick Sort Algorithm which sorts in decreasing order is : [5]

4, 5, 25, 23, 11, 15, 16, 18

Show the sorting process stepwise.

Refer to Ch-5, Q9.

CS-62 : DATA STRUCTURES THROUGH 'C'
JUNE 2002

Note : *There are* **6** *questions in this paper. Question* **1** *is* **compulsory**. *Answer any* **three** *questions from the rest. All algorithms should be written nearer to 'C' language.*

1(a) If A = (a_1, a_2, ..., a_n) and B = (b_1, b_2, ..., b_m) are ordered lists and are represented by Arrays, then write an algorithm for the concatenation of the above ordered lists. [10]

Refer to Ch-2, Q8.

(b) Write an algorithm to transform an infix expression to a postfix expression. [10]

Refer to Ch-2, Q31.

(c) Write an algorithm to count the number of leaves in a tree. [10]

```
// count the leaf node  in tree
int  countleafnode(node *root)
{
     if(root==NULL)
     {
      return 0;
     }
     else if((root→left==NULL)&&(root→right==NULL))
     {
     return 1;
     }
else
{
return (countleafnode(root→left) + countleafnode(root→right));
}
}
```

2(a) Draw the internal memory representation of the following Binary Tree using Sequential Representation. [5]

Refer to Ch-3, Q18.

(b) Write an algorithm to evaluate a prefix arithmetic expression. [5]

1. Read token (operand or operator)
2. If token = operator, push on to stack, set its argument count Ex: if operator takes 2 args then set count = 2, if operator is a 3-ary operator then set count = 3.
3. Else If token = operand, push on to stack
4. If top N entries in stack are operand entries needed for the top n-ary operator, apply operator to these operands Push result onto stack. Repeat this step until there are not enough operands for the top operator, then go back to step 1.

Prefix Evaluation Advantages

• Can evaluate an expression in a single scan.
Need to know the number of arguments for each operation.
Must use unique symbols for the dyadic subtraction and the unary
• No need to use parentheses,
• The usual function call is already written in prefix notation
• Prefix notation can be used to represent operations with any number of operands
• Prefix notation is easy to decode Translation into simple code sequences is easily accomplished.

3(a) Write the postfix form of the following expressions : [5]
(i) (c ÷ d) × (a + b)
(ii) a + b × c ÷ d

Refer to Ch-2, Q32.

(b) Write an algorithm for the addition of two sparse matrices (use proper representation for sparse matrices). [5]

Refer to Ch-2, Q9.

4(a) What is the relationship between the sum of the degrees of the vertices of a graph and the number of edges in the graph? [5]

In case of an undirected graph each edge contributes two degree, therefore the sum of all the degrees will be equal to twice the edges i.e.,

$$\sum_{i=1}^{n} d(V_i) = 2e$$

In case of a directed graph sum of out degree is equal to sum of indegrees, which in term is equal to number of edge i.e.,

$$\sum_{i=1}^{n} d^+ (V_i) = \sum_{i=1}^{n} d^- (V_i) = 2e$$

(b) Write Kruskal's algorithm. [5]

Refer to DEC02, Q5(b)

5(a) Consider the following graph : [5]

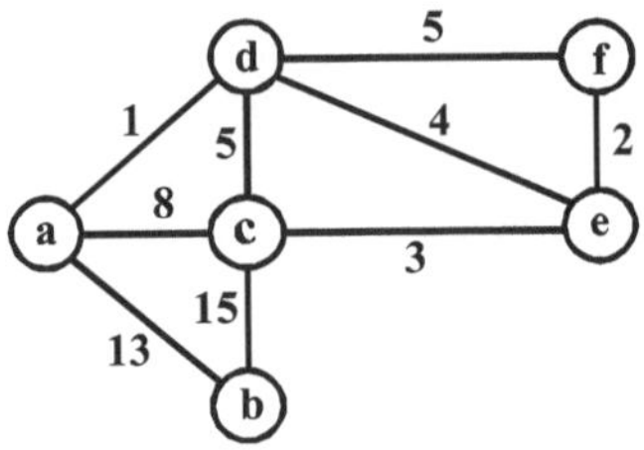

Find the minimum cost spanning tree for the above graph using Prim's algorithm.

Refer to Ch-4, Q11.

(b) Prove that if the edge weights on an undirected graph are distinct, there is only one minimum-cost spanning tree. [5]

Refer to Ch-4, Q12.

6(a) Write an algorithm to implement Quick Sort. [5]

Refer to JUNE03, Q6(a)

(b) The input sequence to a Bubble Sort algorithm which sorts in increasing order is : [5]

6, 5, 39, 32, 11, 41

Show the sorting process stepwise.

Refer to Ch-5. Q7.

CS-62 : 'C' PROGRAMMING AND DATA STRUCTURE
DEC 2002

Note : *There are **6** questions in this paper. Question **1** is **compulsory**. Answer any **three** questions from the rest. All algorithms should be written nearer to 'C' language.*

1(a) Ackermann's function A (m, n) is defined as follows: **[10]**

$$A\,(m, n) = \begin{cases} n+1 & , \text{if } m = 0 \\ A\,(m-1, 1) & , \text{if } n = 0 \\ A\,(m-1, A\,(m, n-1)) & , \text{otherwise.} \end{cases}$$

Write a recursive algorithm for computing this function.

The Ackerman function is a function with two arguments each of which can be assigned any nonnegative integer : 0, 1, 2,...... This function is defined as follows:

(Ackerman Function)

(a) If m = 0, then A (m, n) = n + 1

(b) If m ≠ 0 but n = 0, then A (m, n) = A (m – 1, 1)

(c) If m ≠ 0 and n ≠ 0, then A (m, n) = A (m – 1, A (m , n - 1))

Here, we have recursive definition in (b) & (c). A (m, n) is explicitly given when m = 0. The base criteria are the pairs.

(0, 0), (0, 1), (0, 2), (0, 3)....... (0, n), ...

The ackerman – functions can be recursively expressed as.

Ackerman – function (m, n)

Step-1 : If m = 0
    Print (n + 1)
else
If m ≠ 0 and n = 0
    Set m = m – 1
    Call Ackerman_Function (m, 1)
else
If m ≠ 0 and n ≠ 0
    Call acherman_function (m – 1, Ackerman_Function (m, n – 1))

Step-2 : Return

We can illustrate Ackerman's function by an example : Suppose we have two inputs m & n whose values are m = 1 & n = 3. Then ackerman_function (m, n) will be computed as :

We have Ackerman_Function (1, 3) as A (1, 3) for ease of use.

(1) A (1, 3) = (0, A (1, 2))
(2) A (1, 2) = A (0, A (1, 1))
(3) A (1, 1) = A (0, A (1, 0))
(4) A (1, 0) = A (0, 1)
(5) A (0, 1) = 1 + 1 = 2
(6) A (1, 0) = 2
(7) A (1, 1) = A (0, 2)
(8) A (0, 2) = 2 + 1 = 3
(9) A (1, 1) = 3
(10) A (1, 2) = A (0, 3)
(11) A (0, 3) = 3 + 1 = 4
(12) A (1, 2) = 4
(13) A (1, 3) = A (0, 4)
(14) A (0, 4) = 4 + 1 = 5
(15) A (1, 3) = 5

The forward indention indicates that we are postponing evaluation & are recalling the definition, & the backward indention indicates that we are backtracking.

(b) Let 'P' be a pointer to a doubly linked list. Show how this list may be used as a queue by writing algorithms to add and delete elements. Specify the value for 'P' when the queue is empty. [10]

Refer to Ch-2, Q17.

(c) Write a non-recursive procedure for traversing a Binary Tree in "Postorder". [10]

Refer to Ch-3, Q16.

2(a) Draw the internal memory representation of the following Binary Tree using sequential representation: [5]

Refer to Ch-3, Q17.

(b) Devise a scheme using a stack to convert an infix expression to a postfix expression. [5]

Refer to Ch-2, Q30.

3(a) Write the postfix form of the following expressions: [5]

(i) a + b × (c ÷ d)

Stack	Value	Action	Output
1 [ ]	a	Print	a
2 [+]	+	Push +	a
3 [+]	b	Print	ab
4 [+ | *]	x	Push*	
5 [+ | * | (]	c	Push	
6 [+ | * | (]	c	Print	abc
7 [+ | * | (]	÷	Push ÷	
8 [+ | * | (| ÷]	d	Print	abcd
9 [+ | * | (| ÷]	)	Pop(÷)	abcd ÷
10 [+ | *]	End	Pop stack	abcd ÷ * +

Full postfix expression is abcd÷*+.

(ii) (a + b × c) ÷ d

STACK	VALUE	ACTION	OUT PUT
1 [(]	A	PRINT	A
STACK 2 [(]	+	PUSH +	
STACK 3 [(| +]	B	PRINT	AB
STACK 4 [(| + | *]	*	PUSH*	AB
STACK 5 [(| + | *]	C	PRINT	ABC
STACK 6 [(| + | *]	)	POP STACK	ABC*+
STACK 7 [÷]	÷	PUSH ÷	ABC*+
STACK 8 [÷]	D	PRINT	ABC*+D
STACK 9 [EMPTY]	END	POP STACK	ABC*+D

(b) Write an algorithm for multiplication of two matrices. [5]

Refer to Ch-2, Q7.

4(a) Devise an algorithm to count the number of connected components in a directed graph. [5]

A directed graph is said to be connected, or strongly connected if for each pair U. V of nodes in G there is a path from U to V & there is also a path from V to U.

To know whether a directed graph is connected or not & to count connected nodes of the graph. We check path between the nodes U and V. U & V are representing any node of the graph. A directed graph can be represented through matrix. Rows and columns of the matrix represent nodes of the graph. An entry (either 0 or 1) at the intersection point of Rowi & columnj represents either a path existing or a path not existing between node i and node j.

A graph G is said to be strongly connected only if the path matrix p of G has no zero entries. Here we have to count the connected nodes of graph. The logic here is that if there is a path existing between node i & node j (i.e. Intersection points of row i & column j contains the value 1) & also there is path existing between node j to node i then, we count this as one connected component i & j.

Assumption to the algorithm :-

(a) We are assuming that the directed graph has been represented by adjacency matrix adj [5][5].

(b) The graph contains 5 nodes.

(c) Graph already created & given to us.

(d) Function count( ) will keep total number of connected nodes of the graph.

(e) The variable S will keep total number of connected nodes of the graph.

Count ( ) : This function counts total number of connected nodes of the graph represented through the adjancency matrix adj [5][5].

Step-1 : Set = 0 [I & j is represent node U & V]
Set j = 0
Set s = 0

Step-2 : Repeat step 3 to 4 until I is > = 5
Set j = I

Step-3 : Repeat step 4 until j is > = 5

Step-4 : CHECK [adj[I][j] is not = 0]
CHECK [adj[j][I] is not = 0]
Set s = s + 1;

Step-5 : Print s

Step-6 : End.

(b) Write Prim's Algorithm. **[5]**

Refer to JUNE03, Q5(b)

5(a) Consider the following graph: **[5]**

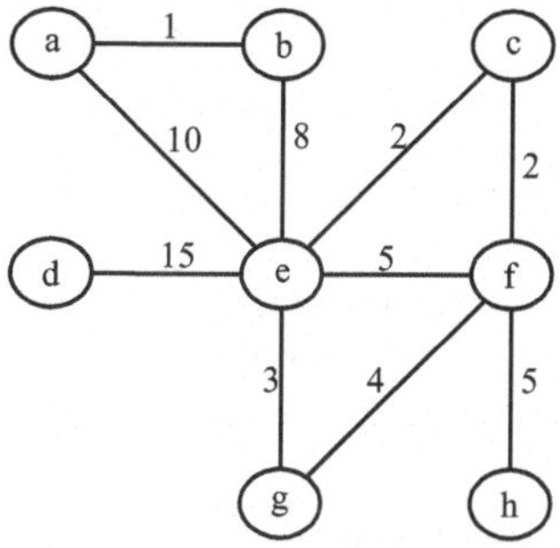

Find the minimum cost spanning tree for the above graph using Kruskal's Algorithm.

Figure (a) :-

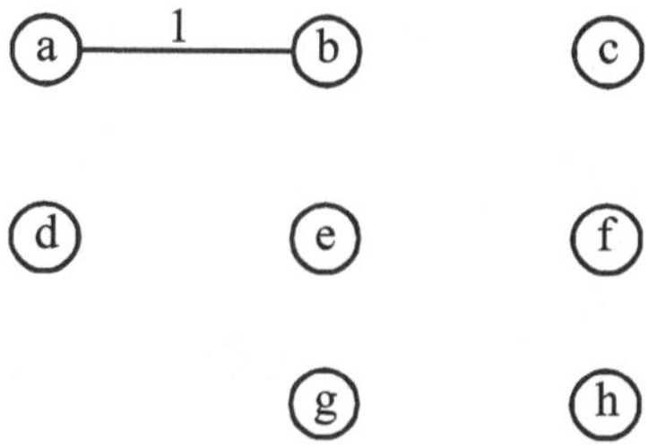

Figure (b) :-

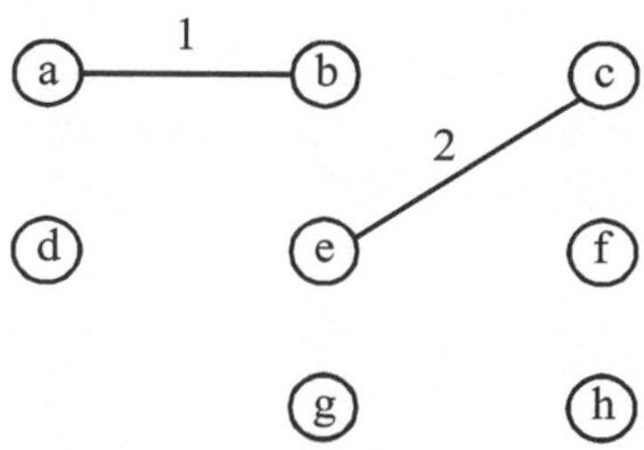

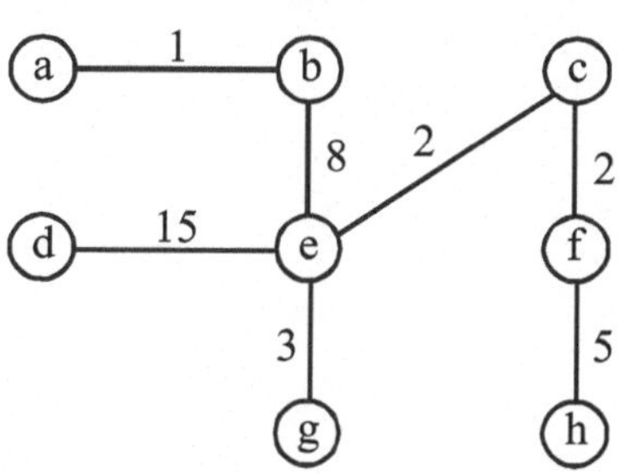

Total minimum cost = 36.

(b) Write Kruskal's Algorithm. **[5]**

```
Kruskal()
{
    T = ∅;
  for each v ∈ V
    MakeSet(v);
  sort E by increasing edge weight w
  for each (u,v) ∈ E (in sorted order)
    if FindSet(u) ≠ Find Set(v)
      T = T ∪ {{u,v}};
      Union(FindSet(u), FindSet(v));
}
```

CS-62 : 'C' PROGRAMMING AND DATA STRUCTURE
JUNE 2003

Note : *There are **6** questions in this paper. Question **1** is **compulsory**. Answer any **three** questions from the rest. All algorithms should be written nearer to 'C' language.*

1(a) Write a function to multiply two polynomials, using a linked list implementation. You must make sure that the output polynomial is sorted by exponent and has atmost one term corresponding to any power. Assume appropriate representation for input polynomials. [15]

Refer to Ch-2. Q16.

(b) Given two Sorted Lists, L_1 and L_2, write an algorithm to compute $L_1 \cup L_2$. L_1 and L_2 are to be implemented as Arrays. [10]

Refer to Ch-2, Q5.

(c) Write a function that takes only a pointer to the root of a binary tree T and computes the number of nodes in T. [5]

Refer to Ch-3, Q12.

2(a) Draw the Internal memory representation of the following Binary Tree using Sequential Representation. Assume that nodes appear in the following physical sequence: [3]

A, B, C, D, E, F, G, H

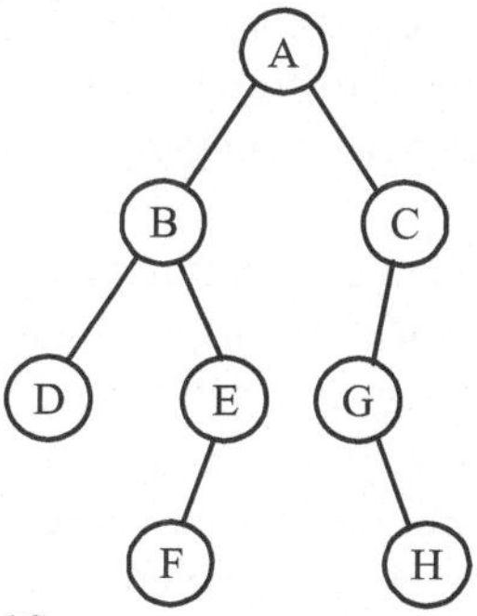

Refer to Ch-3, Q13.

(b) Consider the tree in the following figure: [3]

Refer to Ch-3, Q14.

(c) List atleast 4 differences between Arrays and Pointers in 'C' language. [4]

Refer to Ch-1, Q2.

3(a) Write the Postfix form of the following expression: [2]
(i) (C × D) ÷ (a - b)
(ii) C × D ÷ a - b
i) CD* AB-÷
ii) C D * a ÷ b -

(b) Write an algorithm for the addition of two matrices. The second matrix will be a sparse matrix. The first matrix is not a sparse matrix. [5]

Refer to Ch-2, Q6.

(c) What is an AVL Tree? How does it differ from a Binary Tree? [3]
Refer to Ch-3, Q15.

4(a) Write an algorithm to solve the Single-Source Shortest-Path problem. [5]
Refer to Ch-4, Q8.

(b) Does either Prim's or Kruskal's algorithm work if there are negative edge weights? Justify your answer. [5]
The kruskal algorithm can return different spanning trees for the same graph depending upon how the ties are broken when the edges are sorted into the order. A negative cost will always place the edges with the negative cost, towards the end or to a minimum. This will force the kruskal's algorithm to fail for an edge with a negative cost hence the negative cost edges cannot be managed by the kruskal's algorithm.
The Prims algorithm works on the principle similar to the Dijkrstra algorithm. The only difference being the ends are not fixed for which traversals have to be made. Here the problem starts when we declare a node U to be known but at the same point of time there can be a node which back tracks path to U is negative. In such cases the better solution can be achieved by taking path from any arbitrary node. S to V & back to U rather than going for S to U without going for V. Hence algorithm fails again.
The algorithm for both the cases can be refined by providing some improvement to PRIM's & Krurkal algorithm.

5(a) Consider the following figure: [5]

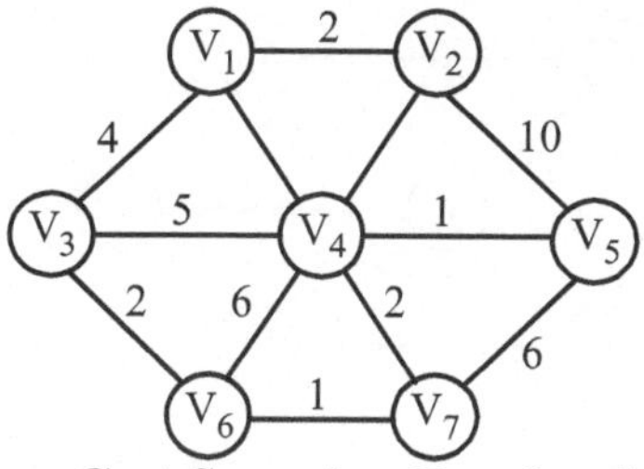

Find the Minimum Cost Spanning Tree for the above graph using Prim's Algorithm.

Step-1 :-

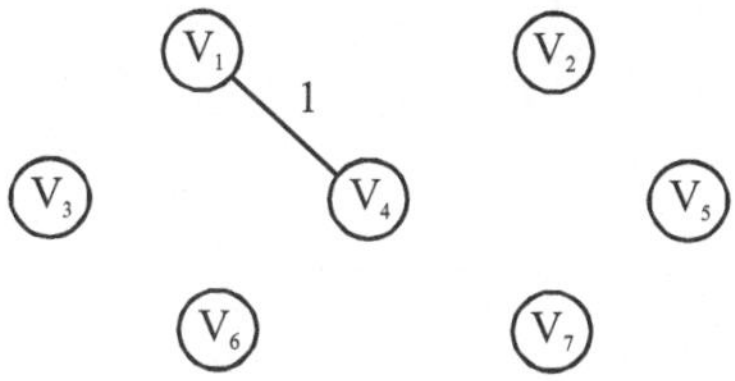

Step-2 :-

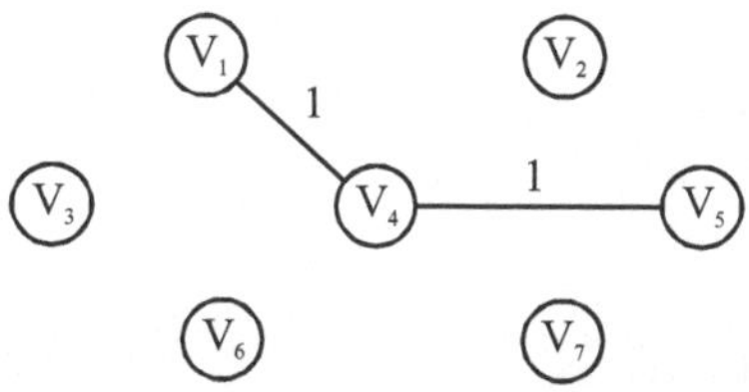

Step-3 :-

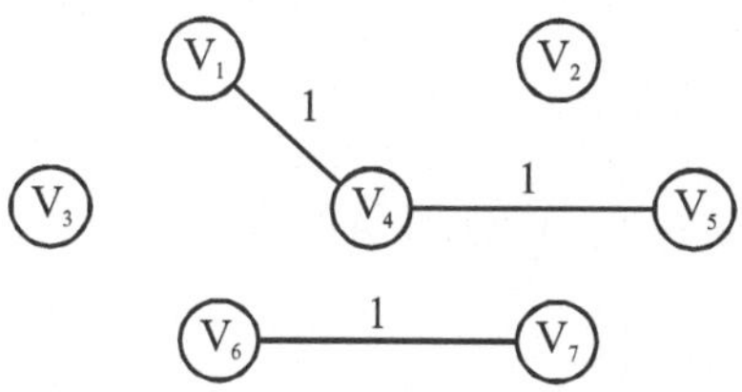

Step-4 :-

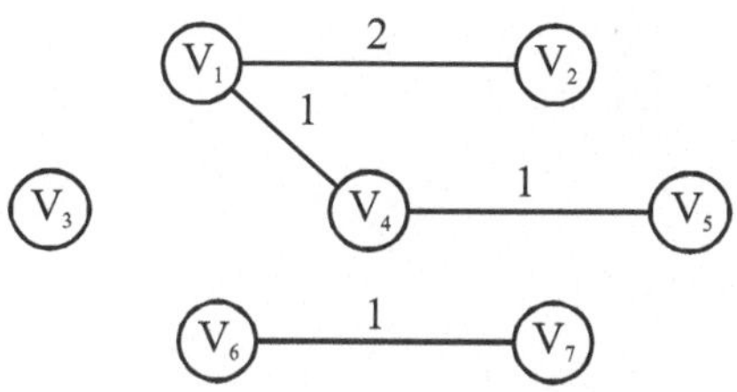

Step-5 :-

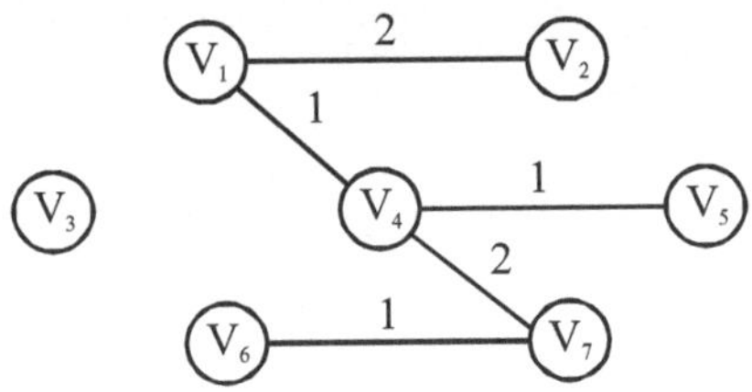

Step-6 :-

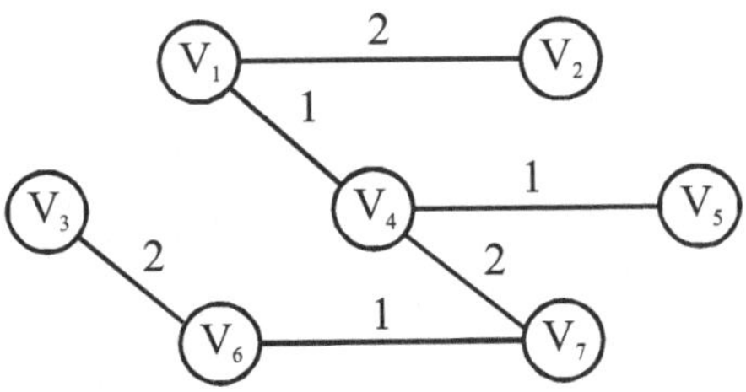

Total cost of above minimum spanning tree = 9

(b) Write Prim's Algorithm. **[5]**

```
root = an arbitrary node choosen as root;
for(every node nd in the graph)
{
distance[nd] = weight(root, nd);
Closet[nd] = root;
}          /*end for*/
distance[root] = INFINITY;
Current = root;
For(i = 1; n < no. of nodes in the graph; ++i)
{
/* find the node closet to the tree */
mindist = INFINITY
for(every node nd in the graph)
          if(distance[nd]<mindist)
          {
          Current = nd;
          mindist = distance[nd];
          }          /*end if*/
addson(closet[current], current);
distance[current] = INFINITY;
for(every node nd adjacent to Current)
```

```
if((distance[nd]<INFINITY)&&(weight(current[nd]<distance[nd]))
{
distance[nd] = weight(current, nd);
closes[nd] = Current;
}            /*    end if  */
}            /*    end for */
```

6(a) Write a recursive algorithm to implement Quick Sort. [5]

Refer to Ch-5, Q2.

(b) The input sequence to a Quick Sort' algorithm which sorts in increasing order is [5]

75, 73, 65, 82, 55, 90

Show the Sorting Process step-wise.

Refer to Ch-5, Q3.

CS-62 : 'C' PROGRAMMING AND DATA STRUCTURE
DEC 2003

*Note: There are 6 questions in this paper. Question **1** is **compulsory**. Answer any **three** questions from the rest. All algorithms should be written nearer to 'C' language.*

1(a) Write an algorithm to add two polynomials. Use the array implementation. If the polynomials have M and N terms respectively, what is the time complexity of your algorithm?
Refer to Ch-2, Q3.

(b) Write an algorithm to convert an Infix Expression which includes the operators (,), +, -, * and / to Postfix Expression. [10]
Refer to Ch-2, Q31.

(c) Write a function that takes a pointer to the root of a binary tree T and computes the number of full nodes in T. What is the running time of your function? [10]
Refer to Ch-3, Q9.

2(a) Draw the internal memory representation of the following Binary Tree using Sequential Representation. [5]

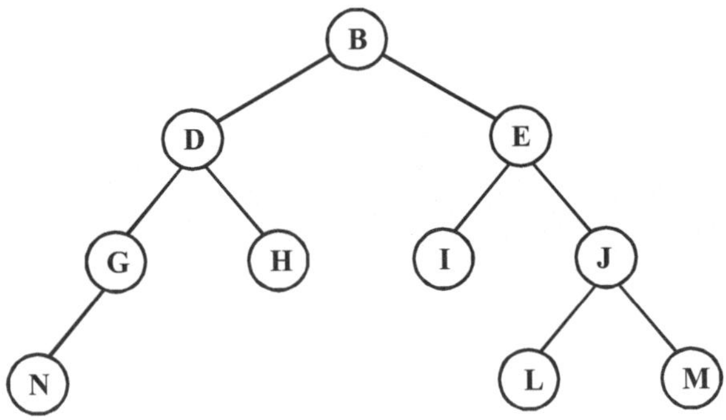

Refer to Ch-3, Q10.

(b) What is the minimum number of external nodes for a Binary Tree with height 'h'? Justify your answer. [5]
Refer to Ch-3, Q11.

3(a) Write the postfix form of the following expression: [5]
(i) a + b - c * d
(ii) (a -b) * (c + d)
Refer to Ch-2, Q29.

(b) Write an algorithm for the multiplication of two Sparse matrices (Use proper representation for the Sparse matrices). [5]
We are implementing sparse matrices through linked list. Function Multiply() will multiple two input sparse matrices & creates and output a sparse matrix Structure of a node of sparse matrix can be declared as:

```
struct sparse_type
{
        int data ;
        int col_no;
        struct sparse_type*Next;
}
```

Now we have two sparse matrices declared using above structure as follows:

```
        struct sparse_type*s1[MAX]
        struct sparse_type*s2[MAX]
```

we have also an output sparse Matrix i.e.

```
        struct sparse_type* s3[MAX]
```

Here MAX is the Maximum number of rows : Here before writing the algorithm, we assume that input sparse Matrices are already created & given to us.
The logic of Multiplications of two sparse Matrices is as follows : If a node with ith row & jth column is present in one sparse matrix & also a node with the same ith row & jth column is present in second sparse matrix then their data values are multiplies & a new node in output sparse matrix is created with new multiplied value & with ith row * jth column. If ith row of two nodes of two input sparse matrix are equal but the jth column of there two nodes are not equal then the node with ith row & smallest jth column values copied to new sparse matrix. Now the algorithm can be written as follows:

MULTIPLY (S1[MAX], S2[MAX])
This function will multiply S1 & S2 to create a third sparse matrix S3.

STEP-1: Set i to Zero
STEP-2: Repeat Step 3 to 8 until to MAX
STEP-3: Repeat Step 4 to 5 until S1[i] is equal to NULL and S2 [i] is equal to NULL
STEP-4: If col_[S1[i]] is equal to Col_no[s2[i]]
then
Set C=col_No[s1[i]]

```
                  Set m=[S1[i]]
                  Set S1 [i] = Next [S1[i]]
                  Set S2 [i] = Next [S2[i]]
                  Set S2 [i] = Next [S2[i]] [Points to next node]
                  else
                  If Col_No [S1[i]] is less than Col_no[S2[i]]
                  then
                  Set C=Col_No [S1[i]]
                  Set m= data[S1[i]]
                  Set S1 [i] = Next [S1[i]]
                  else
                  Set C = Col_No[S2[i]]
                  Set m = data [S2[i]]
                  Set S2[i] = Next [s2[i]] [Points to next node]
                  ENDIF
          ENDIF
STEP-5:           Create Next Node in S3[i]
                  Set Col_no [S3[i]] = C
                  Set data S3[i]] = m
STEP-6:           IF S1[i] is NULL then
                  Repeat following statements until S1[i] is NULL
                     (a) Create Next Node in S3[i]
                     (b) Set Col_No[S3[i]] = Col-No[S1[i]]
                     (c) Set data [S3[i]] = data [S1[i]]
                     (d) Set S1[i] = Next [S1]]
          ENDIF
STEP-7:           If S2[i] is Not NULL then
                  Repeat following statements until S2[i] is NULL
                     (a) Create Next node in S3[i]
                     (b) Set Col_No[S3[i]] = Col-No[S2[i]]
                     (c) Set dat [s3[i]] = data [s2[i]]
                     (d) Set s2[i] = Next[s2[i]]
STEP-8:           Set i = i + 1
                  Set s1[i] to point to first Node of ith row of first sparse
                  matrix
                  Set s2[i] to point to first node of the ith row of second sparse
                  matrix
STEP-9:           END
```

4(a) Draw the transitive closure of the directed graph shown in the following figure: **[5]**

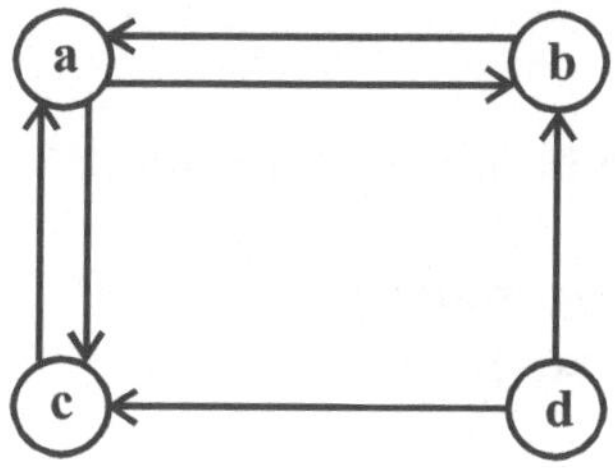

Refer to Ch-4, Q10.

(b) Write Dijkstra's Algorithm. **[5]**

Refer to Ch-4, Q8

5(a) Consider the following figure: **[5]**

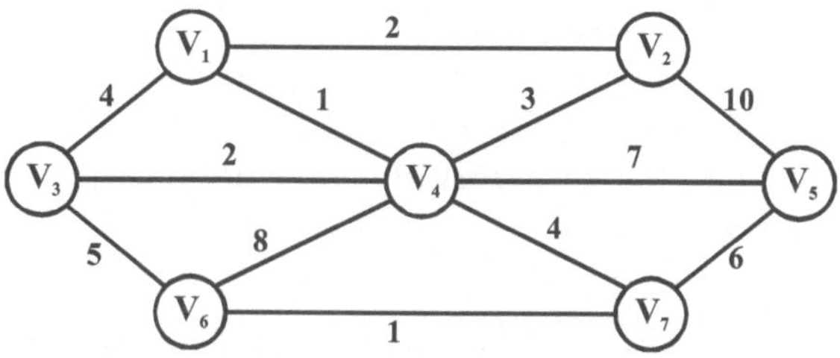

Find Minimum Cost Spanning Tree for the above graph using Prim's Algorithm.

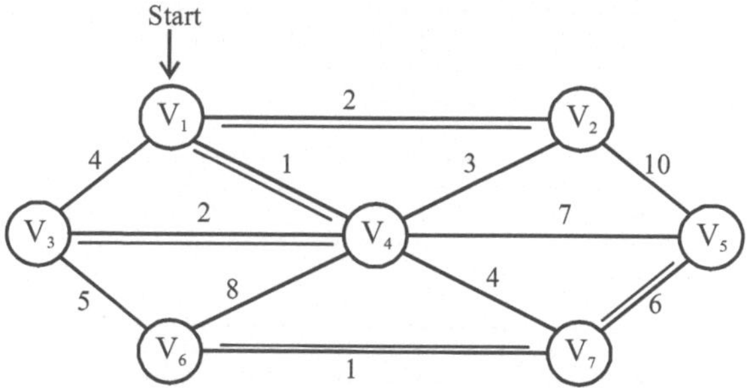

$V_1V_4 = 1$
$V_1V_2 = 2$
$V_4V_3 = 2$
$V_4V_7 = 4$
$V_7V_6 = 1$
$V_7V_5 = \underline{6}$
$\underline{\mathbf{16}}$

(b) Is the Minimum Cost Spanning Tree found by using Prim's Algorithm unique? Justify your answer. **[5]**

Refer to Ch-4, Q9.

6(a) Write an algorithm to implement Bubble Sort technique of sorting. [5]

Algorithm Bubble Sort Algorithm.

1) input n elements of an array a
2) initialize i = 0
3) Repeat through Step 6 while (1 < N)
4) Set j = 0
5) Repeat through Step 6 while (J < N - i - 1)
6) If (a[j] > a[j+1])
    (i) temp = a[i]
    (ii) a[j] = a[j+i]
    (iii) a[j+i] = temp
7) Display the Sorted elements of array a
8) Exit

(b) The input sequence to a Bubble Sort algorithm which sorts in increasing order is [5]

35, 5, 38, 41, 39, 37

Show the sorting process stepwise.

35	5	38	7	41	39	37

5	35	38	7	41	39	37

5	35	38	7	41	39	37

5	35	7	38	41	39	37

5	35	7	38	41	39	37

5	35	7	38	39	41	37

5	35	7	38	39	41	37

5	35	7	38	39	37	41

5	35	7	38	39	37	41

5	7	35	38	39	37	41

5	7	35	38	39	37	41

5	7	35	38	37	39	41

5	7	35	38	37	39	41

5	7	35	37	38	39	41

Final Sort

5	7	35	37	38	39	41

CS62 : "C" PROGRAMMING AND DATA STRUCTURE
JUNE 2004

Note: *There are 6 questions in this paper. Question 1 is* ***compulsory.*** *Answer any* ***three*** *questions from the rest. All algorithms should be written nearer to "C" language.*

1(a) What is the Time and Space complexity of an algorithm? For the binary search algorithm, derive the best, average and worst case time complexities for its execution. **[10]**

Time complexity and space complexity of an algorithm:

Time complexity:

Time complexity of any algorithm is the speed at which manipulation of that algorithm is performed. For example: Bubble sort takes n – 1 passes and n-1 comparison on each pass.

Thus total number of comparison = (n-1) (n-1)

$$= n^2 - 2n + 1$$

So time complexity = $O(n^2)$

Space complexity:

Space complexity is the amount of space taken by data structure used on that program.

Example:- Bubble sort require little additional space. One additional record to hold temporary value for interchanging and several simple integer variables.

Binary search:

Suppose there are n element in an array and 1 element is to be searched.

Best case:

This will be best when array is sorted and we want to search exactly mid element in the array. In this search it will take O(1) constant time.

Average case:

In this case if height of binary tree is logn and so,

Time complexity = O(logn)

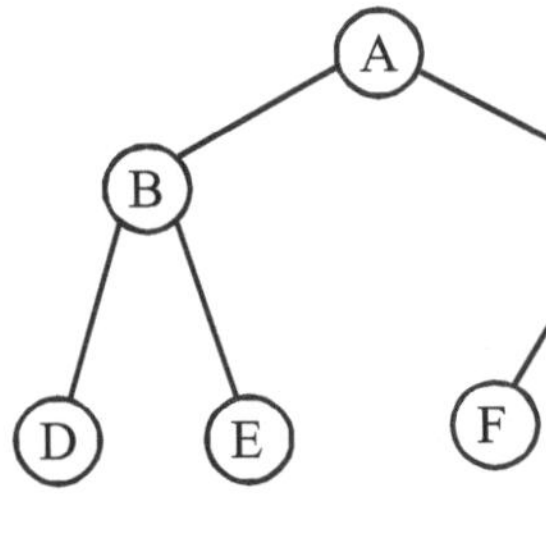

Worst case:

This case will e worst when height of binary search tree is n – 1.
Therefore time complexity = (n – 1)

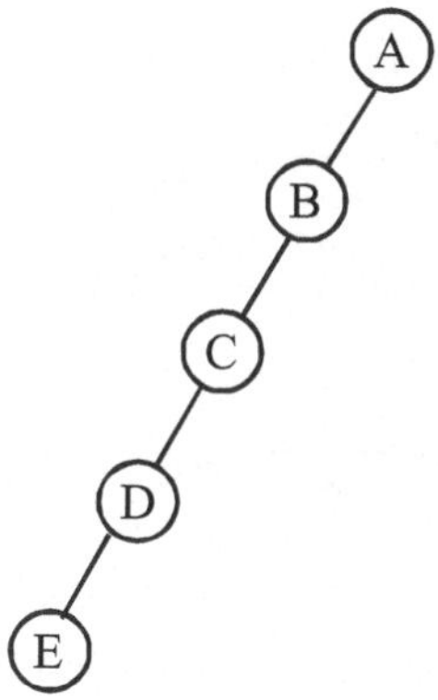

(b) What are Row major and Column major representations of arrays? For a character array defined as A[20] [20], if A[0] [0] is located at memory address 100, where is element A[10] [1] located in Column major representation and in Row major representation. [10]

Refer to Ch-2, Q1.

(c) Write an algorithm that takes a pointer to the root of a binary tree T and another variable which indicates whether preorder, postorder or inorder traversal of the tree is required. Depending on this variable, the function should print the tree in either preorder, poster or inorder. [10]

Refer to Ch-3, Q5.

2(a) What is a Circular Queue? Give an example of its application. Give an algorithm for the addition of a new element to the circular queue. Include necessary validation checks. [5]

Refer to Ch-2, Q27.

(b) Prove that a binary tree with N internal nodes has N+1 external nodes. Preferably, use mathematical induction for this. [5]

Case 1 :

Consider N = 1

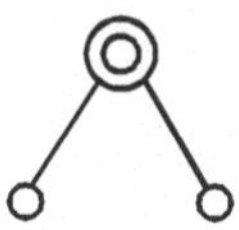

Here, 1 internal and 2 external node.

i.e. 1 + 1 = 2

Hence result is true for N = 1.

Case 2 :

Suppose result is true for N – 1 i.e. N – 1 internal node have n external node.

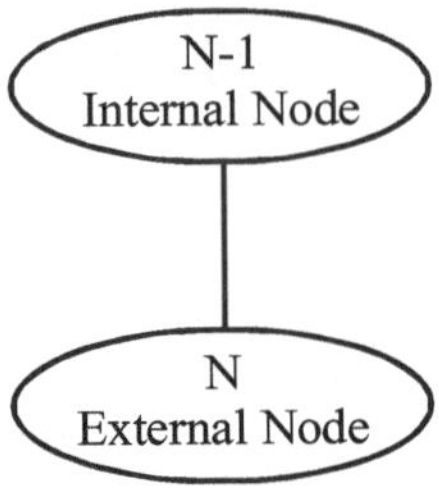

We have to prove that result is also true for N nodes.

For making N internal node we will have situation like this

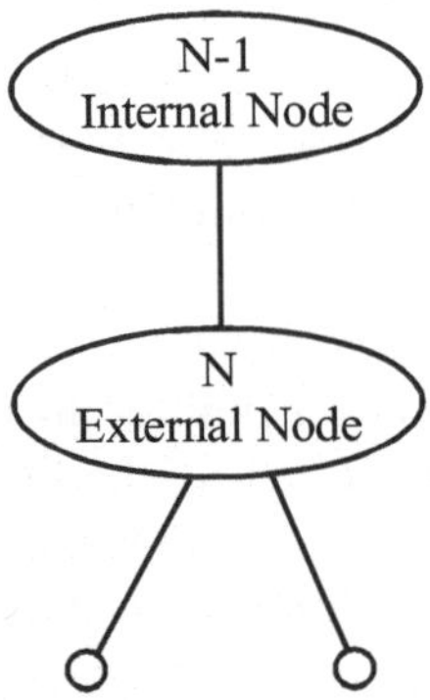

Hence total number of internal nodes

= N – 1 internal + one internal node of N external

= N

Total number of external node = N – 1 + 2 = N + 1

Hence result is true for N + 1

By the mathematical induction result is true for all N.

3(a) The following are the inorder and preorder traversal of a Binary Tree. **[5]**

Inorder : NTCGOISU

Preorder : IGNCTOUS

Construct the Binary Tree.

Refer to Ch-3, Q6.

(b) Define the following: **[5]**

(i) Tree

Refer to Ch-3, Q7.

(ii) Strongly Connected Graph

Refer to Ch-4, Q6.

(iii) Adjacency Matrix

Refer to Ch-4, Q6.

(iv) Binary Tree

Refer to Ch-3, Q7.

(v) Directed Graph

Refer to Ch-4, Q6.

4(a) Write an algorithm for creation of a Singly Linked List. Also write algorithms for insertion and deletion of elements from the Singly Linked List. **[5]**

Refer to Ch-2, Q10.

(b) Write an algorithm to list the nodes of a Binary Tree in the following way:

List the root, then nodes at depth 1, followed by m nodes at depth 2, and so on.

You algorithm should have linear time complexity. **[5]**

Refer to Ch-3, Q8.

5(a) Consider the following graph: **[5]**

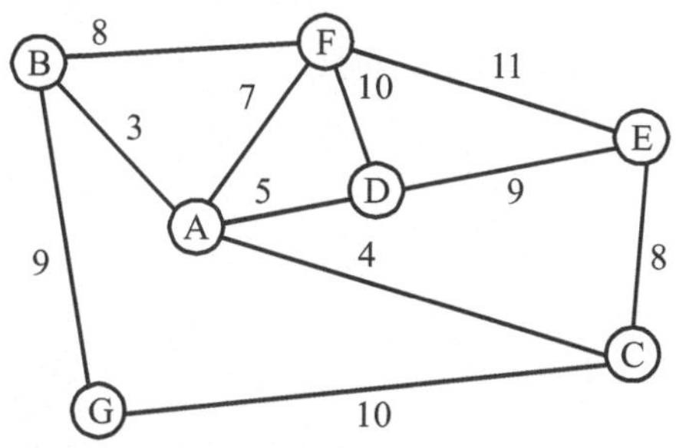

Construct a minimum cost spanning tree. Give the cost.

Refer to Ch-4, Q7.

(b) Write an algorithm to convert a decimal number to binary number using stacks(s). **[5]**

Refer to Ch-2, Q28.

6(a) Using Heapsort, sort the following in Ascending order: [5]
17, 12, 29, 33, 2, 15, 8
Show all the steps involved.

Making heap

Step 1 :

Step 2 :

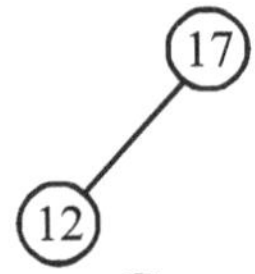

Step 3 :

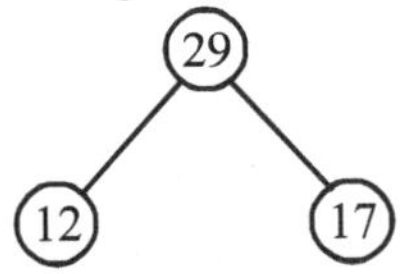

Step 4 :

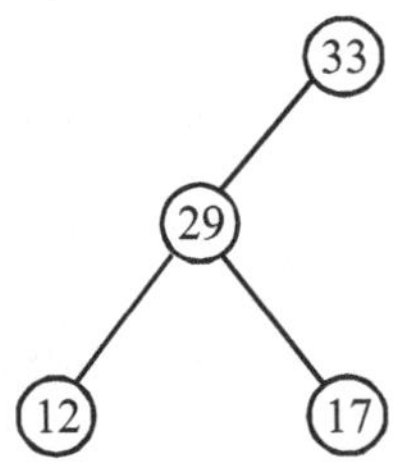

Step 5 :

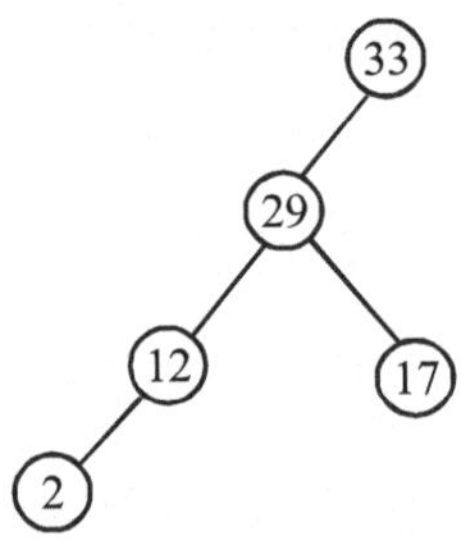

Step 6 :

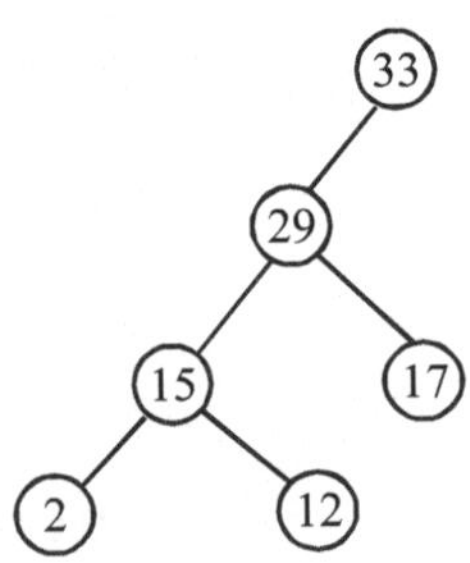

Step 7 :

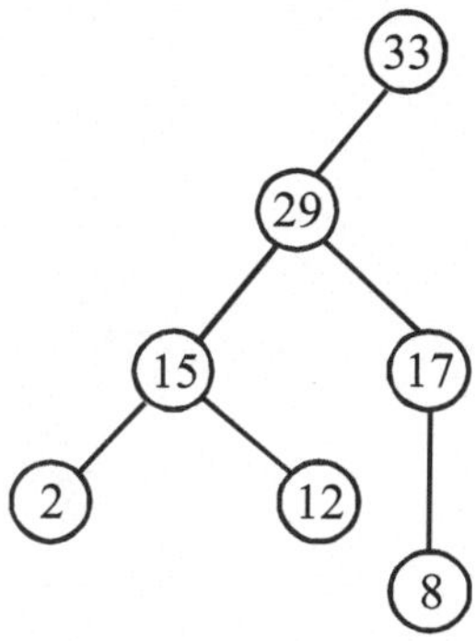

Adjusting heap:
Original Heap

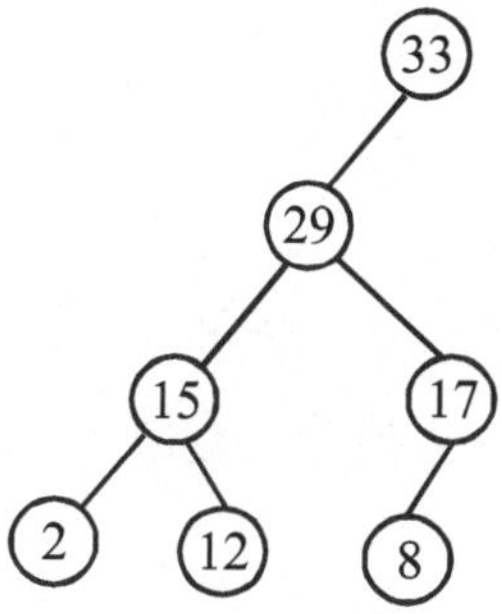

Step 1 :

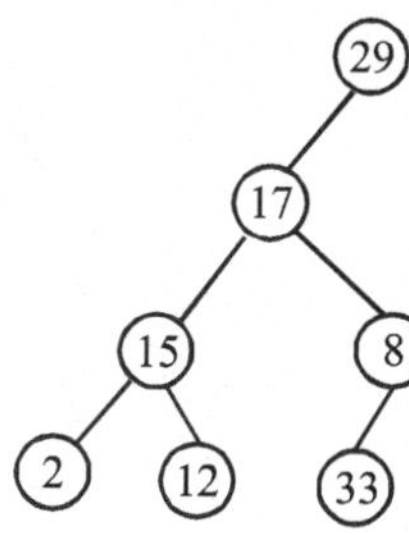

Step 2 :

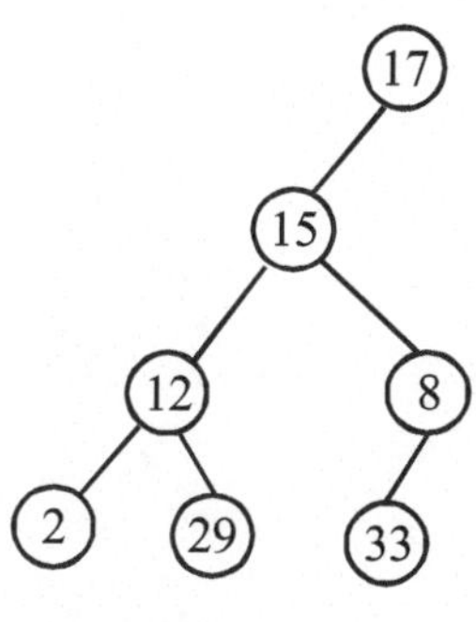

Step 3 :

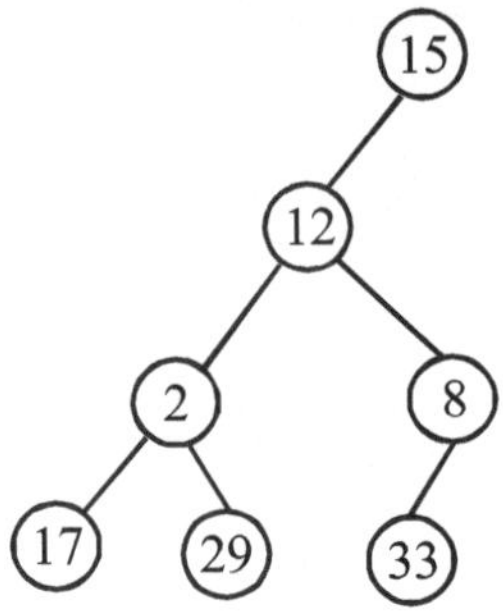

Step 4 :

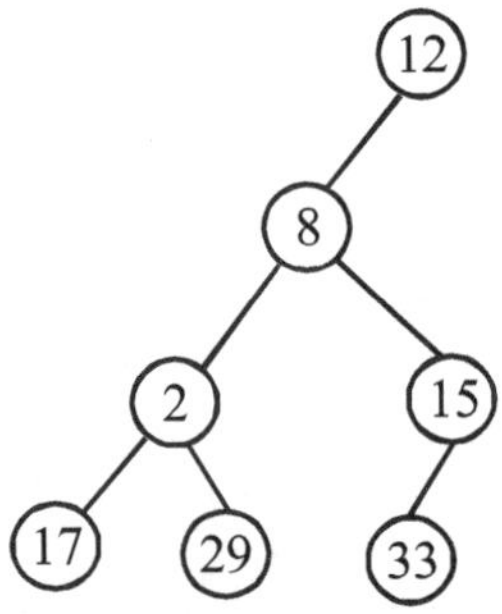

Step 5 :

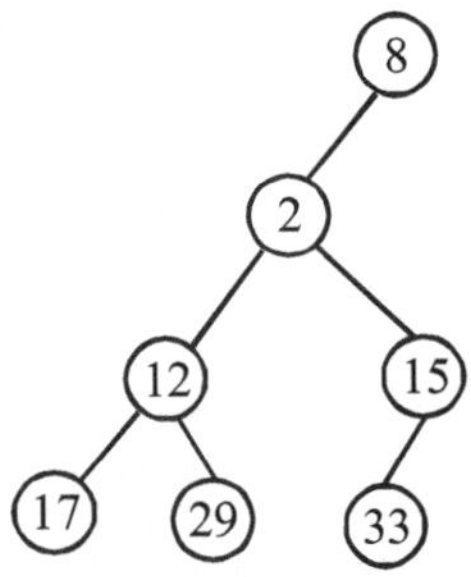

Step 6 :

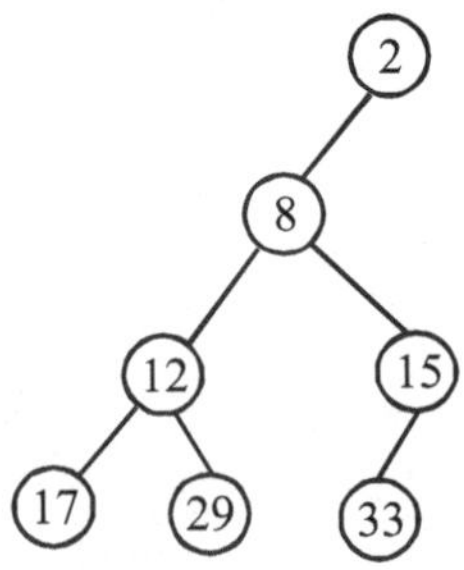

Sorted array is 2, 8, 12, 15, 17, 29, 33.

(b) Write an algorithm for 2-way merge sort. Give an application of it also. [5]

In this algorithm, the two sorted arrays PAR1[n] and PAR2[n] are merged into an array FINAL [M + N]. Two variables Ptr1 and Ptr2 are being used to point *"Yet to be merged parts"* of PAR1 and PAR2.

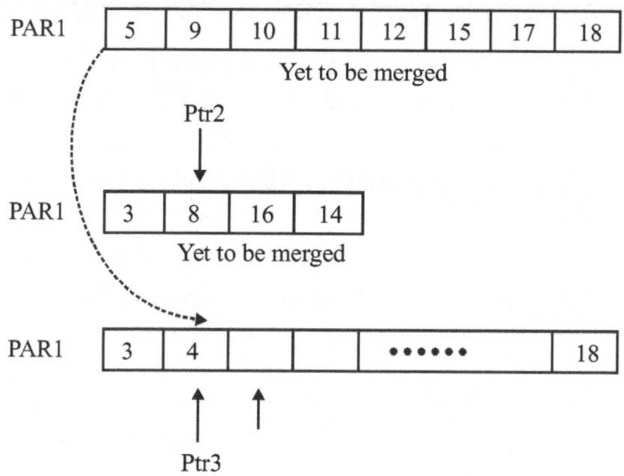

A third variable Ptr3 is used to point the next location in FINAL where the merged element is to added.

Steps : 1. Ptr1 = Ptr2 = 1; Ptr3 = 1;

2. While ((Ptr1 <= N) and (Ptr2 <= M)) repeat step 3

3. If (PAR1 [ptr1] < PAR2 [Ptr2])

    then [FINAL [ptr3] = PAR1 [ptr1];

        Ptr1 = Ptr1 + 1

        Ptr3 = Ptr3 +; 1]

    else

        [FINAL [Ptr3 = PAR2 [Ptr2]

        Ptr2 = Ptr2 + 1;

        Ptr3 = Ptr3 + 1;]

    {end of while loop}

    {copy rest of the elements of array PAR2}

4. While (Ptr2 <= M)

    FINAL [Ptr3] = PAR2 [Ptr2];

CS-62 'C' PROGRAMMING AND DATA STRUCTURE
DEC 2004

Note : *Question no.1 is* **compulsory.** *Answer any* **three** *question from the rest. All algorithms should be written nearer to 'C' language.*

1(a) Represent a polynomial using a circularly inked list. Write an algorithm to subtract two polynomials using the representation above. What is the time complexity of your algorithm to subtract two polynomials using the representation above. What is the time complexity of your algorithm ? [10]

A node of linked list can represent a polynomial expression of one or two variables. Representation of polynomial expression of one variable

The structure of a node of linked list represent polynomial of one variable will be as follows:

```
Structure
{
int power;
int coef;
}* head = NULL;
```

One polynomial term will be mapped to one node of linked list. The field "power" of a node is used represent the power of the term & the "coeff" of the node is used to represent coefficient of the term.

Example :-

Suppose we have a polynomial expression of variable.

$$2x^2 + 3x^3 + 5x^5$$

It will be represented as follows :

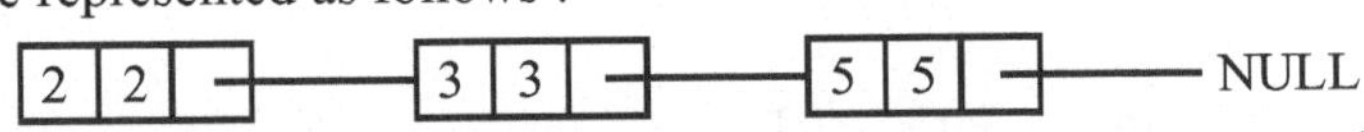

Now the polynomial expression of two variables can also be represented through linked list. The linked list representing two variable-polynomial addition will be a two way list in which a node containing the power of X will also contain all the coefficients & power of Y for which power of X is same. In this way we will maintain two linked list in which the node of first linked list will have the following fields. (i) Power of X (ii) Pointer to next node (iii) pointer to the node of second linked list.

The second list will have the fields. (i) co-efficient (ii) Power of y (iii) Pointer to next node.

Example :-

Suppose we have a two variable polynomial expression $3x^2\ y^2$ then it will be represented as follows:

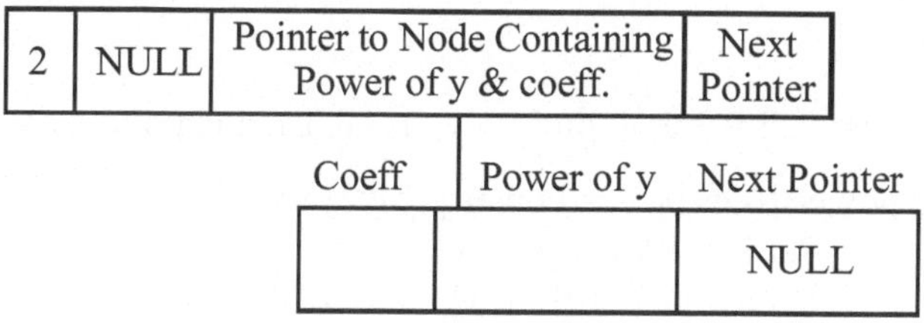

The structure of a node of linked list to represent polynomial of two variable is as follow:

```
Structure list_y              // Structure of second list
{
        int Pow_y ;
        int coeff;
        struct list_y *next_y;
}
structure_X                   //Structure of first list
{
        int pow_x;
        structure list_y *next_xy;
        structure list_x *next_x;
}
struct list_x node_x;
```

Algorithm to add two Polynomials.

Assumption of Algorithm

(i) Here we are performing one-variable polynomial addition

(ii) Poly1 & Poly2 are input Polynomials pointing the head node of two polynomials

(iii) Poly3 is the output Polynomial which is the outcome of addition of two polynomials.

Logic of the algorithm is as follows:-

The logic of one-variable polynomial addition is that if power of corresponding terms of both Polynomials is equal, their coefficient are added and a new output term is created with the power of input term and added coefficient, otherwise, the input term having smallest power becomes new output terms. Now we move to next term of input polynomial. This process continues until any of the two input polynomials end. The rest terms of the polynomial, which did not end are added to output polynomials.

Algorithm :-

STEP-1 : Start

STEP-2 : Repeat STEP 3 to 4 until Poly1 is NULL and poly2 is NULL

STEP-3 : If power [poly1] = = Power [Poly2] then
Set P = Power [Poly1]
Set m = Coeff[Poly1] + Coeff[Poly2]
Set Poly1 = next [Poly1]
Set Poly2 = next [Poly2]

else
if Power [Poly1]<Power [Poly2]then
Set P = Power [Poly1]
Set m = Coeff[poly1]
Set poly1 = next [Poly1]

else
Set P = Power [Poly2]
Set m = Power [Poly2]
Set Poly2 = next [Poly2]

SETP-4 : Create a new node in Poly3
Set power [poly3] = p
Set coeff[Poly3] = m

STEP-5 : If Poly1 is not NULL then repeat following statements until Poly1 is NULL
Create new node in Poly3
Set Power [Poly3] = Power [Poly1]
Set coeff [Poly3] = Coeff [Poly1]
Set poly1 = next[Poly1]

else
If Poily2 is not NULL then repeat following statements until Poly2 is NULL
Set Power [Poly3] = Power [Poly2]
Set coeff[Poly3] = Power[Poly2]
Set Poly2 = next [Poly2]

STEP-6 : Print Poly 3

STEP-7 : END

Time Complexity

When the two Polynomials have m & n terms respectively, then the computing time is O(m+n), because maximum number of executions of any of the statements is bounded by m+n.

This means that if the algorithm is implemented & run on a computer, the time taken will be $C_1m+C_2n + C_3$ Where C_1, C_2, C_3, are constants Since any algorithm that adds two Polynomials Must look at each non zero term at least once, every algorithm must have a time requirement of

$$C_1m+C_2n+C_3$$

(b) A file stores a series of numbers. Write an algorithm using binary search tree that counts the occurrence of different numbers in the file. For example, file containing data 1, 50, 20, 1, 25 would produce output as **[10]**

Number	Occurrence
1	2
20	1
25	1
50	1

We must read numbers from the file and insert these numbers in Binary Search Tree i.e. Parent is > Left child and parent < right child.

Then we write the entries in inorder, thus numbers will be arranged in increasing order with repeating numbers written adjacent. We count of number of occurrences of repeating numbers with a loop and thus result is arrived at.

Algorithm :

```
1. declare tree node with left, right, child. Declare array A[100]
2. open file "ABC.TXT"
3. while(! EOF)
        do read h
        if TREE IS EMPTY,
                then parent = n.
        else
        if n< parent.
                then parent —> left =n.
        else
                parent —> right=n.
        end if.
; Traverse the tree
4. P=parent, i = 0;
5. while (p!=NULL)
        do
        p=p—> left
        A[i]=p—>info
        i=i+1
```

```
        p=p—>right
; count occurrences
6. count = a[j], k=1, occurrence[20], l=0
7. for j=1 to i-1
        do
        if count = a[j]
        k=k+1
        else
        occurrence[l]=k
        l=l+1
        k=1
        print "No :" a[j] "has occurrences" occurrence[l-1]
        end if
8. Stop
```

(c) Write an algorithm to sort a sequence of number of numbers in increasing order using bubble sort. What is the time complexity of this algorithm ? **[6]**

```
1. ar1[20], n, temp
2. Input n; no. of elements
3. for i=0 to n-1
do
input ar1[i]
4. for i=0 to n-2
5. for j=0 to n-2-l
do if ar1[j]>ar1[j+1]
then temp=a[j]
a[j]=a[j+1]
a[j+1]=temp
6. print "Sorted array is"
7. for i=0 to n-1
do print a[i]
8. Stop
```

In this algorithm for n elements we need (n-1) passes and (n-1)+(n-2)+… … … +1 comparisons

=(n-1)(n-1+1) / 2

= (n-1)(n) / 2

$=O(n^2)$

(d) What are the various applications of stacks and queues ? Give at

least two applications of each. **[4]**

Stacks are used in compilers in passing an expression by recursion; in memory management in OS etc.

Queues find their use in CPU scheduling, in printer spooling, in message queueing in compilers, network programming etc.

Two applications of Stacks :

1. Converting number bases
2. Infix to postfix conversion

Two applications of Queues :

1. In breadth first search of a graph.
2. Communication buffer queue with messages.

2(a) What is a graph ? How can it be represented in a C program? Describe two important applications of graphs. **[5]**

A Graph G consists of a set V of vertices (nodes) and a set E of edges (arcs). We write G=(V,E). V is a finite and non empty set of vertices. E is a set of pairs of vertices; these pairs are called edges. Therefore V(G), read as V of G, is set of vertices, and E(G), read as E of G, is set of edges.

An edge e = (v,w), is a pair of vertices v and w, and is said to be incident with v and w. A graph may be pictorially represented as given in Figure 1 below :

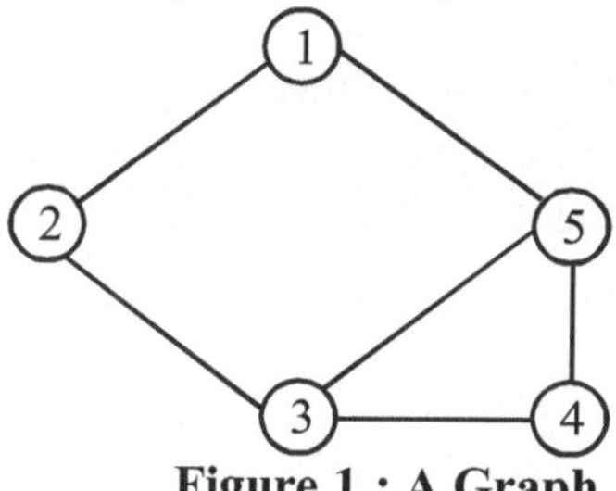

Figure 1 : A Graph

It can be represented in a C program by

1. Adjacency Matrix

The adjacency matrix A for a graph G = (V,E) with n vertices, is an nxn matrix of bits, such that

A_{ij} = 1, iff there is an edge from vi to vj and

A_{ij} = 0, if there is no such edge.

2. Adjacency List

It is a more precise and shorter way of representation. In this representation, we store a graph as a linked structure. We store all the vertices in a list and then for each vertex, we have a linked list of its adjacent vertices.

Two important applications of graph :

1. In finding routes

we use graphs as models of practical situations involving routes: the vertices represent the cities and edges represent the roads or some other links, specially in transportation management, Assignment problems and many more optimization problems.

2. In electronic circuits.

Circuits elements like transistors, resistors, and capacitors are intricately wired together. Such circuits can be represented and processed within a computer in order to answer simple questions like "Is everything connected together?" as well as complicated questions like "If this circuit is built, will it work?"

(b) Write an algorithm to delete a node from a doubly linked list. Show the process with the help of a diagram. [5]

Suppose we have a doubly linked list as shown :

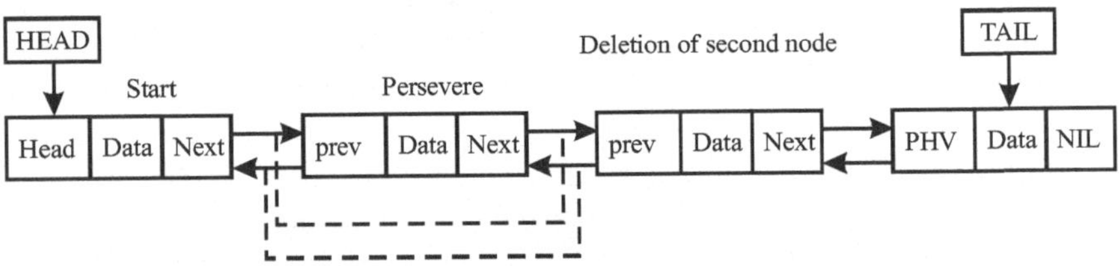

Suppose we have to delete any node

```
1. start = head, preserve=head—>next, ITEM.     ;Traverse the list
2. if start —> data = ITEM
        then start = start —> next
        head=start
        head—>prev=head
end if
3. while start—>next != NIL
        if start—>next = ITEM
                start—>next=preserve—>next
                preserve—>next—>prev=start
        else
                start=start—>next
                preserve=start—>next
        end if
4. print "The list is"
5. start=head
6. while start != NIL
        do print start—>data00
        start=start—>next
```

7. Stop

3(a) How can a queue by represented using an array and a linked list ? Compare the two represented in terms of time and space complexities. [4]

We have give a vector representation of a queue. We define a queue as a record structure containing the vector and two variables front and rear to denote the present position of its front and rear element.

We may define a Queue as given below:

```
Const max = 100
Struct  q_type
{ elementtype    queue [max];
Int front, rear;
};
```

As an example of this representation of a queue, consider a size 6. Assume that the queue is initially empty. It is required to insert element RED, BLACK and BLUE, followed by delete RED and BLACK and insert GREEN, WHITE AND YELLOW.

Following figure give a trace of the queue contents for this sequence of operations.

RED					
RED	BLACK				
RED	BLACK	BLUE			
	BLACK	BLUE			
		BLUE			
		BLUE	GREEN		
		BLUE	GREEN	WHITE	
		BLUE	GREEN	WHITE	YELLOW

The second approach for implementing queues is by using the dynamic storage allocation through the use of pointers. We can define a queue consisting of records where each record contains record that comes after it. Therefore we may declare a queue as

```
Struct  qrec
{ element type data;
Struct qrec * next;};
Struct qrec *qptr;
```

we must also specify the items at the front and rear of the queue. This may be done by the following declaration.

```
Struct qtype
{ Struct qrec * front;
        Struct qrec * rear;
}; qtype q;
```

This kind of an implementation is a singly linked list implementation of the Queue.

Time Complexity :

Searching an item will be of order of number of items in linked list representation whereas in array representation it can be reduced to $\log_2 n$ if binary search is applied.

Space Complexity :

Array representation has more space complexity as even removal of any item will not reduce the number of calls but in linked list representation, node removal leads to decreased memory use in the program.

(b) Write an algorithm construct a binary tree from the given in order as well as preorder traversal. [4]

1. Here we get the root as starting node of preorder.
2. All members to left of that root in inorder come to left and all members to right of that root come to the right.
3. The left subtree sequence in inorder appearing in preorder sets the left subtree root as the first node in the sequence present in preorder.
4. All nodes to left of this node in order form left subtree & on right form right subtree.
5. Repeat step 3 for right subtree sequence from step 2
6. Repeat step 2 to 5 for newly formed left and right subtrees in order till you get single nodes.

Preorder → Root Left Right

Inorder → Left Root Right

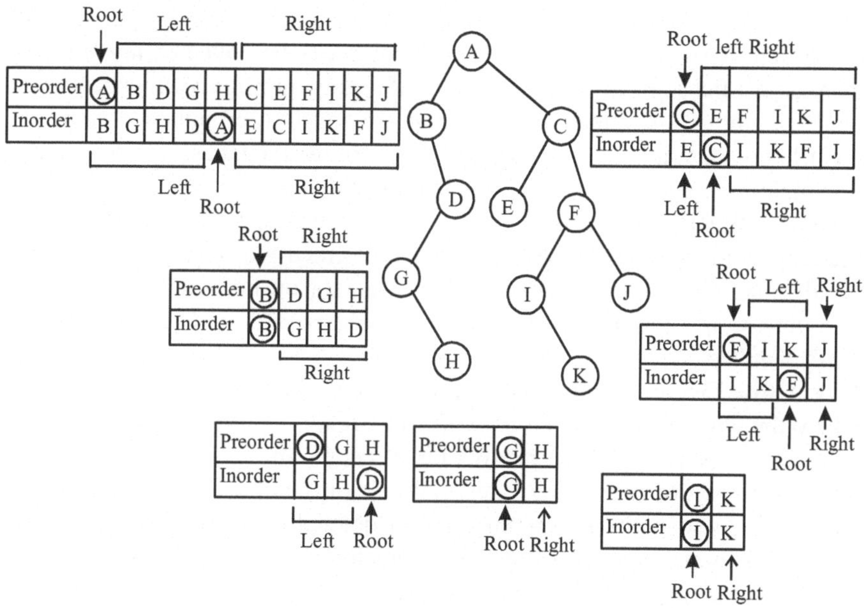

4(a) Differentiate between the following with an example $\left[2\frac{1}{2}\times 2=5\right]$

(i) Arrays vs Pointers

(ii) Sequential file organization vs Direct file organization

(i) Arrays vs Pointers

Arrays	Pointers
(1) Static memory i.e. number of calls remain same. E.g. int a [10] constant malloc	Implement dynamic memory i.e. number of calls can decrease or increase. E.g. int *P; P = (int *) (size of (int) * n);
(2) Overflow of bounds is there	Bounds overflow not there
(3) Array's base address is constant e.g. so you cannot write int a[10]; a = a+1;	Pointer address can be changed int * p = "Gph"; P = P+1;

(ii) Sequential file organization vs Direct file organization

Sequential File Organization : This organization refers to the storage method where the data records are stored in some specific sequence. This sequence may be the order of arrival of records, the ascending sequence of any key etc. Generally a key field is chosen which follows the sequence of insertion and the key field is such that it uniquely processes systems where a certain number of records can be collected and processed in batch which is called batch processing where a certain number of records can be collected together and then stored after some time. Also this kind of file organization requires sequential mode of storage like magnetic tapes and previously used punched cards etc. this file organization is best suited for maintaining a database and its backup. The major disadvantage of this organization is that none of the records can be accessed directly i.e. even if the last records has to be accessed then the process is to move sequentially from the first record only. The second disadvantage is that it can never be use used for on-line transaction, all the transactions are required to be batched together. The updates are also not easily handled.

Direct File Organization : This organization refers to the storage method where the data records are stored with some relative position in the file. This helps in direct access of the records i.e. a record can be accessed directly. A field of the record is fixed as a key that helps in unique identification of the record. The new records to be inserted or deleted is performed through this key field. This organization is suited for interactive processing like the reservation system, booking counters so that the queries are solved as soon as they are raised. Any record can be accessed directly if the key is known. The faster access devices like floppy disk, hard disk etc. used for implementing direct file organization

(b) Write an algorithm to implement a Queue that allows insertion and deletion at both ends. [5]

```
#include<stdio.h>
struct node{
int data;
struct node *link;
};
struct node*rear,*front;
main()
{
int item,p,i;
char ch;
void addq(int,int);
int delq(int);
void traverse();
```

```
front=NULL;
rear=NULL;
clrscr();
do{
printf("\n\nInsert or delete:'i'/'d'.Enter any other character to exit:");
scanf("%c",&ch);
if(ch=='i'||ch=='d')
{
do{
printf("\n\nEnter position:1 for front,2 for rear:");
scanf(" %d",&p);
if(p<1||p>2)
printf("\n\nWrong input.Enter again");

}while(p<1||p>2);
if(ch=='i')
{
printf("\n\nEnter the no:");
scanf("%d",&item);}
}
else
{
getch();
exit(0);
}
if(ch=='i')
{addq(item,p);
traverse(); }
else
{i=delq(p);
printf("\n\nDeleted item is:%d",i);}
printf("\n\nDo you want to continue:'y' for yes,any other character to exit:");
scanf(" %c",&ch);
}while(ch=='y');
getch();
}
void addq(int item,int p)
{
truct node*temp;
temp=(struct node*)malloc(sizeof(struct node));
```

```
temp->data=item;
if(front==NULL)
temp->link=NULL;
else
{
if(p==1)
{temp->link=front;
front=temp;}
else
{
rear->link=temp;
temp->link=NULL;
rear=rear->link;
}
}
if(front==NULL)
{
front=rear=temp;
return;
}
}
int delq(int p)
{
struct node *temp;
int i;
if(front==NULL)
{printf("\n\nQueue is empty!!");
return NULL;
}
if(front->link==NULL)
{i=front->data;
temp=front;
front=rear=NULL;
free(temp);
return i;
}
if(p==1)
{i=front->data;
temp=front;
front=front->link;
```

```
free(temp);
return i;
}
else
{
i=rear->data;
temp=front;
while(temp->link->link!=NULL)
temp=temp->link;
temp->link=NULL;
rear=temp;
return i;
}
}

void traverse()
{
struct node*temp;
if(front==NULL)
{
printf("\n\nQueue is empty!");
getch();
exit(0);
}
else
{
temp=front;
printf("\n\nThe Queue data is:");
while(temp!=NULL)
{
printf("%d",temp->data);
temp=temp->link;
if(temp!=NULL)
printf("->");
}
}
}
```

5(a) Consider the graph :

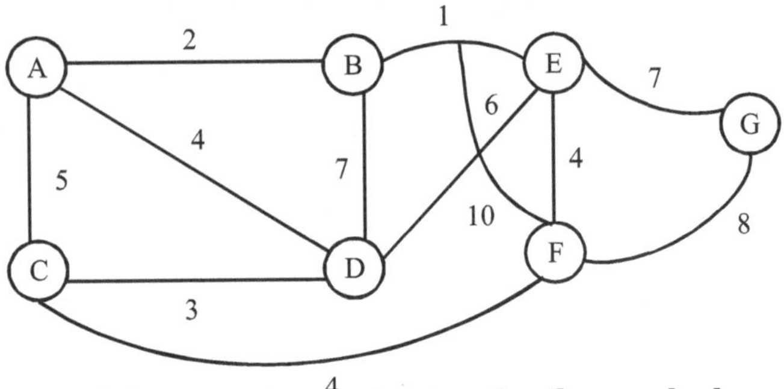

Construct a minimum cost spanning tree for the graph above. Also give the cost of this tree. **[5]**

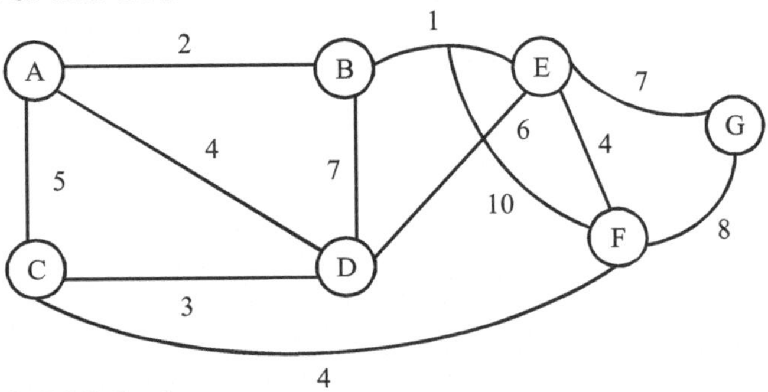

By Kruskal Method

i.e. take minimum weightage in increasing order till all vertices are covered but without a cycle.

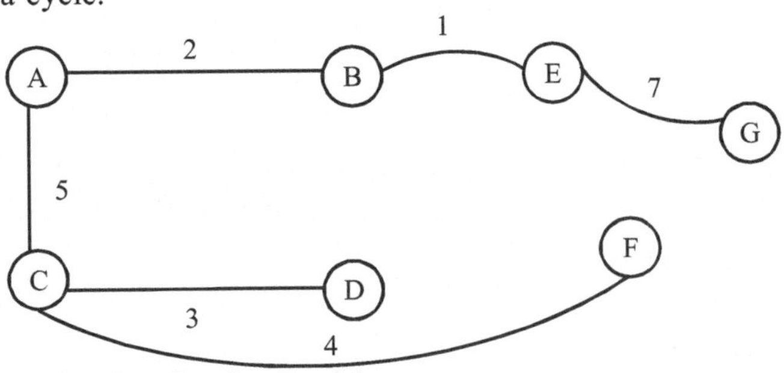

Cost : - 1 + 2 + 3 + 4 + 5 + 7 = 22

(b) Write an algorithm for sorting a sequence of numbers using any merge sort technique. **[5]**

Here we are giving recursive algorithm of merge sort.

Void merge_sort (int low, int high)

{

// a [low:high] is a global array to be sorted

```
// small [p] is true if there is only one element
// to sort. In this case the list is already sorted

int mid;
if (low<high)      // If there are more than one element
// divide p into subprograms
// Find where slit the set
                    mind = (low + high)/2;
// solve the subprograms
                    mergesort(low,mid);
                    mergesort (mid + 1, high);
// combine the solution
                    merge(low, mid, high)
}
}/* end of function

void merge (int low, mid,int high)
{
int h = low, i = low, j = mid + 1, k;
while (h < = mid && j <= high)
{
          If  (a[h] < = a [j])
          {
                    b [i] = a [h];
                    h ++;
          }

          else
          {
                    b[i] = a [j];
                    j ++;
          }
          i ++;
}
if (h > mid)
{
          for (k = j; k< = high; k ++)
          {
                    b [i] = a [k];
i ++;
}
```

```
}
else
{
        for (k = h; k < = mid; k++)
        {
                b [i] = a [k];
                i ++;.
                }
        }
        for (k = low; k < = high ; k ++)
        a [k] = b [k];
}/* end of function */
```

The efficiency of mergesort can be shown by the following table:

Algorithm merge sort	Worst case behaviour n long = o (n long)	Average case n long = O (n long n)	Extra memory n(n)

Where n is the number of input data to be sorted.

6(a) Write ab algorithm to find the first occurrence of the substring of the form 'aab' in an input string. **[5]**

1. str[10], i, istr[50]
2. input str, istr
3. n<—length[istr]
4. m<—length[str]
5. for i=0 to n-m
6. do if P[1…m]=T[s+1…s+m]
1. then print "Pattern occurs with shift" s.

Here istr is input string Str is substring to be found.

The program intimates the shift in input string at which substring occurs.

(b) Define the following terms : **[5]**

(i) Height balanced tree

(ii) Post-order traversal

(iii) Column major order

(i) Height balanced tree

➢ ***AVL tree***

An AVL tree is a binary tree in which the left and right subtrees of any node may differ in height by at most 1, and in which both the subtrees are themselves AVL trees (the definition is recursive). It is also called height balanced tree

1. An AVL tree is constructed in the same manner as an ordinary binary tree,

except that after the addition of each new node, a check must be made to ensure that the AVL balance conditions have not been violated. If all is well, no further action need be taken. If the new node causes an imbalance in the tree, however, some rearrangement of the tree's nodes must be done.

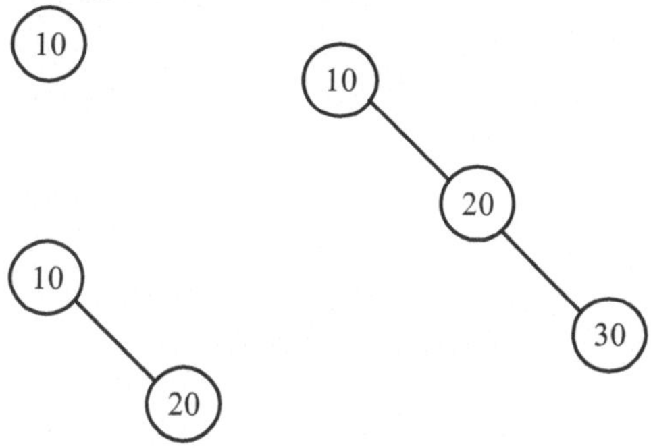

(ii) Post order traversal : This is a particular case of traversing a binary tree T with root R.

Step 1 Traverse the left subtree of R in post order.

Step 2 Traverse the right subtree of R in post order.

Step 3 Process the root R

e.g. Consider the tree given below :

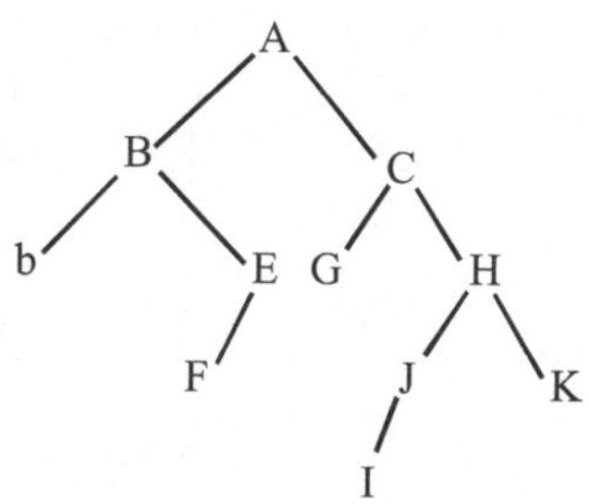

Postorder Traversal will be : D F E B G L J K H C A

(iii) Column major order :

Let us see how the above expressions work out for a column major order. We once again consider a 4x6 array A[4] [6]. Also take B as base address and S as size of each element. Then the address of A[I,J] would be :

B+J*4*S+ I*S

To reach A[I] [J] we shall skip J-1 columns, each of length 4* S and I-1 elements each of lengths. We further generalize it for an array A[U_1] [U_2]. Following the same logic, the address of A[I] [J] would be given as

B+(J*U_1*S)+(I*S)

The column major order varies the subscripts in left to right order. For example the elements of a 2-dimensional array A[4] [3] would be stored in the sequence as given below :

A[0] [0]
A[1] [0]
A[2] [0]
A[3] [0]
.
.
.
.
A[0] [2]
A[1] [2]
A[2] [2]
A[3] [2]

Sparse Arrays

Sparse arrays are special arrays which arise commonly in applications. It is difficult to draw the dividing line between the sparse and non-sparse array. Loosely an array is called sparse if it has a relatively number of zero elements. For example in Figure below, out of 49 elements, only 6 are non-zero This is a sparse array.

0	0	0	0	0	1	0
0	0	0	0	1	0	0
0	0	0	0	0	0	0
0	0	0	0	3	0	0
0	2	0	0	0	0	0
0	0	0	0	4	0	0
0	0	0	0	2	0	0

Figure : A Sparse Array

CS-62 : 'C' PROGRAMMING AND DATA STRUCTURE
JUNE 2005

Note : *Question no. 1 is* ***compulsory.*** *Answer any* ***three*** *questions from the rest. Algorithm should be written nearer to 'C' language.*

1(a) Write the syntax of any five file handling commands supported by 'C'. **[5]**

(i) A call to fopen( ) to read the file **passbook.dat** looks like.
fopen (passbook.dat","r")

(ii) To connect your program to the file that fopen opens, your program must also declare a pointer of type FILE as :

FILE * file_ptr;

Now you can assign to fileptr the pointer that fopen returned: file_ptr = fopen ("passbook.dat", "r');
(iii) fscanf(file_ptr, "control string", list of pointers);
(iv) fwrite(numbers, sizeof(double), NUM_EL, f1)* ;
(v) fread(copy, sizeof(double), NUM_EL, f1);

(b) Write a 'C' program to count the number of characters and lines in a text file whose name is supplied command line. **[5]**

```
#include<stdio.h>
main(int argc,char *argv[])
{
FILE *fs,*ft;
char ch;
int nol=0,noc=0;

if(argc!=2)
{
puts("Insufficient arguments");
getch();
exit(0);
}

fs=fopen(argv[1],"r");
if(fs==NULL)
{
puts("Cannot open file");
```

```
getch();
exit(0);
}
while(1)
{
ch=fgetc(fs);
if(ch==EOF)
break;
noc++;
if(ch=='\n')
nol++;
}
fclose(fs);
printf("Number of characters=%d",noc);
printf("\nNumber of lines=%d",nol);
getch();
}
```

(c) Define an adjacency matrix and an adjacency list. Create an adjacency list and an adjacency matrix for the following graph: [6]

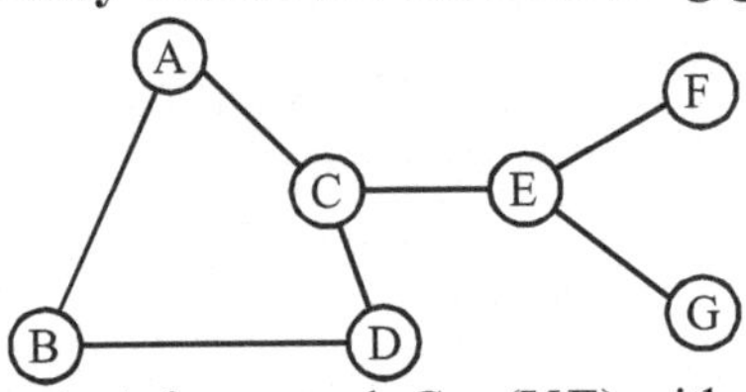

The adjacency matrix A for a graph G = (V,E) with n vertices, is an nxn matrix of bits, such that

A_{ij} = 1, iff there is an edge from vi to vj and

A_{ij} = 0, if there is no such edge.

In this representation, we store a graph as a linked structure. We store all the vertices in a list and then for each vertex, we have a linked list of its adjacent vertices. Let vertex number for A=0, B=1, C=2, D=3, E=4, F=5, G=6

Adjacency Matrix will be :

$$
\begin{array}{c} \\ 0 \\ 1 \\ 2 \\ 3 \\ 4 \\ 5 \\ 6 \end{array}
\begin{array}{c} \begin{array}{ccccccc} 0 & 1 & 2 & 3 & 4 & 5 & 6 \end{array} \\
\begin{bmatrix}
0 & 1 & 1 & 0 & 0 & 0 & 0 \\
1 & 0 & 0 & 1 & 0 & 0 & 0 \\
1 & 0 & 0 & 1 & 1 & 0 & 0 \\
0 & 1 & 1 & 0 & 0 & 0 & 0 \\
0 & 0 & 1 & 0 & 0 & 1 & 1 \\
0 & 0 & 0 & 0 & 1 & 0 & 1 \\
0 & 0 & 0 & 0 & 1 & 1 & 0
\end{bmatrix} \end{array}
$$

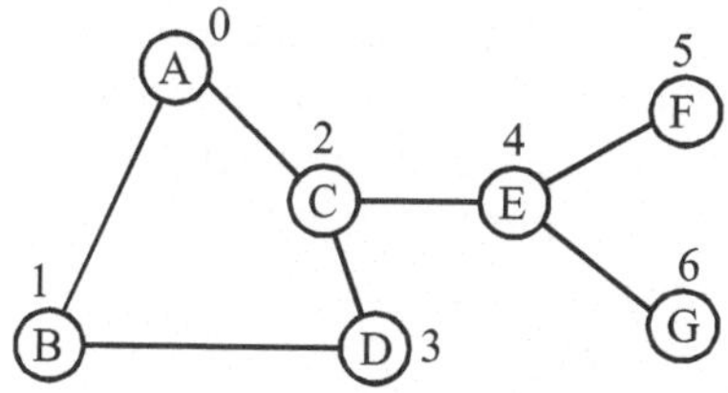

Adjacency List will be :

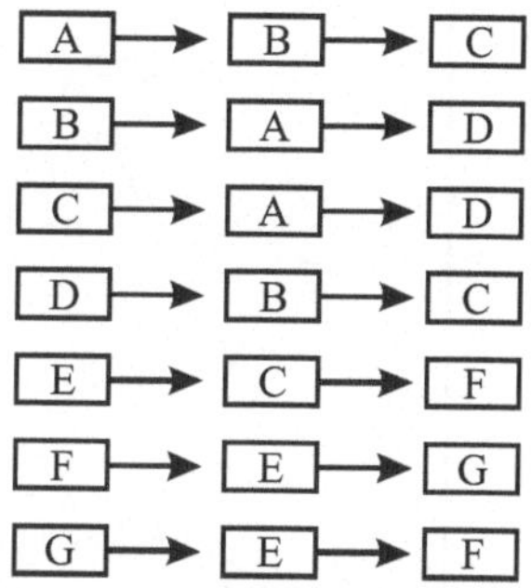

(d) Define a graph. Explain at least two traversal techniques in graphs. [4]

A Graph G consists of a set V of vertices (nodes) and a set E of edges (arcs). We write G=(V,E). V is a finite and non empty set of vertices. E is a set of pairs of vertices; these pairs are called edges. Therefore V(G), read as V of G, is set of vertices, and E(G), read as E of G, is set of edges.

An edge e = (v,w), is a pair of vertices v and w, and is said to be incident with v and w. A graph may be pictorially represented as given in Figure 1.

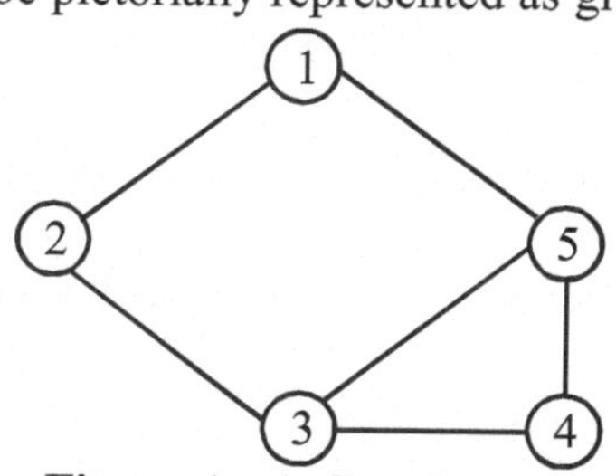

Figure 1 : A Graph

Depth First Search (DFS)

In graphs, we do not have any start vertex or any special vertex singled out to start traversal from. Therefore the traversal may start from any arbitrary vertex. We start with say, vertex v. An adjacent vertex is selected and a Depth First Search is initiated from it, i.e. let V_1, V_2 .. V_k are adjacent vertices to vertex v. We may select any vertex from this list. Say, we select v_1 . Now all the adjacent vertices to v1 are identified and all of those are visited; next V2 is selected and all its adjacent vertices visited and so on. This process continues till all the vertices are visited. It is very much possible that we reach a traversed vertex second time. Therefore we have to set a flag somewhere to check if the vertex is already visited. Let us see it through an example. Consider the following graph on the next page :

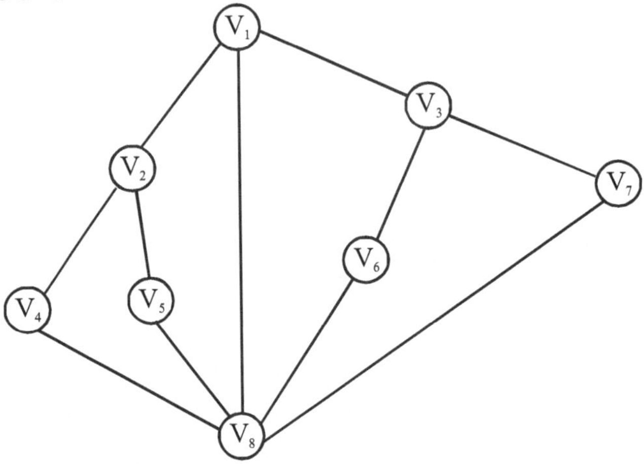

Let us start with V_1.

Its adjacent vertices are V_2, V_8 and V_3. Let us pick on V_2.

Its adjacent vertices are V_1, V_4, V_5. V_1 is already visited. Let us pick on V_4.

Its adjacent vertices are V_2, V_8. V_2 is already visited. Let us visit V_8. Its adjacent vertices are V_4, V_5, V_1, V_6, V_7.

V_4 and V_1, are already visited. Let us traverse V_5. Its adjacent vertices are V2, V_8. Both are already visited Therefore, we back track. We had V_6 and V_7 unvisited in the list of V_8. We may visit any. We visit V6. Its adjacent are V6. and V_3. Obviously the choice is V_3. Its adjacent vertices are V_1, V_7 . We visit V_7.

All the adjacent vertices of V_7 are already visited, we back track and find that we have visited all the vertices.

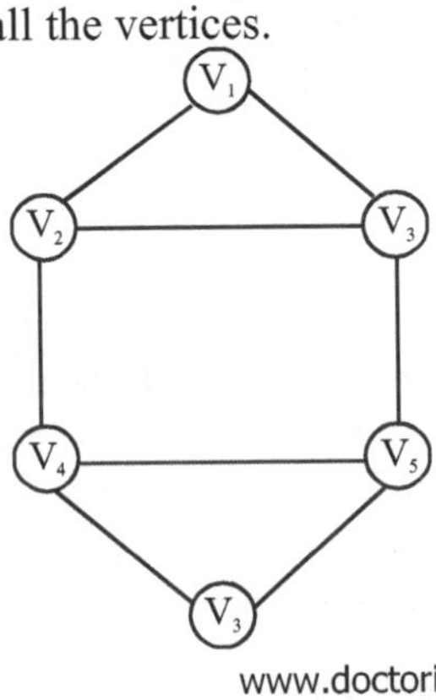

Therefore the sequence of traversal is
$V_1, V_2, V_4, V_8, V_5, V_6, V_3, V_7$.

Breadth First Search (BFS)

In DFS we pick on one of the adjacent vertices; visit all of its adjacent vertices and back track to visit the unvisited adjacent vertices. In BFS, we first visit all the adjacent vertices of the start vertex and then visit all -the unvisited vertices adjacent to these and so on. Let us consider the same example, given in Figure. We start say, with V_1. Its adjacent vertices are V_2, V_8, V_3. We visit all one by one. We pick on one of these, say V_2. The unvisited adjacent vertices to V_2 are V_4, V_5. We visit both. We go back to the remaining visited vertices of V_1 and pick on one of those, say V_3. The unvisited adjacent vertices to v_3 are V_6, V_7. There are no more unvisited adjacent vertices of V_8, V_4, V_5, V_6 and V_7. Thus, the sequence so generated is V_1, V_2, V_8, V_3, V_4, V_5, V_6, V_7.

(e) What do you understand by a height balanced tree. Construct a height balanced tree for the following list : [5]

5, 10, 0, 7, 8, 2, 6, 3

Below is the height balanced tree for the given numbers :

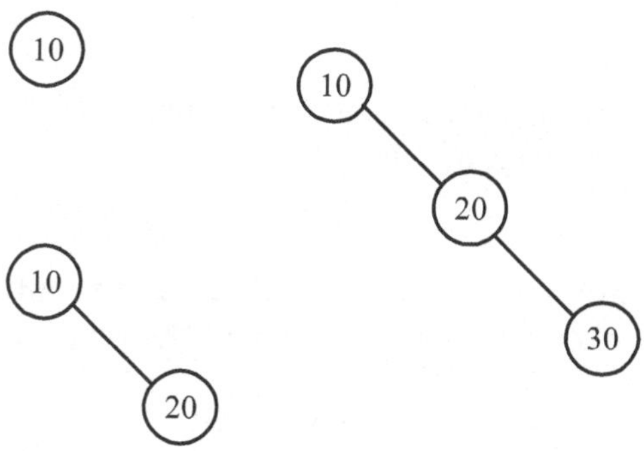

(f) Write an algorithm to sort a list using quick sort. Show it's operations on the following list : [5]

5, 10, 3, 0, 15, 7, 3

```
Quicksort(A, low, high)
        pivot = A[low]
        leftwall = low
        for i = low + 1 to high
                if(A[i] < pivot) then
                                leftwall = leftwall + 1
                                swap(A[i], A[leftwall])
                swap(A[low],A[leftwall])
```

List {⑤,10,3,0,15,7,3}
Let 5 be pivot, start scanning from right i.e. 3 >>5 exchange them.
{7,10,3,0,15,⑤,3}
Let 5 be pivot, start scanning from left i.e. from left i.e. 7
3 < 5 exchange them
{7,10,⑤,0,15,3,3}
Again from right
15 > 5 exchange them
{7,10,15,0,⑤,3,3}
Again from left
0 < 5 exchange them
{7,10,15} 5{0,3,3}
5 gets its position
In left list take 7 as pivot. In right take 0 as pivot
{⑦,10,15} 5 {⓪,3,3}
15 > 7 exchange 15 and 7   3 > 0 exchange 3 and 0
{15,10,⑦} 5 {3,3,⓪}
Again from left. A in both lists
7 and 0 get their positions.
{⑮,10} 7,5 {③,3} 0
Taking left list and 15 as pivot 15 gets its position, so as 10 in right list taking 3 as pivot both 3's get their position.
Final 15,10,7,5,3,3,0

2(a) What is a singly linked list ? Mention any two advantage of singly linked list Give linked list representation of the following sparse matrix: [5]

$$\begin{bmatrix} 0 & 1.2 & 0 & 3 \\ 0 & 0 & 0 & 0 \\ 0.5 & 0 & 1 & 0 \\ 0 & 1.5 & 0 & 0 \end{bmatrix}$$

The primary advantage of Linked Lists over arrays is that Linked Lists can grow and shrink in size during their lifetime. In particular, their maximum size need to be known in advance. In practical applications, this often makes it possible to have several data structures share the same space, without paying particular attention to their relative size at any time.
A second advantage of Linked List is that they provide flexibility in allowing the items to be rearranged efficiently. This flexibility is gained at the expense of quick access to any arbitrary item in the List.

Linked list representation of sparse matrix is given below :
1.2 at row=1 col=2
3 at row=1 col=4
0.5 at row=3 col=1
1 at row=3 col=3
1.5 at row=4 col=2
So, list becomes

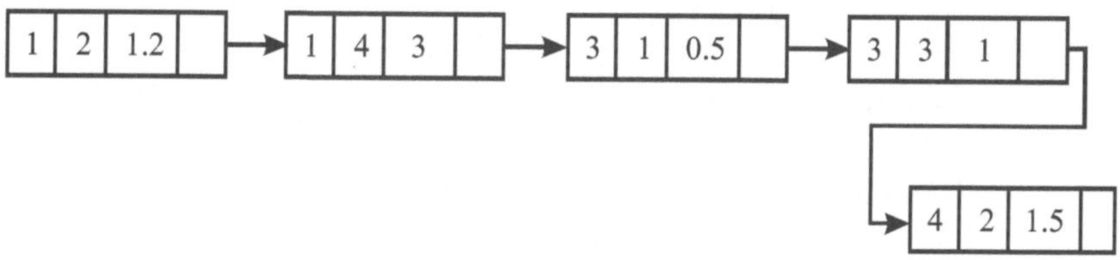

(b) What is a variable length argument ? Give an example of such an argument. How are variable length arguments passed to a function ?[5]

It is frequently necessary to deal with situations where the number of arguments in a function's call may be arbitrary. Two common examples are printf () and scanf (). There are three macros available in the file "stdarg.h" called **va_start, va_arg** and **va_list**

These macros provide a method for accessing the arguments of the functions when a function takes a fixed number of arguments followed by a variable number of arguments. The fixed number of arguments are accessed in the normal way, whereas the optimal arguments are accessed using the macros **va_start** and **va_arg**. Out of these macros **va_start** is used to initialize a pointer to the beginning of the list of optional arguments. On the other hand the macro **va_arg** is used to advance the pointer to the next argument. Let us put these concepts into action using a program. Suppose we wish to write a function **findmax**( ) which would find out the maximum value from a set of values, irrespective of the number of values passed to it.

```
# include "stdarg.h"
        main( )
        {
    int max ;

    max = findmax (5, 23, 15, 1, 92, 50) ;
    printf ("\nmaximum = %d", max) ;
        }

        findmax (int tot_num)
        {
```

```
int max, count_num ;
va_list ptr ;
va_start (ptr, tot_num) ;
max = va_arg (ptr, int) ;

for (count = 1 ; count < tot_nun ; count++)
    {
    nun = va_arg (ptr, int) ;
    if (num > max)
            max = num ;
        }
        return (max) ;
    }
```

Here, we are making two calls to findmax( ) first time to find maximum out 5 values and second time to find maximum out of 3 values. Note that for each call the first argument is the count of arguments that follow the first argument. The value of the first argument passed to **findmax( )** is collected in the values **tot_num. findmax( )** begins with a declaration of a pointer **ptr** of the type **va_list**. Observe the next statement carefully

va_start (ptr) ;

This statement sets up **ptr** such that it points to the first variable argument in the list. If we are considering the first call to **findmax**( ) **ptr** would assign the integer being pointed to by **ptr** to **max**. Thus 23 would be assigned to **max**, and **ptr** would now start pointing to the next argument i.e., 15. The rest of the program is fairly straight forward. We just keep picking up successive numbers in the list and keep comparing them with the latest value in **max**, till all the arguments in the list have been scanned. The final value in **max** is then returned to **main**( ).

3(a) Write a program in 'C' language that accepts a number as input and prints it in words. (For example, if 256 is the input number, then 'Two hundred and fifty six' is the output.) **[5]**

```
#include<iostream.h>
#include<string.h>
#include<conio.h>
#include<stdlib.h>

class hps
{
public:
hps(void);
```

```
~hps(void);
int initno(int x);
int hdred(int x);
};
hps::hps(void)
{}
hps::~hps(void)
{}
int hps::hdred(int x)
{
switch(x)
{
case 1:cout<<" one hundred";
      break;
case 2:cout <<" two hundred";
      break;
case 3:cout <<" three hundred";
      break;
case 4:cout<<" four hundred ";
      break;
case 5:cout<<" five hundred";
      break;
case 6:cout<<" six hundred";
      break;
case 7:cout<<" seven hundred";
      break;
case 8:cout<<" eight hundred ";
      break;
case 9:cout<<" nine hundred"; break;
}
return 0;
}

int hps::initno(int x)
{
switch (x)
{
case 1: cout<<" one";
         break;
case 2: cout<<" two";
         break;
```

```
case 3:  cout<<" three";
         break;
case 4:  cout<<" four";
         break;
case 5:  cout<<" five";
         break;
case 6:  cout<<" six";
         break;
case 7:  cout<<" seven";
         break;
case 8:  cout<<" eight ";
         break;
case 9:  cout<<" nine";
         break;
case 10:cout<<" ten";
         break;
case 20:cout<<" twenty";
         break;
case 30:cout<<" thirty";
         break;
case 40:cout<<" fourty";
         break;
case 50:cout<<" fifty";
         break;
case 60:cout<<" sixty";
         break;
case 70:cout<<" seventy";
         break;
case 80:cout<<" eighty";
         break;
case 90:cout<<" ninety";
         break;
}
return 0;}

main ()
{
clrscr();
hps x;
long x1=0,x2=0,pick,getnext;
char *pr,ix[200];
```

```
 cout<<"Enter number to convert:";
 cin>>ix;
 pr=ix;
 pick=atol(pr);
 long z1=0;
 long z2=0;
 z1=pick/1000;
 getnext =z1*1000;
 if (z1>0 && z1<21 || z1==20 || z1==30 || z1==40 || z1==50
    || z1==60 || z1==70 || z1== 80 || z1==90 )
    {
          x.initno (z1);
          cout<<" thousand";
    }
 else{
 if (z1 >20)
    {
          z2 =z1/10;
          z2 = z2*10;
          x.initno(z2);
          z2=z1%10;
          x.initno(z2);
          cout<<" thousand";
    }}
long y1=0, newx;
newx=pick-getnext;
y1=newx/100;
if(y1>0)
x.hdred(y1);
x1=pick%100;
if (x1>0 && x1<21 || x1==20 || x1 ==30 || x1==40
   || x1==50 || x1==60 || x1==70 || x1==80 || x1==90)
   {
         x. initno (y1);
   }
   else{
if(x1>20)
   {
         x2=x1/10;
         x2=x2*10;
         x.initno (x2);
```

```
        x2=x1%10;
        x.initno (x2);
   }}
cout<<endl;
getche();
return 0;
}
```

(b) Write 'C' program which accepts a stack as input and reverses the elements of stack using one additional queue. [5]

```
#include<stdio.h>
main()
{
struct st_node{int data;
              struct st_node*link;
             }*top;
struct st_node *temp;
struct qu_node{int data;
              struct qu_node*link;
             }*rear,*front;
struct qu_node *t;

int n,i,a[20];
clrscr();
top=NULL;
front=rear=NULL;
printf("How many elements:");
scanf("%d",&n);
printf("Enter the elements");
                                        //filling the stack
for(i=0;i<n;i++)
scanf("%d",&a[i]);
i--;

for(;i>=0;i--)
{
temp=(struct st_node*)malloc(sizeof(struct st_node));
temp->data=a[i];
temp->link=top;
top=temp;
}
```

```
temp=top; //catching the top
printf("The stack elements are:");
while(top!=NULL)
{printf("\n%d",top->data);
top=top->link;}
top=temp;//resetting top
//Filling Queue,emptying stack
while(top!=NULL)
{
temp=top;
t=(struct qu_node*)malloc(sizeof(struct qu_node));
t->data=temp->data;
top=top->link;
free(temp);
t->link=NULL;
if(front==NULL)
{
rear=front=t;
}
rear->link=t;
rear=rear->link;
}

//filling stack,emptying queue
while(front!=NULL)
{
temp=(struct st_node*)malloc(sizeof(struct st_node));
temp->data=front->data;
temp->link=top;
top=temp;
t=front;
front=front->link;
free(t);
}
printf("\nQueue operating");
delay(2000);
printf("\nNow the stack elements are:");
while(top!=NULL)
{
printf("\n%d",top->data);
temp=top;
```

```
top=top->link;
free(temp);
}
getch();
}
```

4(a) What is garbage collection ? Explain the process of Fragmentation, Relocation, and Compaction w.r.t. garbage collection. [8]

Deallocation of nodes can take place in two levels:

1. The application which claimed the node releases it back to the operating system.
2. The operating system calls storage management routines to return free nodes to the free space.

For example, Deallocation as in (1) occurs in a C, program with the statement 'free(x)' where x is space earlier allocated by a 'malloc' call. (2) is usually implemented by the method of **Garbage Collection.** This requires the presence of a 'Marking' bit on each node. It runs in two phases. In the first phase, all non-garbage nodes are marked. In the second phase all non-marked nodes are collected and returned to the free space. Where variable size nodes are used it is desirable to keep the free space as one contiguous block, in this case, the second phase is called Memory compaction.

Garbage Collection is usually called when some program runs out of space. It is a slow process and its use should be obviated by efficient programming methods.

Fragmentation literally means splitting. That the 'Best fit'& 'First fit' algorithms result in creation of small blocks of space. These constitute wastage of space as they can be used to satisfy only requests for small blocks. This can be illustrated by the following example:

Consider the following space divided into three nodes of size 100 each.

A (Size : 100)	
B (Size : 100)	
C (Size : 100)	

The following have to be allocated using first fit:

1. Size 50. This can be allocated from A. So we get.

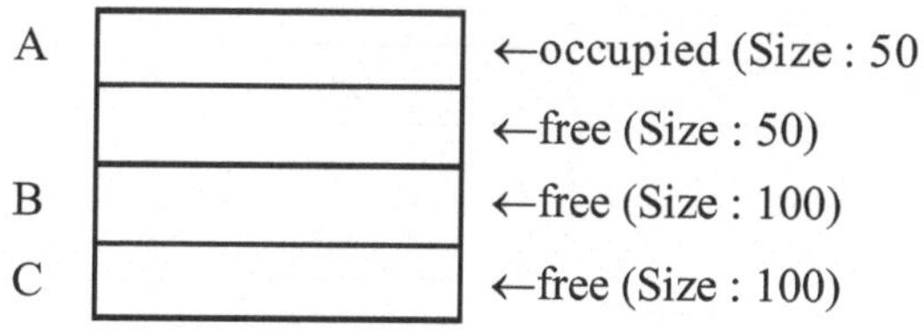

2. Size 80. This can be allocated from B.

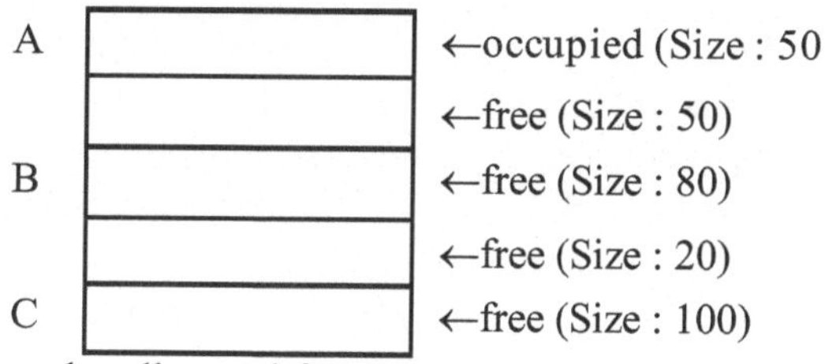

3. Size 20. This can be allocated from A.

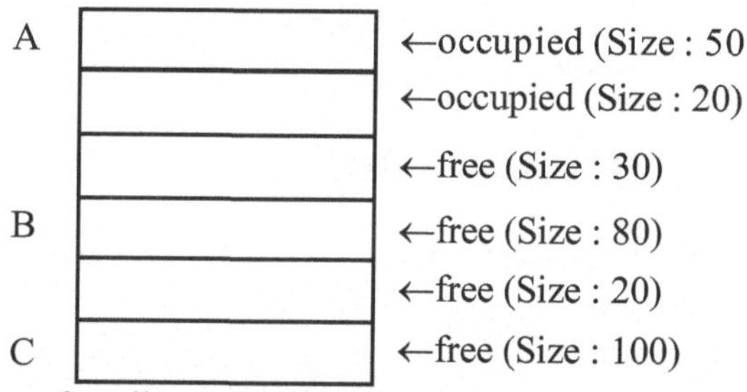

4. Size 50. This can be allocated from C.

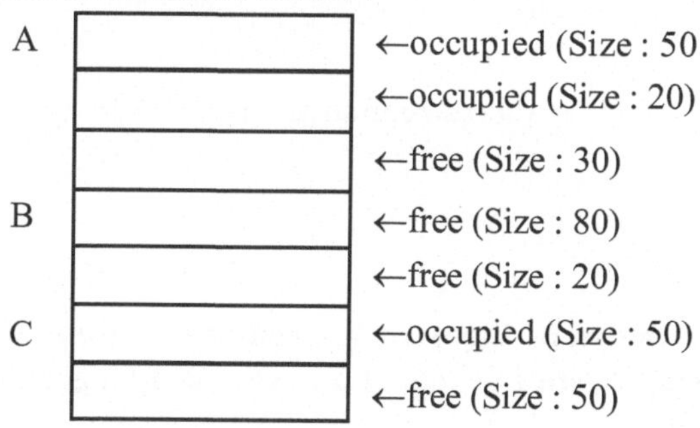

5. Size 75

Now there is no contiguous block of size 75 though the actual space available is 30+20+50=100. In this state of fragmentation, only requests of size<= 50 can be satisfied.

This calls for 'Relocation of the allocated blocks A[0-70], B[0-80], and C[0-50], so that the free blocks A[70-100], B[80-100], and C[50-100] can be 'Compacted' to form one free block of size 100.

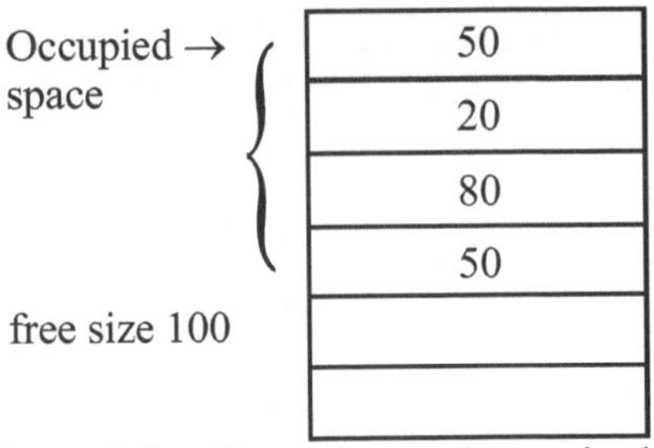

The relocation of B and C will result in a change in their address. This change must be reflected wherever B and C are used.

Relocation & Compaction usually form the second phase of Garbage collection, A[0-70], B[0-80], and C[0-50] constitute the 'non-garbage' nodes or 'marked nodes' which are relocated and A[70-1001, B[80-100], and C[S0-100] are the garbage nodes which are 'compacted' to release space.

(b) Consider the following declaration :

```
struct list_node
  { int data;
        struct list_node link;
  };
```

Write an algorithm to insert a value 'M' after the last node in the Singly Linked List. **[2]**

```
struct list_node *temp, *t;
temp=head;
while(temp—>link!=NULL)
temp=temp—>link;
t=(struct list_node *) malloc(sizeof(struct list_node));
t—>data=M;
t—>link=NULL;
temp—>link=t;
```

5(a) Describe the steps involved in creating a minimum cost spanning tree from a graph with the help of an example of a graph consisting of at least 4 vertices. **[5]**

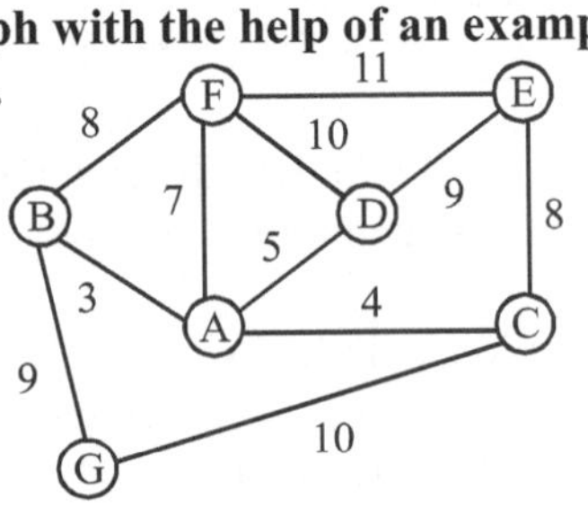

Figure 1

We need to select n-1 edges in G (of n vertices) such that these form an MCST. We begin by first selecting an edge with least cost. It can be between any two vertices of G.. Subsequently, from the set of remaining edges, we can select another least cost edge and so on. Each time an edge is picked, we determine whether or not the inclusion of this edge into the spanning tree being constructed creates a cycle. If it does, this edge is discarded. If no cycle is created, this edge is included in the spanning tree being constructed. Let us work it out through an example. Consider the graph given in Figure 1. The minimum cost edge is that connects vertex A and B. Let us choose that.

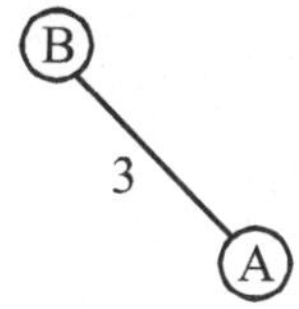

Now we have

Vertices that may be added	**Edge**	**Cost**
F	BF	8
	AF	7
G	BG	9
C	AC	4
D	AD	5

The least cost edge is AC; therefore we choose AC. Now we have

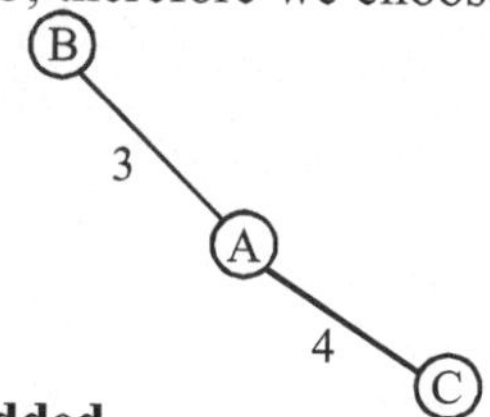

Vertices that may be added	**Edge**	**Cost**
F	BF	8
	AF	7
G	BG	9
	CG	10
D	AD	5
E	CE	8

The least cost edge is AD; therefore we choose AD. Now we have

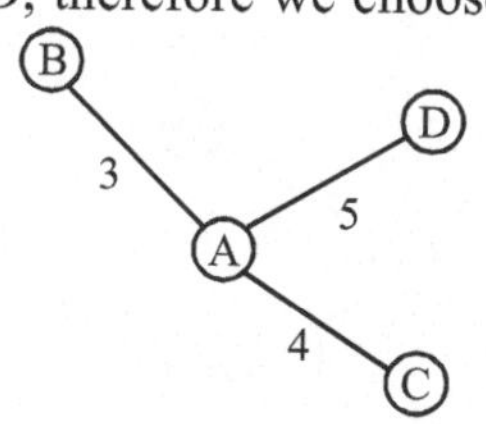

Vertices that may be added	**Edge**	**Cost**
F	BF	8
	AF	8
	DF	10
G	BG	9
	CG	10
E	CE	8
	DE	9

AF is the minimum cost edge; therefore, we add it to the partial tree. Now we have

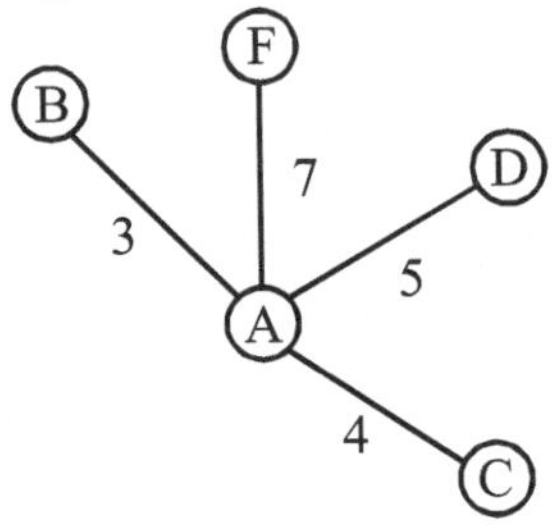

Vertices that may be added	**Edge**	**Cost**
G	BG	9
	CG	10
E	CE	8
	DE	9
	FE	11

Obvious choice is CE

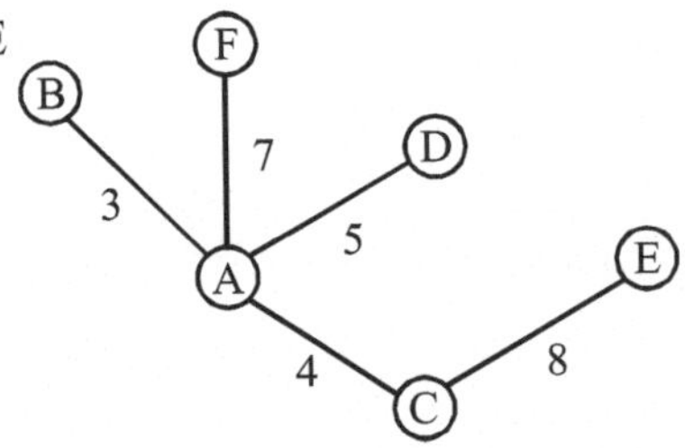

The only vertex left is G and we have the minimum cost edge that connects it to the tree constructed so far is BG. Therefore we add it and the minimal spanning tree constructed would be of the costs 9+3+7+5+4+8 = 36; and is given in Figure below.

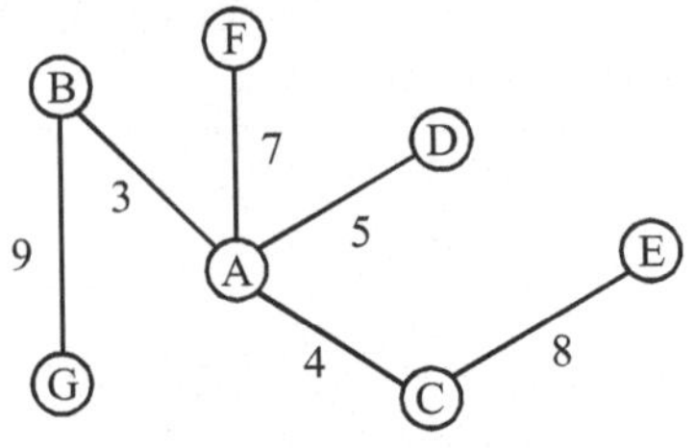

This method is called the Kruskal's method of creating a MST.

(b) Write at least two differences between a Structure and a Union in 'C' language. Give an example each of a structure and Union. [5]

The difference between structures and unions lies in the way their members are stored and initialized, as follows:

- Within a structure, the members have addresses that increase as the declarators are read left-to-right. That is, the members of a structure all begin at different offsets from the base of the structure. The offset of a particular member corresponds to the order of its declaration; the first member is at offset 0. A pointer to a structure points to its first member, so no unnamed holes can reside at the beginning of a structure.
- In a union, every member begins at offset 0 from the address of the union. The size of the union in memory is the size of its largest member. The value of only one member can be stored in a union object at a time. When the storage space allocated to the union contains a smaller member, the extra space between the end of the smaller member and the end of the allocated memory remains unaltered. A pointer to a union member, converted to the proper type, points to the beginning of the union object.
- Several members of a structure can be initialized at once; only the first member of a union can be given an initialiser.

Example of structure :

```
structure book
{
        char name ;
        float price ;
        int pages ;
};
structure book b1 = {'B' 130,00, 550};
```

b1. name	b1. price	b1. pages
'B'	130.00	550

Example of union :

```
Union a
{
        int i ;
        char ch[2] ;
};
```

union a key ;

Representation of this data type in memory is shown below.

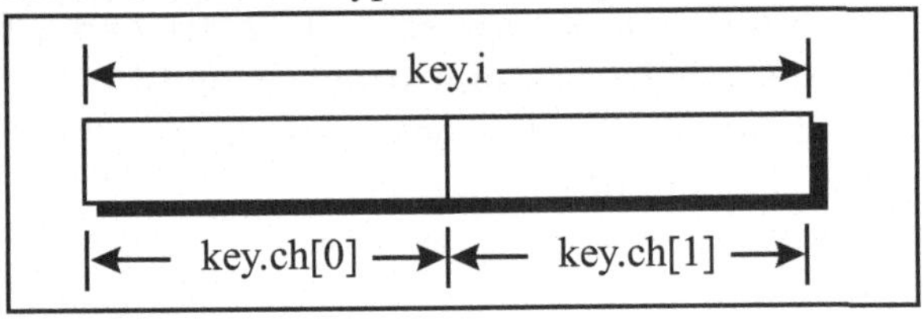

CS-62 : 'C' PROGRAMMING AND DATA STRUCTURE
DECEMBER, 2005

Note : Question no.1 is **compulsory.** Answer any **three** questions from the rest. All algorithms should be written nearer to 'C' language.

Q1(a). Write a non-recursive function to traverse a binary tree using inorder traversal. [10]

Ans. Inord (Info, Left, right, root)

A binary tree is in memory. This algorithm does an in order traversal of T, applying an operation process to each of its nodes. An array STACK is used to temporarily hold the addresses of nodes.

1. [Push NULL onto STACK and initialize PTR]
Set TOP: =1, STACK [1]: =NULL and PTR: = ROOT.
2. Repeat while PTR ≠ NULL :[Pushes left-most path onto STACK]
(a) Set TOP: = TOP=1 and STACK [TOP:=PTR. [Save node]
(b) Set PTR: = Left [ptr]. [update PTR]
[End of loop]
3. Set PTR: =STACK [TOP] and TOP:=TOP-1. [Pops node from STACK]
4. Repeat Steps 5 to 7 while PTR ≠ NULL. [Back tracking]
5. Apply Process to info [ptr]
6. [Right child?] if Right [ptr] ≠ NULL, then:
(a) Set ptr: = Right [ptr]
(b) Go to Step 2
[End of if structure]
7. Set PTR: = STACK [TOP] and TOP: =TOP-1, [Pops node]
[End of step 4 loop]
8. Exit.

(b) What is sparse array? Write an algorithm to represent a sparse array using a linked list. Using the data structure created above, write an algorithm for finding the transpose of the sparse array. [10]

Ans. Refer to Q5(ii), June 2006.

Algorithm to represent a sparse array using a linked list: -

We can represent a sparse array through single linked list where each will have the following information: -

· value
· Link (Pointer) to next non-zero node.

```
Struct node
{
   int val;
   struct node *link;
}
```

Algo :

Step 1: [check the link list is null or not]
Repeat while (P → link | =NULL)
P = P → link;
End while

Step 2: [Allocate memory]
temp =malloc (size of (struct node))

Step 3: Repeat for I=0 to index
If (a[i]>0)
temp → val =a[i]
temp → link =NULL
P → link =temp
[End if]

Step 4: Exit

Algorithm for finding the transpose of the Sparse Array:

Step 1: [Transpose of sparse Array]
Repeat for i= 0,1,2,3,. …….. index-1
Transpose [i] = a [i]

Step 2: Exit

(c) Write an algorithm for the implementation of a 2-way merge sort. What is its time complexity? Sort the following sequence of numbers using 2-way merge sort: [10]

7, 4, 1, 3, 0, 2, 6, 5

Ans. Two way merge_sort (A, start, finish)

Step 1: [Compute the size of the current sub_table]
Size =finish_start+1

Step 2: [Test base condition for sub-tables of size one]
If size<=1
then
Return.

Step 3: [calculate midpoint position of current sub-table]
mid = start + size/2 –1

Step 4: [Recursively sort the first sub_table]

```
        Call two way merge-sort (A, start, mid)
Step 5: [Recursively sort the second sub-table]
        Call two way merge_sort (A, Mid+1, finish)
Step 6: Call simple_merge (A, start, mid+1, finish)
Step 7: Return
```

Merge sort Algo

```
        Merge-sort (A, m,n)
Step 1: [compute middle index value]
            mid =m+n/2
Step 2: [test non equality of M&N]
        If M ≠ N
        Call merge-pass (A, m, mid)
        Call merge –pass (a, mid+1, n)
        Call merge-sort (a, m, mid, n)
Step 3: Return
```

Merge_ Pas Algo.

```
        Merge_ pass (A, Top, size, Bottom)
Step 1: [Initialization]
        F=top
        S=size +1
        T =Top
Start 2: [start merging from here]
Repeat through step while f<=size & size< = Bottom
        If A[f] <=A[S]
        then
        Temp P [T]= A[f]
        f=f+1
        else
        Temp [T] =A[S]
        S=S+1
Step 3: T=T+1
Step 4:
        if f<=size
        then
        Repeat for f=f, f+1,f+2…..size
        Temp [T]= A[f]
        T=T+1
        `else
        Repeat for S= S, S+1, S+2…. Bottom
```

Temp p[T]= A[S]
T=T+1

Step 5:

Repeat for upper= Top , Top+1, Top+2…….Bottom
A[upper] =Temp [upper]

Step 6: Return.

Time Complexity:

Worst case	Average case	Extra memory
n logn = 0 (n logn)	n logn =0 (n logn)	0 (n)

List: 7, 4, 1, 3, 0, 2, 6,5.

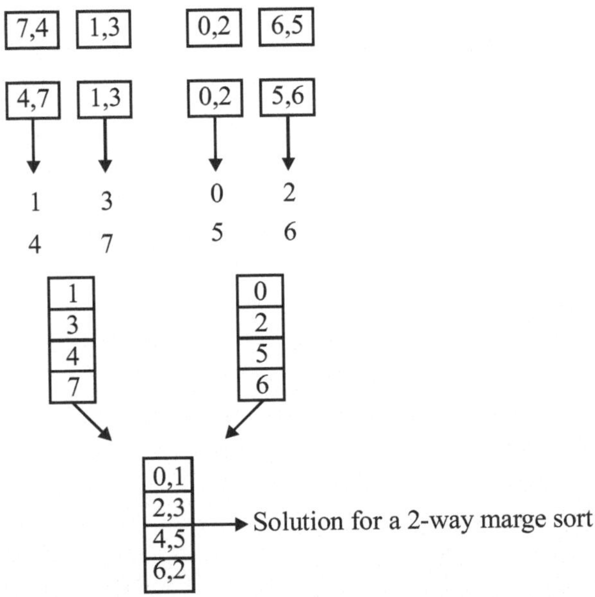

Q2(a). A 3-dimensional integer array X [4] [5] [3] is stored using the column-major order. What will the address of X [2] [3] [1] be if the base address is 100? Also, calculate the address if the array is stored using row-major order. [5]

Ans. Given information:

Array - X[4][5][3]
Base Address –100
Address Calculated for X [2][3][1]?

(i) Column Major order form.

$$\text{Address of } A[i_1,i_2,i_3] = \alpha + \begin{bmatrix} (i_1\text{-}LB_1)(UB_3\text{-}LB_3+1)(UB_2\text{-}LB_3+1) \\ +(i_2\text{-}LB_2)(UB_2\text{-}LB_2+1)+ \\ (i_3\text{-}LB_3) \end{bmatrix} *S$$

In question :

α = base address =100

S = 2 (integer)

$i_1=2$

$i_2=3$

$i_3=1$

$$=100+\begin{bmatrix}(2+1)(3-1+1)(3-1+1) \\ +(3-1)(3-1+1)+(1-2)\end{bmatrix}*2$$

=100+[17]*2

=100+34

=134

Row major Order from:

$$A[i_1,i_2,i_3]=\alpha+\begin{bmatrix}(i_1\text{-}LB_1)(UB_2\text{-}LB_2+1)(UB_3\text{-}LB_3+1) \\ +(i_2\text{-}LB_2)(UB_3\text{-}LB_3)+(i_3\text{-}LB_3)\end{bmatrix}*S$$

$$=100+\begin{bmatrix}(2\text{-}1)(5\text{-}1+1)(3\text{-}1+1)+(3\text{-}1)(3\text{-}1+1) \\ +(1\text{-}1)\end{bmatrix}*S$$

=100+(21*2)

=100+42

=142

(b) Write an algorithm for creation of a doubly linked list. Also, write an algorithm for deletion of elements from a doubly linked list. [5]

Refer to Dec, 2006.

Then Refer to Page No. 204, Q2(b).

Q3(a). Define the following: [5]

(i) Syntax for a typedef statement

* You can create synonyms or aliases to a previously defined data type by using the typedef statement

The syntax of the typedef statement is:

* typedef existingTypeName newTypeName;
* typedef does not create any new data types
* typedef creates an alias to an existing data type

(ii) Digraphs
Refer to Page No. 131.

(iii) Adjacency Matrix
Refer to Page No. 203.

(iv) Garbage Collection
Refer to Page No. 191.

(v) Height-balanced tree
Refer to Page No. 214.

(b) Write an algorithm to evaluate the postfix expression. Draw the expression tree for the following postfix expression: **[5]**

a b + c * d e / f * - g h * +

Ans. Algorithm: POLISH (Q, P)

Suppose Q is an arithmetic expression written in infix notation. This algorithm finds the equivalent postfix expression P.

1. Push "("onto STACK, and add ")" to the end of Q.

2. Scan Q from left to right and repeat Steps 3 to 6 for each element of Q until the STACK is empty.

3. If an operand is encountered, add it to P.

4. If a left parenthesis is encountered, push it onto STACK

5. If an operator ⊗ is encountered, then:

(a) Repeatedly pop from STACK and add to P each operator (on the top of STACK), which has the same precedence as or higher precedence than s.

(b) Add ⊗ to STACK.

[End of If structure.]

6. If a right parenthesis is encountered, then:

(a) Repeatedly pop from STACK and add to P each operator (on the top of STACK until a left parenthesis is encountered.

(b) Remove the left parenthesis. [Do not add the left paren-thesis to P.]

[End of If structure.]

[End of Step 2.loop]

7. Exit.

Postfix=ab+c*de*|f*-gh*+

its

infix=(a+b)*c-(d/e)*f+(g*h)

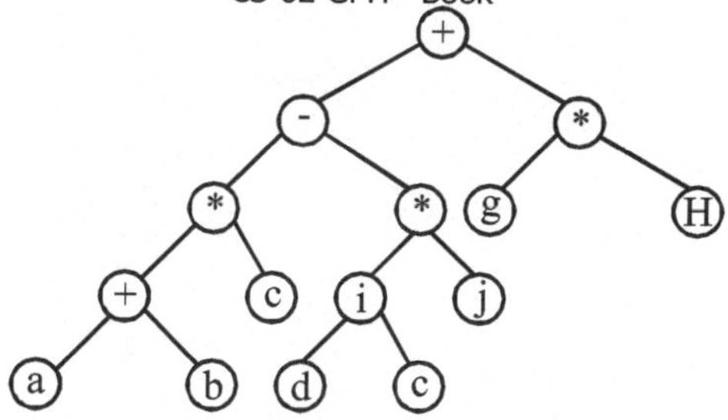

Q4(a). Consider the following graph diagram.

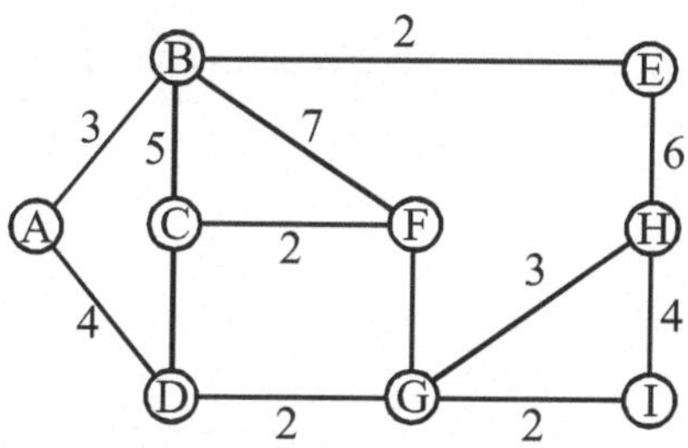

Construct a minimum cost spanning tree. Also, give the minimum cost.

Step1: We take A

Step2: 4

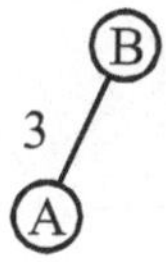

Step3:

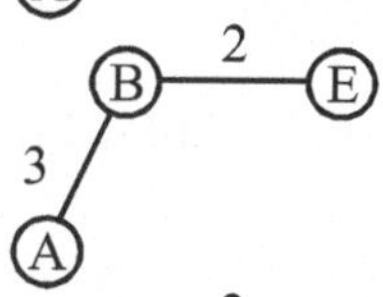

Step 4:

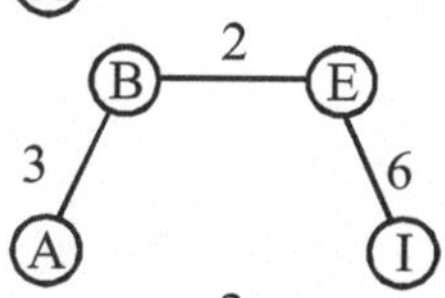

Step 5:

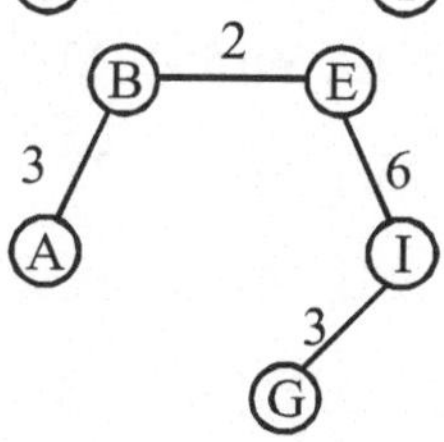

Step 6:

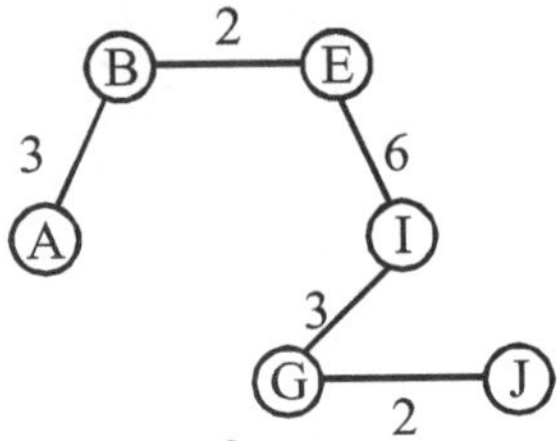

Step 7:

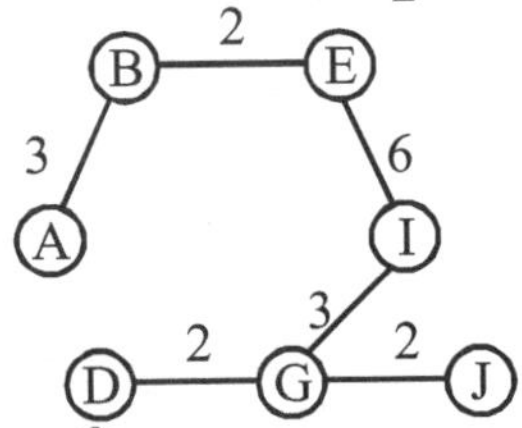

Step 8:

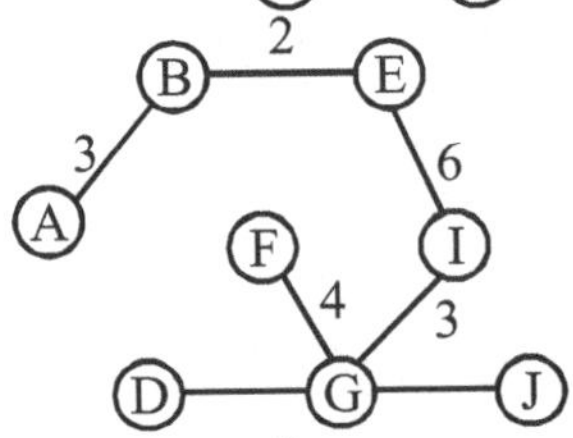

Step9:

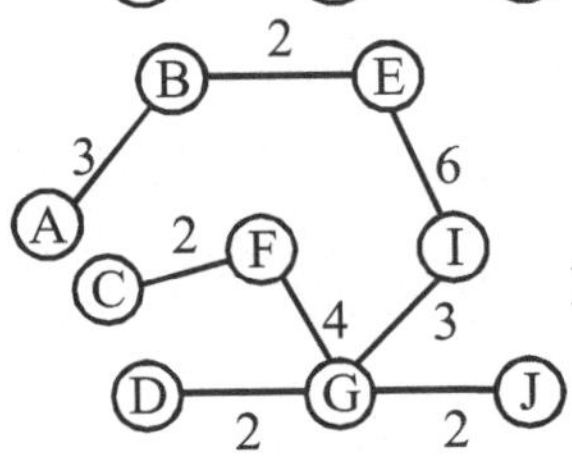

Minimum Cost = 22

(b) Using Quick sort, sort the following sequence in descending order: 25, 12, 9, 30, 15, 50

What is the average run time complexity of Quick sort? [5]

It the list be

$$\{25, 12, 9, 30, 15, 50\}$$

Let pivot=25 and we can initiate from 50

$$\{(25), 12, 9, 30, 15, 50\}\, 50 > 25$$

$$\{50, 12, 9, 30, 15, (25)\}\, 15 < 25$$

$$\{50, 12, 9, 30, (25), 15\}\, 9 < 25$$

$$\{50, 12, (25), 9, 30, 15\}\, 30 > 25$$

$$\{50, 12, 30, (25), 9, 15\}\, 12 < 25$$

{50, (25), 30, 12, 9, 15,} 30 > 25

{50, 30, (25), 12, 9, 15,}

pivot=25 at perfect position so break in two sublist.

{50, 30} 25 {12, 9,15, }

Left sublist   Right Sublist

Pivot = 50 for left sublist
Pivot = 20 for right sublist

{50, 30} 25 {(12), 9,15, }

50, 30, 25, {15, 9, (12)} 15>12

50, 30, 25, {15, 12, 9}9<12

Pivot=12 at perfect position so

| 50 30 25 15 12 9 | sorted

Average runtime complexity of quick sort is O(nlogn)

Q5(a). Write a function which accepts a stack as input and reverses the elements of the stack using one additional queue. [5]
Ans. Refer to Page No. 189.

(b) Write an algorithm to list the nodes of a Binary tree in the following way: List the root, then nodes at depth 1, followed by nodes at depth 2, and so on. [5]
Ans. Refer to Page No. 111.

CS-62 : 'C' PROGRAMMING AND DATA STRUCTURE
JUNE, 2006

Note : Question no.1 is **compulsory.** Answer any **three** questions from the rest. All algorithms should be written nearer to 'C' language.

Q1(a). Write a C function to convert the adjacency matrix of a graph to its adjacency list. Illustrate this C functions, using an example. [7]

Ans. Let G= (V, E) is graph with n vertices. This graph can be represented by $n \times n$ adjacency matrix. The n linked list represents the n rows of the adjacency matrix A and there is one linked list for each vertex in G. The vertices in list L represent the vertices that are adjacent to the vertex L, each vertex represented by two fields: Vertex & link. The vertex field contains the indices of the vertices adjacent to vertex L. The adjacency matrix for G is as follows: -

	V1	V2	V3	V4	V5	V6
V1	0	1	0	0	1	0
V2	0	0	1	1	1	0
V3	0	0	0	0	1	0
V4	1	0	1	0	0	1
V5	0	0	0	0	0	0
V6	0	1	0	0	1	0

The number of distinct unordered pairs (V_i, V_j) with $V_i \neq V_j$ in graph with n vertices is n (n-1)/2

:: function to convert the adjacency matrix of a graph to its adjacency list follows:

```
struct edge node
{
  edge node *next;
  int target;
  int weight;
};

// convert an adjacency matrix to an adjacency list
edge node ** matrix to list (int ** ad matrix, int num vertices)
{
  int i=0, j=0;
edge node ** adj list= (struct edge node*) malloc (size of (struct
```

```
                                        edge node)* (num vertices))
  for ( i =o; i< num vertices; i++)
          adj list  [i] =NULL;
 // for each row in the matrix
 for (i=0; i<num vertices; i++)
    {
     for (j=0; j< num vertices; j++) || convert row into a list
    {
     if (adj matrix [i][j]=0)
     {
          edge node * new node;
     new node = (struct edge node*) malloc (size of (struct edge node));
     new node  → target =j;
     new node  → weight =adj matrix × [i][j];
     new node  → next = adjust [i];
     adj list [i] = new node;
    }
  }
}
return adjlist;
}
```

(b) Explain the concept of representation of a graph. Write an algorithm for graph traversal using breadth first search, with a suitable example. Also, determine its space and time complexity. [10]

Ans. A graph G is defined fast a set of two tuples that is G =(V, E), where B represents set of vertices of G and E represents the set of edges of G. There exists a mapping from the set of edge to a set of pairs of elements of V. We can represent the graph with two types:

1. Adjacency Matrix

2. Adjacency list

If we have a graph

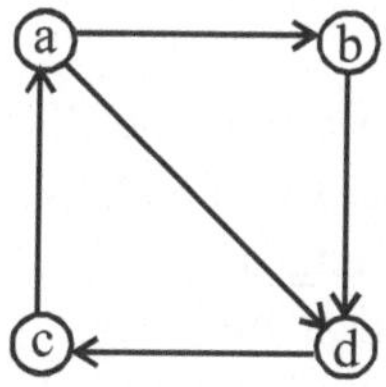

Then

Adjacency Matrix would be

$$\begin{array}{c} \\ a \\ b \\ c \\ d \end{array} \begin{array}{c} \begin{array}{cccc} a & b & c & d \end{array} \\ \begin{bmatrix} 0 & 1 & 0 & 1 \\ 0 & 0 & 0 & 1 \\ 1 & 0 & 0 & 0 \\ 0 & 0 & 1 & 0 \end{bmatrix} \end{array}$$

Adjacency list would be

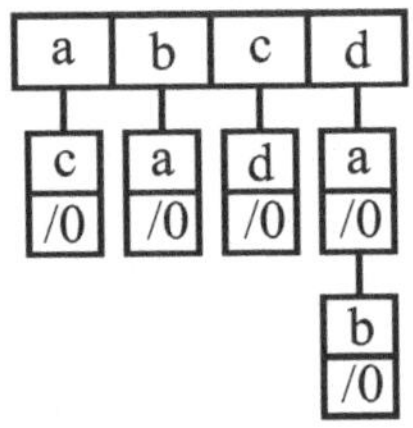

Algorithm for B.F.S (Breadth first Search)

Step1:- Initialize all the vertices be setting flag=1

Step2: Put the starting vertex A in Q and change its status to the waiting state by the setting flag =0

Step3: Repeat through step 5 while Q is not NULL

Step4: Remove the front vertex V of Q. Process V and set the status of V to the processed status by setting flag =-1.

Step5: Add to the rear of Q all the neighbors of V that are in the ready status by setting flag =1 and change their status to the waiting state by setting flag=0

Step6: Exit.

Space Complexity: Since all nodes discovered so far have to be saved, the space complexity of BFS search is O(|V|+|E|) where |V| is the number of nodes and |E| is number of edges in the graph. Another method of saying this is O (B ^ M) where B is the maximum branching factor and M is the maximum path length of the tree.

Time Complexity: Since in the worst case BFS had to consider all paths to all possible nodes the time complexity of BFS is O (|V|+|E|) where |V| is number of nodes and |E| is number of edges. The best case of this search is O(1). It occurs when the node is found at first time.

(c) Write an algorithm for the implementation of insertion sort. Compute the time complexity of insertion sort in accordance to worst, best and

average case, sort the following sequence of numbers by applying insertion sort: [10]

7, 4, 1, 3, 0, 2, 8, 5

Ans. One of the simplest methods to sort on array is an insertion sort. An example of an insertion sort occurs in everyday life while playing cards. To sort the cards in one's hand one extract a card, and shift the remaining cards, and then extracted card in correct place. This process is repeated until all the cards are in correct sequence.

Algorithm of Insertion Sort:

Insertion_ sort (L,n)

Where L $\rightarrow$ represent the list of the element

N $\rightarrow$ represent number of elements in list.

Step1: [Initialize]

L[0]= -0

Step2: repeat through step3 through 5 for i=1,2,3…n

Step3:

(i) temp =L [i]

(ii) pointer= i-1

Step4: while (temp < [pointer])

(i) L[Pointer+1] =L [Pointer]

(ii) Pointer =pointer-1

Step5:

L[pointer]= temp

Step6: Exit

Complexity:

Worst case	Average case	Best case
$\frac{n(n-1)}{2} = o(n^2)$	$\frac{n(n-1)}{4} = o(n^2)$	o(n)

Number of Sequence for sort:

7	4	1	3	0	2	8	5

Step1 -0	7	(4)	1	3	0	2	8	5
Step2 -0	4	7	(1)	3	0	2	8	5
Step3 -0	1	4	7	(3)	0	2	8	5
Step4 -0	1	3	4	7	(0)	2	8	5
Step5 -0	0	1	3	4	7	(2)	8	5
Step6 -0	0	1	2	3	4	7	(8)	5
Step7 -0	0	1	2	3	4	7	8	(5)
Step8 -0	0	1	2	3	4	5	7	8

(d) How is circular queue better than a linear queue? Explain this with an example. [10]

Ans. Linear Queue: A Queue is a kind of data structure or type of list in which all additions to the list are made at one end, and all deletions from the list are made at one end. Queue is defined as waiting line. Queue also called FIFO list.

Circular Queue: A circular Queue is one in which the insertion of a new element is done at the very first location of the queue if the last location of the queue is full. In other words, if we have a queue Q of say n elements, then after inserting an element last (i.e. in the n-1 the) location of array the next element will be inserted at the very first location.

Circular queue is better than the linear queen because

(i) Circular queue utilize the space in comparison to linear queue.

(ii) Circular queue implement wrapping around.

(iii) Circular queue is known as "Ring Buffer"

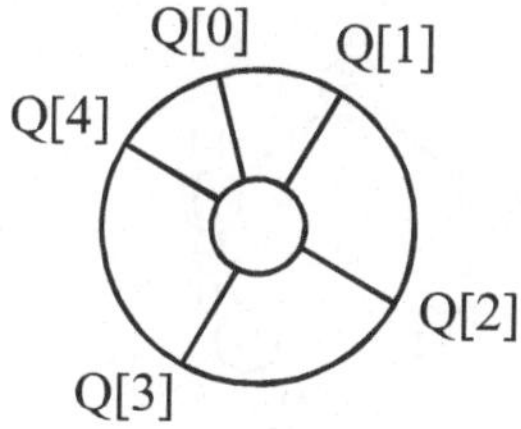

Q2(a). Define an AVL Tree. Construct a Height Balanced Tree for the following list of elements: [7]

3, 5, 11, 9, 4, 2, 15, 7, 2, 6, 10,

Ans. An AVL tree is a binary tree in which the left and right sub trees of any node may differ in height by at most 1, and in which both the sub trees are themselves AVL trees (the definition is recursive). It is also called height balanced tree. It is discovered by Adelson, Velskii, Londis. One first letter of the scientist name it comes AVL. It has the following properties.

(i) T_L and T_R are heighted balanced. Where

$T_L \rightarrow$ left subtree

$T_R \rightarrow$ Right subtree

(ii) $|H_L - H_R| <= 1$

(iii) Balance factor is –0,0, +1.

List of Elements:-

3, 5, 11, 9, 4, 2, 15, 7, 2, 6, 10

Its AVL tree as follows:-

New Identifier **After Insertion** **After Rebalancing**

(i) 3

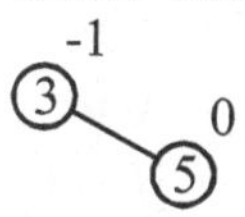

No Rebalancing

(ii) (5)

No Rebalancing

(iii) 11

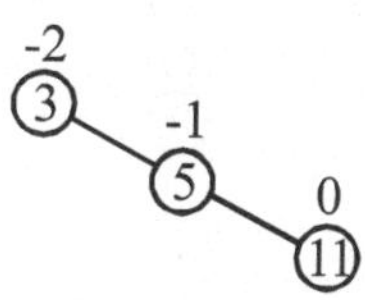

RR →

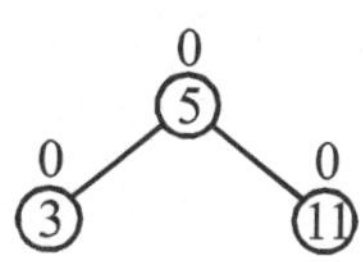

(iv) 9

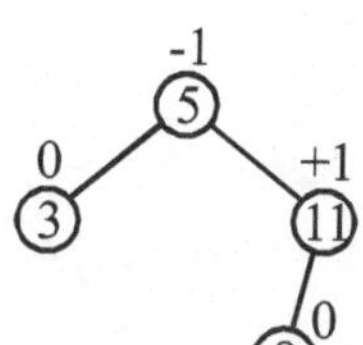

No Rebalancing

(v) 4

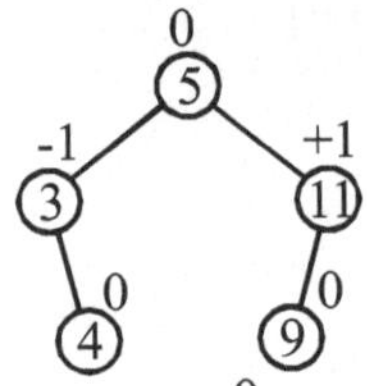

No Rebalancing

(vi) 2

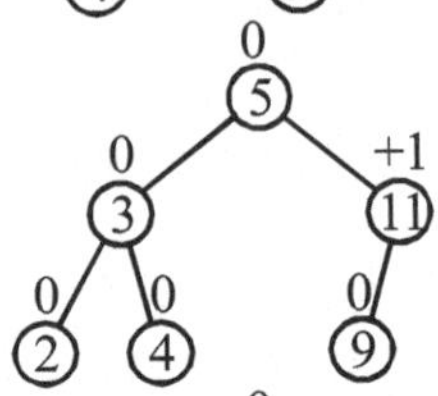

No Rebalancing

(vii) 15

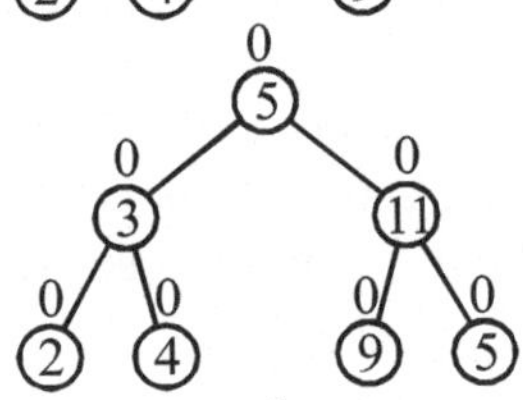

No Rebalancing

(viii) 7

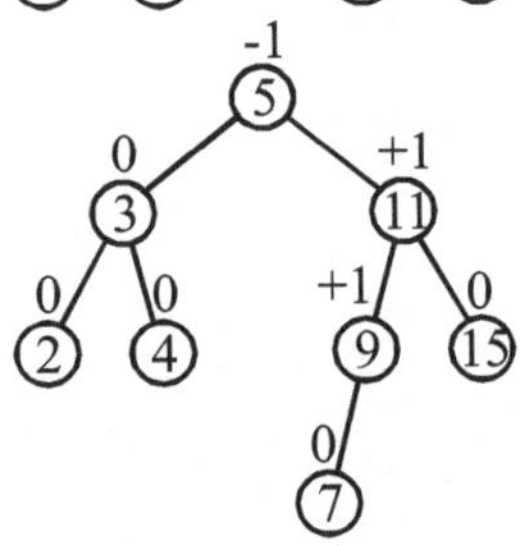

No Rebalancing

(ix) 2

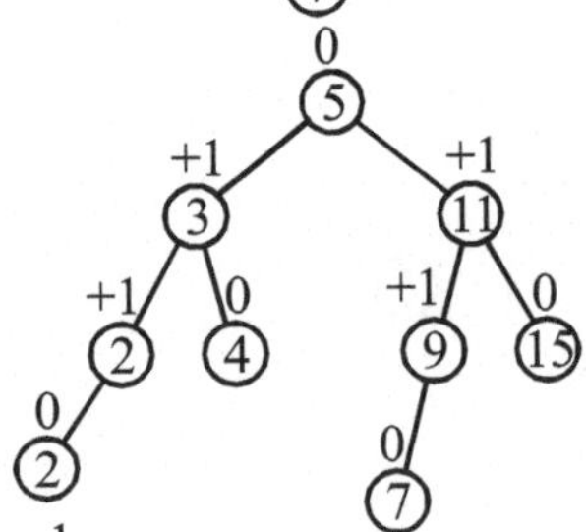

No Rebalancing

(x) 6

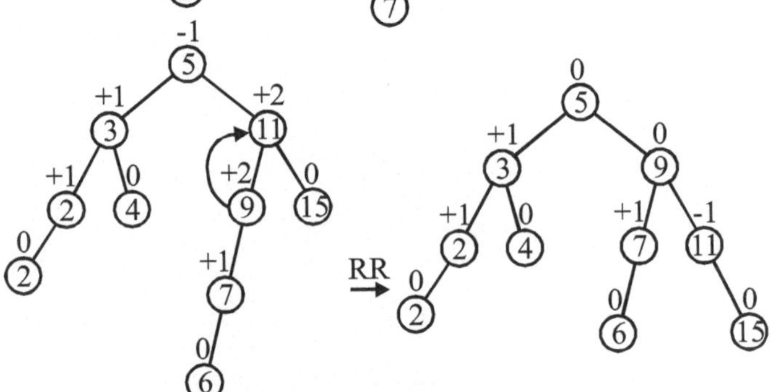

(xi) 10

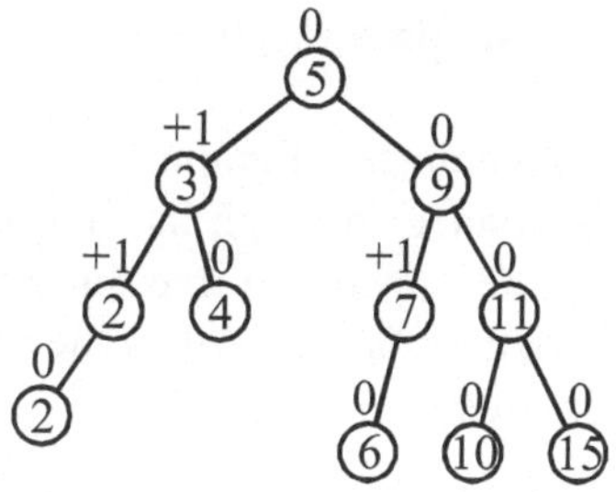

(b) Write a recursive function to generate the Fibonacci series? [3]

Ans.
```
int S1, S2
    Int fibonacci (int n)
    {
      if (n = = 0)
        return 1;
    else if (n = = 1)
        return 1;
    else
      {
      S1 = fibonacci (n-1);
      S2 = fibonacci (n-2);
         Return S1+S2;
    }
  }
```

Q3(a). Explain any three advantage of a singly linked list over arrays? [3]

Ans. Refer to Page No. 64, Q21.

(b) Consider the graph:

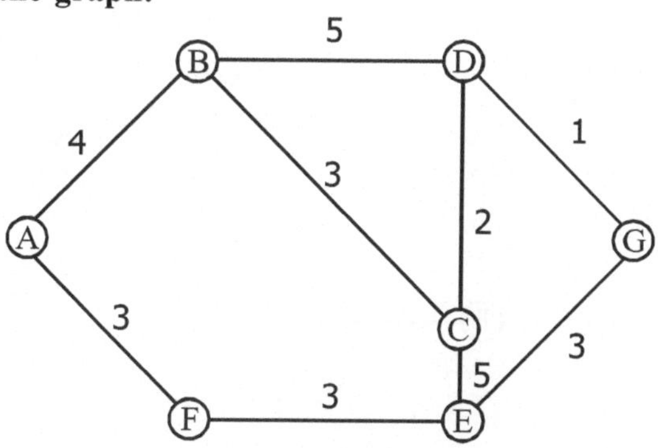

Construct a minimum cost spanning tree for the graph above. Also give the cost of this tree.

Ans. A spanning tree of a connected graph G is a connected subgraph of G having no cycles. Every connected graph has a spanning tree.

We construct a minimum cost spanning tree through Kruskal's method.

According to Kruskal's method first we select the minimum cost edge and no cycle (loop) occur in the tree.

Graph is:-

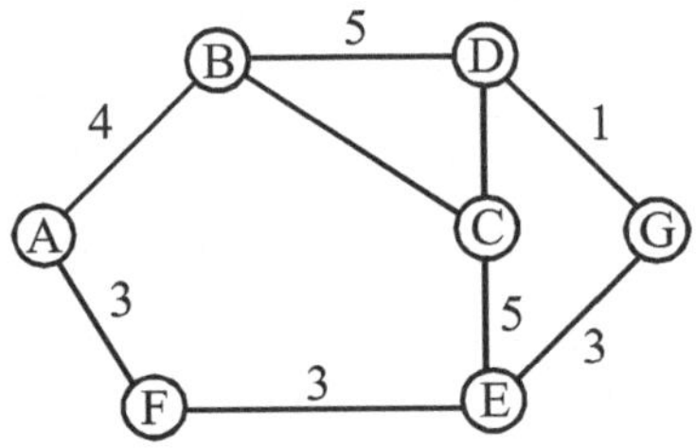

Step1:-

choose minimum
cost edge DG=1

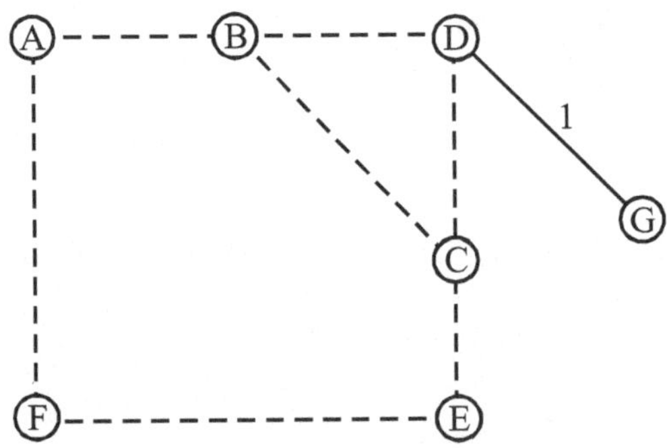

Step2:-

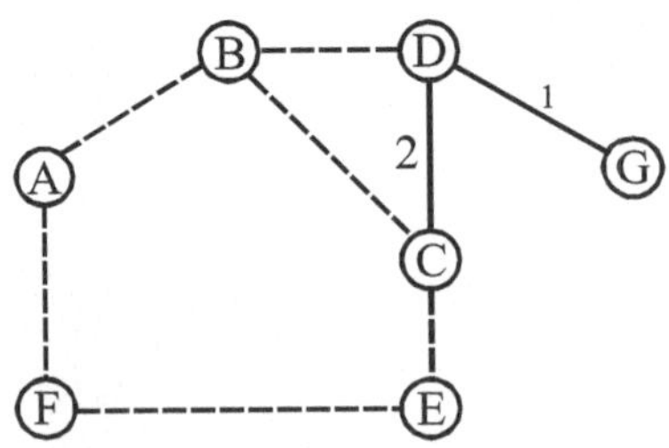

Step3:-

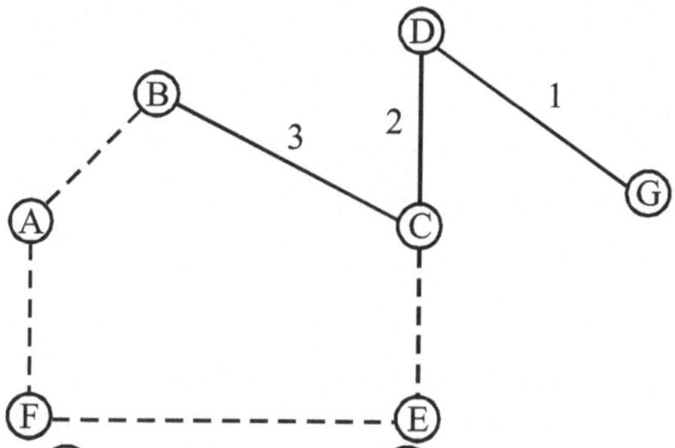

Step4:-

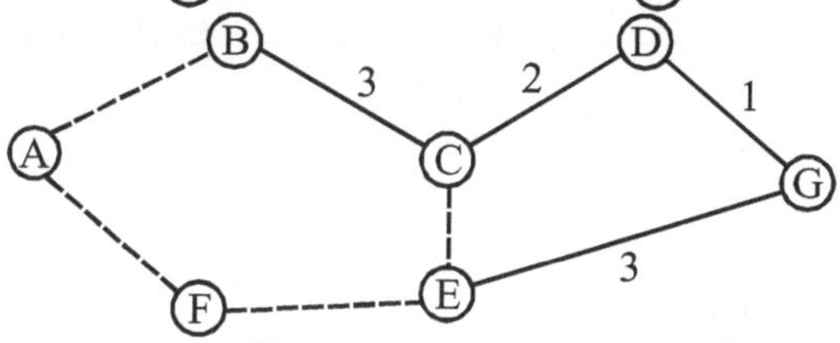

Step5:-

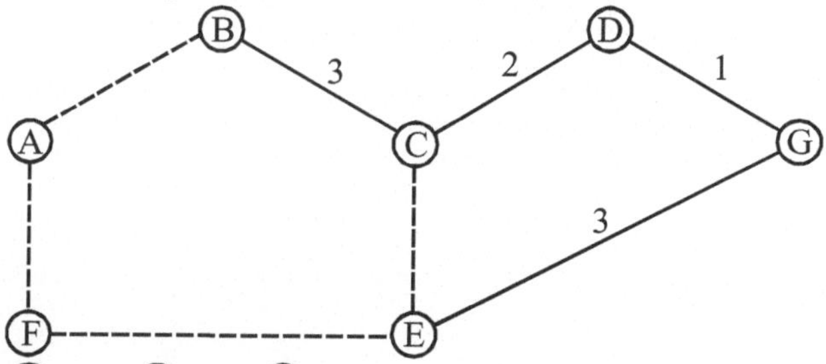

Step6:-

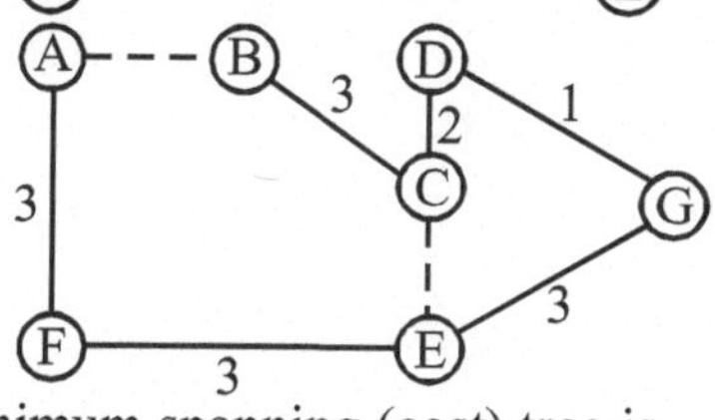

The required minimum spanning (cost) tree is

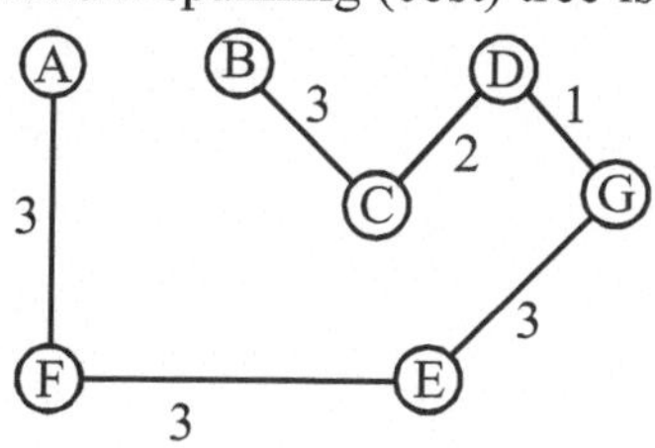

The cost is

DG =1

CD=2

BC=3
EG=3
EF=3
AF=3

The minimum cost of spanning tree is
= 1+2+3+3+3+3
=15

Q4. Suppose there is a singly linked list of integers. The linked list is implemented by pointers in 'C' write 'C' functions of the following: [10]
(i) Delete a node in the list, given a pointer to that node.

Ans. /* Delete a node in the list */

```
void delete_ node (struct link *node)
 {
  int node_number =0;
         node =start→next';
         previous=& start;
         if (node = = NULL)
       {
         Printf ("In underflow");
       }
       else
         while (node)
       {
           node = node→next;
           previous = previous →next;
           node_number++;
       }
   printf ("In Total Nodes-%d", node_ number);
   node = Start→next;
   previous = &start;
   while (node_number!= 1)
   {
    node = node → next;
    previous = Previous → next;
    node_number- -;
   }
   if (node_number = = 1)
   {
   previous → next = node →next;
```

```
    free (node);
  }
```

(ii) Reverse the list.

Ans.
```
/ * Reversing the list *|
    struct link * (struct link *struct)
    {
    current1= start;
    previous = NULL;
       while (current!=NULL)
    {
    counter = (struct link *)malloc (size of (struct link));
    counter = current1 → next;
    current 1 → next = previous;
    previous = current 1;
    current 1 = counter;
  }
    start = previous;
    return (start);
  }
```

Q5. Explain the following with an example each: [10]

(i) Dynamic Memory Allocation

Ans. Dynamic Memory Allocation: Reserving memory in a program moment to moment, as needed, without having to reserve a fixed amount when the program startup. All modern operating systems perform dynamic memory allocation for their own use as well as providing an API function such as "malloc" (memory allocate) to allow applications to do the same. Dynamic memory allocation is provided in the linked list. Array does not provide the dynamic memory allocation so we used linked list. The main advantage of dynamic allocation is prevent memory wastage. We can do dynamically allocation by following ways: -

1. Malloc
2. Relloc
3. Tree

(ii) Sparse Array

Ans. A sparse array in computing is an array where most of the elements have the same value (called the default value… usually 0) and a few elements have a non-default value. Arrays are data structures used in programming language, databases, and other computer systems. They use a value, called a subscript or and index, that indicates a position to locate a particular value.

A typical implementation may allocate space for the entire array, but this is inefficient since there are only a few non-default values. If the sparsity is known in advance, more space- efficient implementation can be used which allocate space only for the non-default values.

Example:- An array with length of one million, where only the indices 1,320 and 9999999 have non-default values, is sparse. It would be inefficient to allocate any spacer for 999996 array element with default values.

(iii) Pre-order Traversal

Ans. Pre-order Traversal: Traversing means visiting each node exactly once. A full traversal of a binary tree T produces a liner order of elements existing in T.

in pre-order traversing, first of all we process the root R of the binary tree T. Then we traverse the left sub–tree T_1 of R in preorder, which means that we traverse root of the sub-tree T_1 first and then its left sub-tree. After traversing left sub-tree of R then we take over right sub tree of R and process all the nodes in preorder. For example:-

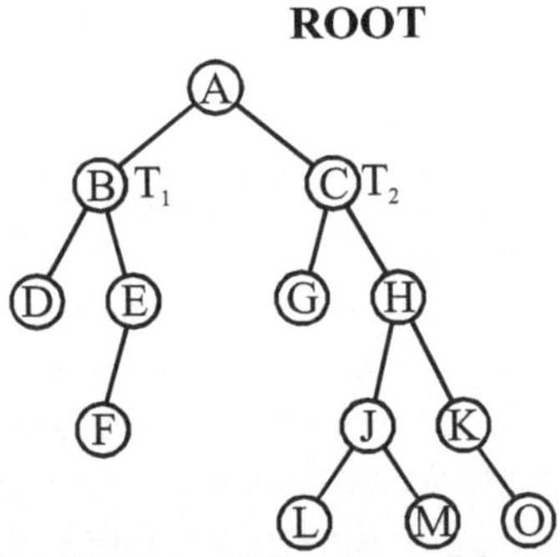

Pre-Order Traversal in above binary Tree is
DBFC AGCL JMHOK

(iv) Indexed Sequential File Organization

Ans. Refer to Q26, Page 127.

(v) Macros

Ans. MACROS: It is technique that allows the user to combine several keywords into one. Macros are simply mini programs that allow the user to design a menu to include in a Template. An assembly language that allows macros to be defined and used.

CS-62 : 'C' PROGRAMMING AND DATA STRUCTURE
DECEMBER, 2006

Note : Question no.1 is **compulsory.** Answer any **three** questions from the rest. All algorithms should be written nearer to 'C' language.

Q1(a). Show how the array,

$$A = \begin{bmatrix} 3 & 4 & 9 & 2 \\ 0 & 1 & 6 & 8 \\ 7 & 8 & 4 & 5 \\ 9 & 9 & 2 & 3 \end{bmatrix}$$

Would appear in memory when stored in
(i) Row major order
(ii) Column major order
(ii) Logical representation **[10]**

Ans.

(i) Row-Major Order:

$$\begin{bmatrix} A[0][0]=3 \rightarrow A[0][1]=4 \rightarrow A[0][2]=9 \rightarrow a[0][3]=2 \\ A[1][0]=0 \rightarrow A[1][1]=1 \rightarrow A[1][2]=6 \rightarrow A[1][3]=8 \\ A[2][0]=7 \rightarrow A[2][1]=8 \rightarrow A[2][2]=4 \rightarrow A[2][3]=5 \\ A[3][0]=9 \rightarrow A[3][1]=9 \rightarrow A[3][2]=2 \rightarrow A[3][3]=3 \end{bmatrix}$$

(ii) Column-Major Order:

$$\begin{array}{cccc} A[0][0]=3 & A[0][1]=4 & A[0][2]=9 & A[0][3]=2 \\ \downarrow & \downarrow & \downarrow & \downarrow \\ A[1][0]=0 & A[1][1]=1 & A[1][2]=6 & A[1][3]=8 \\ \downarrow & \downarrow & \downarrow & \downarrow \\ A[2][0]=7 & A[2][1]=8 & A[2][2]=4 & A[2][3]=5 \\ \downarrow & \downarrow & \downarrow & \downarrow \\ A[3][0]=9 & A[3][1]=9 & A[3][2]=2 & A[3][3]=3 \end{array}$$

(iii) Logical Representation:

$$\begin{bmatrix} A[0][0]=3 & A[0][1]=4 & A[0][2]=9 & A[0][3]=2 \\ A[1][0]=0 & A[1][1]=1 & A[1][2]=6 & A[1][3]=8 \\ A[2][0]=7 & A[2][1]=8 & A[2][2]=4 & A[2][3]=5 \\ A[3][0]=9 & A[3][1]=9 & A[3][2]=2 & A[3][3]=3 \end{bmatrix}$$

(b) What is a Binary Search Tree (BST)? Write algorithms for inserting and deleting nodes in a BST. Explain them with the help of an example each. [10]

Ans. Refer to Q22, Page No.122.

Algorithm for insertion of node in BST.

Insbst (Info, Left, Right, Avail, Item, loc)

A binary search tree is in memory and an ITEM of information is given. This algorithm finds the location LOC item int or adds ITEM as a new node in T at location LOC.

1. Call Find (info, left, Right, Root, item, LOC, PAR)

2. If LOC $\neq$ NULL, then Exit

3. [copy ITEM into new node in AVAIL list.]

(a)If AVAIL= NULL, then: Write: OVERFLOW, and Exit

(b) Set NEW: =AVAIL, AVAIL: left [AVAIL] and INFO [NEW]: =ITEM

(c) set LOC: = NEW, Left [NEW]: =NULL and right [NEW]: =NULL

4. [Add item to tree]

if PAR= NULL, then: =

Set ROOT: = New

else if item< info [par], =then;

Set left [par]: =new.

else

Set Right [par]:=New.

[End of if structure]

5. Exit

(c) Assume A is a N × N square matrix. Write the algorithm for the following operations in the matrix A. [10]

(i) Find the product of the diagonal elements of A.

(ii) Find the sum of the elements above the diagonal elements.

Ans. Product of diagonal element of A

(i) 1. Set Prod: = 1

2. Repeat for K = 1 to N

Set Prod: = Prod * A [k]
[End of loop]
3. Return

(ii) Sum of elements above the diagonal elements.
1. Set SUM: = 0
2. Repeat for j =2 to n
3. Repeat for I =I to J-1
Set SUM: = SUM+ A [i, j]
[End of inner step 3 loop]
4. Return.

Q2(a). Construct a Height Balanced Tree for the following list of elements **[5]**

2, 6, 13, 8, 4, 3, 18, 7, 1, 8, 11

Ans. List is :- 2,6,13,8,4,3,18,7,1,8,11

	Inserted Value	**Tree**	**Rotation**
Step1:-	2		**No Need**
Step2:-	6	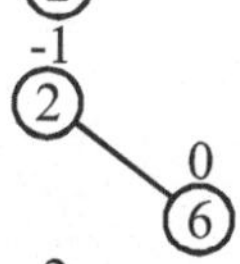	**No Need**
Step3:-	13	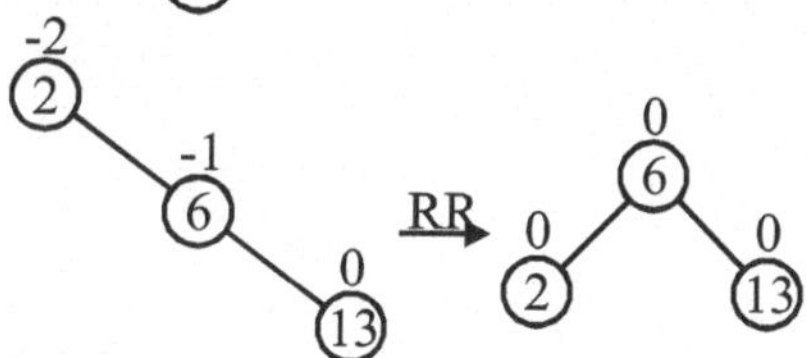	
Step4:-	8	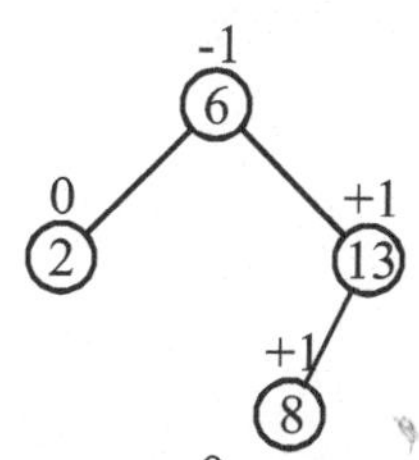	**No Need**
Step5:-	4	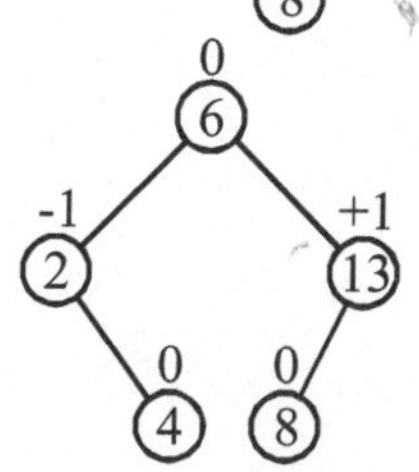	

Step6:- 3

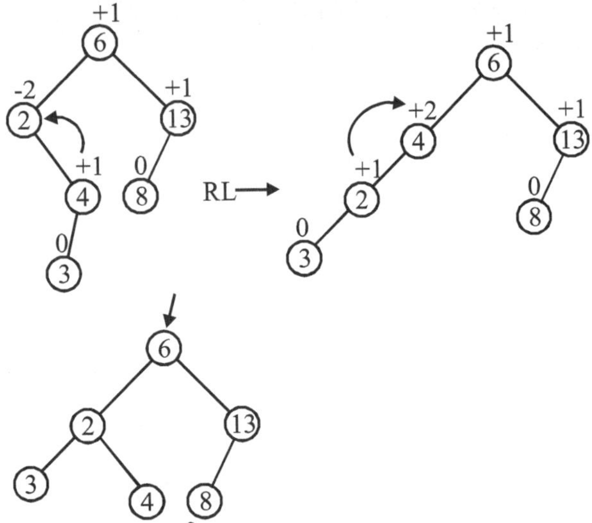

Step7:- 18

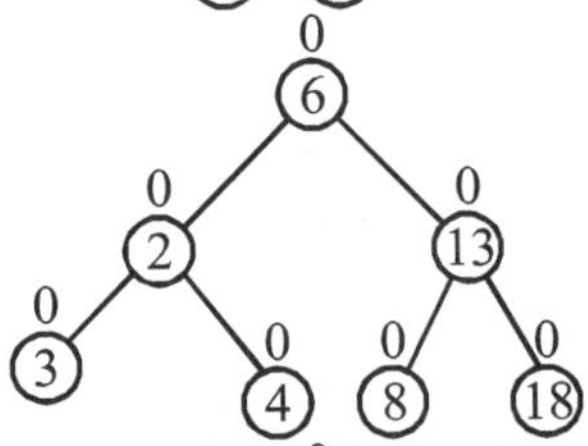

No Need

Step8:- 7

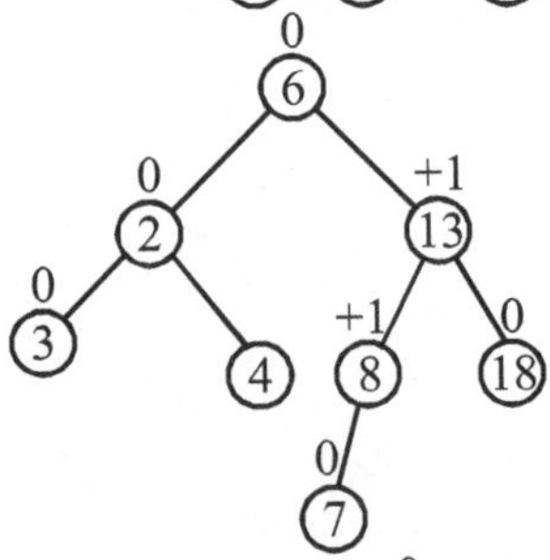

No Need

Step9:- 1

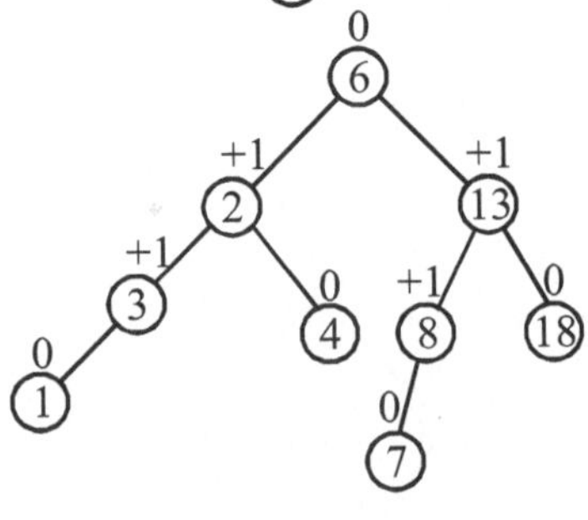

No Need

Step10:- 8

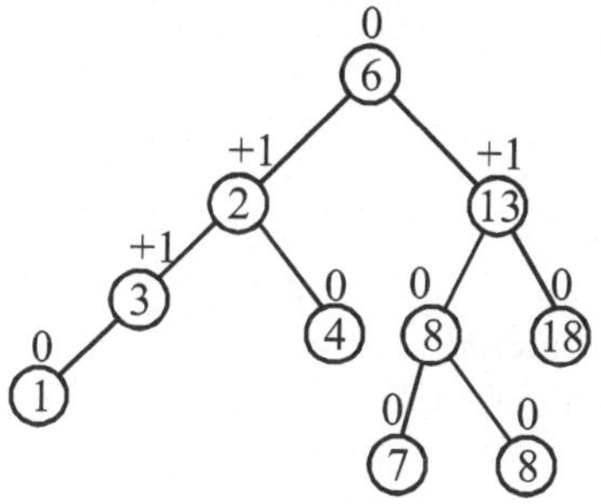

No Need

Step 11:- 11

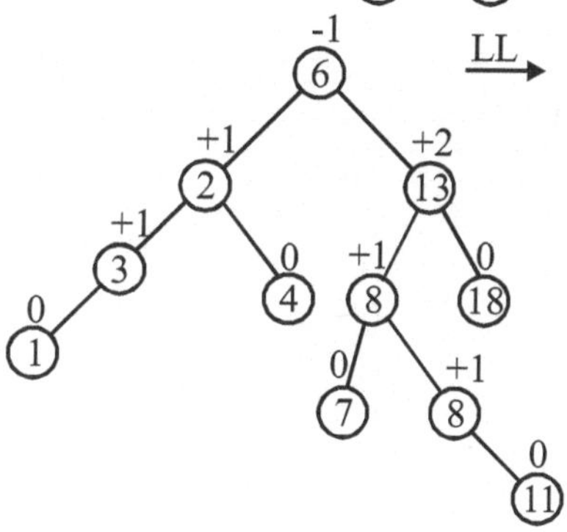

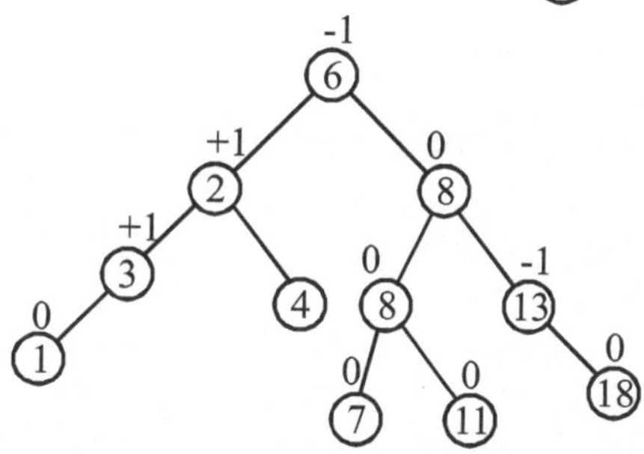

(b) Write an algorithm to convert an infix expression to as postfix expression. Also explain the logic with the help of an example. (Use stack implementations) **[5]**

Ans. **<u>Algorithm to convert in fire expression to post fine polish (Q, P)</u>**

Suppose Q is an arithmetic expression written in infix notation.

1. Push "("onto stack, and add")" to the end of a

2. scan Q from left to right and repeat steps 3 to 6 for each statement of Q until the stack is empty.

3. if an operand is encountered, add it to P.

4. if a left parenthesis is encountered, push it onto stack.

5. if an operator ⊗ is encountered, then:

(a) Repeatedly pop from stack and add to p each operator (on the top of stack) which has the same precedence as or higher precedence than ⊗

(b) Add ⊗ to stack

[end of if structure]

6. If a right parenthesis is encountered, then:

(a) Repeatedly pop stack and add to P each operator (on the top of stack) until a left parenthesis is encountered.

(b) Remove the left parenthesis [Do not add the left parenthesis to p]

[End of step loop]

7. Exit.

Example

Infix Expression : (A+B)* D

Symbol	Stack	expression P
(	((	
A	((	A
+	((+	A
B	((+	AB
)	(	AB+
*	(*	AB+
D	(*	AB+D
)	-	AB+D*

Algorithm for find position

Find (info, Left, Right, Root, Item, LOC, Par)

1. [Tree Empty?]

If root= NULL, then: Set LOC: = NULL and Par: = NULL, and Return

2. [Item at root?]

If them = info [root], then set LOC: =Root and Par: =NULL, and return

3. [Initializes pointer PTR and SAVE]

if Item< info [root], then:

Set PTR: = Left [Root] and SAVE: = ROOT

else:

Set PTR: = Right [root] and save: =Root

[End of if structure]

4. Repeat steps 5 to 6 while PTR $\neq$ NULL;

5. [ITEM found?]

if ITEM = INFO [PTR], then set LOC:=PTR and PAR:= SAVE, and Return

6. if item< info [ptr], then

set SAVE:= PTR and ptr: = Left [ptr]

else

set Save: = PTR and PTR: =Right [ptr]
[End of if structure]
[End of step 4 loop]

7. [Search unsuccessful] set LOC: =NULL and PAR: = SAVE

8. Exit.

Algorithm for Deletion:

```
    Dele (LOC, Parent)
Step1 : [initialization]
        If left child [LOC] = NULL then
           Dnode = Right_child [LOC]
        else
            Dnode  = Left_child [LOC]
Step2: if parent ≠ NULL then
       If LOC=Left_child [parent]
         Then Left_child [parent] = Dnode
       else Right_child [parent] = Dnode
       else  Root = Dnode
Step3. Return .
```

Q3(a). Write and explain the hash function method, "Division–Remainder Hashing". Also explain where this can be used. [5]

Ans. The two principle criteria is used in selecting a HASH function H : K → are as follows. First of all, the function H should be very easy and quick to compute, second the function H should, as far as possible, uniformly distribute the hash addresses throughout the set so that there are a minimum number of collisions. Naturally, there is no guarantee that the second condition can be completely fulfilled without actually knowing before hand the keys and addresses. One technique is to 'chop'

A key into pieces and combine the pieces in some way to form the hash address H (k)

Division Method:

Choose a number in large than the number of n keys to k (the number in is usually choosen to be prime number or a number without small divisors, since this frequently minimizes the number of collisions). The hash function H is defined by

H (k) K (mod m) or H (k)- k (mod m)+1

Here K (mod m) denotes the remainder when K is divided by m. The second formula is used when we want the hash addresses to range from 1 to m rather than from o to m-1

For example

Consider the company, each of which 68 employees is assigned a unique 4-

digit employee number. Suppose L consists of 100 two –digit addresses: 00,01,02- - - - 99.

We apply the division –remainder hashing method to each of the following employee numbers.

3205,7148,2345

⇒ firstly choose a prime number m close to 99, such as=97 them

H (3205)=4, H (7148)=67, H (2345)=17

That is dividing 3205 by 97 gives ad remainder of 4, dividing 7148 by 97 gives a remainder of 67, and dividing 2345 by 97 gives a remainder of 17. In the case that the memory addresses begin with 01 rather than OO, we choose that the function H (K) = k (mod m)+1 to obtain:

H (3205)=4+1=5, H (7148)= 67+1 =68, H (2345)=17+1=18

(b) For the digraph shown below find **[5]**

(i) the indegree and outdegree of each vertex

(ii) its adjacency matrix representation

(iii) its adjacency list representation

(iv) its strongly connected component

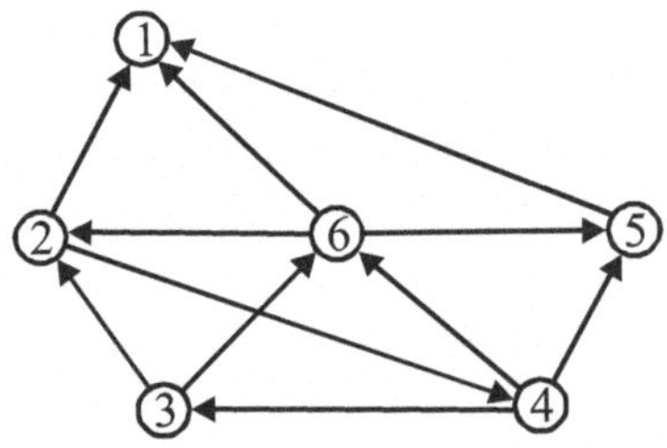

Ans. (i)

Vertex	1	2	3	4	5	6
In degree	3	2	1	1	2	2
Outdegree	o	2	2	3	1	3

(ii) **Adjacency Matrix representation:**

	1	2	3	4	5	6
1	0	0	0	0	0	0
2	1	0	0	1	0	0
3	0	1	0	0	0	1
4	0	0	1	0	1	1
5	1	0	0	0	0	0
6	1	1	0	0	1	0

(iii) Adjacency List Representation:

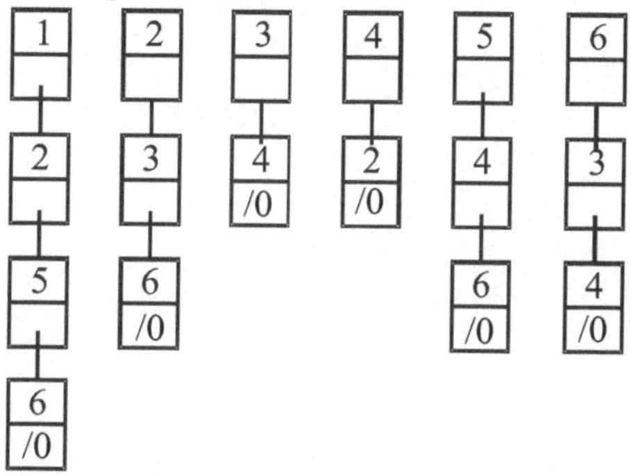

(iv) Its Strongly connected graph is:

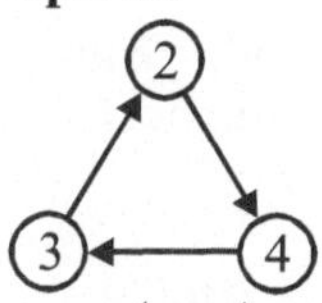

Q4(a). Write an algorithm to construct a doubly linked list and search for data. **[5]**

Ans. Algorithm for creation of double linked list

Step: [initialization]

(i)start.Next=NULL

(ii) Previous Next= NULL

Step 2 [Assign address of start variable to node]

Node = address of start

Step 3: [make left and right links of node]

(i) Next [node]= node [make link to node]

(ii) Previous [Node]= Node [Make link to node]

(iii) Node =Next [Node][move pointer to next node]

(iv) info[node]=value [information value of node]

(v) Next[Node]=NULL [Assign NULL to the address field]

Step4: [call step3]

Repeat step 3 to create required number of nodes for linked for linked list

Step5: End.

Algorithm for searching

Step1: [Initialization]
Node =Start. Next
Previous = address of first node in list
Node_number = 1

Step2: [set the flag]
Flag=0

Step3: [Read the information of node to which we want to search]
Search_node=value

Step4: [check the list]
If Node=NULL
Output "list is empty" and Exit

Step5: [Perform search operation]
Repeat through step6 while Node $\neq$ NULL
If info[Node] = Search_ Node
(i) output "search is successful" and
position is equal to value of
(ii) Node = Next [Node]
(iii) Previous = Next [Node]
(iv) Flag = 1
else
(i) Node = Next [node]
(ii) Previous = Next[Previous]

Step6: [Increment the value of Node _Number]
Node_ Number = Node_Number+1

Step7: [check the flag]
If flag = 0
Output "search is unsuccessful".

Step8: Exit.

(b) Write an algorithm for addition and deletion of an element into a queue. [5]

Ans. Refer to Q30, Page No. 76.

Q5. Define the following and give an example for each: [10]
(i) UNION in C language (ii) Circular linked list (iii) Post order traversal of a binary tree (iv) Insertion Sort (vi) K-way merging

Ans. (i) Refer to Page No. 24 **(ii)** Refer to Page No. 48 **(iii)** Refer to Page No. 92 **(iv)** Refer to Page No. 153

(v) K-Way Merging : This also is improvement on one-way or two merging. In this K-Way merging we can increasing the number of input and output files. The number of runs in each file is decreased, with the result that fewer merges have to be performed.

The merging phase is more complicated with K input files because K-way merge needs to distributed merged runs into K output files.

In this K-way merging we can divide unordered list into k parts then each part we make in ordered way then perform the merging operation. The execution of k-way merging is too fast.

CS-62 : 'C' PROGRAMMING AND DATA STRUCTURE
June, 2007

Note : Question no. 1 is **compulsory**. Answer any **three** questions from the rest. All algorithms should be written nearer to 'C' language.

---

1. (a) Write a 'C' function to compute the total number of nodes in a binary tree.

Ans. /*'C' function to compute the total number of nodes in a binary tree*/

Suppose the Binary tree is represented in memory with following declaration:

```
typedef struct BTREE_node
{
struct BTREE_node * left;
int item;
struct BTREE_node * right;
} BTREE;
BTREE * root;
int count_nodes(BTREE * tree)   /* 'C' function to count number of nodes
in Binary Tree*/
{
if(tree = = (BTREE *) NULL)
return O;    // zero
else
return(count_nodes(tree → left) + count_nodes(tree → right) + 1);
}
```

(b) Write an algorithm to sort 'N' numbers using Bubble sort. Also, show that bubble sort algorithm, on average, makes O(N^2) comparisons while sorting a list of N elements.

Ans. Algorithm: (Bubble Sort) BUBBLE(NUM, N)

Here NUM is an array with N elements. This algorithm sorts the elements in NUM array is ascending order.

Step 1: Repeat Steps 2 and 3 for K = 1 to N – 1.

Step 2: SET PTR:=1

Step 3: REPEAT while PTR $\leq$ N – K

(a) IF NUM[PTR] > NUM[PTR + 1], THEN:

INTERCHANGE NUM[PTR] and NUM[PTR + 1]

(b) SET PTR:=PTR + 1

Step 4: EXIT

The time for sorting algorithm is measured in terms of the number of

comparisons. The number f(n) of comparisons in the bubble sort is easily computed.
There are n – 1 comparisons during the first pass of bubble sort algorithm, which places the largest element in the last position; there are n – 2 comparisons in the second pass and so on. Thus

$$f(n) = (n - 1) + (n - 2) + \text{----------} + 2 + 1$$

$$= \frac{n(n-1)}{2}$$

$$= \frac{n^2}{2} + O(n)$$

$$= O(n^2)$$

∴ The time required to execute a bubble sort algorithm is proportional to n^2, where n is the number of input items.

(c) What is indexed sequential file organisation? Name the data structure which is most appropriate for this file organisation. Justify the answer.

Ans. Indexed Sequential File Organisation : This organization refers to the storage method where the data records are stored with some relative position in the file. This helps in direct access of the records i.e. a record can be accessed directly. A field of the record is fixed as a key that helps in unique identification of the records. The new record is to be inserted or deleted through the key field. This organization is suited for interactive processing like reservation system, booking counters so that the queries are solved as soon as they are raised. Any record can be accessed directly if the key value is known.
The most suitable data structure for Indexed Sequential File Organization is Linked List representation. As Linked List representation allow us to insert new records in the beginning, at the end or in the middle of the list. So, if we are maintaining Indexed Sequential File as a Linked List representation, then it will be easy for us to maintain the order of key field.
We can access the data stored in a Linked List in both the ways: Sequentially or Directly (using specific memory address). So, Linked List representation will help in accessing the records of the file in sequential as well as in Direct manner. Indexed Sequential Files are stored in Memory Devices like floppy disk, hard disk etc. which are maintaining the data in Indexed Sequential File Organization manner to provide direct access as well as sequential access on the stored data.

(d) Write a program in 'C' language that counts total number of characters, words, white-spaces and lines in a given text file.

Ans.
```
#include <stdio.h>
#include <stdlib.h>
main( )
{
char line[81], ch;
int i, j = 0, word_count = 0, line_count =  0, space_count  = 0, char_count =
0;
FILE *fptr;
if((fptr = fopen("test.txt", "r")) = = NULL)
{
printf("File doesn't exist\n");
exit(1);
}
else
{
while((ch = fgetc(fptr))!=EOF)
j = j + 1;
}
char_count = j;
while((fgets(line, 81, fptr))!=NULL)
{
for(i = 0; line[i]!='\0'; i++)
if(is_end(line[i]))
word_count ++;
}
printf("Number of character in the File = %d\n", char_count);
printf("Number of words in the File = %d\n", word_count);
fclose(fptr);
}
is_end(int ch1)
{
switch(ch1)
{
case '\n': line_count ++;
case ' ': space_count ++;
return 1;
}
printf("Number of Lines in File = %d\n", line_count);
printf("Number of white spaces in File = %d\n", space_count);
return 0;
}
```

(e) Construct a binary tree from the following preorder and inorder traversal sequence:
Preorder: A B C D E F
Inorder: C B A E D F

Ans. PREORDER : A B C D E F

INORDER : C B [A] E D F

The root of the Binary Tree to be constructed is [A].

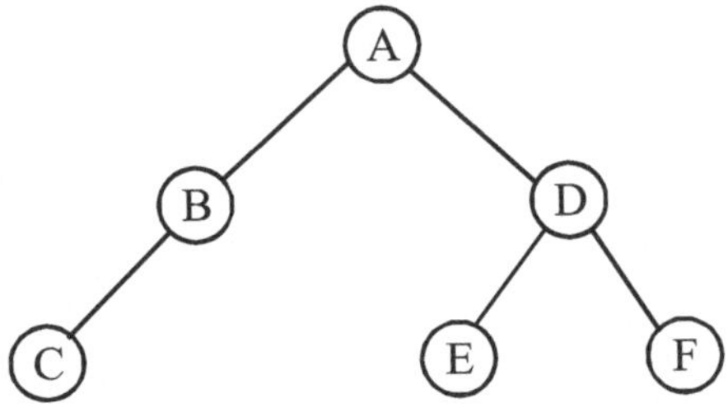

Fig :- Binary Tree

2. Write a 'C' language that sorts a given linked list of integers. Also, write a function that splits this linked list into a linked list of even integers and a linked list of odd integers.

Ans. The Merge sort translate the unsorted linked list of integers into a sorted linked list.

```
/*Program of Merge sort to sort a linked list*/
List_type *Mergesort(List_type*p)
{
List_type *q;
List_type *head = p;
If(p && p→next)
{
q = Divide(p);
p = Mergesort(p);
q = Mergesort(q);
head = Merge(p, q);
}
return head;
}

/*The definition for List_type Linked list*/
typedef struct item_tag
{
key_type key;
} Item_type;
```

```
typedef struct list_tag
{
Item_type info;
Struct list_tag *next;
} List_type;

/*Divide algorithm divides the list into two lists. p points to the first half of the
list. The function returns a pointer to the second half of the list*/
List_type *Divide(List_type*p)
{
List_type *q, *r;
q = p;
r = p → next → next;
while(r)
{
r = r → next;
q = q → next;
if(r)
r = r → next;
}
r = q → next;
q → next = NULL;
return r;
}

/*Merge two sorted linked list into one linked list*/
List_type *Merge(Link_type *p, List_type *q)
{
List–type *head, *r; Pvt underscare
if (p ¦¦ !q)
Error("Merge called with empty list(s)");
If(LE(p → info.key, q → info.key))
{
head = p;
p = p → next;
}
else
{
head = q;
q = q → next;
```

```
}
r = head;
while(p && q)
if(LE(p→info.key, q→info.key))
{
r = r→next = p;
p = p→next;
}
else
{
r = r→next = q;
q = q→next;
}
if(p)
r→next = p;
else
r→next = q;
return head;
}
```

→C function to split this sorted linked list into a linked list of even integers and a linked list of odd integers.

```
List_type *split(List type *p)
{
List_type *even, *odd;
List_type *head = p;
while(p→next≠NULL)
{
if(p→info%2 = = 0)
{
if(even = = NULL)
create_node();
{
even = p;
even→info = p→info;
even→next = NULL;
}
else
{
create_node();
```

```
even → next = p;
even → next → info = p → info;
even → next → nextNULL;
}
}
else if(odd = = NULL)
{
create node();
odd = p;
odd → info = p → info;
odd → next = NULL;
}
else
{
create node();
odd → next = p;
odd → next → info = p → info;
odd → next → next = NULL;
}
p = p → next;
}        //while loop ends
}        //split function ends
```

3. (a) What is a height-balanced tree? Construct an AVL tree for the following elements:
5, 9, 12, 10, 6, 1, 20, 8, 4, 15

Ans. Height-balanced Tree or AVL Tree :

Refer to Dec-04, Q6(b)(i), Page No.-214

The AVL Tree for following elements 5, 9, 12, 10, 6, 1, 20, 8, 4, 15 is as follows:

1) Insert 5 :

Here balancing factor = 0 ∵ No left subtree and no right subtree.

2) Insert 9 :

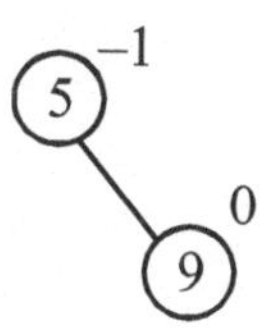

⑦ AVL Tree is Right High
⑧ BF of Root =–1

3) Insert 12 :

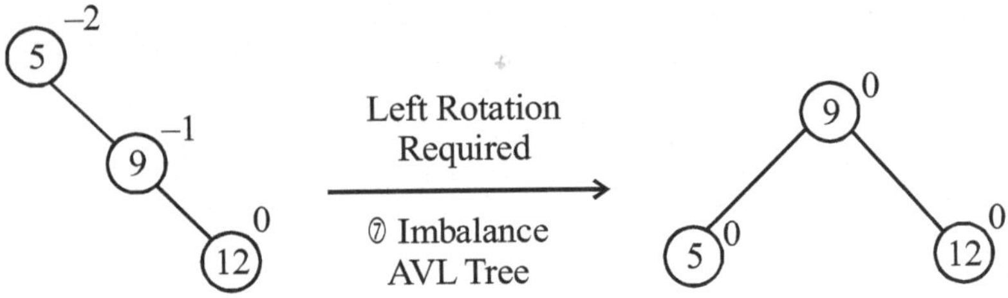

4) Insert 10 :

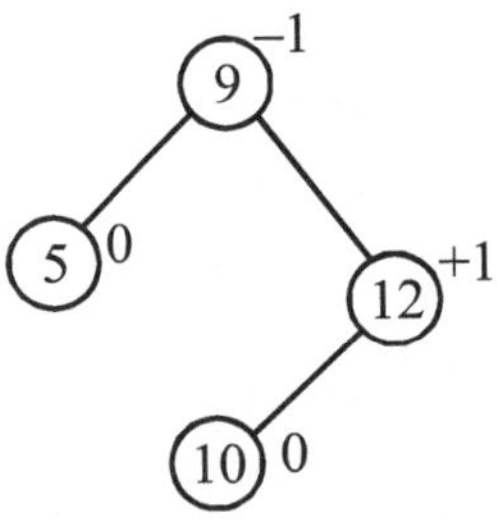

5) Insert 6 :

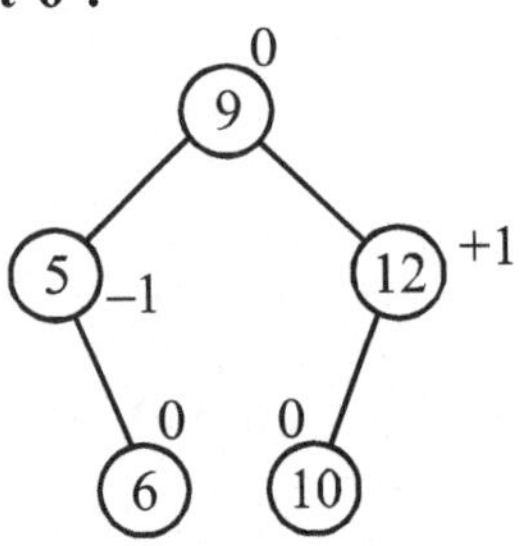

6) Insert 1 :

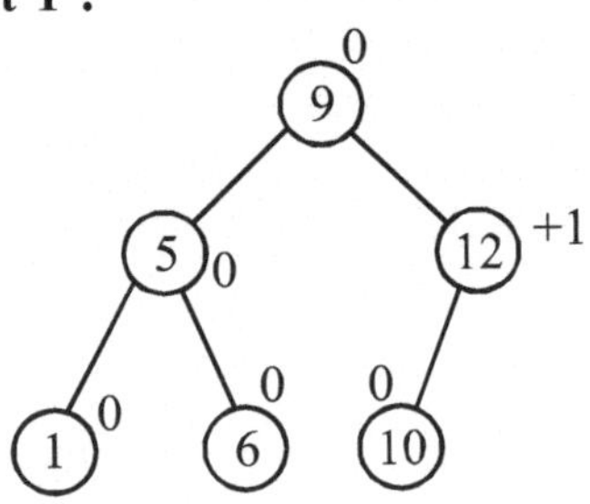

7) Insert 20 :

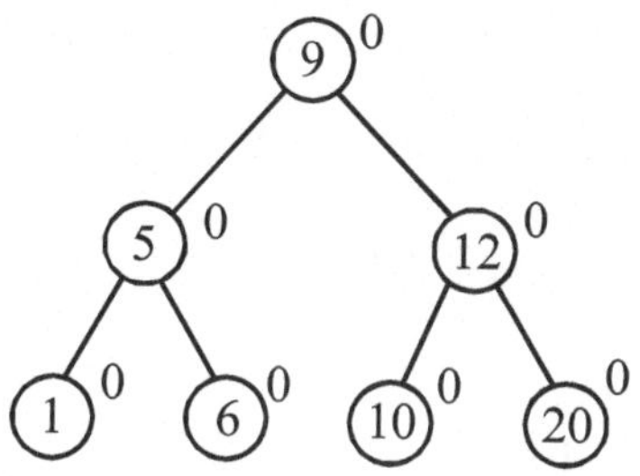

8) Insert 8 :

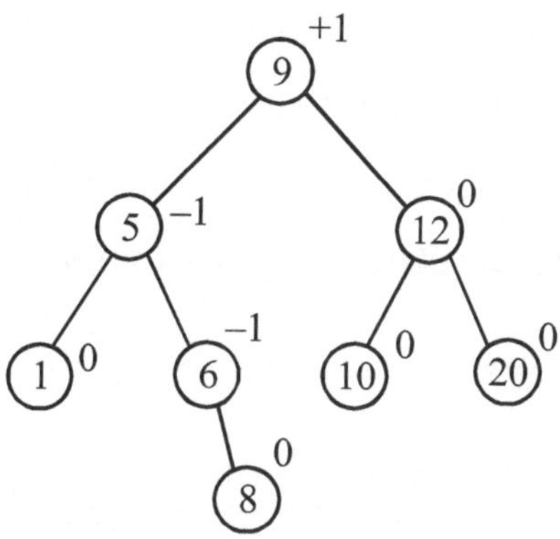

9) Insert 4 :

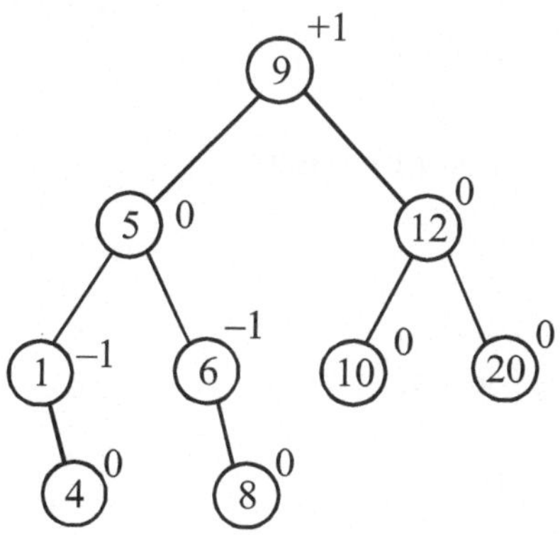

10) Insert 15 :

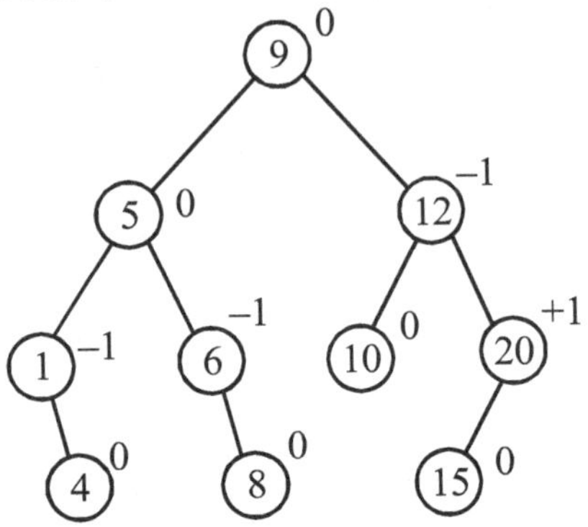

Note : Value of Balancing Factor for Left High AVL Tree = +1
Value of Balancing Factor for Right High AVL Tree = -1
Value of Balancing factor for an equal AVL Tree = 0

(b) Write a recursive function to calculate the 'gcd' of a number.

Ans. General Logic for GCD

$$GCD(x, y) = \begin{cases} x & \text{if } y = 0 \\ GCD(y, x\%y) & \text{if } y \neq 0 \end{cases}$$

```
int gcd(int x, int y)          //Recursive function for gcd
{
if(y = = 0)
return(x);
else
return(gcd(y, x%y));
}
main( )                        //main function of program
int a, b, ans = 0;
printf("Enter two numbers");
scanf("%d%d", &a, &b);
ans = gcd(a, b);
printf("The GCD of %d and %d is %d", a, b, ans);
}
```

4. (a) Consider the following graph:

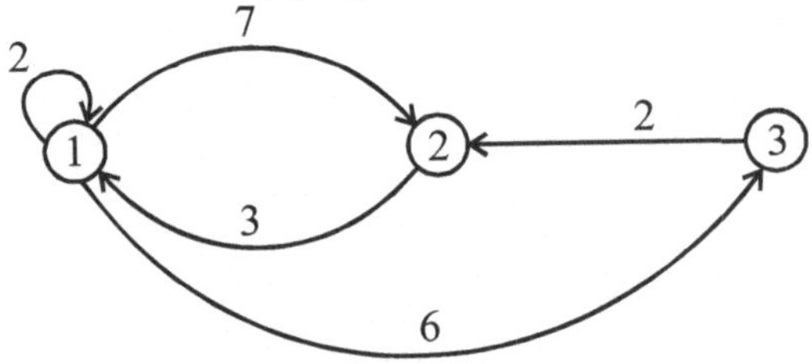

Make the adjacency matrix for the given graph. Also, write an algorithm to compute the transpose of the matrix.

Ans. Adjacency Matrix for given graph is as follows :

$$\begin{array}{c} \\ 1 \\ 2 \\ 3 \end{array}\begin{array}{c} \begin{array}{ccc} 1 & 2 & 3 \end{array} \\ \begin{bmatrix} 1 & 1 & 1 \\ 1 & 0 & 0 \\ 0 & 1 & 0 \end{bmatrix} \end{array}$$

Algorithm to compute the transpose of a Matrix

Note: We can take transpose of a Matrix which is a square matrix.

$\therefore$ We are considering a two dimensional array MAT[N × N] where No. of Rows = No. of Columns = N

Algorithm: TRANSPOSE OF MATRIX MAT[N × N]

Step 1: REPEAT STEPS 2 to 3 FOR I = 1 To N

Step 2: REPEAT STEPS 3 FOR J = 1 To N

Step 3: SET MAT[I, J]:= MAT[J, I]

Step 4: REPEAT STEPS 5 to 6 FOR I = 1 To N

Step 5: REPEAT STEP 6 FOR J = 1 To N

Step 6: PRINT MAT[I, J]

Step 7: EXIT

(b) What is the difference between Sequential and Direct file organisations? Under what condition, if any, is it advantageous to have the file organized as a direct file rather than sequential file?

Ans. Refer to Dec-2004, Q.No.-4(ii), Page No.-207

5. Explain the following with example:

(a) Column-major order

Ans. Refer to Dec-2004, Q.No.-6(iii), Page No.-215

(b) Structures vs Unions

Ans. Refer to June-2005, Q.No.-5(b), Page No.-196

(c) Complete binary tree

Ans. Refer to Chapter-3, Page No.-95

(d) m-way merging

Ans. Refer to Dec-2006, Q.No.5(v), Page No.-290

(e) Spanning tree

Ans. Refer to Chapter-4, Page No.-133

CS-62 : 'C' PROGRAMMING AND DATA STRUCTURE
December, 2007

Note : Question no. 1 is **compulsory**. Answer any three questions from the rest. All algorithms should be written nearer to 'C' language.

1. (a) Define an AVL tree. Construct a height balanced tree for the following list of elements

4, 6, 12, 8, 4, 15, 7, 3

Ans. AVL Tree i.e. Adelson – Velskii – Landis Tree. If T is a non-empty binary tree with T_L and T_R as Left and Right subtrees, than T is an AVL tree if and only if:

(i) $|h_L - h_R| \leq 1$ where h_L is height of Left subtree T_L and h_R is height of Right subtree T_R

(ii) T_L and T_R are independently AVL trees.

Every node in an AVL tree has a field Balancing factor i.e. bf. The value of bF is chosen as:

$$bf = \begin{cases} -1 & \text{if } h_L < h_R \\ 0 & \text{if } h_L = h_R \\ +1 & \text{if } h_L > 1 \end{cases}$$

The AVL tree of given elements 4, 6, 12, 8, 4, 2 15, 7, 3 is given below:

Step 1) Insert 4

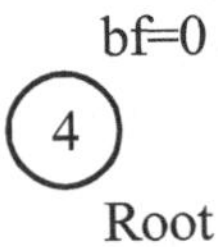

Step 2) Insert 6

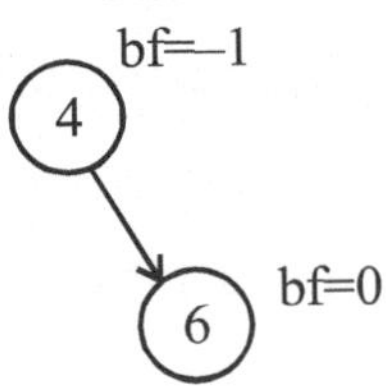

Step 3) Insert 12

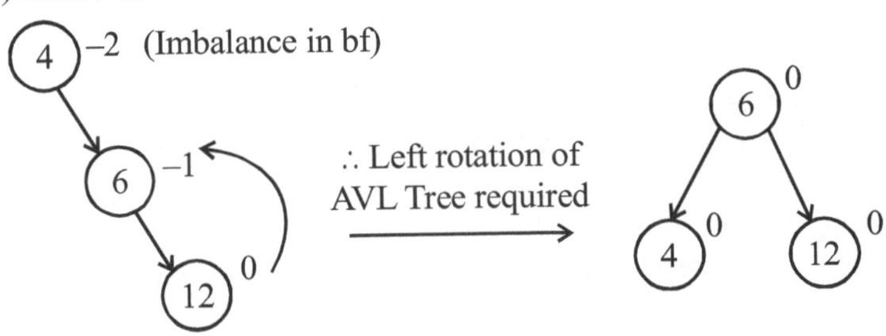

Step 4) Insert 8

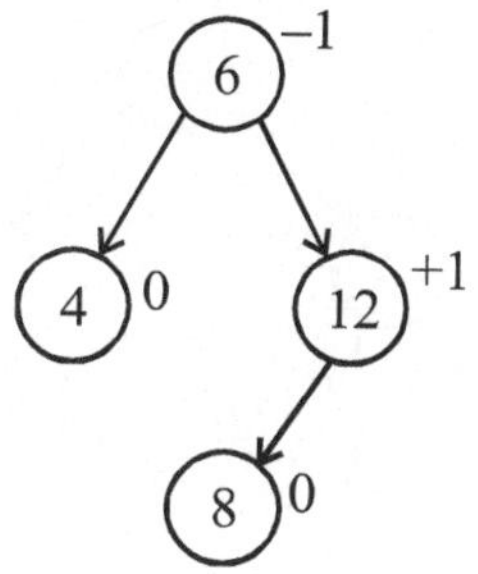

Step 5) Insert 4

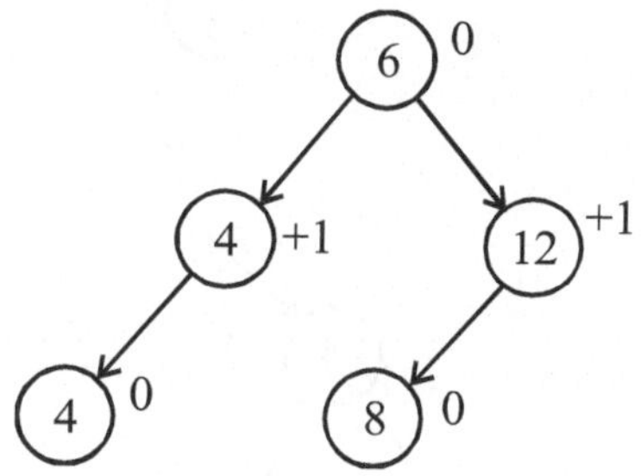

Step 6) Insert 2

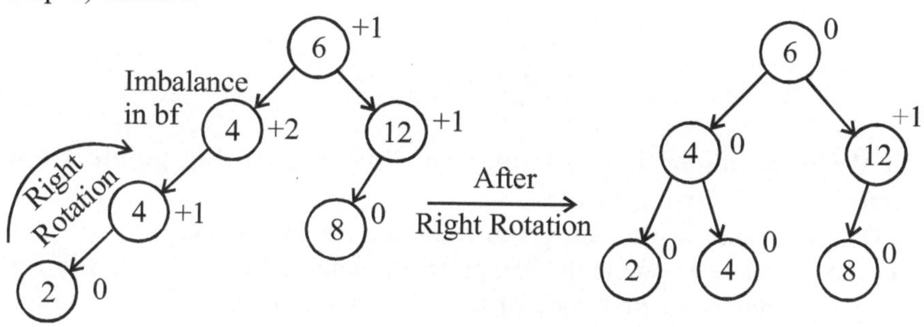

Step 7) Insert 15

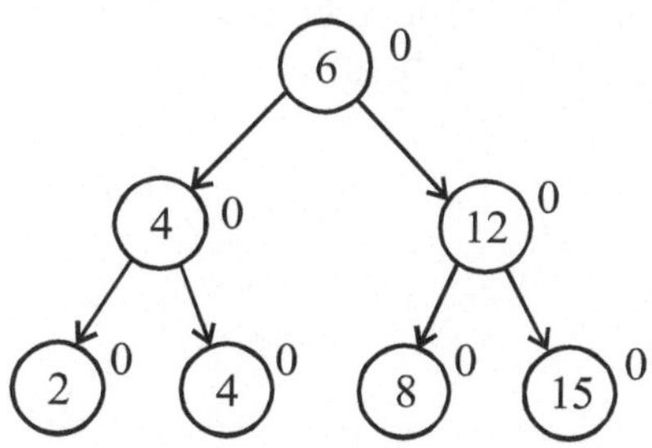

Step 8) Insert 7

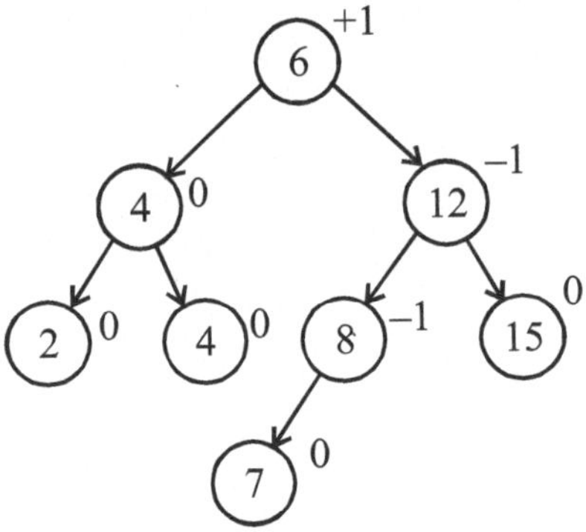

Step 9) Insert 3

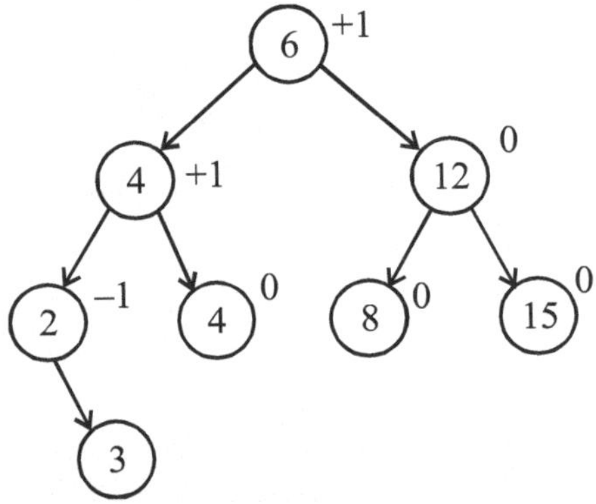

(b) Write an algorithm to implement linked list using pointers and perform the following tasks:

(i) Delete a node in the list, given a pointer to that node.

Ans. (i) To delete a node in the list, given a pointer to that node, we will first assign the address of first node of the list to the pointer variable head and assign the address of the node to be deleted to pointer variable pos.

```
void deleteptr (node *head, *pos)
{
node *ptr, *loc;
ptr = head;
while(ptr != pos)
ptr = ptr → next;
loc = ptr → next;
loc → next = ptr → next → next;
Free(ptr);
}
```

(ii) Write a function to reverse the linked list.

Ans. To reverse a linear linked list, three pointer fields are used.

1) previousNode: it holds the address of previous node

2) currentNode: current node address and

3) nextNode: it holds the address of next node.

Here the first node will become the last node of the list and the link field of first node is set to NULL

```
void reverseList (node **head)
{
node *previousNode, *currentNode, *nodeNode;
currentNode = *head;
nextNode = currentNode → next;
previousNode = NULL;
currentNode → next = NULL;
while(nextNode != NULL)
{
previousNode = currentNode;
currentNode = nextNode;
nextNode = currentNode → next;
currentNode → next = previousNode;
}
*head = currentNode;
}
```

(c) Write an algorithm that reads m × n matrix "A" and p × q matrix "B", checks whether these matrices are multipliable in either order or not. (e.g. whether A × B or B × A is defined). Further, if A × B or B × A is defined then calculate the product.

Note : Show proper error handling also.

Ans. Two matrices of order a × b and c × d can be multiplies when number of columns in first matrix are equal to the number of rows in second matrix i.e.

if $\boxed{b = c}$ in this case then we can multiply these two matrices of order a × b and c × d

Program for matrices multiplication:

```
# include <stdio.h>
# include <conio.h>
main ( )
{
int mat1[3][4], mat2[4][2], mat3[3][2];
int i, j, k;
```

```
printf("Enter matrix mat1");
for(i = 0; i < 3; i++)
for(j = 0; j < 4; j++)
scanf("%d", &mat1[i][j]);
printf("Enter matrix mat2");
for(i = 0; i < 4; i++)
for(j = 0; j < 2; j++)
scaf("%d", &mat2[j][j]);
/*MULTIPLICATION*/
for(i = 0; i < 3; i++)
for(j = 0; i < 2; j++)
{
mat3[i][j] = 0;
for(k = 0; k < 4; k++)
mat3[i][j] += mat1[i][k] * mat2[k][j]
}
printf("The Resultant Matrix Mat3 is: \n");
for(i = 0; i < 3; i++)
{
for(j = 0; j < 2; j++)
printf("%5d", mat3[i][j]);
printf("\n");
}
}
```

(d) Calculate the time complexity of the following code by using Big 'O' notation:

1. Scanf ("%d", &n);
2. Scanf ("%d", &m);
3. for (i=0; i<m+n; i+=2)
4. Prinf ("%d \n", i-1);
5. for (j=m • n/100; j<=m • n; j++)
6. Prinf ("%d \n",j);

Ans. The time complexity of above code using Big 'O' notation is:

$$f(m,n)=O\left[(m+n)\left(m*n-\frac{m*n}{100}\right)\right]$$

$$=O\left[(m+n)(m*n)\left(1-\frac{1}{100}\right)\right]$$

$$= O\left[(m+n)(m*n)\left(\frac{99}{100}\right)\right]$$

2. (a) Write an algorithm, that accepts 12 words of different string-size. Arrange the words in descending order based on the sum of ASCII values of the characters in the string.
e.g. : If string is "ABCD", its ASCII mapping is 65, 66, 70, 68 respectively and sum is 65 + 66 + 70 + 68 = 269
***Hint :* ASCII value of 'A' starts with 65, and 'a' starts with 97.**
Ans. Refer www.Gullybaba.com/ignou/bca/cs62.htm

(b) Write an algorithm to implement bubble sort technique. Also, show the steps of bubble sort on the following given number:

"5, 12, 38, 7, 3, 18, 68, 115"

Ans. Algorithm in 'C' Language

```
bubble_sort(int a[n])
{
int i, j, temp, n;
for(i = 0; j < n – 1; i++)
for(j = 0; j < n – 1 – i; j++)
if(a[j] > a[j + 1])
{
temp = a[i];
a[j] = a[j + 1];
a[j + 1] = temp;
}
}
```

Interaction 1:

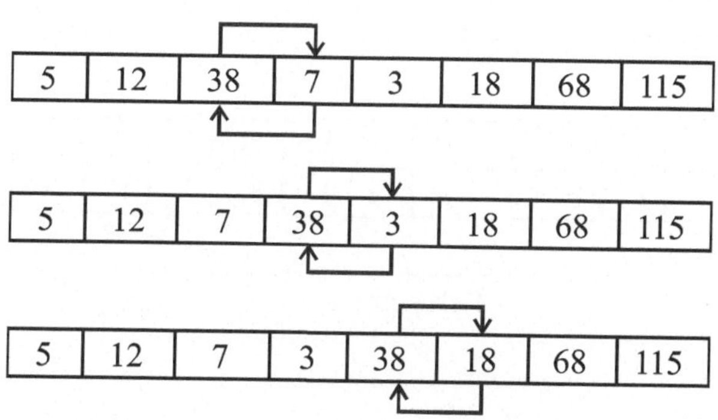

5	12	7	3	18	38	68	115

Interaction 2:

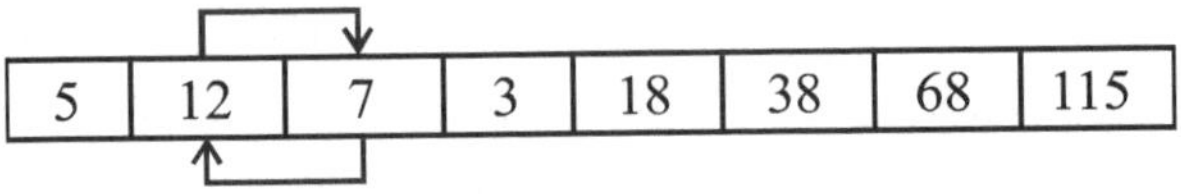

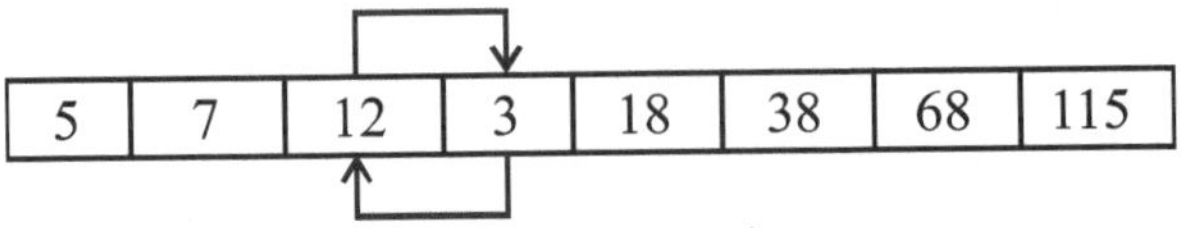

5	7	3	12	18	38	68	115

Interaction 3:

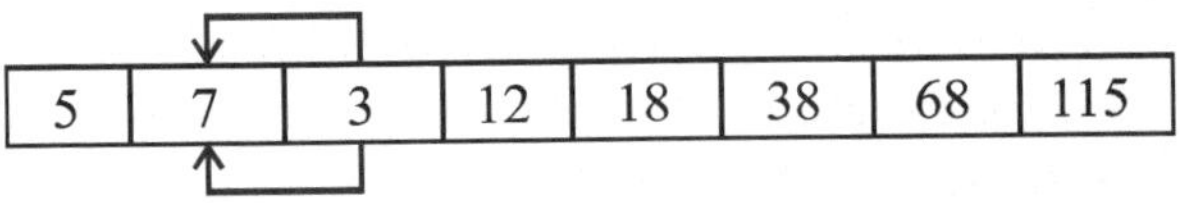

5	3	7	12	18	38	68	115

Interaction 4:

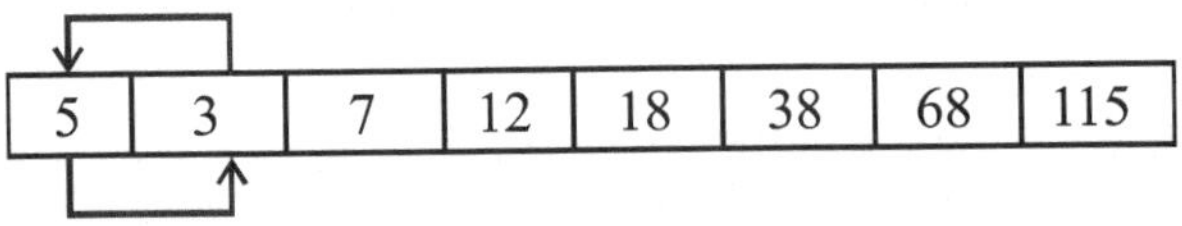

3	5	7	12	18	38	68	115

3. (a) Construct the binary tree using the following preorder and inorder sequences:
Preorder : A B C E I F J D G H K L
Inorder : E I C F J B G D K H L A
Also, write the postorder sequence of it.

Ans.

Preorder	A	B	C	E	I	F	J	D	G	H	K	L
Inorder	E	I	C	F	J	B	G	D	K	H	L	A

Left subtree (E I C F J B G D K H L) — Root (A)

Insert :A

Preorder	A	B	C	E	I	F	J	D	G	H	K	L
Inorder	E	I	C	F	J	B	G	D	K	H	L	A

Left subtree　　Root　　Right subtree

Insert B :

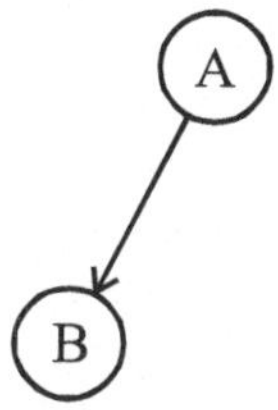

Insert C :

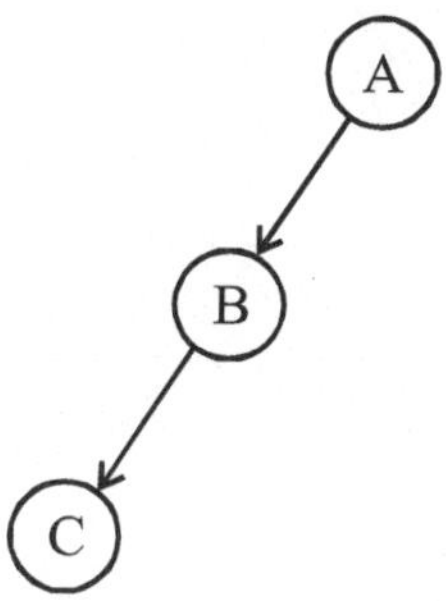

Insert E :

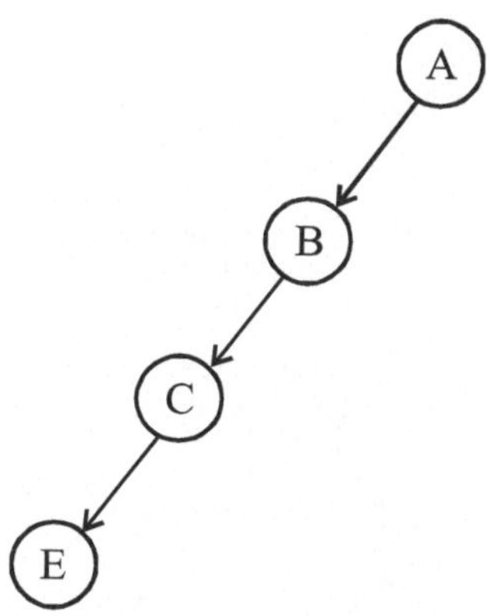

Insert I :

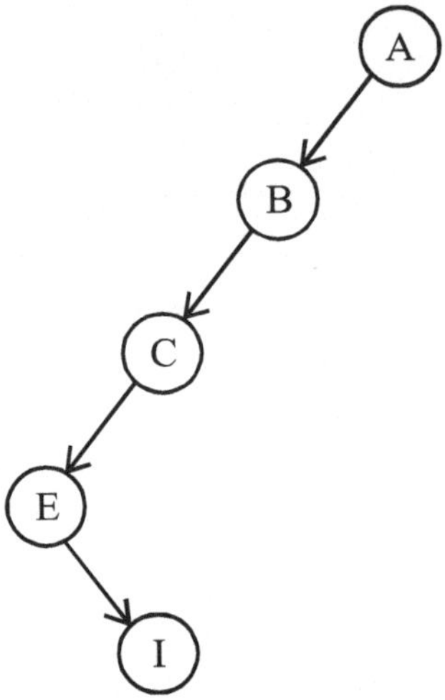

Insert F :

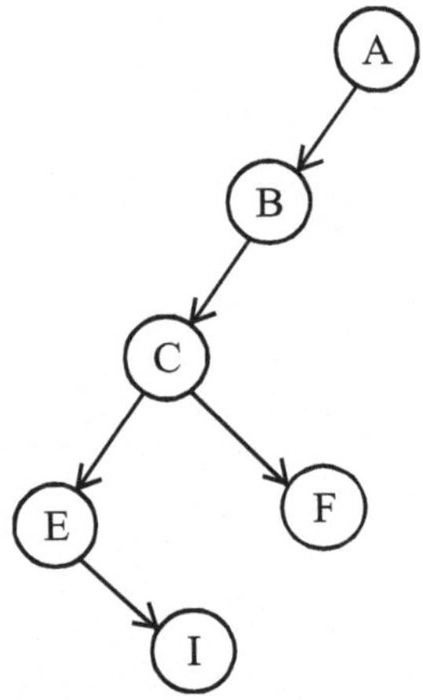

Insert J :

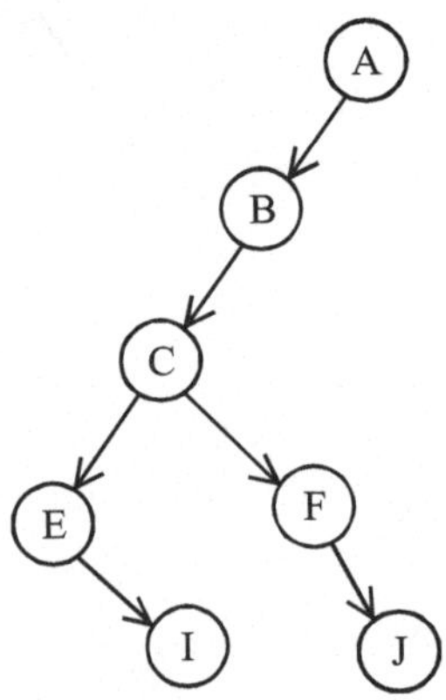

Insert D :

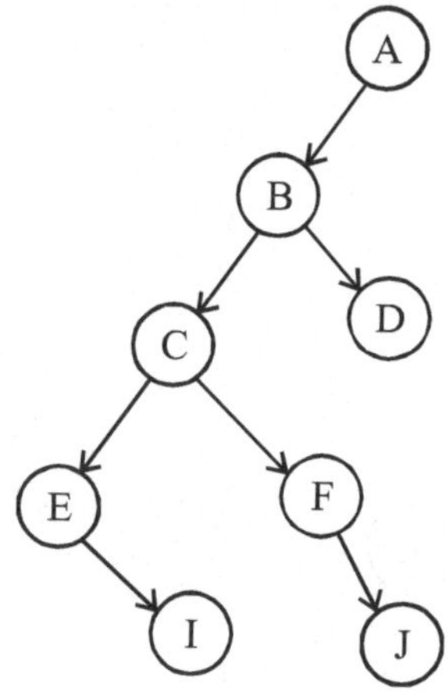

Insert G :

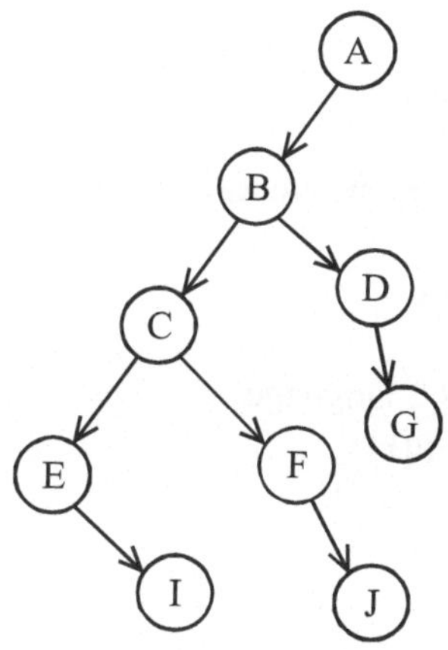

Insert H :

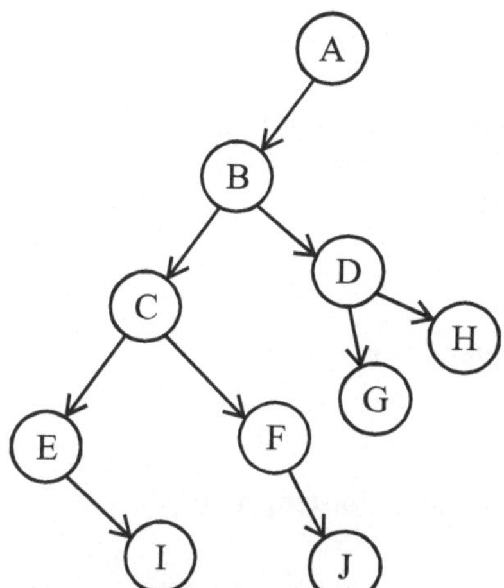

Insert K, L :

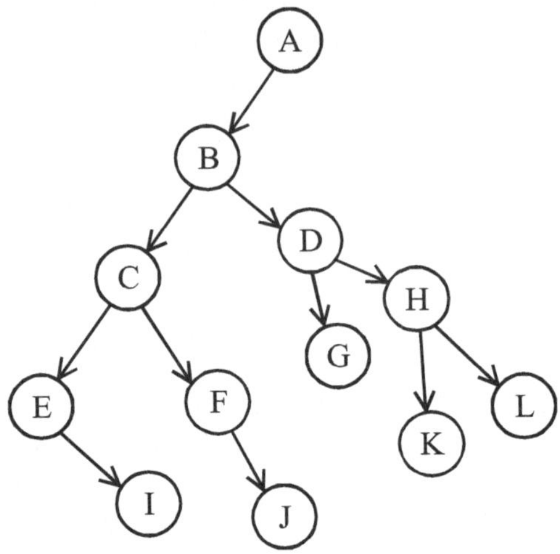

Postorder of tree

Postorder: IEJFCGKLHDBA

(b) Write algorithms to perform the following operations in circular queue:

(i) Create a circular queue

Ans. (i)

Create a circular queue ('C' language)

```
void createqueue(queue *pq)
{
pq → front = 1;
pq → rear = –1;
}
```

Note : Here the queue which we have created is an empty queue.

(ii) Check whether a queue is empty

Ans. Check whether a queue is empty ('C' language)

```
void eqempty(void)
{
if(front = = φ)
{
printf("Circular queue is empty");
}
else
{
printf("Circular queue is not-empty");
}
```

```
}
```

(iii) Insert an element in a queue

Ans. Insert an element in a queue

```
void eqinsert(void)
{
int i;
if(front = = -1)
{
front = rear = 0;
printf("\n Enter the item to be inserted");
scanf("%d", &equeue[rear]);
}
else
{
if(rear = = size – 1)
i = 0;
else
i = rear + 1;
if(i = = front)
{
printf("\n !!Queue overflow!! \n");
}
else
{
rear = i;
printf("\n Enter the item to be inserted");
scanf("%d", &equeue[rear]);
}
}
}
```

4. (a) Consider the following graph:

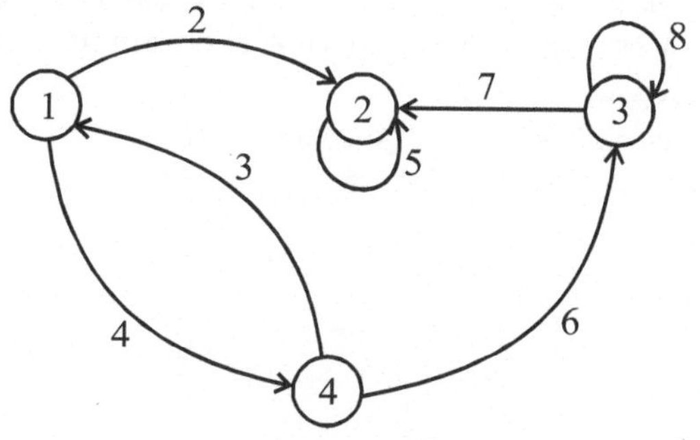

Make the adjacency matrix for the given graph. Also, write an algorithm to compute the transpose of the matrix.

Ans.

	1	2	3	4
1	0	1	0	1
2	0	1	0	0
3	0	1	1	0
4	1	0	1	0

Algo for transpose of Matrix :

```
# define Row3
# define Col4
main ( )
{
int mat1[Row][Col], mat2[Col][Row], i, j;
printf("Enter matrix mat1(%d%d);
for(i = 0; i < Row; i++)
for(j = 0; j < Col; j++)
scanf("%d", &mat1[i][j]);
for(i = 0; i < Col; i++)
for(j = 0; j < Row; j++)
mat2[i][j] = mat1[j][i];
printf("Transpose of matrix is: \n");
for(i = 0; i < Col; i++)
{
for(j = 0; j < Row; j++)
printf("%5d", mat2[i][j]);
printf("\n");
}
}
```

(b) What is a sparse matrix? Which method is used to represent its non-zero elements? Also, write the algorithm corresponding to this method, explaining its steps.

Ans. An m × n matrix A is said to be sparse if many of its elements are zero. The best method to represent its non-zero elements is linked list.

Example:

$$\begin{bmatrix} 0 & 0 & 0 & 2 & 0 \\ 0 & 0 & 1 & 0 & 5 \\ 0 & 4 & 0 & 0 & 0 \\ 0 & 0 & 0 & 0 & 0 \\ 0 & 0 & 0 & 0 & 0 \end{bmatrix}$$

A 5 × 6 sparse matrices

* A linked list of columns containing non-zero terms, in the ascending order of their column values. Each node of this lists has three fields: col (column number for corresponding row list), term (a non-zero value in column col) and link (a pointer to the next column having non-zero element).

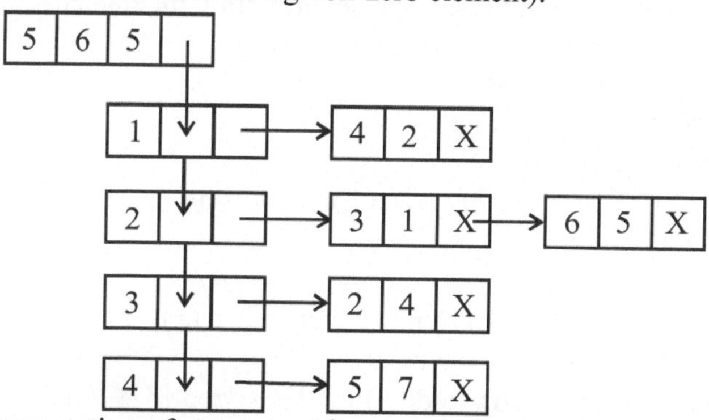

Linked representation of sparse matrix

```
/* Structure of column node */
typedef struct columnNodeType
{
int col;
float element;
struct columnNode *link;
}
columnNode;

/*Structure of row Node */
typedef struct rowNodeType
{
int row;
struct rowNode * next;
struct columnNode * first;
}
```

```
rowNode;

/*Structure of header node */
typedef struct headerNodeType
{
int nrow;
int ncol;
int num;
struct rowNode * head;
}
headerNode;

void storeElement(headerNode * sparse, int i, int j, int element)
{
rowNode *rptr, *pptr1, *ptr1;
columnNode *cptr, *pptr2, *ptr2;
sparse → num++;
cptr = (columnNode *) malloc (sizeof(columnNode));
cptr → col = j;
cptr → element = element;
if(sparse → head = = NULL) /*sparse matrix is empty*/
{
sparse → head = rptr = (rowNode *) malloc (sizeof(rowNode));
rptr → next = (rowNode *) NULL;
rptr → row = i;
rptr → first = cptr;
cptr → link = (columnNode *) NULL;
return;
}
pptr1 = (rowNode *) NULL;
ptr1 = sparse → head;
while((pptr != (rowNode *)NULL) &&(ptr1 → row < i))
{
pptr1 = ptr1;
ptr1 = ptr1 → next;
}
if(ptr1 → ow = = i) /*if row already exists*/
{
pptr2 = (columnNode *)NULL);
ptr2 = ptr1 → first;
```

```
while((pptr2 != (columnNode *)NULL)&&(ptr2 → col < j))
{
pptr2 = ptr2;
ptr2 = ptr2 → link;
}
/*insert as first column node*/
if(pptr2 = = (columnNode *)NULL)
{
cptr → link = ptr1 → first
ptr1 → first = cptr;
}
else
{
cptr → link = ptr2;
}
pptr2 → link = cptr;
}
return;
else if(ptr1 = = (rowNode *)NULL) /*insert new row at end*/
{
rptr = (rowNode *) malloc (sizeof(rowNode));
pptr1 → next = rptr;
rptr → next = (rowNode *)NULL);
rptr → row = i;
rptr → first = cptr;
cptr → link = (columnNode *)NULL;
return;
}
else
{
rptr = (rowNode *) malloc (sizeof(rowNode));
rptr → row = i;
rptr → next = ptr1
pptr1 → next = rptr;
rptr → first = cptr
cptr → link = (columnNode *)NULL);
}
}
```

5. Explain the following with an example of each:

(a) Direct file organisation

Ans. Refer to Chapter-3, Page No. 127

(b) Depth first search

Ans. Depth First Search : It is a searching method in graph. The edges are explored out of the most recently discovered vertex V that still has unexplored edges leaving it.

Depth First Search is an that search backtracks to explore edges leaving the vertex from which V was discovered. This process continues till we have discovered all the vertices that are reachable from the source vertex. This algorithm reaches both in directed as well as in undirected graphs.

- DFS makes use of stack structure to maintain the order in which the vertices are to be processed, instead of queue.
- DFS algorithm also uses the same colouring scheme as described for BFS i.e. white, gray or black; where WHITE color indicates that vertex which is still undiscovered, GRAY color indicates that vertex that is discovered but not yet processed and BLACK color indicates that vertex which has been processed in the graph.

(c) B-tree

Ans. B-tree : B-tree was discovered by R. Bayer and E. McCreight of Boeing Scientific Labs.

Later B-tree has become one of the most popular techniques for organizing an index structure.

A B-tree of order m is an m-way search tree with the following properties:

(1) Each node of the tree, except the root node and leaves, has at least m/2 subtrees and no more than m subtrees.

(2) Root of the tree has at least two subtrees unless it is a leaf node.

(3) All leaves of the tree are on the same level.

Most popular B-trees are:

(1) B^+ Tree : It is a B-tree in which the leaves nodes are linked to each other from left to right to form a linked list of the keys in sequential order.

(2) B* Tree : It is a B-tree in which each interior node is at least two third full rather than just half full.

(d) Column major order

Ans. Refer to June-2007, Q.No.-5(a), Page No.-301

CS – 62 : 'C' Programming and Data Structure
June, 2008

Note : Question number 1 is **compulsory.** Answer any **three** questions from the rest. All of the above algorithms should be written nearer to 'C' language.

Q1. (a) What is sparse matrix? Discuss methods of representation of sparse matrix in memory. Explain row-major and column-major order with example.

Refer to Page-314, Q.No.-4(b) and Page-281, Q.No.-1(a)

(b) What is a binary search tree? Write an algorithm to find an element in a binary search tree.

First Refer to Q22, Page No.122.

The algorithm to find an element in a binary search tree is as follows; Each node contains four fields: k which holds the record's key value, r, which holds the record itself, and left and right, which are pointers to the sub trees.

```
p = tree;
while ( p!= null &&  key!= k(p))
   p = ( key < k(p)) ? left(p) :right(p):
return(p);
```

(c) Define a circular queue. What is the condition that a circular queue is full (if queue is implemented using array)? Write an algorithm for inserting a node at given location in a circular queue.

Refer to Page-74, Q.No.-27

(d) Differentiate between internal and external sorting. Which sorting algorithm is preferred for external sorting? Write an algorithm for K-way merge sort.

Ans. Refer Page No.-153, First two paragraphs.

A K-way Merge Algorithm Assumptions :

Suppose that we want to merge k lists: list0, list1, list2, listk-1

Lists list0…listk-1 are sorted.

A K-way Merge Algorithm : Initialize all lists to the point to the first item (call this item *item(listi)*)

```
Loop until there are items to be processes.
   Select the minimum item (minItem) among the k elements.
   Output this item
   Loop from i=0 to k-1
    if minItem = item(listi) then advance listi
  EndLoop
EndLoop
```

Q2. (a) Write a program in C for binary search tree.

Ans. /* binary search tree: bst.c */

```
#include <stdio.h>
#include <stdlib.h>
#define compLT(a, b) (a < b)
#define compEQ(a, b) (a = = b)
/* implementation dependents declarations */
typedef enum { STATUS_OK,
STATUS_MEM_EXHAUSTED,
STATUS_DUPLICATE_KEY,
STATUS_KEY_NOT_FOUND
} statusEnum;

typedef int keyType;                /* type of key */

/* user data stored in tree */
typedef struct {
int stuff;                          /* optional related data */
} recType;

typedef struct node Tag
{ struct nodeTag *left;             /* left child */
struct nodeTag *right;              /* right child */
struct nodeTag *parent;             /* parent */
keyType key;                        /* key used for searching */
recType rec;                        /* user data */
} node Type;

nodeType *root = NULL;              /* root of binary tree */

statusEnuminsert(keyType key, recType *rec)
{ nodeType *x, *current, *parent;
/* Allocate node for data and insert in tree. Find future parent.* /
current = root;
parent = 0;
while(current)
{ if(compEQ(key, current->key))
return STATUS_DUPLICATE_KEY;
parent = current;
current = compLT(key, current->key) ?
current->left : current->right; }
/* setup new node */
if((x = malloc(sizeof(*x))) = = 0)
{ return STATUS_MEM_EXHAUSTED; }
x->parent = parent;
x->left = NULL;
x->right = NULL;
x->key = key;
x->rec = *rec;
```

```
/* insert x in tree */
if(parent)
if(compLT(x->key, parent->key))
parent->left = x;
else
parent->right = x;
else
root = x;
return STATUS_OK;
}

statusEnumdelete(keyTye key) { nodeType *x, *y, *z;
/*Delete node from tree. Find node in tree. */
z = root;
while(z != NULL)
{ if(compEQ(key, z->key)
break;
else
z = compLT(key, z->key) ? z->left : z->right;
}
if(!z) return STATUS_KEY_NOT_FOUND;

/* find tree successor */
if(z->left = = NULL || z->right = = NULL)
y = z;
else
{ y = z->right;
while(y->left != NULL) y = y->left;
}

/* x is y's only child */
if(y->left != NULL)
x = y->left;
else
x = y->right;

/* remove y from the parent chain */
if(x) x->parent = y->parent;
if(y->parent)
if(y = = y->parent->left)
y->parent->left = x;
else
y->parent->right = x;
else
root = x;
```

```
/* if z and y are not the same, replace z with y */
if(y != z)
{ y->left = z->left;
if(y->left) y->left->parent = y;
y->right = z->right;
if(y->right) y->right->parent = y;
y->parent = z->parent;
if(z->parent)
if(z = = z->parent->left)
z->parent->left = y;
else
z->parent->right = y;
else
root = y;
free(z);
} else
{ free(y);
}
return STATUS_OK;      }
statusEnum find(keyType key, recType *rec) {

/*Find node containing data */
nodeType *current = root;
while(current != NULL)
{ if(compEQ(key, current->key))
{
*rec = current->rec;
return STATUS_OK;
} else {
current = compLT(key, current->key) ?
current->left : current->right; }
} return STATUS_KEY_NOT_FOUND; }
int main(int argc, char **argv)
{ int i, maximum, random;
recType *rec;
keyType *key;
statusEnum status;
maxnum = atoi(argv[1]);
random = argc > 2;
if((rec = malloc(maxnum * sizeof(recType))) = = 0)
{ fprintf(stderr, "insufficient memory (rec)\n");
exit(1); }
if((key = malloc(maxnum * sizeof(keyType))) = = 0)
{ fprintf(stderr, "insufficient memory (key)\n");
exit(1); }
if(random) {                          /* random */
```

```
/* fill "key" with unique random numbers */
for(i = 0; i < maxnum; i++) key[i] = rand( );
printf("ran bt, %d items\n", maxnum);
} else {
for(i = 0; i < maxnum; i++) key[i] = i;
printf("seq bt, %d items\n", maxnum);
}
for(i = 0; i < maxnum; i++)
{ status = insert(key[i], &rec[i]);
if(status) printf("pt1, i = %d: %d\n", i, status);
}
for(i = maxnum-1; i >= 0; i-)
{ status = find(key[i], &rec[i]);
if(status) printf("pt2, i = %d: %d\n", i, status);
}
for(i = maxnum-1; i >= 0; i-)
{ status = delete(key[i]);
if(status) printf("pt3, i = %d: %d\n", i, status);
} return 0; }
```

(b) Apply Binary search for elements in array P to find the element 40, 11, 22, 30, 33, 40, 44, 55, 60, 66, 77, 80, 88, 99.

Ans. Array elements are 11, 22, 30, 33, 40, 44, 55, 60, 66, 77, 80, 88, 99

As Array elements are in sorted order we can search an element using Binary Search method.

int A =

11	22	30	33	40	44	55	60	66	77	80	88	99

First Comparison: Beg = 0, End = 12

Mid = (Beg + End)/2 = 6

∴ A [Mid] = 60 and Item to be searched is 40

∴ Item < A [Mid]

∴ End will become Mid – 1 for 2nd comparison.

Second Comparison :

Beg = 0, End = Mid – 1

⇒ End = 6 – 1 = 5

Now, Mid = (Beg + End)/2 = 2

∵ A [Mid] = 30 and Item to be searched is 40

∵ Item > A [Mid]

∴ Beg will become Mid + 1 for 3rd comparison.

Third Comparison: Beg = Mid + 1, End = 5 = 3

Mid = (Beg + End)/2 = (3 + 5)/2 = 4

∵ A [Mid] = 40 and Item to be searched is 40

∴ Item will be found in 3rd comparison.

(c) What are the various disadvantages of sequential file organisation?

Ans. Refer Q26, Page No.-126

Q3. (a) Convert the following postfix expression into infix using stack:
A B C * D E F ↑ / G * - H * +

Ans. Infix:

Operand/ operator	Operation on stack	Stack	Operand/ operator	Operation on stack	Stack
1) A	PUSH A	A	10) G	PUSH G	G R3 R1 A
2) B	PUSH B	B A	11) *	POP G POP R3 R4 = R3 * G PUSH R4	R3 / R1 / A — POP G R1 / A — POP R3 R4 / R1 / A — PUSH R4
3) C	PUSH C	C B A	12) –	POP R4 POP R1 R5 = R1 – R4 PUSH R5	R1 / A — POP R4 A — POP R1 R5 / A — PUSH R5
4) *	POP C POP B R1 =B*C PUSH R1	B / A — POP C A — POP B R1 / A — PUSH R1	13) H	PUSH H	H R5 A
5) D	PUSH D	D R1 A	14) *	POP H POP R5 R6 = R5*H PUSH R6	R5 / A — POP H A — POP R5 R6 / A — PUSH R6
6) E	PUSH E	E D R1 A	15) +	POP R6 POP A R7 = A + R6 PUSH R7	R7
7) F	PUSH F	F E D R1 A			
8) ↑	POP F POP E R2 = E ↑ F PUSH R2	E / D / R1 / A — POP F D / R1 / A — POP E R2 / D / R1 / A — PUSH R2			
9) /	POP R2 POP D R3 D/R2 PUSH R3	D / R1 / A — POP R2 R1 / A — POP D R3 / R1 / A — PUSH R3			

(b) What is AVL tree? Construct an AVL search tree by inserting the following elements in order of their occurrence. (Show each of the rotations).

64, 1, 44, 26, 13, 110, 98, 85

Ans. Refer Page No.-95

The AVL tree of given elements 64, 1, 44, 26, 13, 110, 98, 85 is as follows:

(a) Inserting 64

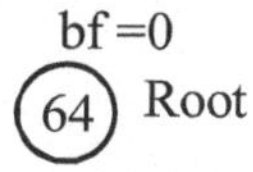

(b) Inserting 1

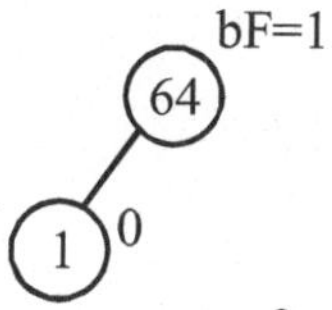

(c) Inserting 44

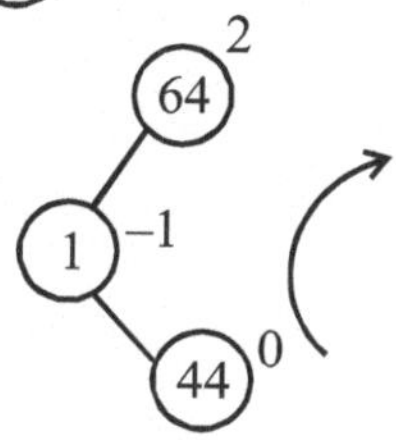

∴ bF of Root = 2
∴ Right Rotation is required

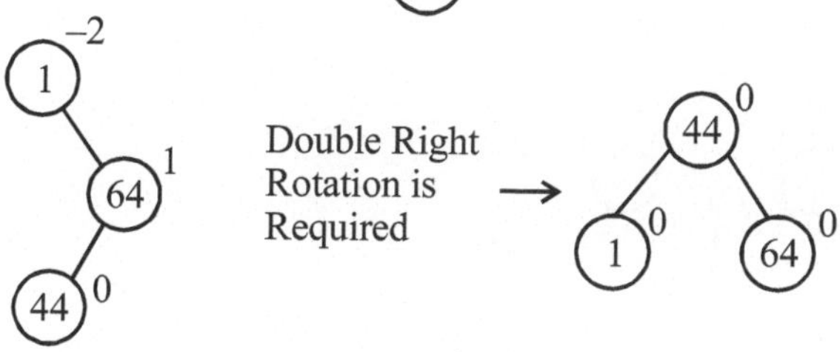

(d) Inserting 26

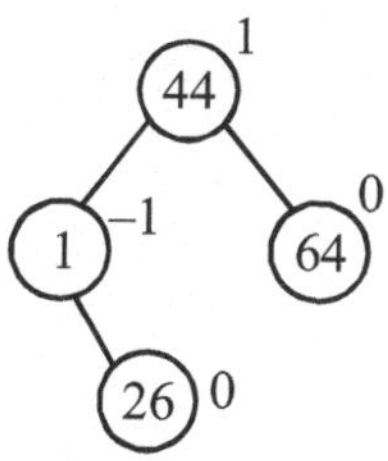

(e) Inserting 13

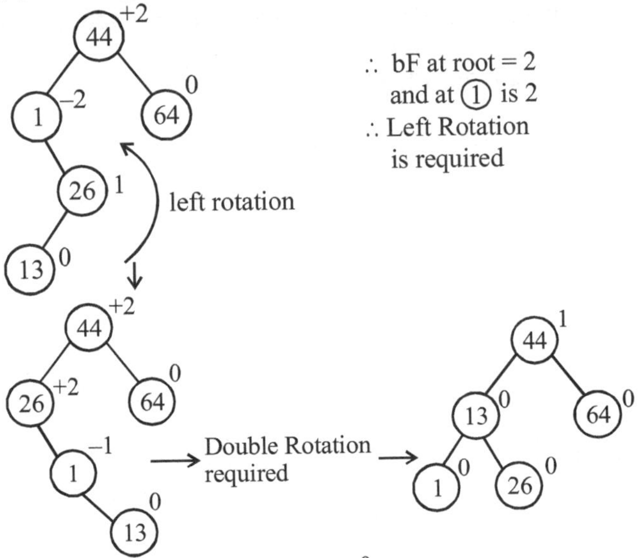

(f) Inserting 110

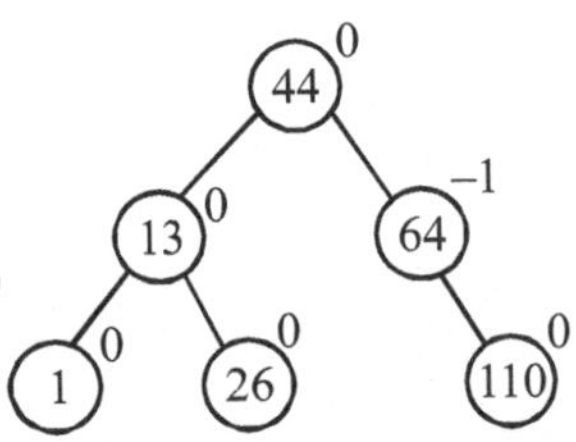

(g) Inserting 98

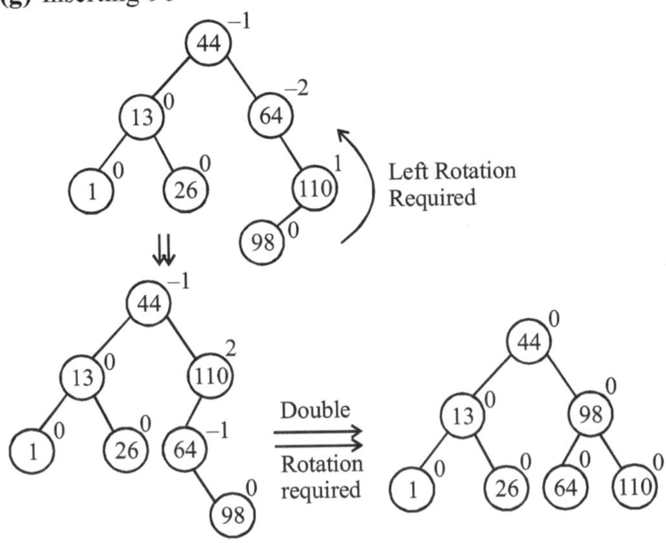

(h) Inserting 85

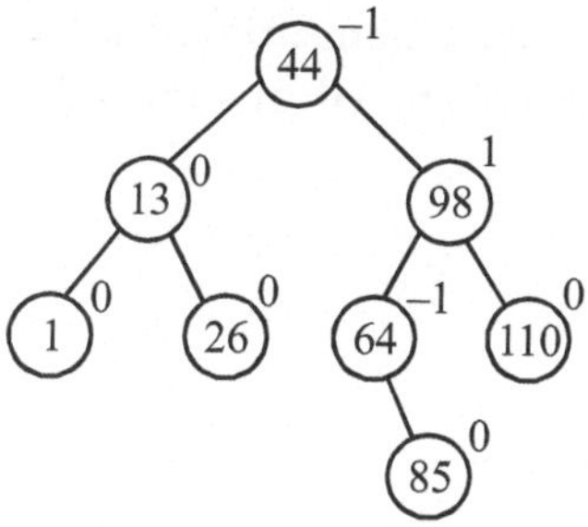

Final AVL Tree

Q4. Write short notes on the following:
(i) Directed graph

Ans. (i) Directed Graph or Digraph: Refer to Page-131, Chapter-4, Q.No.-1

(ii) Compaction: Refer Q4(a), Page No.-191

(iii) Complete Binary Tree: Refer to Chapter-3, Page No.-95

(iv) Hash Function: Refer Q3(a), Page No.-287

(v) Height Balanced Tree: A tree whose subtrees differ in height by no more than one and the subtrees are height-balanced, too. An empty tree is height-balanced.

Q5. (a) Write a program in C for bubble sort.

Ans. Program in C for Bubble Set

```
# include <stdio.h>
# define SIZE 10
main ( )
{ int arr[SIZE];
int i, j, temp;
printf ("Enter elements of the array\n");
for (i = 0; i < SIZE - 1; i++)
{ for (j = 0; j < SIZE - 1; i; j++)
{         if (arr[j] > arr[j + 1])
{                   temp = arr[j];
                    arr[j] = arr[j + 1];
                    arr[j + 1] = temp;          }          }          }
printf("Sorted array is: \n");
for (i = 0; i < SIZE; i++)
printf("%d", arr[i]);
printf("\n");       }
```

(b) Explain indexed-sequential file organisation. Under what conditions is it advantageous to have file organized as indexed-sequential rather than direct file?

Refer to Page-126, Q.No.-26

CS – 62 : 'C' Programming and Data Structure
December, 2008

Note : Question number 1 is **compulsory.** Answer any **three** questions from the rest. All of the above algorithms should be written nearer to 'C' language.

Q1. (a) Using Quick sort method, sort the following sequence in descending order : 07, 62, 54, 03, 94, 01, 100
What is the average run time complexity of the quick sort?

Ans.

7	62	54	3	94	1	100
a[0]	a[1]	a[2]	a[3]	a[4]	a[5]	a[6]

Let
loc = first
left = first
right = last

Pass: 1

7	62	54	3	94	1	100

loc   right
left

(In this statement condition is true now interchange)
while a[loc] < a[right]
tmp = a[loc]
a[loc] = a[right]
a[right] = tmp
loc = right

100	62	54	3	94	1	7

left   loc
                        right

Pass: 2

100	62	54	3	94	1	7

left   loc
                        right

Now check while a[loc] < a[left] condition true than left + +

100	62	54	3	94	1	7

     left   loc
                        right

Pass: 3

100	62	54	3	94	1	7

     left   loc
                        right

Now check while a[loc] < a[left] condition true than left + +

100	62	54	3	94	1	7

left loc
right

Now check while a[loc] < a[left] condition true then left + +

Pass: 4

100	62	54	3	94	1	7

left loc
right

Now check while a[loc] < a[left] condition is false.
In this Pass condition is false. So, we will check
while a[loc] > a[left] (Condition is true now interchange)
tmp = a[loc]
a[loc] = a[left]
a[left] = tmp
loc = left

100	62	54	7	94	1	3

left right
loc

Pass: 5

100	62	54	7	94	1	3

left right
loc

Now we will check while a[loc] > a[left] condition false. Now we will check while a[loc] > a[right] condition is true then right + +

100	62	54	7	94	1	3

left right
loc

Pass: 6

100	62	54	7	94	1	3

left right
loc

Now we will check while a[loc] > a[right] if condition is true than right + +

100	62	54	7	94	1	3

left right
loc

Pass: 7

100	62	54	7	94	1	3

left right
loc

while a[loc] > a[right] => Condition is false
Therefore, we will check
while a[loc] < a[right] (If condition is true than interchange)
tmp = a[loc]
a[loc] = a[right]
a[right] = tmp
loc = right

100	62	54	94	7	1	3

left right
loc

Pass: 8

100	62	54	94	7	1	3

left right
loc

Now we will check while a[loc] < a[left] if condition is true then left + +

100	62	54	94	7	1	3

right
loc
left

Now this list will be divided in two parts

100	62	54	94

left right
loc

7

1	3

left right
loc

100	94	62	54

7

1	3

left right
loc

While a[loc]< a (right)
True
Now Inter change
tmp = a[loc]
a[loc] = a[right]
a[right] = tmp
loc = right

Pass : 10

100	62	54	94

7

1	3

left right
loc

Now check a [loc] <a [left]
true left ++

100	94	62	54	7	3	1

right
loc left

Descending Order of Array:

100	94	62	54	7	3	1

Average runtime complexity of quick sort is = 0(n log n)

(b) Define stack? Implement PUSH and POP operations using pointers in 'C'.

Ans. Refer Page No.-67

Push Operation:

```
# include <stdio.h>
# include <malloc.h>
# include <conio.h>
void push (int data);       // function declaration //
struct node
{ int info;
  struct node * link;
} * top;

void main ( )
{int m
 printf("Enter your choice: \n");
 scanf("%d", & choice);
 push (m);                  // function call //
 getch ( ); }

void push (int data)        // function definition //
{ struct node * tmp
 tmp = (struct node *) malloc (sizeof(struct node));
 tmp → info = data;
 tmp → link = NULL;
 if (top = = NULL)
 top = temp;
 else {
tmp → link = top;
top = tmp;
} // end of else //
} // end of definition //
```

Pop Operation :

```
# include <stdio.h>
# include <conio.h>
# include <malloc.h>
void pop ( );               // function declaration //
struct node
{ int info;
```

```
struct node * link;
} * top;

void main ( )
{ pop ( );                              // function call //
 getch ( ); }

void pop ( );                           // function definition //
{ struct node * tmp
 if (top = = NULL) {
printf("Stack Empty"); }
while (top != NULL) {
 tmp = top;
 top = tmp → link;
 free(tmp);
} // end of while //
} // end of definition //
```

(c) Write a program in 'C' to implement the following Binary Tree Traversals.

(i) Inorder Traversal

Ans. void inorder (tree * root)

```
{ if (root)
{ inorder (root → lptr)
printf("%d", root → info);
inorder (root → rptr);    }        }
```

(ii) Preorder Traversal

Ans. struct node

```
{ int info;
struct node *lptr, *rptr; }
function for PREORDER
void preorder (tree * root)
{ if (root)
{ printf("%d\t", root → info);
preorder (root → lptr);
preorder (root → rptr); }        }
```

(iii) Postorder Traversal

Ans. void postorder (tree * root)

```
{ if (root)
{ post order (root → lptr)
post order (root → rptr)
printf("%d\t", root → info); }     }
```

Q2. (a) Discuss the following file organization methods w.r.t. the structure, operations like insertion of records, deletion of records, updation of records and retrieval :
(i) Sequential files
(ii) Indexed files
Give the applications of above two file organization techniques.

Refer to Page-126, Q.No.-26

(b) Write a program in 'C' to count :
(i) Number of words in a given string

Ans.
```
# include <stdio.h>
main ( )
{ char line[100];
int count = 0, i = 0;
printf("Enter the line of text:");
gets(line);
while(line [i] != '\0')
{ if (line[i] = = 32)
count ++;
i++;
}
if(line[i] = = '\0')
count ++;
printf("The number of words in line = %d\n", count);
}
```

(ii) Number of vowels in a given string

Ans.
```
main ( )
{ char line[50];
int count = 0, i = 0;
printf("Enter a string:");
gets(line);
while(line [i] != '\0')
{ if (line[i] = = 'a' || line[i] = = 'e' || line[i] = = 'i' || line[i] = = 'o' || line[i] = =
'u')
```

```
count ++;
i++;
}
printf("The number of vowels in line string = %d\n", count);
}
```

Q3. (a) Write a program in 'C' to insert an element into singly linked list at :
(i) Beginning of list
(ii) Middle of list
(iii) End of list

Ans.

```
# include <stdio.h>
# include <conio.h>
# include <malloc.h>
struct node                          // structure define //
{
int info;
struct node * link;
} * start;

void Beginning of list (int data);   // function declaration //
void Middle of list (int data);      // function declaration //
void End of list (int data);         // function declaration //

void main ( )
{
int m, n
printf("Enter the element:");
scanf("%d", &m);
Beginning of list (m);               // function call //
printf("Enter the element");
scanf("%d", &m);
Middle of list (m);                  // function call //
printf("Enter the element");
scanf("%d", &m);
End of list (m);                     // function call //
}

Insert at beg (int data)             // function definition //
{
struct node * tmp;
```

```
tmp = (struct node *) malloc (sizeof (struct node));
tmp → info = data;
tmp → link = start;
start = tmp;
}

Middle of list (int data)            // function definition //
{
struct node * tmp;
tmp = (struct node *) malloc (sizeof (struct node));
tmp → info = data;
tmp → link = start → link;
start → link = tmp;
}

End of list (int data)               // function definition //
{
struct node * tmp;
q = start
while (q → link != NULL)
{ q = q → link;
}

tmp = (struct node *) malloc (sizeof (struct node));
tmp → info = data;
tmp → link = NULL
q → link = tmp;
}
```

(b) Explain the following parameter passing mechanisms to functions:
(i) Call-by-value
(ii) Call-by-reference

Ans. A function can be invoked in two manners:

(a) Call by Value and

(b) Call by Reference

The **Call by Value** method copies the values of actual arguments into the formal argument. i.e., the function creates its own copy of argument values and uses them.

Here, the arguments that appear in a function call statement are Actual Arguments and the arguments that appear in Function definition are called

Formal arguments.

We can alter the variables that are used to call the function in call by value method.

Call by Reference Method: The call by reference method uses a different mechanism. In place of passing a value to the function being called, a reference to the original variable is passed. A reference is an alias for a predefined variable. The same variable's value can be accessed by any two names: the original variable's name and the reference name.

When a function is called by reference, then the formal parameters become references to actual parameters in the calling function. In the call by reference method, the called function does not create its own copy of original values, rather it refers to the original values only by different names i.e. the references.

Q4. (a) Compare the performance of the following sorting techniques:
(i) Bubble sort
(ii) Merge sort

Bubble sort is known to have a predictable N square iterations before the array is fully sorted. Here, N refers to the number of elements in the array.

Performance of Bubble Sort : Excellent performance in some cases and very poor performances in other cases. Best case : Array already sorted, O(n) comparisons and O(1) exchanges. Worst case : Array is in descending order, (n-1) + (n-2) + ... + 2 + 1 comparisons and exchanges, $O(n^2)$ comparisons and $O(n^2)$ exchanges. **Performance of Merge Sort** : Merge sort is only applicable to certain situations. It's great when you want to combine a couple of sorted data sets, but not terribly appropriate otherwise. For two input sequences that contain a total of n elements, we need to move each element's input sequence to its output sequence. Merge time is O(n). We need to be able to store both initial sequences and the output sequence. The array cannot be merged in place. Additional space usage is O(n).

(b) Write a program in 'C' to implement static and dynamic allocation for a STUDENT structure with following fields :
char name [10],
int marks and
long int mobile_no.

Ans.
```
# include <stdio.h>
# include <conio.h>

struct student
{
char name[10]
```

```
int marks
long int mobile_no.
}
void main ( )
{
int i
struct student stu arr(3);
for(i = 0; i < 3; i++)
{
printf("Enter name");
scanf("%d", stu arr[i]);
printf("Enter total marks");
scanf("%d", & stu arr[i].marks);
printf("Enter mobile number");
scanf("%d", stu arr[i].mobile_no);
}
printf("Name %d, Marks %d \n :: Mobile no, stu arr[i].name, stu arr[i].Marks,
stu arr[i] Mobile No.);
}
```

(c) Compare structure and union.
Ans. Refer to Page No.-23

Q5. Write short notes on the following :
(a) AVL - Tree
Ans. Refer June-2008, Q3(b)

(b) Breadth First Search (BFS)
Ans. Refer to Page No.-133

(c) Circular Queue
Ans. Refer Q(d), Page No.-272

(d) Doubly Linked List
Ans. Refer to Page No.-47

(e) Binary Search Trees
Ans. Refer to Q22, Page No.122.

CS – 62: 'C' PROGRAMMING AND DATA STRUCTURE

June, 2009

*Note: **Question number 1** is **compulsory**. Answer any **three** questions from the rest. All algorithms should be written nearer to 'C' language.*

Q1. (a) What do you mean by Sparse Matrix. Write a program to compute the transpose a sparse matrix.

Ans. Sparse Matrix: Refer to Dec-2007, Q.No.-4(b)

Now Refer to Dec-2001,. Q.No.-3(b)

(b) List the advantages and disadvantages of doubly linked list over singly linked list. What is a priority queue? Write an algorithm for inserting an element into circular queue.

Ans. Advantages and Disadvantages of Doubly Linked List over Singly Linked List: Refer to Chapter-2, Q.No.-20

Priority Queue: A priority queue is a type of queue in which each element is assigned a priority and the order in which elements are deleted and processed comes from the following rules:

1. An element with highest priority is processed first before any element of lower priority.

2. Two or more elements with the same priority are processed according to the order in which they were added to the queue.

'C' function for inserting an element into circular queue:

```
void cqinsert( )
{
int i;
if(front = = -1)
{
front = rear = 0;
printf("\n Enter the item to be inserted:");
scanf("%d", &cqueue[rear]);
}
else
{
if(rear = = size)
i = 0;
```

```
else
i = rear + 1;
if(i = = front)
{
printf("\n !!! Queue is overflowing");
}
else
{
rear = i;
printf("\n Enter the item to be inserted:");
scanf("%d", &cqueue[rear]);
}
}
```

Algorithm for inserting an element in circular queue:

/* Assuming that circular queue is stored in QU with size N. */

Algorithm: CQUEU_INSERT

Step 1: IF(FRONT = 0 AND REAR = N – 1)
OR (FRONT = REAR + 1) THEN
{ PRINT "OVERFLOW!!"

Step 2: ELSE { (IF FRONT = NULL) THEN
{
SET FRONT = 0
REAR = 0
}

Step 3: ELSE IF REAR = N – 1 THEN
SET REAR = 0
ELSE

Step 4: SET REAR = REAR + 1
}

Step 5: SET QU[REAR] = I_ITEM

Step 6: END

(c) Write an algorithm for insertion sort. Apply insertion sort algorithm for the following list of elements.
17, 36, 95, 25, 54, 72, 68

Ans. Algorithm for Insertion Sort: Refer to Chapter-5, Page No.-174

Insertion Sort Algorithm for the following list of elements is as follows:

17 36 95 25 54 72 68

Number of items = 7

∴ Number of iterations required = 7 – 1 = 6

Iteration 1: J = 1, compare A(J) and A(J-1)

17 36 95 25 54 72 68

A(0) A(1) ⇒ No interchange required

Iteration 2: J = 2

J = 2

17 36 95 25 54 72 68

NO (A [1], A [2]) **Compare A [2] and A [1]**

Iteration 3: J = 3

J = 3

17 36 95 25 54 72 68

Inter Change (95, 25) **Compare A [3] and A [2]**

17 25 36 95 54 72 68

No (17, 25) **Compare A [1] and A [0]**

Iteration 4: J = 4

J = 4

17 25 36 95 54 72 68

17 25 Inter Change (95, 54) **Compare A [4] and A [3]**

17 25 36 54 95 68

17 25 36 No (36, 54) **A [3] and A [2] 68**

17 25 36 54 95 72 68

No (25, 36) **Now Compare A [2] and A [1] 68**

17 25 36 54

No (17, 25) **Now Compare A [1] and A [0]**

Iteration 5: J = 5

17 25 36 54 95 72 68 A [4]

Inter Compare A [5] and

17 25 36 54 72 95 68

No Compare A [4] and A [5]

17 25 36 54 72 95 68

No Compare A [3] and A [2]

17 25 36 72 95 68

No Compare A [2] and A [1]

17 25 36 54 72 95 68

No Compare A [1] and A [1]

Iteration 6: J = 6 compare A[6]

17 25 36 54 72 Compare A [6] and AL
95 68
Inter Change

17 25 36 54 72 68 95 A [4]
Inter Change Compare A [5] and

17 25 36 54 68 95
No Compare A [4] and A [3]

17 25 36 54 72 95
No Compare and A [2]

17 25 36 54 68 72 95
No Compare A [2] and A [1]

17 25 36 54 68 72 95
No Compare A [1] and A [0]

Shorted List → **17 , 25 , 36 , 54 , 68 , 72 , 95 ,**

Sorted List: 17, 25, 36, 54, 68, 72, 95

(d) Define Postorder and Preorder traversal of tree. Given the following Postorder and Preorder traversals, construct the corresponding Binary Tree.

Post order: J H D E B I F G C A

In order: D J H B E A F I C G

Ans. Post Order Traversal: In Binary Tree, in post-order traversal of Binary Tree, first traverse the left subtree, then traverse the right subtree and finally process the root of Binary Tree.

Pre Order Traversal: In Binary Tree, in pre-order traversal of tree, first process the root of Binary Tree, then traverse the left subtree and finally traverse the right subtree.

Example: In given Binary Tree T

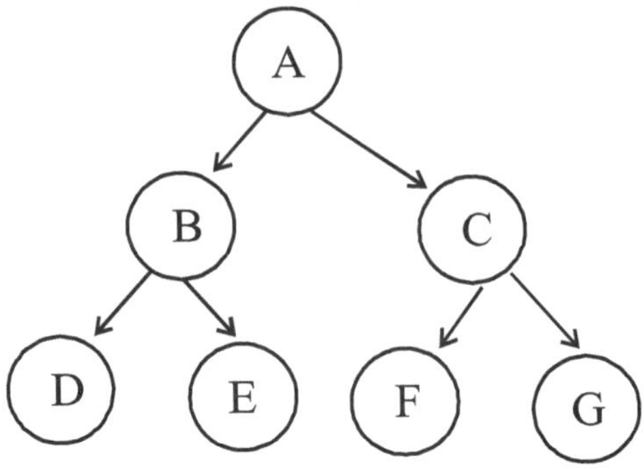

PREORDER TRAVERSAL: A B D E C F G

POSTORDER TRAVERSAL: D E B F G C A

Binary Tree Construction:
Post Order: J H D E B I F G C A

In Order: D J H B E A F I C G

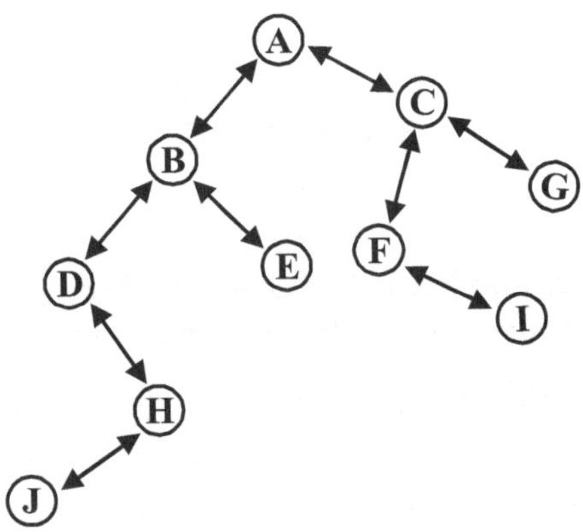

Q2. (a) What is recursion? Write a recursive function to find factorial of a number.

Ans. Recursion: The function that calls itself is known as recursive function and recursion is a powerful technique of solving a complicated problem in an easy way. According to this technique, a problem is solved by dividing it into smaller problems, which are similar in nature to the original problem. In recursion, the call function and the called function are same.

Program to find factorial of a number using recursion:

```
main( )
{ int num;
long fact(int n);
printf("Enter a number:")
scanf("%d", &num);
printf("Factorial of %d is %ld\n", fact(num));
getch( );
}
long fact(int n)
{ if(n = = 0)
return(1);
else
return(n * fact(n – 1));
}
```

(b) Convert the following infix expression into postfix. Write an algorithm for the same.
(i) ((A – (B + C) * D)/(E + F))
(ii) (A ^ (B * C) – D) + (E/F) * (G + H)

Ans. (i) ((A – (B + C) * D) / (E + F))
Step 1: ((A – ((B + C) * D)) / (E + F))
Step 2: ((A ((BC) + D) *) – (EF) +) /
Step 3: ABC + D * - EF + / Post fix Ans.

(ii) (A ^ (B * C) – D) + (E/F) * (G + H)
Step 1: [((A ^ (B * C)) – D) + ((E/F) * (G + H))]
Step 2: (((A (BC) *) ^ D) – ((EF) / (GH) +) *) +
Step 3: ABC * ^D – EF / GH + * + Post fix Ans.
Algorithm to convert infix into postfix form: Refer to Chapter-2, Q.No.-4

Q3. (a) What is B-Tree? What are the properties of B-Tree of Order M?
Ans. B-Tree: A B-Tree of order M is an M-way tree such that each node, except the root and leaves, has at least [1 / (2M)] subtrees and no more than M subtrees. The root has at least two subtrees unless it is itself a leaf and all the leaves are on the same level.
Properties of B-Tree of Order M:
1. Each node of the B-Tree, except the root node and leaves, has at least M/2 subtrees and no more than M subtrees.
2. Root of the tree has at least two subtrees unless it is a leaf node.
3. All leaves of the tree are on the same level.

The first property ensures that each node of the tree is at least half full, second one forces the tree to branch early and the third property keeps the tree balanced.

(b) Write a program in C for implementing Breadth First Search (BFS).

Ans. Program for implementing Breadth First Search:

```
#include<stdio.h>
#include<conio.h>
#include<malloc.h>
#define MAXNODE 80
#define TRUE 1
#define FALSE 0
struct EDGE
{
int dest;
struct EDGE *next;
};
typedef struct EDGE EDGE;
struct NODE
{
int reach;
int nodenum;
char data;
int dist;
struct NODE *edgeptr;
};
typedef struct NODE NODE;
struct QUEUE
{
int data;
struct QUEUE *next;
};
typedef struct QUEUE QUEUE;
EDGE *insertnode(int nodenum, EDGE *start)
{
EDGE *n, *cur=start;
```

```
N=(EDGE*)malloc(sizeof(EDGE));
n->dest=nodenum;
n->next=NULL;
if(!start)
return(n);
while(cur->next!=NULL)
cur=cur->next;
cur->next=n;
return(start);
}
QUEUE *qinsert(int nodenum,QUEUE *f)
{
QUEUE *n,*cur;
N=(QUEUE*)malloc(sizeof(QUEUE));
n->data=nodenum;
n->next=NULL;
if(!f)
return(n);
while(cur->next!=NULL)
cur=cur->next;
cur->next=n;
return(f);
}
QUEUE *qdelete(int nodenum,QUEUE *f)
{
QUEUE *pred;
if(!f)
return(NULL);
nodenum=f->data;
pred=f;
f=f->next;
free(pred);
printf("%d",nodenum);
return(f);
}
void createnode(int numnode,int mat[MAXNODE][MAXNODE],NODE
```

```
node[MAXNODE])
{
int i,j;
for(i=0,i<numnode;i++)
{
node[i].reach=FALSE;
node[i].nodenum=i+1;
node[i].data='A'+i;
node[i].dist=0;
node[i].edgeptr=NULL;
}
for(i=0;i<numnode;i++)
for(j=0;j<numnode;j++)
if(mat[i][j]= =1)
node[i].edgeptr=insertnode(j,node[i].edgeptr);
}
void bfs(int ind, NODE node[MAXNODE])
{
QUEUE *q=NULL;
EDGE *link;
node[ind].reach=TRUE;
q=qinsert(ind,q);
while(q)
{
q=qdelete(ind,q);
for(link=node[ind].edgeptr;link;link=link->next)
{
if(node[link->dest].reach= =FALSE)
{
node[link->dest].reach=TRUE;
node[link->dest].dist=node[ind].dist+1;
q=qinsert(link->dest,q);
}
}
}
}
```

```
void main( )
{
int i,j,n,ind;
int mat[MAXNODE][MAXNODE];
NODE node[MAXNODE];
EDGE *list;
Printf("\n How many vertices \n");
Scanf("%d", &n);
For(i=0;i<n;i++)
```

Q4. (a) What is a File? Write a 'C' program to copy the contents of one file to another file.

Ans. File: A file is a collection of related records on the disk. For e.g., A student file contains the records of students in a class.

Program to copy contents of one file to another file:

```
void main(int argc, char *argv[ ])
{
FILE *source, *dest;
int c;
if(argc!=3)
{
printf("Enter 3 arguments");
exit(1);
}
if((source=fopen(argv[1] "r") = = NULL)
{
printf("Cannot open the source file");
exit(1);
}
if((dest=fopen argv[2], "w") = = NULL)
{
printf("Cannot open the destination file");
exit(1);
}
while(ch=fget(source)!=eof)
{
fputc(dest, ch);
}
fclose(source);
```

```
fclose(dest);
getch( );
}
```

(b) Define Binary Search Tree (BST). Write an algorithm to insert a node in a BST.

Refer to Chapter-3, Q.No.-22

Q5. Write short notes on the following:

(a) Stack

Refer to Chapter-2, Page No.-67

(b) Circular Linked List

Refer to Chapter-2, Page No.-48

(c) Complete Binary Tree

Refer to Chapter-3, Page No.-95

(d) Storage Pool: An area of storage reserved for use in performing I/O operations, into which data is read and written. A storage pool is used to compensate for a difference in the rate of flow of data between devices. For e.g. between a CPU and a peripheral device.

(e) Pointers

Refer to Chapter-1, Page No.-18

CS – 62: 'C' PROGRAMMING AND DATA STRUCTURE

December, 2009

Note: ***Question number 1*** *is* ***compulsory****. Answer* ***any three*** *questions from the rest. All algorithms should be written nearer to 'C' language.*

Q1. (a) Distinguish between linear queues and circular queues.

Refer to June-2006, Q(d), Page No.-272

Write a 'C' program (i) To insert an element at the rear end of a queue. (ii) To delete an element from the front end of the queue.

```
void qinsert( );
void qdelete( );
void qdisplay( );
int queue[50], front = -1, size;
void main( )
{
int choice;
clrscr( );
printf("Enter the size of queue:");
scanf("%d", &size);
printf("Enter your choice:\n");
printf("\n 1: Insert \n 2: Delete \n 3: Display \n 4: Quit…");
scanf("%d", &choice);
while(choice)
{
switch(choice)
{
Case 1: qinsert( );
break;
Case 2: qdelete( );
break;
Case 3: qdisplay( );
break;
Case 4: exit( );
default: clrscr( );
```

```
printf("\n! Invalid Choice!!!");
break;
getch( );
}
printf("\n Enter your choice! \n");
printf("\n 1: Insert \n 2: Delete \n 3: Display \n 4: Quit...")
scanf("%d", choice);
}
}
void qinsert( )
{
int item;
if(rear = = size – 1)
{
printf("\n!! Queue overflow!!!\n");
getch( );
}
else
{
printf("\n Enter the item to be inserted");
scanf("%d", &item);
if(front = = -1)
front = rear = 0;
else
rear = rear + 1;
queue[rear] = item;
}
}
void qdelete( )
{
if(front = = -1)
printf("\n!! Queue underflow!!\n");
else
{
printf("\n The deleted element is: %d", queue[front]);
if(front = = rear)
```

```
front = rear = -1
else
front = front + 1;
}
}
void display( )
{
int i;
if(front = = -1)
printf("\n!! Queue underflow!!\n");
else
{
printf("\n The recent element in queue are…\n");
for(i = front; i <= rear; i++)
printf("%d \t", queue[i]);
}
}
```

(b) For the following tree traversals, construct the corresponding Binary Tree.

Inorder: B C A E G D H F I J

Preorder: A B C D E G F H I J

Ans. INORDER: B C A E G D H F I J

PREORDER: A B C D E G F H I J

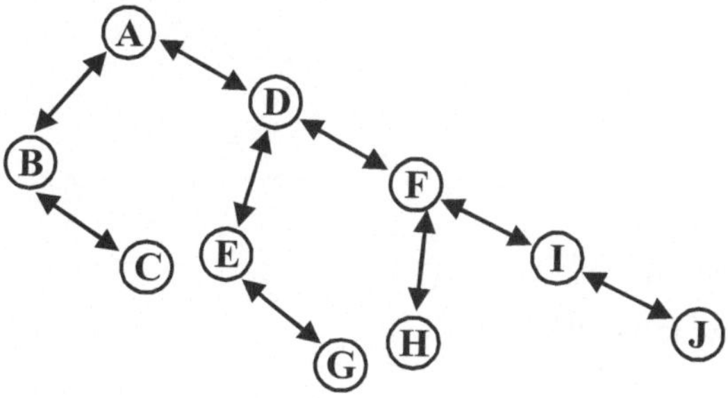

(c) What do you mean by Sorting? Explain Internal and External Sorting methods.

Ans. Refer to Page No.-152

(d) Define Pointers. List the advantages of using linked lists over Arrays. Write a 'C' program to merge two linked lists.

Ans. Pointers: Refer to Chapter-1, Page No.-18

Advantages of Using Linked Lists Over Arrays: Refer to Chapter-2, Q.No.-21

C Program to merge two linked lists:

```
#include <stdio.h>
#include <malloc.h>
struct Dlink_list
{
        struct Dlink_list *previous;
        int info;
        struct Dlink_list *next;
};
typedef struct Dlink_list Dnods;
/* Global declaration */
int num;
Dnode *lp=NULL, *lp2=NULL, *lp=NULL;
Dnode *list1=NULL, *list2=NULL, *list=NULL, *new1;

/* Prototype of various functions */
void Create(Dnode *);
void display (Dnode *);
void Merge (Dnode *, Dnode *);

/* Function main */
void main( )
{
        lp1 = (Dnode *) malloc (sizeof(Dnode));
        lp2 = (Dnode *) malloc (sizeof(Dnode));
        Create(lp1);
printf("\n first list is as follows\n");
display(lp1);
Create(lp2);
printf("\n second list is as follows\n");
display(lp2);
```

```
Merge(lp1, lp2);
printf("\n After merging two lists resulting linked list is as follows\n");
display(lp);
getchar( );
}

/* Function create */
void Create(Dnode *ptr)
{
        char ch;
        num = 0;
        ptr->previous = NULL; /* set previous pointer of ptr to NULL */
        printf("\n Enter e for Exit any other key for continue:");
        ch = getchar( );
        if(ch = = 'e')
        {
                free(ptr);
                exit(0);
        }
        printf("\n Enter first list:");
        do
        {
                printf("\n Input the values of the node: %d:", (num+1));
                scanf("%d", &ptr->info);
                fflush(stdin);
                printf("\n want to continue(y/n)->:");
                ch = getchar( );
                if(ch = = 'y')
                {
                        ptr->next = (Dnode *) malloc(sizeof(Dnode));
                        ptr->next->previous = ptr;
                        ptr = ptr->next;
                }
                 num++;
}
```

```
while(ch = = 'y');
ptr->next=NULL;
printf("\n Total nodes = %d", num);
printf("\n Enter second list:");
}

/* Function insert */
void Merge (Dnode *list1, Dnode *list2)
{
        if(lp1 = = NULL)          */ if list1 is empty */
        lp = lp2;                        */ resultant list will be list2 */
        else if(lp2 = = NULL)     */ if list2 is empty */
        lp = lp1;                        */ resultant list will be list1 */
         else
         {
                lp=list = (Dnode *)malloc(sizeof(Dnode));
                lp->previous=lp->next=NULL;    */ set previous and next
 pointer of LP to NULL */
 while(list1!=NULL&&list2!=NULL)
         {
                if(list1->info<=list2->info)
                 {
                        list->info=list1->info;
                        list1=list1->next;
                 }
                 else
                 {
                        list->info=list2->info;
                        list2=list2->next;
                 }
                list->next = (Dnode *)malloc(sizeof(Dnode));
                list->next->previous=list;
                list=list->next;
         }
         if(list1= = NULL)
         while(list2 != NULL)    */ copy the remaining element of list2 */
```

```
    {
            list->info=list2->info;
            list2=list2->next;
            list->next = (Dnode *)malloc(sizeof(Dnode));
            list->next->previous=list;
            list=list->next;
    }
    else
    while(list1 != NULL)     */ copy the remaining element of list2 */
    {
            list->info=list1->info;
            list1=list1->next;
            list->next = (Dnode *)malloc(sizeof(Dnode));
            list->next->previous=list;
            list=list->next;
    }
    list->previous->next=NULL;
    free(list);
}
}
/* Display the list */
void display (Dnode, *ptr)
{
    while(ptr != NULL)      /* Traverse up to end of the list */
    {
            printf("\n 0x%x", ptr);
            printf("%d", ptr->info);
            ptr = ptr->next;
    }
}
```

Q2. (a) Show the detailed concepts of the stacks to evaluate the following postfix expression.
632 - - 5*1^7+
Ans. Postfix Expression: (632 - - 5 * 1 ^ 7 +)

Sr. No	Character Scanned	Operation on STACK	STACK
1	C	Push C	C
2	6	Push 6	6 C
3	3	Push 3	3 6 C
4	2	Push 2	→ 2 3 6 C
5	—	Pop 2 Pop 3 E×P=3-2 =1 Push1	1 6 C
6	—	Pop 1 Pop 6 E×P=6-1 =5 Push 5	5 C
7	5	Push 5	5 5 C
8	*	Pop 5 Pop 5 E×P=5×5 =25 Push 25	25 C
9	1	Push 1	1 25 C
10	^	Pop 1 Pop 25 E×P=25^1 =25 Push 25	25 C
11	7	Push 7	7 25 C
12	7	Pop 7 Pop 25 E×P=5+7 =32 Push 32	32 C
13	2		Pop = 32 | Pop = C

(b) Write a 'C' program to perform a search operation in a Binary Search Tree.

Refer to June-2008, Q.No.-2(a)

Q3. (a) What do you mean by Command-line Arguments? Write a program to reverse a string using Command-line Argument.

Ans. Command Line Arguments: Refer to Chapter-1, Page No.-30

Program to reverse a string using Command Line Argument:

```
#include <stdio.h>
#include <string.h>
#include <conio.h>
void main(int argc, char, *argv[ ])
{ int len;
char str[20];
if(argc != 2)
{
printf("You have not entered 2 arguments");
exit(1);
}

strcpy(str, argv[1]);
len = strlen(str) – 1;
while(len >= 0)
{
printf("%c", str[len]);
len —;
}
printf("\n");
getch( );
}
```

(b) Define the following w.r.t. Disk access:
(i) Seek time
(ii) Latency time
(iii) Transfer time

Ans. (i) Seek Time: The time required to position the access mechanism of a direct access storage device at a specified position, such as the time needed to position the read/write head in a drive over the specified track of the disk is known as **seek time**.

(ii) Latency Time: The time required for an addressed block to appear under the read/write head of rotating disk is known as **latency time**.

(iii) Transfer Time: The time required to transfer the request record/file from secondary storage to primary memory is known as the **transfer time**.

Q4. (a) Explain Union data type. How does it differ from a structure data type? Give example of each.
Refer to Chapter-1, Page No.-196

(b) Construct an AVL tree by inserting the following elements in order of their occurrence (show each of the rotations). 5, 6, 8, 3, 2, 4, 7
Ans. AVL Tree: Step 1: Insert 5. It will become root node

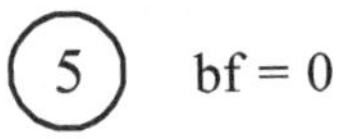

Step 2: Insert 6

Step 3: Insert 8

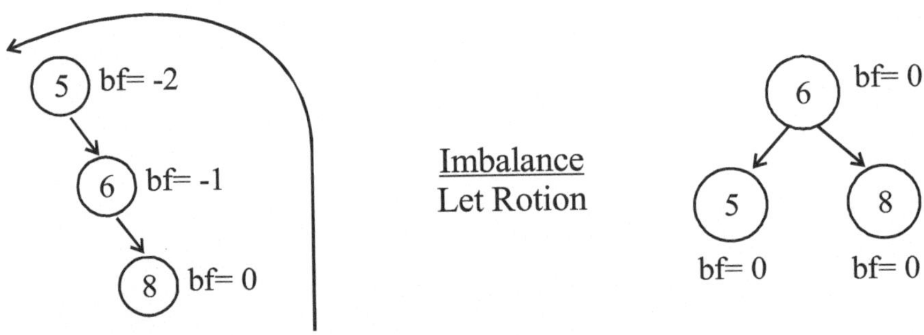

Step 4: Insert 3

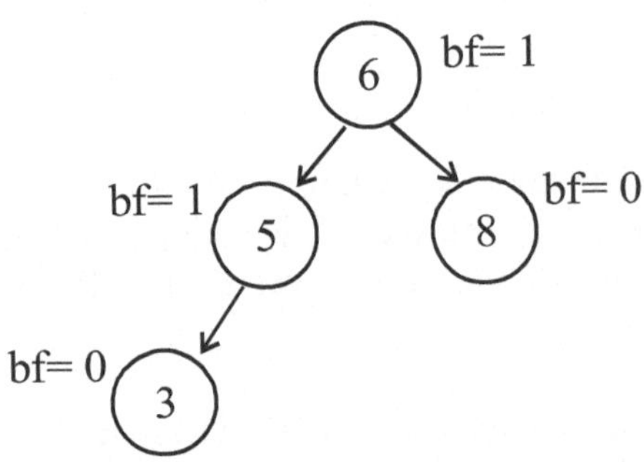

Step 5: Insert 2

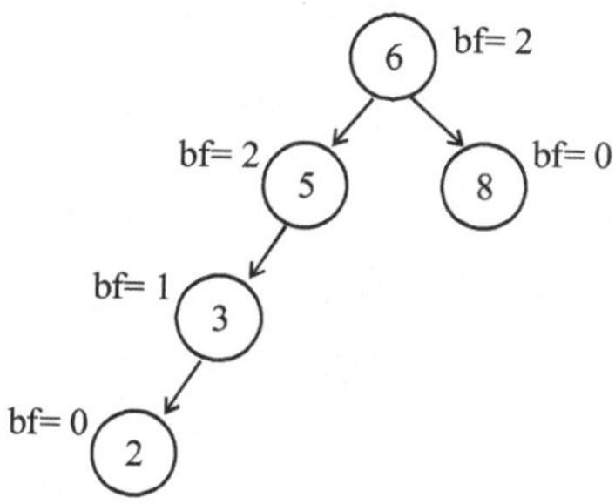

Imbalance

Right Rotion

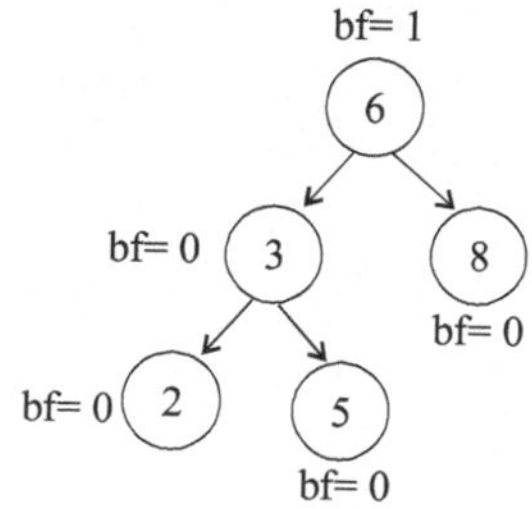

Step 6: Insert 4

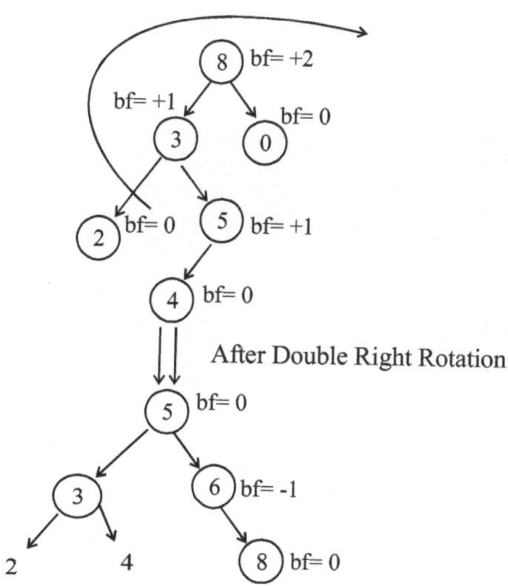

Imbalance

Right Rotation

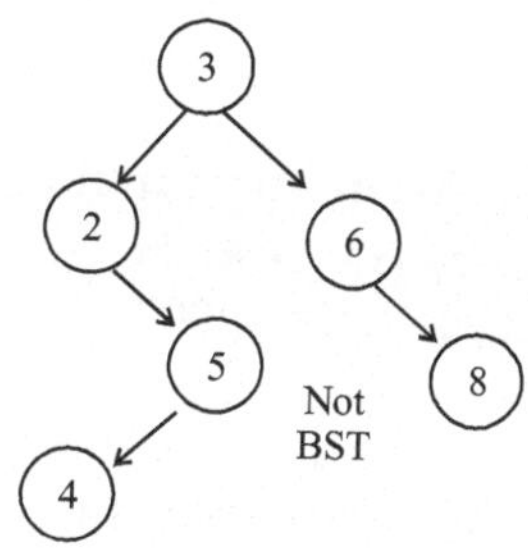

Double Rotation Required

Step 7: Insert 7

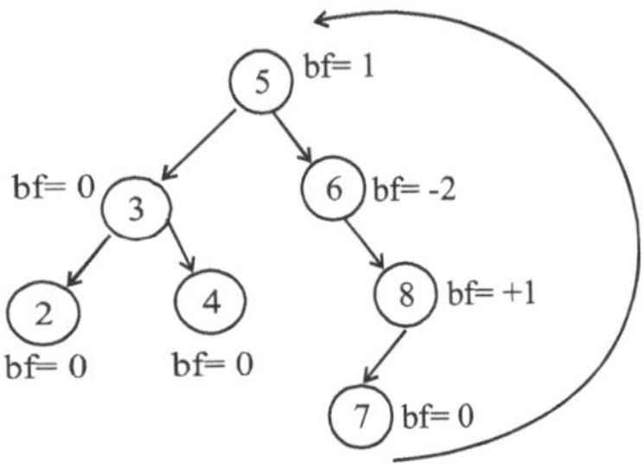

Left Rotation
Reuired Inblance

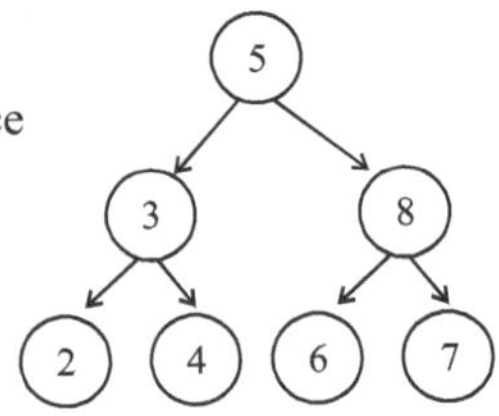

After Double Left Rotation

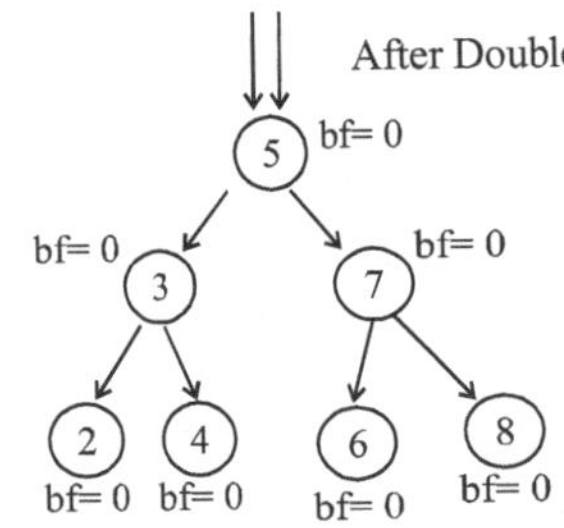

Double Rotation Required

Q5. Write short notes on the following:

(a) Sparse Matrix

Refer to Dec-2007, Q.No.-4

(b) Breadth First Search

Refer to Page No.-133

(c) Complete Binary Tree

Refer to Chapter-3, Page No.-95

(d) Indexed Sequential File Organization

Refer to June-2007, Q.No.-1(c)

(e) Switch Case Default Statement

Refer to Chapter-1, Page No.-9

CS – 62: 'C' PROGRAMMING AND DATA STRUCTURE
June, 2010

*Note: **Question number 1** is **compulsory**. Answer any **three** questions from the rest. All algorithms should be written nearer to 'C' language.*

Q1. (a) Write an algorithm to implement bubble sort, and sort the following list in descending order by using the algorithm.
15, 12, 4, 16, 9, 10, 94
What is the average run-time complexity of the bubble sort.

(b) What do you mean by Traversal of a tree? Explain the difference between preorder and postorder traversal with the help of illustrations.

(c) Show how a polynomial can be represented using linked list. Write an algorithm to add two polynomials containing minimum of four terms.

Q2. (a) Write an algorithm which accepts a stack as input and reverses the elements of the stack using one additional queue.

(b) Write at least two differences between a structure and a union in 'C' language. Given an example of each.

Q3. (a) Find a minimum cost spanning tree of the following graph using PRIM's algorithm.

(b) Explain indexed sequential file organization. Name the data structure most appropriate for this file organization.

Q4. (a) Write an algorithm for implementation of Breadth First Search (BFS).

(b) What is a Binary Search Tree? List its advantages.

Q5. Given two sorted lists L1 and L2, write an algorithm to compute L1 ∪ L2.

CS – 62: 'C' PROGRAMMING AND DATA STRUCTURE
December, 2010

*Note: **Question number 1** is **compulsory**. Answer any **three** questions from the rest. All algorithms should be written nearer to 'C' language.*

Q1. (a) Write a non-recursive algorithm for calculating power of an integer 'm' raised by another integer 'n' i.e. m^n.

Ans.

Power (int m, int n)
1. if (n = 0) then return 1;
2. if (n = 1) then return m;
3. Result = 1
4. if m > 1 & n > 1) then Repeat Step 5 n times;
5. Result = Result*m;
6. Return result,
7. end.

(b) Write an algorithm to multiply two sparse matrices using pointers.

Refer to Page No.-226, Dec-2003, Q.No.-3(b)

(c) Explain indexed sequential file organization.

Refer to Page No.-292, June-2007, Q.No.-1(c)

(d) Write an algorithm for finding $L1 \cap L2$ where L1 and L2 are two sorted lists.

Refer to Page No.-38, Chapter-2, Q.No.-5

Q2. (a) Construct a Binary tree from the given Preorder and Inorder traversals.

Preorder: * - + E A B + C D

Inorder: E + A – B * C + D

Ans.

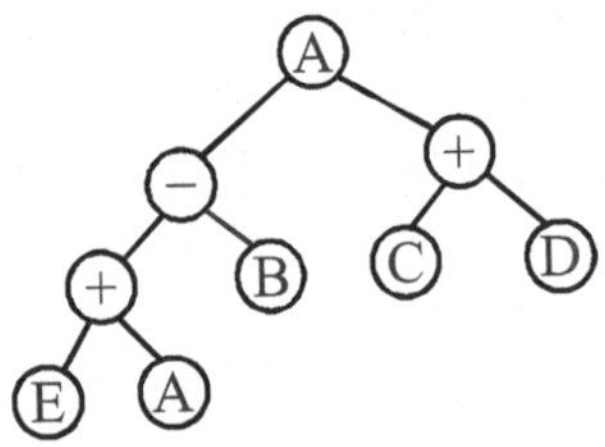

(b) Write an algorithm that computes the height of a Binary Tree.

```
int height (node * curNode) {

int cur Height = 0;
int curMax = 0;
return height (curNode, curHeight, curMax);
}
int height(node * curNode, int curHeight, int curMax) {
if (curNode ! = NULL) {
if (curHeight> curMax) { curMax = curHeight;}
// Traverse the left subtree
if (curNode->left != NULL){
curMax = height(curNode->left, curHeight + 1, curMax);
}
// Traverse the right subtree
if (curNode->right != NULL){
curMax = height (curNode->right, curHeight + 1, curMax);
}
}
return curMax
}
int main (void) {
node * root;
//Initialize tree
int h = 0;
h = height (root);
}
```

Q3. (a) Write an meant by "Death First Search" of a graph? Consider the following graph:

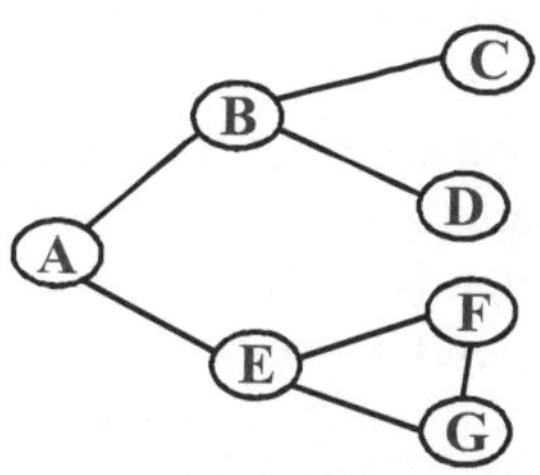

Explain how a Depth First Search Scheme will Traverse the graph starting at node A?

Ans. Refer to Page No.-131 (Depth First Search)
Depth First Search of the graph is
A, E, G, F, B, D, C

(b) List any five advantages of a Doubly Linked List.

Ans. Following are the advantages of a Double Linked List:

(i) A doubly linked list can be traversed in both directions (forward and backward).

(ii) A node on a doubly linked list may be deleted with little trouble, since we have pointers to the previous and next nodes.

Now, Refer Page No.-21

Q4. (a) Write a program in 'C' language for reading a file and displaying its contents on the standard output.

Ans.
```
/* Program to display the contents of a file on screen */
#include <stdio.h>
void main ()
{
FILE *fopen(), *fp;
int c;
fp = fopen ("prog.c", "r");
c = getc(fp):
while (c! = EOF)
{
Putchar (c);
c = getc(fp);
}
fclose(fp);
}
```

(b) List any two features of a Deque.

Deque features:

(i) Individual elements can be accessed by their position index.

(ii) Iteration over the elements can be performed in any order.

(iii) Elements can be efficiently added and removed from any of its ends (either the beginning or the end of the sequence).

Q5. Write short note on the following:

(a) Adjacency list representation.

Ans. A representation of a directed graph with n vertices using an array of n lists of vertices. List i contains vertex j if there is an edge from vertex i to vertex j. A weighted graph may be represented with a list of vertex/weight pairs. An undirected graph may be represented by having vertex j in the list for vertex i and vertex i in the list for vertex j.

Refer to Page No.-144, Q.No.-17(c)

(b) Direct File Organisation.

Refer to Page No.-127